Celebrating Indigenous Voice

T0246662

Anthropological Linguistics

Edited by
Svenja Völkel and Nico Nassenstein

Advisory board

Volume 5

Celebrating Indigenous Voice

Legends and Narratives in Languages
of the Tropics and Beyond

Edited by
Alexandra Y. Aikhenvald, Robert L. Bradshaw,
Luca Ciucci and Pema Wangdi

ISBN 978-3-11-162716-8
e-ISBN (PDF) 978-3-11-078983-6
e-ISBN (EPUB) 978-3-11-078989-8
ISSN 2701-987X

Library of Congress Control Number: 2022945401

Bibliographic information published by the Deutsche Nationalbibliothek
The Deutsche Nationalbibliothek lists this publication in the Deutsche
Nationalbibliografie; detailed bibliographic data are available on the internet at
http://dnb.dnb.de.

www.degruyter.com

Preface

Narratives are the key to indigenous cultural heritage and knowledge. They are a repository of millennia-long traditions, reflecting the intricate relationships between language and culture in their multifaceted ecologies. This volume centres on linguistic and cultural aspects of narratives in the hot-spots of linguistic diversity across the tropics and beyond, the ways of framing discourse of varied genres, and salient grammatical features which make each story-telling tradition so special.

The volume starts with an introduction which weaves together the multiple threads in the twelve contributions – how narratives are organized, how the protagonists and the narrator interact, how the art of narration is taught to children, how the impact of post-colonial experience results in the creation of new genres, and many more issues. The idea for the volume was sparked by the Workshop "Celebrating indigenous voice: Legends and narratives in languages of the tropics" (25–27 November 2020) organized by the editors within the then Language and Culture Research Centre. The Workshop served as an impetus for this project, which took shape and was prepared for publication within the nurturing environment of the Jawun Research Centre at Central Queensland University.

It is our hope that this volume will contribute to creating a consolidated conceptual and analytic framework, for further work on how narratives and their grammatical features reflects the world around us and the features of the societies in which we live. Our aim is to highlight what is special about the narrative means deployed, opening further perspectives on how languages work and why they are the way they are. Each contributor has undertaken intensive fieldwork and has firsthand in-depth knowledge of the languages under discussion. This is what makes the discussions and the results within this volume particularly reliable.

We are grateful to all the participants of the 2020 Workshop and colleagues who took part in the discussion. Many thanks to Joe Blythe and Dineke Schokkin for their fascinating contributions. Thanks are also due to the editors of the series, and the reviewer, for their incisive comments. We owe a debt of gratitude to Brigitta Flick and Bruce Allen, for their invaluable support during the preparation of this volume.

Last but not least, we would like to express our appreciation to Professor Adrian Miller, member of the Jirrbal Nation, Deputy Vice-President Indigenous Engagement, BHP Chair in Indigenous Engagement, and Director of the Jawun Research Centre at Central Queensland University without whose on-going support this enterprise would have not been feasible.

https://doi.org/10.1515/9783110789836-202

Contents

List of figures

https://doi.org/10.1515/9783110789836-204

List of tables

https://doi.org/10.1515/9783110789836-205

Alexandra Y. Aikhenvald

1 Introduction. Legends and narratives in language and culture

Every society thrives on stories, legends, and myths. The intricate fabric of every culture is reflected in how people relate the lore to each other, what they talk about, how they make sure the audience is involved and how the art of storytelling is taught to their children. Narratives, legends, and stories of various kinds are a key to cultural knowledge and cultural heritage, across languages of the world. A legend may offer a cautionary tale. A myth might tell a story about how people came to be the way they are now, and where they come from. In Ellen Basso's (1987: 1) words,

> narrative traditions are a vital, dynamic, and productive art form, an elaborate means of preserving, reworking, and sharing between generations knowledge, insight, and understanding of their world.

Across the world, traditional narratives vary in their genres, the ways they are told, and the linguistic means they are couched in. Narratives are hardly static. New genres and new ways of telling stories evolve, as people are exposed to new media and to the impending pressure from mainstream cultures and languages. What could be a better way of catching a glimpse of the unprecedented diversity of narratives and their structures than to turn to linguistic traditions in the very hotspots of linguistic diversity and to focus on the voices of minority First Nations languages – reflected in the many facets of the stories, told and documented?

The present volume is an attempt to do just that. Its aim is to address a selection of linguistic and cultural facets of the narratives in areas of linguistic diversity across the tropics and a few adjacent areas. These span New Guinea, Northern Australia, and the Tibeto-Burman domain, with an additional foray into traditional narratives in Siberia.

A narrative will have a structure and will evolve as the plot evolves. Traditional stories usually begin, and end, in a particular way. In many European languages, a folk tale will start with an introductory formula along the lines of *once upon a time*. Estonian folktales start with the expression *Elanud kord . . .,* 'literally, there is reported to have lived once . . . .' An ancestral myth in Tariana, from north-western Amazonia, would open with the time word *walikasu* 'at the beginning, back in the old days'. Stories in Manambu, a Papuan language, tend

Alexandra Y. Aikhenvald, Jawun Research Centre, Central Queensland University

https://doi.org/10.1515/9783110789836-001

to start with a statement of the participants and their actions. Reference to a place is another typical way of starting a story (Dingemanse, Rossi, and Floyd 2017). In each case, the scene will be set for the narrative to unravel. The formulaic beginnings offer the audience a sneak preview into the genre to be expected.

A formula will also conclude a story. In Tariana, any story (a folktale, a myth, or a narrative dealing with a historical event) would end in a verbless clause with the adverb *kida* or *kaida* 'finished, ready', or the possessed noun *kewhidana* 'the end' (literally 'head'). A typical ending of a legend or a myth in Manambu is quite different: it translates as 'the story goes back to its base'; for some, it is 'the story enters an enclosure' – as if, when told, the story was let out of where it is kept, and when it is finished, it goes back to its resting place. For a real-life narrative, a speaker would just say "it is finished".

Different speech genres may have their distinct features – both grammatical and lexical. A grammaticalised marker of information source (that is, an evidential) is often chosen depending on the genre of a story – whether it is an ancestral tale, an account of what had actually happened to the narrator, or something they know because someone else told them that. Switching evidentials highlights multiple information sources and multiple layers of access to – and knowledge of – what one is talking about (Aikhenvald 2015: 280–281). In several Indigenous Australian languages, artful use of quotations reflects layers of representation of speech and thought through voices of different characters (Rumsey et al., this volume). In telling a story in English or in North Khanty (an Ob-Ugric language), a speaker may choose to switch to what is known as "historic present". This is a way of describing "the past as if it is happening now", and of conveying "something of the dramatic immediacy of an eye-witness account" (Quirk et al. 1985: 118; Skribnik, this volume). Speakers of every language will exploit whichever means are available to them, weaving a complex fabric of a narrative.

Which linguistic devices are the key to the narratives of varied genres in different languages? How to make a story flow, and keep the listeners on track? And how do cultural changes and new means of communication affect narrative genres and the way speakers structure them? What are the themes and the genres which come up time and time again? We now turn to these, and other, common threads in the analysis of narratives which permeate the twelve contributions within this volume. We start with the person of the narrator and the representation of multiple voices through quoted speech and thought in Australian languages – the topic of the first two chapters.

Storytellers in Yidiñ, an indigenous language from North Queensland (Australia), had a special way of recounting traditional tales. The speaker would often take on the identity of the main character and tell the tale as if they were the protagonist – 'I', the first person. This is the topic of Chapter 2, "First person orientation in Yidiñ narratives and its implications", by R. M. W. Dixon. The stories about several characters were told in first person.

The fusion of the character and the narrator resonates with Silverstein's (1999: 107) remarks:

> imagine a so-called "first-person" narration, that is, a narration – generally marked, where explicit, by the use of *I/we* personal deixis – in which the incumbent of the narrator role is also one of the characters inhabiting the narrated world. Imagine further that there happens to be no clear and distinct metapragmatic framing apparatus: at the level of text-sentences, for example, there is not the constant reminder of the dual roles the communicating narrator/communicated-about narrative subject is occupying in first-person narration. Finally, imagine that we are not encountering deliberate, aesthetically theorized verbal art, so much as that vast folk-art that is constituted intuitively every time a speaker of a language achieves a text-in-context.

This fusion of the narrator and the ancestral protagonist can be compared to other traditional extensions of 'I' or 'us' as a cover term for a ritually – or traditionally – defined unit, or segment (be it a clan, or a subclan; known as "segmentary" person: Merlan and Rumsey 1991: 96–98; Rumsey 2000; Henry 2013: 282). The narrator, the ancestral character, and oftentimes the whole clan or tribe are fused into one. In each case, the narrator speaks as a protagonist. And in other parts of the Pacific (including the Maori and the Fijians) people use first person to identify themselves not just with a particular group, but with a particular ancestral chief or an ancestor within it (but not a group: Rumsey 1999). The autobiographical component of public speeches and oratories cast in "segmentary person" is one of the topics of Chapter 11, by Rosita Henry – we return to this shortly.

For Yidiñ, in a legend where the initial main character passes away, the narrator takes on the first person reference of another character who now becomes the principal actor. This technique is absent from Dyirbal, Yidiñ's southerly neighbour, where non-autobiographical narratives are all told in third person.

Yidiñ and Dyirbal are similar in both having split case marking – nouns are marked as absolutive (S and O functions) versus ergative (A function) whereas first and second person pronouns are shown as nominative (S and A) versus accusative (O). In Dyirbal all clausal coordination is on an S/O basis, whether the clauses are linked through shared noun or pronoun. Yidiñ differs in that coordination based on a pronoun is on an S/A basis, reflecting the morphology of pronouns. This correlates with the first person orientation of narratives in Yidiñ, giving it a higher frequency of first and second person pronouns than Dyirbal. Accordingly, Dixon argues that there is a strong interdependency between the infrastructure of a grammar and the ways narratives are organized (to which we return further on in this introduction).

The multiplicity of voices reflected in the use of quotations and re-enactment of various characters and the narrator is the topic of Chapter 3, "The sound of one quotation mark: Quoted speech in Indigenous Australian narrative", by ALAN RUMSEY, JOHN MANSFIELD, and NICHOLAS EVANS.

In Silverstein's (1999: 108) words, "complex indexicalities [. . .] bespeak complexity of crisscrossing and overlapping voicings" with which speakers and members of speech communities articulate themselves to each other within the context of relating stories, legends, and myths. A special feature of narrative traditions in many Australian languages is the predominance of quotations in representing much of the action, the talk, the thoughts, the feelings and the attitudes of the characters and the narrator through speech reports – and especially direct quotes.

Quotations often appear without an overt segmental introducer, or a "quote framer", and set off from the rest of the text by intonation and other, suprasegmental, means (in contrast to a few languages from other parts of the world: see a typological overview in Aikhenvald 2011: 314–321). They offer more than the content of what is said. In Clark and Gerrig's (1990: 772) words, quotations are "demonstrations", so much so that "the internal structure of quotation is really the structure of what is being depicted". Quotations represent actions, in a lively and dramatic way – as can be heard and enjoyed in the linked online audio recordings that accompany many of the narrative texts discussed in this chapter. The meanings of speech reports go beyond speech representation: they express internal thoughts, feelings, and perception – similar to numerous languages across the world, spanning New Guinea and the Andes (Adelaar 1990; de Vries 1990; Aikhenvald 2012a: 348–349). The speech verb, 'say', is polysemous with 'do' in most languages discussed. This relatively uncommon feature is shared with a few Austronesian languages and languages of the Horn of Africa (Cohen, Simeone-Senelle, and Vanhove 2002; Aikhenvald 2011: 318–319).

The preponderance of quotations, with their prosodic features, stereotyped use of interjections, and person shifts, signal the inclusion of multiple voices in the traditional stories from six Indigenous languages from northern Australia – Kayardild, Bininj Kunwok, Dalabon, Ngarinyin, Wurla, and Bunuba. The expert manipulation of represented speech interspersed with quotations and speech reports of other sorts reflect "the heteroglossic mastery – including the harnessing of multilingualism to narrative – which is displayed in the oral cultures of Indigenous Australia" (§5 of Chapter 3).

The ways of describing events and organizing a narrative vary across the world's languages. Many languages of Asia-Pacific, Amazonia and the Tibeto-Burman region have a special device, known as "clause chains" – a special type of complex sentence unavailable in many familiar Indo-European languages like English. A sequence of backgrounded subevents will be expressed by a chain of dependent – or "medial" – clauses leading up to a main, typically "final" clause. This technique contrasts with the ways a speaker of English – or of many Indo-European and Austronesian languages – will describe a sequence of related sub-events, with several independent sentences (linked by intonation or by conjunctions: an up-to-date synthesis is in Sarvasy and Aikhenvald forthcoming). Clause chaining is often a feature of various narrative genres. In many languages it goes together with "switch-reference" marking. Switch reference indicates whether or not the subject of a clause is identical with that of another clause, oftentimes signalling topical continuity within the stretch (more on this in Sarvasy and Aikhenvald forthcoming, and references there). Clause chains, and switch reference, are a well-attested feature of numerous languages of Papua New Guinea. Three languages from this hotspot of extreme linguistic diversity discussed in this volume are Manambu, a Ndu language from East Sepik Province (Chapter 4), Doromu-Koki, a Manubaran language from Central Province (Chapter 5), and Nungon, a Huon-Finisterre language from Morobe Province (Chapter 6).

Organizing clauses into chains is a means of packaging information and structuring the representation of an event. In a canonical situation the final clause – or a focal clause, following the terminology in Dixon (2009) – will carry the main event line. Non-main clauses – also known as medial clauses – carry backgrounded information, in line with their status as supporting clauses. The person of the narrator – and their interface with the addressee – underlie the interactive powers of a narrative and of a conversation. Both the narrator and the addressee are woven into the fabric of the narrative. This is done by artful manipulation of clause chains. Medial verb forms in Manambu can occur in non-canonical positions (along the lines mapped out by Sarvasy 2015). A free-standing medial clause occurs in addressee-oriented commands and questions. Or it can mark completed action, inviting the addressee to join in and start over again. A sentence-final medial clause may serve as a clarification; or it may mark a completed action with an invitation to the addressee to join in and take their turn. The non-canonical uses of medial clauses are a means of keeping up the interaction between the speaker and the interlocutors, making the stories and the conversations flow. This is the topic of Chapter 4 "The medial clause does it all: Coherence, continuity, and addressee involvement in Manambu", by ALEXANDRA Y. AIKHENVALD.

The ways of telling a story and the means of linking clauses and sentences are likely to be affected by language contact (see, for instance, Haig 2001; Aikhenvald 2002: 153–175, Sarvasy and Aikhenvald forthcoming). Doromu-Koki has been in intensive contact with Hiri Motu, an Oceanic language, for a long time. This has resulted in borrowing numerous lexical and grammatical items and techniques. Doromu-Koki preserves its original system of clause chains with a robust system of switch-reference – which co-exist with numerous clausal and sentential conjunctions, many of which have a transparent Hiri Motu origin. Relatively recent contact with English, a major language of communication within the part of Papua New Guinea where Doromu-Koki is spoken, has resulted in an increase of code-switching. The advent of new genres of communication – writing, internet, and social media, all influenced by English – has seen an expansion of conjunctions and a reduction of clause chains as a means of linking sentences within these newly emergent discourse genres. On-going changes in media-based communication among the Manambu point in the same direction. New genres create new ways of saying things, oscillating towards convergence and levelling with English as the mainstream language. In a nutshell: social media and mobile phones are transforming the ways the Doromu-Koki, from Central Province, and also the Manambu from East Sepik, communicate: short and clipped sentences are becoming the way to go. These issues are the topic of Chapter 5, "Contact-induced changes in Doromu-Koki clause linking: New genres, new strategies", by ROBERT L. BRADSHAW.

How do children acquire narrative techniques in a Papuan language with an elaborate system of clause chains, and switch-reference tracking the identity of who-did-what-to whom? Speakers of Nungon, from Morobe Province in Papua New Guinea, learn how to tell a story at a fairly early age. An in-depth longitudinal study of child language acquisition of Nungon in Chapter 6, "Verbatim narrative prompting to children in Nungon", by HANNAH SARVASY, shows the pre-eminence of verbatim prompting by mothers and carers. Children are prompted to repeat lengthy clause chains, aimed at reporting their own personal experiences, word-by-word and clause-by-clause. Following the principles of organization of Nungon narratives, and their tense-iconicity, the verbatim prompting sequences involve clause chains for extended stretches. This is where medial clauses are the most prevalent. The process of prompting reflects a high degree of planning of a story which is to be fed to the child by the carers, alongside the "impressive maintenance of switch-reference relations that accord with grammatical rules". The children readily comply with verbatim prompting of narratives – which may last for as long as five or six minutes. This indicates their familiarity with, and acceptance of, this kind of interaction, and accounts for their early mastery of clause-chaining, ready to be manipulated for discourse-organizing purposes at a later age. The constituency of prompts may point towards psychological salience of phrases and clauses, even for speakers with minimal literacy and little if any formal schooling (as is the case for care-givers among the Nungon). Sarvasy's is the first-ever case study of verbatim narrative prompting as a way of teaching children to produce narratives in a clause-chaining language.

The next four chapters focus on grammatical devices which keep a narrative going, ensure its coherence, and signal its progress, its focal points and climaxes.

The fabric and the flow of a narrative are seen and expressed through the variety of clause-linking devices. Chapter 7, "Adjoining clauses in Brokpa narratives", by PEMA WANGDI, focuses on the internal structure of sentences and their combinations in stories and conversations in this Tibeto-Burman (or Trans-Himalayan) language of Bhutan. In Genetti's (2011: 5) words, "many languages . . . possess a feature, or a set of features, which is remarkable in systematic efficiency and central to its design, an axis around which other grammatical subsystems revolve". For Brokpa, as for Dolakha Newar (Genetti 2011: 6), its "essential structural core is found in the combination of clauses, which produces sentences with remarkable levels of syntactic complexity". Clause-chaining, nominalizations, and embedded clauses expresses the full gamut of semantic types of clause-linking to specify relations between clauses and between sentences, within a coherent narrative. A feature Brokpa shares with many Tibeto-Burman, Papuan and Australian languages is a pervasive heterosemy of case markers (within noun phrases) and clause-linking morphemes on verbs within dependent clauses. The organization of a narrative is mirrored by the status of dependent clauses as supporting clauses transmitting backgrounded information and of main clauses as focal clauses, which carry the principal story line. The discourse function of clause types is iconically reflected in their linear order: supporting clauses – which serve as a lead-up to the main line – typically precede the main, focal clauses.

Anaphoric devices are a further means of making a story flow and maintaining its coherence. Demonstratives in their anaphoric function help keep track of referents throughout discourse. They help establish major discourse participants and distinguish between those referents which are backgrounded and less salient, and those which will be foregrounded and even unexpected. A substantial body of literature focuses on discourse use of demonstratives in languages with relatively simple systems, with a binary opposition between 'this' and 'that' (see, for instance, Dixon 2010: 223–254). What happens if a language has a complex system of demonstratives with a consistent distinction between visible and non-visible terms and more than two degrees of distance? This is the topic of Chapter 8, "Discourse functions of 'visible' and 'nonvisible' demonstratives in Tiang (New Ireland) and in a cross-linguistic perspective", by CHRISTOPH HOLZ. Tiang has three degrees of distance – proximal, medial, and distal – and distinguishes visible and nonvisible forms. Visible forms tend to be a functionally unmarked choice; nonvisible forms tend to emphasise that the referent is not seen.

The use of visible forms correlates with speaker's knowledge. The geography of the Tiang-speaking island of Djaul is known to everyone, and so place names are always referred to with visible demonstratives, even when out of sight. In this way, demonstratives in Tiang express non-propositional evidentiality – information source concerning a noun phrase or just a noun (along the lines of Aikhenvald 2018; Jacques 2018). A careful study of a large corpus of Tiang narratives shows that nonvisible forms are the preferred choice for anaphors, while cataphors tend to be expressed by visible demonstratives. This statement is corroborated by a careful study of twenty-two languages with visible versus nonvisible distinctions in their demonstrative systems, from various parts of the world. The sample covers all the languages for which information about anaphoric uses of visible and nonvisible forms is available at this point in time. The link between lack of visibility and participant anaphora correlates with conceptual distance. For instance, in Nivkh, a Paleo-Siberian isolate, the immediate anaphor is expressed with visible demonstratives, while nonvisible demonstratives appear to be reserved for anaphoric reference to those referents which are either not seen or were mentioned much earlier in the narrative. That visible demonstratives are preferred for marking cataphoric referents may have to do with the way cataphora works – deictically referring to something immediately following the demonstrative. Holz's chapter, in its depth and breadth, opens a new avenue for typological research – to be taken up by linguists working on other languages with visibility distinctions in their demonstrative systems and their deployment in discourse.

Some grammatical devices are particularly prominent in framing a narrative, foregrounding its salient features, and leading up to an unexpected climactic peak. Mirativity – or grammaticalized expectation of knowledge, which covers unprepared mind and surprise – is a relatively recent arrival in the field of linguistics. It is not that individual scholars of numerous languages had not been aware of the existence of the phenomenon. But having a cross-linguistic overview of mirative, by DeLancey (1997), alerted grammarians across the world to its validity as something more than an exotic curiosity. New types of mirative systems (distinct from tense, aspect, modality and evidentiality) – as exponents of what Hyslop (2014) aptly called "expectation of knowledge" – and new mirative extensions of other categories keep being discovered (see also Aikhenvald 2012b and DeLancey 2012).

The use of mirative forms within narratives remains somewhat of a moot point in most grammars. Mirative forms and mirative extensions of other categories (be it evidentials or aspects) tend to be illustrated with isolated sentences produced as a spontaneous reaction to something. Two further chapters in this volume take a different approach – focusing on how miratives play out in actual narratives, and how a context leading up to a mirative is structured.

Mirativity, the grammatical marking of unexpected information, is a core feature of many a Himalayan language, and particularly so of Kurtöp, from Bhutan. This is the focus of Chapter 9, "Miratives and magic: On 'newness' as iconic grammar in Kurtöp narratives", by GWENDOLYN HYSLOP. Mirativity is encoded in perfective and imperfective aspects, and in affirmative and negative existential and equational copulas. Mirativity is distinct from evidentiality (the marking of information source) and egophoricity (access to information). Mirative forms express the information the speaker did not have before the speech act. They are not uncommon in conversations and other speech genres – as the need arises. But a real hotspot of miratives are Kurtöp narratives all of which appear to involve something magical and whose key characters possess special, supranatural powers. The overall percentage of miratives in such stories is strikingly high. In two of the stories analysed by Hyslop, miratives were used within the first three clauses – "setting the tone for the introduction of the characters and place". When asked about the choice of forms in the stories, the speakers remarked that the mirative forms made the stories "interesting", and that using them was the way to tell a story.

Miratives appear to act like attention-getting devices – as if telling the audience to expect the unexpected, and to keep listening: something new is coming. The strength of novelty and lack of expectation expressed in Kurtöp mirative forms correlates with another feature – their relatively recent origin. It is as if the novel forms encode very novel information – an example of historical iconicity of sorts. And quite likely, older and more archaic miratives in a language will tend to wear out, giving way to new mirative forms, which would express stronger newsworthiness, and novelty. The necessity for constant renewal of mirative forms and the iconic correlation between the age of a form and its force is reminiscent of Jespersen's cycle of renewal for negative expressions across languages (see, for instance, Miestamo 2017: 431). A similar point is taken up in Chapter 10.

As a narrative evolves, the audience is gradually being prepared for a new and surprising turn of events, and a focal point of a stretch of discourse. The ways in which the narration is structured shows an iconic correlation with the presentation of events leading to a focal point, or a climax in a story – be it a folktale, a legend, a myth, or an account of any event worth talking about. In many languages of Western and Central Siberia, such a focal point requires mirative marking. This is the topic of Chapter 10, by ELENA SKRIBNIK, "Reading Siberian folklore: Miratives, premirative contexts, and Proppean 'Hero's Journey'".

The sequence of actions leading to the climax of a story paves the way for an unexpected outcome. In other words, a discourse context for a mirative meaning is created by a conventionalised series of actions reflecting what Propp (1929) called "A Hero's Journey". The set typically involves
(i)   a verb of motion towards the speaker or point of reference, 'come',
(ii) a verb of visual perception 'see', potentially also followed by a verb of comprehension and then a verb of speech.

The sequence of verbs and of actions goes along the formula *veni vidi* 'I came I saw', which can be expanded by *comprehendi* 'I understood' and then *dixi* 'I said (it)'. This is the essence of what Elena Skribnik calls "premirative contexts": a set of background events leading to a climax in a narrative. The formulaic organization of the story line in its lead-up to an unexpected outcome creates the context for the use of dedicated "mirative" forms. Examples come from Mansi and Khanty, two Ob-Ugric languages (from the Uralic family). Or an essentially non-mirative form will acquire a mirative extension – as is the case in Selkup, from the Samoyedic branch of Uralic, which has no conventionalised special forms with just a mirative meaning. The organization of a tale with its build-up towards a surprising outcome creates the appropriate context and the motivation for the emergence, and concomitant renewal, of mirative forms and meanings across the discourse genres captured by the corpora of narratives of indigenous languages of Siberia (analysed by Skribnik).

The renewal and salience of mirative meanings in specific discourse genres resonates with Hyslop's conclusions in Chapter 9. In Du Bois' (1985: 363) adage, "grammars code best what speakers do most". New, surprising, and unexpected facets of magic, the supranatural, and folk tales across the board are conducive to continuous renewal of mirative forms, pivotal for telling a story the way it is to be told.

The three final chapters focus on a selection of topics, and types, of narratives in Northern Australia and in Papua New Guinea.

Across many languages and many story-telling traditions, from Amazonia to North America and Australia, a Trickster is a well-attested character, and "an intriguing puzzle to anthropologists and folklorists" (Basso 1987: 4). In Ellen Basso's (1987: 4–5) words, what appears to be impressive are "the contradictions in Trickster's moral character", in "what Boas called 'the troublesome psychological discrepancy' between the apparently incongruous attributes of the 'culture hero' (who makes the world safe and secure for human life) and the 'selfish buffoon' (who ludicrously attempts the inappropriate)" – that is, the Trickster. Tricksters come in different guises. It is human-like for the Kalapalo, a Carib-speaking group from the Xingu area of Brazil (Basso 1987: 225–226) and for the Wakuénai, an Arawak-speaking variety of Kurripako from Venezuela (Hill 2009). Trickster comes in the shape of Wanali (a large bird of the genus of Anhingidae) for the Tariana, who speak a closely related Arawak language. In a magic tale by the Kurtöp a trickster is a frog (Hyslop, Chapter 9 of this volume). Across North American traditions, Trickster takes the shape of a variety of birds and animals (Raven, Mink, Coyote, Hare, and so on). The Trickster is ambiguous: he can be a deceiver and a trick-player, a shape-shifter, a lewd improviser and a bricoleur, and also a messenger-imitator of the god, transcending "the ordinary in a way that is both destructive and creative" (evoking the figure of Trickster-creator among some northern Amazonian groups who never does, or bestows anything on anyone, in a straightforward way).

In Chapter 11, "Jawoyn Trickster stories, Southern Arnhem land", FRANCESCA MERLAN offers a brief discussion of what the image of a Trickster is like in a variety of traditions. She then defines "trickerism" as "a narrative complex of character and events in which the trickster figure does things which become understood by the audience as beyond the knowledge of another or others within the story, in a way that advances the story line". Trickster stories are part of the personal repertoires of male speakers of Jawoyn, of the Northern Territory (originally from the Arnhem land), and are shared with their former neighbours, the Bininj Kunwok.

In one story, the Trickster figure is Najik 'owlet nightjar', a rather menacing looking bird. Najik is a shape-shifter, a deceiver, a disrupter, and also an establisher of norms. A Jawoyn story tells how women used to hunt but, due to Najik's action, only men now hunt. The other story involves Balukgayin, 'the guardian': this is a man charged with taking care of boys during their initiation and making them into adults. But instead of acting in a responsible manner, he does the opposite, transgressing every norm of acceptable and ethical behaviour, and is killed as a result. Depicting the Tricksters as norm-breakers and norm-inverters is a matter of mirth for the narrators – the stories are interspersed with laughter at Tricksters' tricks and mischief. The readers can accompany the flow of the stories themselves: the stories are provided in the Appendix, and the running commentary is within the chapter itself. Trickster stories are perhaps among the oldest and the most traditional ones for the Jawoyn, and appear to be the exclusive domain of male narrators.

In contrast, Chapter 12, "Narratives of self and other: Auto/Biography in PNG", by ROSITA HENRY, addresses a genre believed to be a relatively new arrival – that of autobiography. People tend to construct selfhood through narratives about themselves and about others. The novelty of autobiography as a genre in the context of the Papua New Guinea has its roots in the traditional conceptualization of self and of person. Traditionally, people "did not acknowledge themselves as the autonomous, ego-oriented entities, imbued with temporal continuity, which we might call 'individuals'. Consequently, they could not have an autobiographical consciousness" (Goddard 2008: 40). Such consciousness must have started to appear only within the postcolonial context which saw the rise of the autobiographical genre, written predominantly in English.

However, it would be too simplistic to assume that autobiographical motives are solely a post-colonial innovation. Numerous traditional oral narrative genres across Papua New Guinea can be autobiographical in some way and be employed as a means of self-representation. One such example is segmentary person, whereby an orator will use the first person singular in reference to their entire tribe (as mentioned above). This use of first person can be considered autobiographical, no matter whether the orator is speaking of his own personal lived experiences as one man or of the shared experiences of his whole tribe, or "segment". Another oral genre which appears to be autobiographical in nature is confession – a traditional practice which involves getting together to give members of a lineage opportunity to confess and "straighten" any wrong done to others. This practice is now merging with Christian practices. Songs and myths can also be a vehicle for autobiographical stories: through the rendition of a myth, a skilled narrator will construct their own identity and put their own, autobiographical, imprint on it.

The concept of self and the construction of personhood is viewed, by Rosita Henry, with reference to the memoir of the late Maggie Wilson (2019 with additions by Henry). The narrative within the book is in part an unfinished memoir by Maggie herself, and in part a collective biography, with an interplay of many life stories and memoirs of Maggie, herself a prominent member of the Highlands community.

Maggie's memoir is considered to be a true PNG autobiography, that is, a retrospective telling of her own life in written form. But it goes well beyond just that. Even the use of the first person singular 'I' within the memoir does not necessarily imply an 'I' "that is an egocentric, self-reflective, introspective individual self" (Henry, this volume).

As Rosita Henry puts it, "Maggie's narrative is event-dominated rather than characterised by introspective self-reflection": she presents herself through her "practical deeds, exchanges, temporarily emplaced social actions, and her relational engagement with others". Maggie's memoir is an "auto/biography in which the distinction between both self and other, and self and person collapse" and fuse together – perhaps implicitly following the traditional embeddedness of autobiographical motives into genres which go beyond just one person's life and experience. In a nutshell, Maggie's narrative about herself can be viewed as a continuation of autobiographical traditions which constitute part and parcel of traditional narrative genres of the Highlands with which Maggie was intimately familiar. We are faced with a continuity of ways of talking about oneself – not just with a postcolonial expansion of "autobiography" as an imported genre.

Chapter 13. by MICHAEL WOOD, "The origin of death in Kamula futures", focuses on the analyses of a Kamula narrative recorded and transcribed in 2019 – after decades of close interaction between the traditional Kamula of Western Province of PNG, White Australian colonial powers, and Christianity. Powerful ancestral beings continue to play a creative role in the constitution of social life among the Kamula. The narratives about the origins of death position the dead as a salient political concern, and reflect Kamula on-going engagement with the Europeans in terms of their differences and similarities. A narrative overflows into interaction with the audience and the addressees (including the researcher), and has to be supplemented by the context of other events beyond the limits of the narration, and include the history of speakers. The current events to do with logging in the area – the collapse of social order into violence and the long-awaited renewal of logging, so as to provide the community with financial resources – are reflected in the stories about the origin of death. Even the figure of Christ is understood, by some, as already "prefigured" in ancestral myths about the Hero and his son – similarly to the ways in which the White Invader was integrated into the evolving ancestral mythologies across Amazonia (see Aikhenvald 2013 on the evolution and change in structure of Origin myths among the Tariana and other groups in north-west Amazonia within several decades, as a response to the pressures of market economy).

The polyphony of voices is underscored by the ways in which the narrator alternates between his own voice, the voice of the ancestral being (the protagonist), and the sound of the birds as additional participants in the events. The use of quotations – often marked only by changes in voice and in prosody – is reminiscent of the manipulation of different voices and quotations in Chapter 3 of this volume. The ancestral stories of the Kamula are far from set and static: they include future projections, expectations, and evolving attitudes towards what is happening around. In Michael Wood's words (this volume), "the various retellings of the narratives depended on, and were held together, by an emergent community of narrators and characters . . . who all interacted in different ways to create various partial and contingent instantiations of the story". The presence of the speakers' selves in the narration echoes the autobiographical motives and experiences as part and parcel of ancestral myths and legends, outlined in Chapter 11.

As Rosita Henry puts it (Chapter 11, this volume), "narratives of various kinds are an important part of the way people communicate with both humans and non-humans in their worlds. Both the nature of the narrative form and the interpretation of the messages encoded in narratives" are what the chapters within this volume focus on.

The volume is held together by multiple threads which form a multi-coloured tapestry of polyphonous narratives – from grammatical forms and categories deployed in organizing the narrative and interweaving the protagonists and the narrator, to the kinds of narratives told, their organization and evolution in time and space, incorporating the impact of post-colonial languages and post-colonial experience. Each author has undertaken intensive fieldwork and has firsthand in-depth knowledge of the languages under discussion. This is what makes the conclusions – and the generalizations within this volume – particularly reliable.

Last but not least – as many minority languages become obsolescent and gradually slide into disuse, so do the intricate fabrics of their stories and their lore. Documenting them and making them available to younger generations is vital for the survival of millennia-old traditions, ways of life and worldviews. And for maintaining dignity and identity, by preserving First Nations' voices and making them heard, documented, and remembered. Our focus on narrative traditions of indigenous minorities is a further way to serve this purpose. It is fortuitous and appropriate that the preparation and publication of this volume coincide with a decade-long international event – UNESCO's Decade of indigenous languages (2022–2032).

References

Adelaar, W. F. H. 1990. The role of quotations in Andean discourse. In Harm Pinkster & Inge Genee (eds.), *Unity in diversity: Papers presented to Simon C. Dik on his 50th birthday*, 1–12. Dordrecht: Foris.

Aikhenvald, Alexandra Y. 2002. *Language contact in Amazonia*. Oxford: Oxford University Press.

Aikhenvald, Alexandra Y. 2011. Speech reports: A cross-linguistic perspective. In Alexandra Y. Aikhenvald & R. M. W. Dixon (eds.), *Language at large: Essays on syntax and semantics*, 290–326. Leiden: Brill.

Aikhenvald, Alexandra Y. 2012a. *The languages of the Amazon*. Oxford: Oxford University Press.

Aikhenvald, Alexandra Y. 2012b. The essence of mirativity. *Linguistic Typology* 16. 435–485.

Aikhenvald, Alexandra Y. 2013. The language of value and the value of language. *HAU: A Journal of Ethnographic Theory* 3(2). 55–73.

Aikhenvald, Alexandra Y. 2015. *The art of grammar: A practical guide*. Oxford: Oxford University Press.

Aikhenvald, Alexandra Y. 2018. Evidentiality: The framework. In Alexandra. Y. Aikhenvald (ed.), *The Oxford handbook of evidentiality*, 1–46. Oxford: Oxford University Press.

Basso, Ellen B. 1987. *In favor of deceipt: A study of tricksters*. Tucson: The University of Arizona Press.

Clark, Herbert H. & Richard J. Gerrig. 1990. Quotations as demonstrations. *Language* 66. 764–805.

Cohen, David, Marie-Claude Simeone-Senelle & Martine Vanhove. 2002. The grammaticalization of 'say' and 'do': An areal phenomenon in the Horn of Africa. In Tom Güldemann & Manfred von Roncador (eds.), *Reported speech: A meeting ground for different linguistic domains*, 227–251. Amsterdam/Philadelphia: John Benjamins.

DeLancey, Scott. 1997. Mirativity: The grammatical marking of unexpected information. *Linguistic Typology* 1. 33–52.

DeLancey, Scott. 2012. Still mirative after all these years. *Linguistic Typology* 16. 529–564.

Dingemanse, Mark, Giovanni Rossi & Simeon Floyd. 2017. Place reference in story beginnings: A cross-linguistic study of narrative and interactional affordances. *Language in Society* 46. 129–158.

Dixon, R. M. W. 2009. The semantics of clause linking in typological perspective. In R. M. W. Dixon & Alexandra Y. Aikhenvald (eds.), *The semantics of clause linking: A cross-linguistic typology*, 1–55. Oxford: Oxford University Press.

Dixon, R. M. W. 2010. *Basic linguistic theory*, vol. 2, *Grammatical topics*. Oxford: Oxford University Press.

Du Bois, J. 1985. Competing motivations. In John Haiman (ed.), *Iconicity in syntax*, 343–366. Amsterdam: John Benjamins.

Genetti, Carol. 2011. The tapestry of Dolakha Newar: Chaining, embedding, and the complexity of sentences. *Linguistic Typology* 15. 5–24.

Goddard, Michael. 2008. From "My story" to "The story of myself" – colonial transformations of personal narratives among the Motu-Koita of Papua New Guinea. In Brij V. Lal & Vicki Luker (eds.), *Telling Pacific lives: Prisms of process*, 35–50. Canberra: Australian National University Press.

Haig, Geoffrey. 2001. Linguistic diffusion in present-day Anatolia: From top to bottom. In Alexandra Y. Aikhenvald & R. M. W. Dixon (eds.), *Areal diffusion and genetic inheritance: Problems in comparative linguistics*, 195–224. Oxford: Oxford University Press.

Henry, Rosita. 2013. Being and belonging: Exchange, value, and land ownership in the Western Highlands of Papua New Guinea. In Alexandra Y. Aikhenvald & R. M. W. Dixon (eds.), *Possession and ownership: A cross-linguistic typology*, 274–290. Oxford: Oxford University Press.

Hill, Jonathan D. 2009. *Made-from-the bone: Trickster myths, music, and history from the Amazon*. Urbana: University of Illinois Press.

Hyslop, Gwendolyn. 2014. The grammar of knowledge in Kurtöp: Evidentiality, mirativity, and expectation of knowledge. In Alexandra Y. Aikhenvald & R. M. W. Dixon (eds.), *The grammar of knowledge: A cross-linguistic typology*, 108–131. Oxford: Oxford University Press.

Jacques, Guillaume. 2018. Non-propositional evidentiality. In Alexandra Y. Aikhenvald (ed.), *The Oxford handbook of evidentiality*, 109–123. Oxford: Oxford University Press.

Merlan, Francesca & Alan Rumsey. 1991. *Ku Waru: Language and segmentary politics in the Western Nebilyer Valley, Papua New Guinea*. Cambridge: Cambridge University Press.

Miestamo, Matti. 2017. Negation. In Alexandra Y. Aikhenvald & R. M. W. Dixon (eds.), *The Cambridge handbook of linguistic typology*, 405–439. Cambridge: Cambridge University Press.

Propp, Vladimir. 1929. *Morphology of the folk tale*. Austin: University of Texas Press.

Quirk, Randolph, Sidney Greenbaum, Geoffrey Leech & Jan Svartvik. 1985. *A comprehensive grammar of the English language*. London: Longman.

Rumsey, Alan. 1999. The personification of social totalities in the Pacific. *Journal of Pacific Studies* 23. 48–70.

Rumsey, Alan. 2000. Agency, personhood and the "I" of discourse in the Pacific and beyond. *The Journal of the Royal Anthropological Institute* 6(1). 101–115.

Sarvasy, Hannah. 2015. Breaking the clause chains: Non-canonical medial clauses in Nungon. *Studies in Language* 39. 664–696.

Sarvasy, Hannah & Alexandra Y. Aikhenvald. Forthcoming. Clause-chaining in typological perspective. In Hannah Sarvasy & Alexandra Y. Aikhenvald (eds.), *Clause-chaining across the world's languages*. Oxford: Oxford University Press.

Silverstein, Michael. 1999. NIMBY goes linguistic: Conflicted 'voicings' from the culture of local language communities. In S. J. Billings, J. P. Boyle & A. M. Griffin (eds.), *CLS 35. The Panels. Language, identity and the other*, 101–123. Chicago: Chicago Linguistic Society.

Vries, Lourens J. de. 1990. Some remarks on direct quotation in Kombai. In Harm Pinkster & Inge Genee (eds.), *Unity in diversity: Papers presented to Simon C. Dik on his 50th birthday*, 291–309. Dordrecht: Foris.

Wilson, Maggie. 2019. *A true child of Papua New Guinea: Memoir of a life between two worlds*. (Edited, and with additions, by Rosita Henry). Jefferson, North Carolina: McFarland Press.

R. M. W. Dixon

2 First person orientation in Yidiñ narratives and its implications

Whereas traditional legends in the Australian language Dyirbal would be told in 3rd person, in its southerly neighbour, Yidiñ, 1st person was often preferred. That is, the narrator would take on the identity of the central character. In one legend the initial main character (telling the tale in 1st person) departs from the story (he dies), then another character takes over, and continues the story from their perspective, in 1st person. As a consequence of this narrative style, 1st (and 2nd) person pronouns are extraordinarily frequent in Yidiñ narratives, occurring two to four times more often than pronouns in Dyirbal narratives. (The narrator takes on 1st person and uses 2nd person for anyone addressed.) This helps explain a syntactic difference between the two languages. Both have split morphology – ergative case marking for nominals and accusative marking for 1st and 2nd person pronouns. Coordination in Dyirbal is on an S/O (ergative) basis whether based on nominals or pronouns. In contrast, coordination in Yidiñ is on an S/O basis for nominals but on an S/A (accusative) basis for pronouns – reflecting the case marking on pronouns – due to the greeter frequency of pronouns in this language.

2.1 Introduction

Storytellers in Yidiñ had an unusual way of recounting traditional stories. They would often take on – as it were – the identity of the central character and tell the tale in 1st person. Speakers of Dyirbal, Yidiñ's southerly neighbour, employed a quite different technique; as in most other languages, traditional tales were told in 3rd person (examples are in Dixon 1972: 368–382, 387–397; 2022: 407–15).

By examining these contrasting styles of story-telling, I shall show how they determine the different syntactic profiles of the two languages; that is, the contrasting specifications of the pivot (grammaticalised topic) for coordination.

The Yidiñ language was spoken by the Yidiñ-ji (lit. Yidiñ-WITH) people from Cairns down to Babinda, east onto the Cape Grafton Peninsula (and Yarrabah), west up the Mulgrave River to the tablelands (including Yungaburra and Kairi). I worked with the last few fluent speakers, recording texts from Dick Moses (died

R. M. W. Dixon, Jawun Research Centre, Central Queensland University

https://doi.org/10.1515/9783110789836-002

in 1977) and Tilly Fuller (died in 1974). The last fluent speaker (George Davis) died in 2002. The phonemes of Yidiñ and Dyirbal are provided in the appendix.

Dyirbal was spoken from south of Babinda to north of Cardwell and inland as far as Herberton. There were several score fluent speakers when I started fieldwork on the language in 1963 and texts were recorded from more than a dozen people. The last fluent speaker (Jack Muriata) died in 2011. (Yidiñ and Dyirbal are not closely genetically related but do show typological similarities.)

2.2 Storytelling in Yidiñ

Some of the texts recorded in Yidiñ were personal reminiscences, and they were necessarily in 1st person. A number of traditional tales featured several people, no one of them more central than the other(s); for example, the story of the two creator beings Guyala and Damarri. These tales were necessarily told in 3rd person.

But when a legend was oriented to just one ancestor character, the storyteller would take on the identity of that person and the whole text would be told in first person.

For instance, when DICK MOSES recounted Text 1 (see Dixon 1991: 28–32), the story of WUNGUL, the carpet snake (an incarnation of the rainbow), the storyteller was Wungul, right from the first line:

Line 1 *ŋayu*$_S$ *gana* *galii-na*
1sg.NOM TRY go-PURP
'I have to try to go.'

Line 2 *bamaa-n*$_O$ *gali-ŋa-lna* [*miya-miya* *gujuuga*
person-GEN go-COMIT-PURP REDUP-cowrie.shell someone.else's
yuma]$_O$; *ŋayu*$_A$ *galii-ŋa-l* *bamaa-n*$_O$
promised 1sg.NOM go-COMIT-PRES person-GEN
'I have to take these cowrie shells which belong to some other people and have been promised to them (lit. people's someone else's promised cowrie shells); I am taking [the shells] belonging to these people (taking them to the people).'

Line 3 *ŋayu*$_S$ *gana* *yiŋguurruň* *galii-na* *guwa*;
1sg.NOM TRY HERE.ALL.DIRECTION go-PURP west
ŋayu$_S$ *gali-ŋ*
1sg.NOM go-PRES
'I should try to go in this direction, to the west; I am going.'

Line 4 *gima-ŋ,   galii-ŋa-l   muguy   ŋanjaa-da*
       carry-PRES go-COMIT-PRES all.the.time creek-LOC
       '(I) was carrying (the shells), taking them along a creek all he time.'

Line 5 *ŋayu$_S$ guwa wulŋgu+jana-ŋalii-ñ;*
       1sg.NOM   west   sing.wulŋgu.style-GOING-PAST
       wulŋgu+janaa-ñ
       sing.wulŋgu.style-PAST
       'I went to the west and sang a Wulŋgu-style song; I sang a Wulŋgu-style
       song.' (Note that "+" joins the two components of a compound.)

As the story continues, Wungul is waylaid by three bird people who ask to be
given some of the shells. He refuses and is finally slain by the birds.

    The first person style is continued up to line 69, the penultimate line of the
text, where Wungul describes his own death:

Line 61 *ŋayu$_A$ gurrga$_O$ budi-l*
       1sg.NOM   neck   put.down-PRES
       'I put my neck down.' (The carpet snake comes to a log across the path;
       as he is climbing up he puts his head on the log, preparatory to pulling
       himself over it.)

Line 62 *[ŋañañ   gurrga]$_O$ gundaa-l, [ŋañañ   gurrga gulga]$_O$,*
       1sg.ACC   neck   cut-PAST 1sg.ACC   neck   short
       gaymbii-ñ   gilbii-l;   guwal$_O$ jarraa-l   bulmba$_O$;
       do.to.all-PAST throw-PAST   name   assign-PAST Place
       [ŋajin   gulga-gulga   gula]$_O$; [ŋañañ   gulga]$_O$ gundaa-l
       1sg.GEN   REDUP-short   body   1sg.ACC   short   cut-PAST
       'My neck was cut off (by the three bird people), my neck (cut up) in short
       pieces, (the pieces) were all thrown out; names were given to each place
       (where the short pieces landed); many short pieces of my body, my short
       pieces were cut up.'

Line 63 *bama$_S$ bani-baniiji-ñu, guli-dagaa-ñ   [wirraa-gu*
       person   grumble-PAST   angry-INCH-PAST   moveable.object-DAT
       milgaa-gu];   bamaa-n   gujuga
       cowrie.shell-DAT person-GEN someone else's
       'The people (the three birds) grumbled and got angry over the cowrie
       shells; (the shells) belong to other people (not to the three birds, or to
       the carpet snake).'

Just the final line is told in 3rd person.

Rather than commencing in 1st person style, a story will often begin with a few sentences in 3rd person which set the scene. This is found in TILLY FULLER's Text 8 (see Dixon 1991: 58–62), an account of how the ancestral hero GULNYJARUBAY travelled around Yidiñ country naming places according to whatever he saw or experienced there.

The initial three sentences are told in 3rd person and describe the first three places that Gulnyjarubay visited. From sentence 4 onwards, the narrator assumed the identity of Gulnyjarubay with all the remainder of the legend being told in 1st person:

Line 1   *gubii-ja*   *Gulñjarubay$_S$*   *judaa-ñ*   *gambil-jilŋgu,*
         storytime-LOC Gulnyjarubay   descend-PAST   ridge-DOWN
         bulmba   *Wuŋal*
         place   Wungal
         'In the storytime Gulnyjarubay went down along a ridge (to) a place (called) Wungal.'

Line 2   *ŋuŋgu-m*   *judaa-ñ*   *yarrbi-i,*   *bulmba*   *Wuwuy,*
         THERE-ABL   descend-PAST   basalt.rock-LOC   place   Wuwuy
         gubu$_O$ *wawaa-l*   *wuwuy$_O$*
         leaf   look.at-PAST   wuwuy
         'From there (he) went on downhill along flat basalt rocks (to) a place (called) Wuwuy (named after *wuwuy*, a small bean tree, *Pongamia pinnata*, which grows there); (he) looked at the leaves of the bean tree.'

Line 3   *galii-ñ*   *ŋuŋgu-m,*   *jilŋgu* *Bindabalgaal*   *bulmba*   *wawaa-l*
         go-PAST   THERE-ABL   down   Bindabalgaal   place   see-PAST
         balgal-ŋunda
         build-DAT.SUBORD
         '(He) went on from there, down to a place (called) Bindabalgaal (and) saw a house being built there.' (*Binda* is 'shoulder' and *balga-l* 'make, build', the place name *Binda+balgaal* referring to the fact that sticks had been set up there, to make a house frame.)

Line 4   *ŋayu$_S$*   *yiŋurruy*   *naga gali-ŋ,*   *bulmba$_S$*   *wuna-ŋ*
         1sg.NOM   HERE.ALL.DIRECTION   east   go-PRES   place   lie-PRES
         guwa,   *guwal* *Gurragulu;*   *yiŋu*   *ŋañji*   *Gurramiña*
         west   name   Gurragulu   THIS   1pl.NOM   Gurraminya
         'Now I go on in this direction to the east; the place lying to the west is of the moiety named Gurragulu; this (place) of ours is of the Gurraminya moiety.'

Line 5   *ŋayu$_S$*   *gali-ŋ*   *jubu,*   *ŋayu$_A$*   *baja-ari-ñu,*
       1sg.NOM   go-PRES   walking.stick   1sg.NOM   leave-GOING-PAST
       bulmba   *Jubugaraa*
       place   Jubugaraa
       'I am going (with) a walking stick; I went and left it (at) a place (called)
       Jubugaraa (from *jubu* 'walking stick' and suffix *-garaa* 'from, as a result
       of').'

Line 6   *ŋayu$_S$*   *dangil-naga*   *galii-ñ,*   *bulmba*   *Wuwuy*
       1sg.NOM   creek.bank-EAST   go-PAST   place   Wuwuy
       ŋayu$_S$ *Wuwuy-mu*   *galii-ñ*   *Buruburuy,*
       1sg.NOM   Wuwuy-ABL   go-PAST   Buruburuy
       bulmba   *yiŋu*   *Buruburuy*
       place   THIS   Buruburuy
       'I went along the bank of the creek to the east, (to) a place (called) Wuwuy;
       I went from Wuwuy (to) Buruburuy, this place is Buruburuy (named from
       buruburu 'watergum tree', *Syzygium tierneyanum*, and suffix *-y* 'with').'

This continues to the end of the story:

Line 31   *ŋayu$_A$*   *wawaa-l*   *bama$_O$*   *ñamba-ñunda*   *warrma,*
       1sg.NOM   see-PAST   person   dance-DAT.SUBORD   dance.style
       bama$_S$ *ŋaru+ñamba-ñunda*
       bama   dance.shake.a.leg.style-DAT.SUBORD
       'I saw people who were dancing warrna-style, people who were dancing
       shake-a-leg style.'

Line 32   *ŋuŋgu-m*   *ŋayu$_S$*   *ñina-ŋgalii-ñ=ala,*
       THERE-ABL   1sg.NOM   stay-GOING-PAST=NOW
       ŋayu$_S$ *ŋuju=la*   *gana*   *biba-aji-ñu,*
       1sg.NOM   NOT=NOW   TRY   look.back.at-
       ŋajin   *yiŋu*   *bulmba,*   *ŋayu$_S$*   *gadaa-ñ=ala*   *ñinaa-lna*
       1sg.GEN   THIS   place   1sg.NOM   come-PAST=NOW   stay-PURP
       'From there I now went to settle down (in my own place); I tried not to
       look back now, this place is mine, I've now come to stay here.'

I recorded one legend in which the initial main character departs from the story
(he dies), and then another character takes over, and continues the story from
their perspective, in 1st person. DICK MOSES told, in Text 4 (Dixon 1991: 44–48),
how the Yidiñji people first arrived in their present-day territory. Unlike in the

Gulnyjarrubay tale, there is here no 3rd person introduction. The recording commences with GULMBIRA, an old Yidiñji man, speaking:

Line 1   *ŋayu_S*   *gana*   *burrgii-na*   *galii-na* ...
         1sg.NOM   TRY   go.walkabout-PURP   go-PURP
         'I tried to go walkabout, to go off ...'

For the next 38 lines, the story is told by Gulmbira, in 1st person. He travels around
and meets GINDAJA, THE CASSOWARY, who was a legendary man. Then Gulmbira
dies; he describes this himself:

Line 37   *ŋayu_S*   *galii-ñ,*   *ŋayu_S*   *wulaa-ñ*
          1sg.NOM   go-PAST   1sg.NOM   die-PAST
          'I've gone, I've died.'

Line 38   *Gindaja-ŋgu_A*   *ŋañaño*   *bujii-ñ:*   '*ñundu_S*   *gali-n,*   *wula-n*'
          Cassowary-ERG   1sg.ACC   tell-PAST   2sg.NOM   go-IMP   die-IMP
          'Cassowary told me: "You go!, die!"'

Line 39   *Gindaaja_S*   *galii-ñ*
          Cassowary   go-PAST
          'Cassowary went on.'

Line 40   *Baŋgilan-ña_O*   *wawa-ali-ñu*   *wala*   *galii-ñ*
          Baŋgilan-ACC   look.for-GOING-PAST CEASED   go-PAST
          'Stopped looking for Baŋgilan, and went on.'

Line 41   *ŋayu_S*   *yiŋgu*   *guya*   *wujaa-na* ...
          1sg.NOM   HERE   across.the.river cross.river-PURP
          'I (Gindaja) should cross the river here ...'

Gulmbira continued telling the story until line 38, when he recounts how Cassowary told him to die. Line 39 is in 3rd person, introducing the new narrator,
Cassowary, who – from line 41 – tells the last 18 lines of the story from his perspective, in 1st person.

(No subject is stated for line 40. It could either be taken to be 'he', with this
line continuing the 3rd person linking from line 39. Or is could be taken to be 'I',
commencing Cassowary's story-telling.)

As a consequence of this narrative style, 1st (and 2nd) person pronouns are
extraordinarily frequent in Yidiñ narratives, occurring two to four times more

often than pronouns in Dyirbal narratives. (The narrator takes on 1st person and uses 2nd person for anyone addressed.)

2.3 Identical case systems

Like many Australian languages, Yidiñ and Dyirbal, have a split system of case marking on core clausal arguments. 1st and 2nd person pronouns have one case, nominative, for transitive subject (A) and intransitive subjects (S) and another case, accusative for transitive object (O). In contrast, for nominals – nouns, adjectives, and demonstratives, which partly fulfil the function of 3rd person pronouns in other languages – absolutive case is used for S and O and ergative case for A. That is:

Dyirbal			Yidiñ		
pronouns, e.g. 2sg	core functions	nominals, e.g. 'man'	pronouns, e.g. 2sg	core functions	nominals, e.g. 'man'
ŋinda	A	yara-ŋgu	ñundu	A	waguja-ŋgu
	S			S	
ŋinuna	O	yara	ñuniñ	O	waguuja

2.4 Contrasting pivots for coordination

2.4.1 Coordination in Dyirbal

In Dyirbal, two clauses may only be joined to constitute a sentence if they share an argument which is in S or O function in each clause. We say that the language operates with an "S/O pivot". It can be seen that, in the case of nominals, the linking of S and O as pivot corresponds to the one case, absolutive, being used to mark S and O functions. (Absolutive has zero realisation and is left unmarked.)
    Consider the two clauses:

(1) yibi$_O$ yara-ŋgu$_A$ bura-n
     woman   man-ERG   see-PAST
     'The man saw the woman.'

(2) *yibi$_S$*   *miyanda-ñu*
    woman   laugh-PAST
    'The woman laughed.'

Since they share an argument which is in pivot function in each – in O function in (1) and in S function in (2) – these can be combined to form a sentence. Note that the occurrence of the pivot argument is typically omitted from the second clause (its place is shown by Ø). Thus we get:

(3) *yibi$_O$*   *yara-ŋgu$_A$* *bura-n*   Ø   *miyanda-ñu*
    woman   man-ERG   see-PAST   laugh-PAST
    'The man saw the woman and the woman laughed.'

(Note that neither Dyirbal nor Yidiñ use a conjunction similar to *and* in English. Coordination just involves juxtaposition of clauses and is marked by intonation.)

If one wanted to coordinate two clauses which did share a common argument, but it was in A – a non-pivot function – in one clause, then an antipassive derivation would have to be applied, putting the underlying A argument into surface S function and thus satisfying the pivot condition.

We have seen that if a shared argument linking two clauses to be coordinated has a nominal head (which has the same case inflection for S and O functions) then this must be in S or O function in each clause. That is, there is an S/O pivot.

But what if, in Dyirbal, the shared argument linking two clauses to be coordinated has as its head a (1st or 2nd person) pronoun, which has the same case inflection for S and A functions? What then is the pivot constraint? Somewhat surprisingly, there is again an S/O pivot.

Consider the following two clauses:

(4) *ŋaja$_A$*   *ŋinuna$_O$* *bura-n*
    1sg.NOM   2sg.ACC   see-PAST
    'I saw you.'

(5) *ŋinda$_S$*   *miyanda-ñu*
    2sg.NOM   laugh-PAST
    'You laughed.'

These two clauses share a common argument, the 2sg pronoun, which is in an S/O pivot function in each – in O function for (4) and in S function for (5). The two clauses may then be coordinated to form one sentence. The occurrence of the shared argument in the second clause may be retained but is more often omitted. Thus:

(6) ŋaja$_A$ ŋinuna$_O$ bura-n (ŋinda$_S$) miyanda-ñu
      'I saw you and you laughed.'

If one wanted to say "I(A) saw you and I(S) laughed" then – even though the 2sg pronoun has the same form for A and S functions – a different construction would have to be used.

2.4.2 Coordination in Yidiñ

Yidiñ behaves in exactly the same way as Dyirbal with respect to the coordination of two clauses sharing a nominal argument which is in S or O function in each clause. There is again an "S/O pivot". That is, for nominals the linking of S and O as pivot corresponds to the one case, absolutive, being used to mark S and O functions for nominals. Consider the following two clauses:

(7) buña$_O$ waguja-ŋgu$_A$ wawaa-l
      woman   man-ERG   see-PAST
      'The man saw the woman.'

(8) buña$_S$ maŋgaa-ñ
      woman   laugh-PAST
      'The woman laughed.'

Since they share an argument which is in pivot function in each – in O function in (7) and in S function in (8) – these can be combined to form a sentence. As in Dyirbal, the occurrence of the pivot argument is typically omitted from the second clause (its place is shown by Ø):

(9) buña$_O$ waguja-ŋgu$_A$ wawaa-l Ø$_S$ maŋgaa-ñ
      'The man saw the woman and the woman laughed.'

Also as in Dyirbal, if a shared argument was in A function in one clause, then an antipassive derivation would be needed to place it in surface S function so as to satisfy the S/O pivot constraint for coordination involving a nominal shared argument.

Whereas Yidiñ is identical to Dyirbal in having an S/O pivot constraint where nominals are involved, it differs in the case of (1st and 2nd person) pronouns. Here an S/A pivot applies, mirroring the fact that pronouns have one case covering S and A functions.

Consider the two clauses:

(10) ŋayu$_A$ ñuniñ$_O$ wawaa-l
      1sg.NOM   2sg.ACC   see-PAST
      'I saw you.'

(11) ŋayu$_S$ maŋgaa-ñ
      1sg.NOM   laugh-PAST
      'I laughed.'

In Yidiñ, two clauses involving a shared argument which is a pronoun may combine these clauses into a sentence if the shared argument is in S or A argument in each clause – there is here an S/A pivot.

Clauses (10) and (11) share a pivot – the 1sg pronoun ŋayu 'I' – which is in A function in the first and in S function in the second clause. The two clauses can thus be joined to constitute a sentence. As before, the pivot argument is typically omitted from the second clause. Thus:

(12) ŋayu$_A$ ñuniñ$_O$ wawaa-l Ø$_S$ maŋgaa-ñ
      'I saw you and I laughed.'

This difference in pivot between the two languages correlates with their contrasting narrative techniques. The "1st person orientation" of Yidiñ legends leads to pronouns being two to four times more common than in Dyirbal. The predominance of pronouns in Yidiñ gives rise to an S/A pivot for clause coordination where the shared argument is a pronoun. This reflects the case marking on pronouns.

Dyirbal has an S/O pivot for all types of coordination. The syntax is straightforward but this does mean that it is out-of-step with the case marking on pronouns. Yidiñ goes in a different direction. Pivots directly reflect case marking and this leads to more complex syntax with split pivots – S/O for nominals and S/A for pronouns – reflecting the split in case marking. This reflects the different roles of pronouns when telling traditional stories in the two languages.

2.5 The common argument in a relative clause construction

A relative clause modifies the head of an NP in a main clause. One argument in the relative clause must be identical to the head of the NP in the main clause. This is called the "common argument" (CA).

Consider:

(13) Mosquitoes_A bit [the people]_O

(14) [The people]_S were sleeping

There is a CA, *the people*, enabling these two clauses to be combined into a relative clause construction:

(15) Mosquitoes_A bit [the people [who_S were sleeping]_RC]_O

In a number of languages (see Dixon 2010: 318–319), a 1st or 2nd person pronoun may not function as CA in a relative clause construction. English is of this type. One cannot say, for instance:

(16) *Mosquitoes_A bit [me [who_S was sleeping]_RC]_O

Instead, an adverbial clause would have to be employed; something like: *Mosquitoes bit me when/while/as I was sleeping.*

Dyirbal and Yidiñ are unlike English in that a relative clause can have any kind of 1st or 2nd person pronoun as CA. An example from Dyirbal with the 1sg pronoun as CA is:

(17) [ba-ŋgu-l   yarraman-du]_A ñunju-n   [ŋayguna bani-ŋu_RC]_O
      THERE-ERG-MASC horse-ERG   snort.at-PAST   1sg.ACC   come-REL
      'The horse snorted at me as I came.' (Lit. 'The horse snorted at me who came.')

And one from Yidiñ with the 1pl pronoun as CA is:

(18) murii-du_A   ŋañjiiñ_O bajaa-l   [ŋañji_S   wuna-ñuunda_RC]_O
      mosquito-ERG   1pl.ACC   bite-PAST   1pl.NOM   sleep-DAT.SUBORD
      'The mosquitoes bit us as we slept.' (Lit. 'The mosquitoes bit us who slept.')

In most languages there are restrictions on the functions permissible for the CA in main clause and in relative clause. Those in Dyirbal and Yidiñ are set out in Table 2.1. For ease of comparison the pivots for coordination are included alongside.

Table 2.1: Contrasting syntactic orientations for Dyirbal and Yidiñ.

	COORDINATION function of pivot		RELATIVE CLAUSE CONSTRUCTION function of common argument in:	
	nominal pivot	pronoun pivot	main clause	relative clause
Dyirbal	S/O		almost any	S, O
Yidiñ	S/O	S/A	S, O	

In a main clause for Dyirbal the CA may be in almost any function – S, O, A, instrumental, dative, locative, but not allative or ablative. In the relative clause the CA must be in S or O, which are the pivot functions for coordination.

Yidiñ shows stricter constraints: the CA must be in S or O function in both main and relative clauses. In (18) it is O function for the main clause and in S function for the relative clauses (as it is in (17) from Dyirbal).

The question now to be addressed is: since Yidiñ has an S/A pivot for pronouns and an S/O one for nominals in coordination, why does it not carry this through into relative clause constructions? The answer lies in the fact that, although a pronoun can function as common argument in a relative clause construction, it does so relatively rarely.

As mentioned, many languages cannot have a 1st and 2nd person pronoun as CA in a relative clause construction. For those that do allow this, such as Yidiñ and Dyirbal, it is fairly uncommon. It is surely because of this that Yidiñ has a single straightforward constraint on a CA – it must be in S and O function in both main and relative clauses – rather than having a more complex mixture of constraints.

2.6 Conclusion

The infrastructure of a grammar can best be understood if approached in terms of the role of the language within the culture which it serves. We have shown how the nature of discourse organisation in the two languages sheds light on why they employ differing syntactic pivots. The fact that stories in Yidiñ are often told from a 1st person perspective means that this language uses a pronoun as shared argument in coordination far more frequently than does Dyirbal. This helps explain why, while Dyirbal has an S/O pivot for all kinds of coordination, Yidiñ operates with a split system – an S/A pivot for pronouns and an S/O one for nominals. And the observation that 1st and 2nd person pronouns are only rather seldom modified by a relative clause is the key to understanding why Yidiñ has a single constraint on the functions allowed to the CA in a relative clause construction.

Notes

The 24 texts recorded in Yidiñ are set out in Dixon (1991). Only some relevant portions of the grammars of Dyirbal and Yidiñ are mentioned here; full details are in Dixon (1972, 1977a, 2015).

In both languages, proper names and kin terms behave in some ways like pronouns, taking accusative suffix -*ña* for O function, as *Baŋgilan* does in line 40 of Text 4. See Dixon (1972: 43–44; 1977a: 150–151).

English may have a restrictive relative clause with a non-singular pronoun, as in: *You who voted for me will be rewarded, while you who voted against will come to regret it.* However, English may not have a relative clause to a singular pronoun.

The ideas discussed here were first aired in Dixon (1977b). They were then refined as a chapter of Dixon (2015: 141–158). The present paper is a further mild revision with some new examples.

Abbreviations

1	1st person
2	2nd person
A	transitive subject function
ABL	ablative
ACC	accusative
ALL	allative
APASS	antipassive
CA	common argument in relative clause construction
COMIT	comitative
DAT	dative
ERG	ergative
IMP	imperative

INCH   inchoative
LOC   locative
MASC   masculine
NOM   nominative
NP   noun phrase
O   transitive object function
pl   plural
PRES   present
PURP   purposive
REDUP   reduplication
S   intransitive subject function
sg   singular
SUBORD   subordinate

Appendix: Phonology

Both Yidiñ and Dyirbal have 13 consonants set out in Table 2.2.

Table 2.2: The consonant system in Yidiñ and Dyirbal.

	apico-alveolar	apico-postalveolar	lamino-palatal	dorso-velar	bilabial
stop	d		j	g	b
nasal	n		ñ	ŋ	m
lateral	l				
rhotic	r	ɽ			
semi-vowel			y	w	

Dyirbal has just three vowels: *i*, *u*, and *a*. Yidiñ has the same three with a length contrast: *i*, *ii*, *u*, *uu*, *a*, and *aa*. Yidiñ has a complex set of rules for lengthening vowels, omitting final syllables, etc. See Dixon (1977a: 31–107).

References

Dixon, R. M. W. 1972. *The Dyirbal language of North Queensland*. Cambridge: Cambridge University Press.

Dixon, R. M. W. 1977a. *A grammar of Yidiñ*. Cambridge: Cambridge University Press.

Dixon, R. M. W. 1977b. The syntactic development of Australian languages. In Charles N. Li (ed.), *Mechanisms of syntactic change*, 365–415. Austin: University of Texas Press.

Dixon, R. M. W. 1991. *Words of our country: Stories, place names and vocabulary in Yidiny, the Aboriginal language of the Cairns/Yarrabah region*. St Lucia: University of Queensland Press.

Dixon, R. M. W. 2010. *Basic linguistic theory*, vol. 2, *Grammatical topics*. Oxford: Oxford University Press.

Dixon, R. M. W. 2015. *Edible gender, mother-in-law style, and other grammatical wonders: Studies in Dyirbal, Yidiñ, and Warrgamay*. Oxford: Oxford University Press.

Dixon, R. W. 2022. *A new grammar of Dyirbal*. Oxford: Oxford University Press.

Alan Rumsey, John Mansfield, Nicholas Evans

3 The sound of one quotation mark: Quoted speech in Indigenous Australian narrative

A common feature of storytelling around the world is the artful use of quotation to enact the speech of characters in the stories. Here we examine how that works in Indigenous languages across northern Australia. After presenting introductory examples, we map out the main typological dimensions along which languages organise different solutions to the problems of representing speech and thought, and show how those dimensions figure in our sample of Indigenous-language texts. For six of the languages we quantify the proportions of quoted vs non-quoted speech within selected texts, and the proportion of the quoted speech that is explicitly framed as quotation. For comparative purposes the sample also includes two popular English-language narrative texts by non-Indigenous authors. We conclude by addressing the question of what is most distinctive about quotation in Indigenous Australian storytelling, and suggesting how our analysis of it can help to advance understandings of "voice" and multivocality in general.

3.1 Introduction

Talk about talk – incorporating what other people say into your narratives – is something done in all cultures, and all languages (cf. McGregor 2019). But there are considerable differences in how it is done, which can greatly alter the flavour of particular languages, speakers, and genres – e.g., novels alternating between the narrator's voice and conversation between characters, versus plays, which are almost all conversation except for a few stage directions and identifications of characters.

Narrative traditions in many Australian languages are striking because of the way so much of the action, and especially so much of the talk, the thought, the feelings and the perceptions, are presented as direct quotation, often in a very lively and dramatic way. The written version of this chapter captures only a fraction of this liveliness, so for a better feeling of what these artful narratives sound like we recommend you listen to the sound files where indicated.

What's more, these quotations are often "unframed", without being introduced by an expression such as "she said (that)" or "he thought", in what Mathis

Alan Rumsey, Nicholas Evans, The Australian National University
John Mansfield, University of Melbourne

https://doi.org/10.1515/9783110789836-003

and Yule (1994) call "zero quotatives" (cf. Spronck and Nikitina 2019 on "defenestration"). Quotation may be indicated by a number of other narrative techniques, from intonation to getting different characters to speak different languages, to just making the listener work to understand, drawing on their knowledge of the context. However, at the same time it introduces many problems in rendering, and faithfully translating, these texts into English, partly because of English reader expectations, and partly because of the classic translator's problem of how much extra information they can legitimately add.

Let's make this more concrete by looking at an initial example from the north of Western Australia. Text excerpt (1) exemplifies most of the main aspects of quotation that we will be discussing in this chapter. It comes from a story told by Campbell Ellenbrae in 1975, in Wurla, a language of the Central Kimberley region that is closely related to Ngarinyin, as described in Rumsey (1982).[1] The main character in the story – the one referred to in the first two lines, was a white man named Harry, who had been living in the bush "like a blackfella" wearing only a loincloth and living off of the land. At this point in the story Campbell and some other Aboriginal stockmen have just come across Harry when they are mustering cattle. He welcomes them into his camp, and says "Sorry I've got nothing to give you". But this is overly modest of him, as shown by what happens next:

Wurla

(1) a. *ngara   yarrij   andumindan   mejerri bajilarri mejerri*
       honey move.downward 3PL<1SG-take:PRS two   bucket   two
       He takes down two buckets of honey, two of them

   b. *di   nyadungurlun-nyina*
      honey 1PL.EXCL.OBJ-give-PRS-PAUC
      and gives them to us

   c. *'a   bunda-nga birri bunda anja   gundaangurlu-n-na-ngarri*
      uh these-only they these what 2PL.OBJ:IRR:give-PRS-PAUC-SUB
      'These are all I've got to give you.

   d. *dimu   burray   dimu*
      that one nothing   that one
      That's all there is, nothing else.

1 For a link to the sound file for excerpt (1) see ◀⟩ https://www.degruyter.com/document/isbn/9783110789836/html

e. *dorr   ngurrayirri   muna-nga' ama-nyarrigana*
   chop 1SG:be:PST   there-only 3m:do:PRS-1.PAUC.EXCL:IO
   I've just been chopping over there' he says to us.

f. *'waw'   nyarrimenanga   'wali   wali'*
   hang.on 1PL.EXCL:do:PST:3SG:IO wait   wait
   'Hang on!', we said to him 'Wait a minute!'.

g. *'ya ngunju   warda-ga   binjon'*   *ngume-nangga*
   and tobacco like-Q   3PL<2SG-act.upon:PRS 1SG: do:PST:3SG:IO
   'And do you like tobacco?' I said to him.

h. *'yu   wandim   bidinungarri'*
   you   want   some
   'Do you want some?'

i. *'wana   warda   winjon-ngarri   janungurlu-ga   di'*
   if   like   3n_w<2SG:PRS-SUB 1SG<2SG:FUT:give-Q   then
   'You can give me some if you'd like to'

j. *'arri nyunungurlu'*   *ngume-nangga,*   *ngin*
   O.K. 2SG<SG:FUT:give 1SG:do:PST-3SG:IO 1SG
   'OK, I'll give you some' I said to him.

Eight of the ten lines in this excerpt – all but the first two – consist mainly or entirely of quotation. The fact that lines (c), (d) and (e) comprise an extended quote is explicitly indicated at the end of line (e) by the word *amanyarrigana*, a verb which is based on the root *ma* 'do' (the most usual sense of which is 'say'), with a prefix *a-* indicating that its subject – the represented speaker – is masculine, and a suffix *-nyarrigana* indicating that the addressee is first person paucal exclusive (i.e., 'me and a few others, not including you'). This use of a verb or other grammatical device to indicate that a given utterance is to be attributed to another speaker or speech event is what we (e.g. Rumsey 1982: 157–166) and other linguists (e.g. Wiesemann 1990; Spronck and Nikitina 2019) call "framing", because they frame the words being spoken as coming from another person or time. Other examples of framing in text (1) can be seen in lines (f), (g), and (j), which all include forms of the verb *ma* that do the framing as in line (e). Line (i) is also quoted speech rather than the narrator's, but it is not explicitly framed, by the verb *ma* or any other grammatical device. Rather, from the beginning of line (i) there is an implicit change of attributed speaker that goes along with the move from a question (by Campbell) in lines (g) and (h) to a reply (by Harry) in line (i). That fact (along with others to be discussed below) makes it fairly easy to recognize that line (h) is to be attributed to Harry rather than Campbell, even though the change of speaker is not explicitly indicated by a framing verb as it is in line (j). Speaker attribution is not always so straightforward, especially when the quote is unframed, as shown in §3.2–§3.4 below. Whether or not it is explicitly framed, the use of quotation in oral narratives such as 1) enhances their dramatic effect by allowing the narrator to *enact* the speech of the characters, enabling their voices and personae to stand out from his own and the other characters' through the use of intonation – as can be heard on the linked audio – facial and manual gestures, and other markers be discussed below.

It would be wrong to regard the narrative use of quotation as something that is equally common, either across different Australian Indigenous languages or across different speakers of the same language, or even within the speech of one person across different genres or texts. Nor is it by any means unique to Indigenous Australian languages or narrative styles, or to oral as opposed to written narrative. This is illustrated by text (2), a passage from (non-Indigenous) Australian author Tim Winton's (2013) novel *Eyrie*.

English (Winton 2013: 125)

(2) a. Keely felt as soft as a chamois, perilously vulnerable. He was suddenly apprehensive about what the old fella might say next.
      b. Your mum orright?
      c. Keely nodded.
      d. Bloody fine woman.
      e. She is.
      f. How old are ya, exactly?
      g. Forty nine.
      h. Truly, ya do look like him, son. At the end.
      i. Keely felt the jab in his guts.
      j. And I don't say it to make a prick of meself.
      k. No? he asked, smarting.
      l. As a mate, son.
      m. Really.

Like many fiction writers nowadays, Winton makes no use of quotation marks to explicitly set off the speech of his characters from those of the narrator. And as in Wurla example (1), many of the utterances by Winton's characters are unframed. But just as in (1), in (2) it is always clear who is saying what – partly from the question-answer sequences, as in (1), and partly on other grounds to be discussed below. In (2) as a written text, this is enabled in part by the use of indentation to mark a change of speaker – a convention that we generally follow in a modified form in our transcripts by beginning a new line with every clear change of speaker. But the matter is not always so clear, even in the written narrative of novelists such as Winton, as we will see below in §3.3.3.

We have introduced this example from written English fiction to show how general the phenomena of framed and unframed quotation are in narrative across genres and cultures. They show that the written medium offers particular ways of managing the framing relations through line breaks and indentation (and of course through quotation marks, although they are not used by Winton). As we shall see below, the spoken medium offers other affordances for framing devices that are not available in writing. More specifically, we will be showing that there are particular patterns of framing and uses of framed and unframed quotation that have a distinctively Indigenous-Australian flavour to them.

The rest of this chapter is structured as follows. In §3.2 we map out the main typological dimensions along which languages organise different solutions to the problems of representing speech and thought. In §3.3 we illustrate how these dimensions impact on specific problems of understanding how speech and thought are represented, but also look at some examples where it is difficult if not impossible to work out who is saying (or thinking) the quoted passages. In §3.4 we quantify what is going on by looking at existing text collections for some of the languages in our sample (Dreamtime stories, historical narratives, autobiographical reminiscences), and determining the proportions within them of speech which is quoted vs non-quoted vs indeterminate between the two, and within the quoted speech, the amount of is which is framed vs unframed. We conclude in §3.5 with some summary remarks.

3.2 Dimensions of difference

Languages differ widely in their methods for representing speech and thought. In this section we discuss four main dimensions on which they differ:
- direct vs indirect (§3.2.1);
- overtly framed vs unframed (§3.2.2);
- the framing word or construction (§3.2.3), which may clearly distinguish speech from thought or leave this unspecified;

- the way of marking the change between characters or from narrator to character (§3.2.4), whether by intonation, special interjections, switch of language or dialect, or other grammatical or inferential characteristics.[2]

To keep things clear as we move around these narratives, we'll use the following terms. The *narrator*, sometimes also called "primary speaker", is the person actually telling the story, in the *primary speech event* – e.g., Campbell Ellenbrae for Wurla in (1) and Tim Winton or his implied narrator in (2). A *character*, sometimes also called reported speaker, is someone in the story, whose speech, thought, feeling etc. about the *reported speech event* is being quoted. Examples are Harry and the stockmen in text in (1), and Keely and his interlocutor Wally in (2). Note that a character may be the same person as the narrator, as in text except (1), where Campbell extensively quotes himself as a character in the story about a past series of narrated events that he was involved in.

3.2.1 Direct vs indirect

Simplifying somewhat, direct speech (a.k.a. "quotation") purports to represent what was actually said by the character themself, while in indirect speech the portrayal of what is said is assimilated to the narrator's point of view. This generally entails shifts in a number of "deictic" categories that depend on the place, time, speech roles and other factors – cf. the direct speech version *Jack said "**I'll go** back to **your** place **tomorrow**"* and its indirect-speech equivalent *Jack said **he would come** back to **my** place **the next day**,* where the bolded words change their "deictic values" in the indirect-speech version.

In fact it is rare in languages for all deictic values to shift in indirect speech. For example, Russian adjusts person (e.g., *I* in direct speech becomes *he* in indirect speech) but not tense, and Japanese only adjusts honorifics, but does so at all sites where honorificity can be coded, reassessing them from the viewpoint of the reporting speaker rather than the original speaker (Evans 2013, analysing examples from Hasegawa 2005: 113). This makes "indirect speech" an idealised or "canonical" category. The fewer the deictic shifts a language makes, the less often we can make a clear ruling on whether direct or indirect speech is being used (Aikhenvald 2011b). For example, in the Bininj Kunwok language of Western

---

2 Another strategy that some languages adopt in reporting speech is to compress what is said to an abstract word or noun phrase, e.g. *Winston Churchill **declared victory*** (where his words might have been something like "we have won" or even "we can finally declare victory"). These strategies are not typical at all of Indigenous Australian narrative and we ignore them here.

Arnhem Land (Evans 2003: 605) it is tempting to say that only direct speech is used, but when reporting a negative command the regular "declarative negative" *djama* or *minj* (isn't/aren't/didn't) is used instead of the special "prohibitive" *yuwun* or *bayun* 'don't!' Since the choice of negator has been assimilated to the speaker's perspective (as it is in the recasting of *They told him:* **don't** *come!* vs *They told him* **not to** *come*) this is arguably an example of indirect speech, but the relevant grammatical diagnostic can only be applied in the rather rare case that it is negative imperatives which are being reported.

Moreover, instead of the classic dichotomy between direct and indirect speech it is also helpful to posit a third type, "biperspectival speech" (Evans 2013), which shows a situation from both perspectives, the primary and the reported speech event. We have a bit of this in English – we would say "Jack said he **would** come to my place the next day" if his arrival had been planned for after Jack's initial statement, but before the time the narrator is reporting this, while if the narrator was reporting this right after Jack's announcement (say, the afternoon of the same day) we would say "Jack said he **will** come to my place tomorrow". In other words, the choice of *would* vs *will* here triangulates the time of his arrival off the dual perspectives of the primary speech act and the reporting speech act. Following on from this, Evans (2013) argues that it is better to posit three types of reported speech – direct speech (presented as the words of the character), indirect speech (presented from the viewpoint of the narrator) and biperspectival speech (presented from both viewpoints at once).[3] These are idealised types and it is rare, perhaps impossible, to find "pure examples" of indirect or biperspectival speech. But pure examples of direct speech are reasonably common, especially among the languages we are dealing with here.

3.2.2 Overt framing vs no framing

We have already seen above how speech or thought may be overtly framed by a verb such as, to use Wurla examples, *amanyarrigana* 'he says to us' (1e) or *ngu-menangga* 'I said to him' (1g, j). On the other hand, it is often the case (figures will be given in §3.4) that there is no such overt framing material, as in (1, i).

---

3 Cross-cutting the direct/indirect distinction, in some languages, including Athabaskan ones, there is a distinction between quotes and direct speech reports. See for example, Saxton (1998) for Dogrib, and Schauber (1979: 19–29) for Navajo; cf. also Aikhenvald (2011a: 301–302). For an interesting alternative approach to reported speech which dispenses with the direct/indirect opposition altogether and instead operates in terms of a notion of "figure composition" see Zuckerman (2021).

An example from Kayardild (South Wellesley Islands, Queensland) is the following – the transcription here gives the originally recorded text, but when going over the transcription with the speaker, Darwin Moodoonuthi, he suggested that an overtly framing clause *jathaa dangkaa nathawanda barthawanda kamburij* 'another man from the same camp said' be included before the quoted speech starting in line (c). Even allowing for that clarification, the second line could be interpreted either as an exclamation by the narrator, or by the character whose blood is coming out.

Kayardild (Evans 1995: 576–577)

(3) a. *minyi   thaatha   natha-ya   bartha-y*
       Towards   returned   camp-at   at.main.camp-at
       (He) came back home (to Mornington Island).

   b. *(')ngarrkuru   kandu   burrij,   ngarrkuru   kandu   burrij(')*
       strongly   blood   came.out   strongly   blood   came.out
       '(He) came back home (to Mornington Island).'

   c. *'Nyingka   rabatha   dathinki   ngilirri   rar*
       You   trespassed   in.that   in.cave   south
       'You trespassed in that cave in the south,

   d. *Dathinki   rangurrng   rabatha   ngilirri*
       There   Bentinck.Island trespassed   in.cave
       you trespassed in that cave in the south,

   e. *Nyingka   marrwaya   wuranki   dathinki   diyaj.*
       you   close.by   food   there   ate
       You ate food right up close.'

In at least some Australian languages, and for some speakers, such "unframed quotes" are common, raising the issue mentioned above – how do we know which character is supposed to be talking? We return to that issue in §3.2.4. And how do we even know when we are dealing with quoted speech, and when this is just the narrator's commentary? That issue will be addressed in §3.3.3.

3.2.3 Represented speech, thought, feeling or perception?

A further question relates to whether the quoted material is spoken out loud by characters, or merely thought by them. In this chapter we call these "quoted speech" and "quoted thought" respectively. In the latter function, quotation can serve as a way of representing character motivation and emotion in an unfolding narrative: consider how the same narrative development could be represented either by primary narrative such as "She was surprised to see her son had returned", or by quoted thought as in "She thought, 'Ah, my son is back already!'." In English, quoted speech and thought are often distinguished by framing verbs, such as *say, shout, whisper* versus *think, imagine, suppose*. This certainly happens sometimes in Australian languages as well, as in the following example from the Kuninjku dialect of Bininj Kunwok.

Bininj Kunwok, Kuninjku dialect (Evans 2003: 695)

(4) a. *benbengkang*   *ngaldahdaluk,*
      he.thought.about.them   his.sisters
      He was thinking about the sisters.

    b. '*birriyoy*   *kumekke*' *ben-bengka-ng*
      they.were.sleeping   there   he.thought.about.them
      '*birri-yo-y*   *ngaldahdaluk*'
      they.were.sleeping   his.sisters
      'They were sleeping there', he was thinking about them then, 'the sisters were sleeping/have gone to sleep'.

However, what is much more common in many Australian languages is to have a framing verb that does not distinguish speech from thought – a single say/think verb that is ambiguous between external and internal articulations (McGregor 2021).[4] For example, in Marri Tjevin the most frequent framing verb is *gimiya* '(s)he said/thought', as seen in this account of cycad nut processing:[5]

Marri-Tjevin

(5) a. *miyi*   *yinaltjen*
      fruit   there.now
      The fruit is down there [under the water, where it has been left to soak].

---

4 Regarding somewhat similar strategies that are now widely used on colloquial English see Streeck (2002).
5 This text is told by Malviyin Claver Dumoo, recorded by Jeff Hardwick, and transcribed by Malviyin together with John Mansfield. The complete text can be found at https://catalog.paradisec.org.au/collections/JM5

b. *'mi   viwet   gagantja'   giminykiya   gu*
   fruit   cycad.nut   here   they.both.said   GU
   'Here are the cycad nuts', the two of them said/thought.

c. *nada   mi   gulinngkiparrmasrivinidal   guninya*
   next   fruit   they.both.put.inside   they.went
   Then they were putting them in [to bags]. (DSC_2775)

In this example, the two cycad-nut collectors may have announced out loud their recognition of the cycad nuts under the water; or this may instead represent their internal realisation.

Most of the languages we draw on in this article have a framing verb that can mean either 'do', 'say' or 'think', also taking in mental states and reactions: *yime* 'do, say' in Bininj Kunwok, *yin* in Dalabon, *mam* in Murrinhpatha, *ma* in Ngarinyin, Wurla (as exemplified in 1) and Bunuba. Among the languages discussed, only Kayardild does not have a verb which colexifies these two meanings: *kamburija* specifically means 'speak, talk', though the demonstrative *dandananganda*, which spans both actions and utterances: 'do/say like this', is frequently used to frame utterances as well as actions and thoughts. Some of the languages have verbs of cognition including ones for 'think', but these are not generally used by themselves as framing verbs, though Bininj Kunwok is an exception (see (4) above).

The common use of verbs which can mean either 'say' or 'think' introduces a potential ambiguity in how 'quotations' framed by this verb are to be interpreted: 'X said Y' or 'X thought/felt/realised, etc. Y'? In many cases, as will be discussed in §3.3.2, such examples are unspecified to the core: it doesn't actually matter whether the author of the utterance is speaking out loud, or voicing their thoughts to themselves. But there are ways of making the distinction clear where necessary. One is the use of a verb of thinking in a separate sentence either before or after the sentence that contains the framing verb and the framed thought. An example from Ngarinyin is (6).

Ngarinyin (Spronck 2016: 1)

(6) *nini   e   'kunya   ngima   kanda'   ama*
    ni-ni a_1-y_2i-ø   kunya   nga$_1$-yi-ma   kanda   a$_1$-ma
    think-think   3M-be-PRS   what   1SG-FUT-do   3SW.PROX   3M-do
    He is thinking. 'What can I do here'? he thinks.

As we will see below, in Ngarinyin there is wide range of expressions of speaking and thinking that can occur in the same position as *nini e*[6] in (5), i.e., immediately preceding a clause which includes the framed locution or thought and the multi-purpose framing verb *ma* 'say', 'do'. Spronck (2016) calls the first clause in such sequences the "framing-introducing" clause. That is an apt term for them, as they do not in themselves frame the locution or thought, but introduce the following, framing clause by specifying the *kind* of framing it is – in this case of a thought rather than of a locution.

Conversely, some Australian languages have pronominal marking on the verb that indicates an addressee, and thus implies that the quote is spoken out loud. In Murrinhpatha (and other Daly languages) the addressee marker is directly added to the 'say' verb (7a, 7b).[7] In other languages the addressee marking also requires a "benefactive applicative" suffix on the verb.

Murrinhpatha

(7) a. *'Ngarra   wangu   warda?'   mam*
         where   towards   now   he.said
         'Where (will I go) now?' he said/thought.

    b. *'Mere   the   mabath',   mam-**nga***
        not   ear   carry   he.said-to.me
        'I don't know', he **said to me**. [1981_CS1–03A_GM]

A similar example from the Dalabon language of Central Arnhem Land (see Evans 2017: 28 for the full passage) is shown in (8):

---

6 Most of these are not independent inflecting verbs but two-word verbal expressions of the kind illustrated in (7) by *nini e*. The first word in them is what is called a "co-verb" (Spronck 2015) or "verbal particle" (Rumsey 1982) i.e., a semantically specific word that specifies what kind of action is being described – in this case thinking. The second word is an inflecting verb that has a more abstract lexical meaning, and takes prefixes and suffixes that express grammatical categories such as tense, mode, and the person and number of the subject and object – in this case indicating that the thinker is third-person singular masculine ('he') and that the thinking takes place in the present time of the narrated event. This kind of two-word verbal expression is very common in Ngarinyin (Rumsey 1982), and in many languages of northern Australia (McGregor 2002).

7 The full text from which this example is taken, as well as other Murrinhpatha examples in this article, can be found at https://catalog.paradisec.org.au/collections/JM4

Dalabon (Evans 2017: 28)

(8) *'Marrûhmah   djahbon?'*   *bûkahmarnûyininj.*
     Where.to   you.are.going   he.said.to.him
     'Where are you going?', he said to him,

It is our impression that most Australian languages make little use of locutionary verbs to describe a manner of speaking at the same time as they frame a discourse. This is in contrast to English, where locutionary verbs frequently specify the manner of speech, e.g. *drawled, sighed, sputtered*, just as English motion verbs have also been noted to encode manner (Talmy 1985). In Australian languages, perhaps the fact that direct speech is performed with such dramatic style makes it unnecessary to characterise manner-of-speech on the framing verb as well. However, verbs that describe the main type of speech act do get deployed: the collection of Bininj Kunwok texts in Appendix A of Evans (2003) includes, in addition to the ubiquitous *yime* 'say/do' (15 occurrences) and its benefactive form *marneyime* 'say to, tell' (11 occurrences), the speech verbs *djawa* 'ask' (x 3), *manjh-manjhbun* 'thank profusely' (x 1) and *mulewan* 'inform' (x 1); to put these framing speech act verbs into perspective, this total of 31 stretches of direct speech framed by speech act verbs must be set against 50 instances of direct not framed by any speech act verb.[8] This is representative of the relative frequency of speech verbs in Bininj Gun-wok, though there are just a couple more verbs, such as *kayhme* 'cry out, call out', which can also frame speech.

Moreover, there is usually a reasonably wide set of framing verbs of cognition and feeling. In Dalabon, for example, attested quote-framing verbs are *bengdinj* 'was thinking', *yolhwehmun* 'feels bad, worries' (9), *bengkang* 'thought', *kurnh-*

---

8 Making these counts involves many analytic decisions, not always straightforward – in particular this count does not include:

(a) instances where the quoted speech was preceded by *wanjh* 'then, next', on the basis that this is used for a much wider range of setting up sequences in narrative, so is not specific to framing quotations;

(b) (one case only) where the quotation was followed by the verb *djurlhmeng* 'shook (object) awake', again on the grounds that this is simply a sequence-of-events structure ('"[X]", (and he) shook him awake);

(c) several examples in text (9) where an expression (a multi-word place name like 'the python sank down') is followed by *bolk-ngei-gurrme* 'gave a place name to', on the grounds that this is simply mention of an expression, not quotation.

Though each of these analytic decisions could be overturned individually, it would not have a substantial effect on the figures cited above.

bengkabengkang 'thought, worried', as well as other lexical framing devices like *men-no* 'his/her mind' (for more detailed discussion see Evans 2017).

Dalabon

(9) *kahyolhwehmun* *'ngahdudjkeyhwoyan'* *kirdikirdnokah,* *wurdurdnokah*
    he.feels.bad I.will.have.to.go.back to.his.wife to.his.child
    He felt terrible, 'I have to go back' to his wife, to his child. (More freely: 'He suffered terribly, wanting to go back to his wife and child.') [MTDL1 3.05–3.10][9]

In Bunuba (Southern Kimberley region), in addition to the multi-purpose framing verb *ma*, other verbs of speaking[10] include *wurla+ma* 'talk', *ngayaga+ra2* 'ask (someone)', *matha+ra2* 'tell' (someone) and *waya+ma* 'call out' (Rumsey 2000: 141). In Ngarinyin, some of the more common ones are *barra+wu* 'tell', *burrgaj+ma* 'ask', *dali+ma* 'name', *jigal+yi* 'lie' (Rumsey 1982: 141; Coate and Elkin 1974).[11]

In Murrinhpatha, the framing verb is almost always *mam* 'say' (7 above), and only one other option, *dantharrpu* 'ask' is attested (10). Other locution verbs such as *kanamkay* 'call out', *dantherr* 'inform', *damngurru* 'provoke' and *pampeyithi* 'express resignation after unsuccessfully rebuking children' have not been observed in quotative constructions. However, Murrinhpatha perception verbs may effectively play a framing role, much like the Dalabon emotion verbs noted above. For example, in (11) the verb *memmirl* 'look around' frames the following quotation (speech or thought), because the quoted question clearly results from or coincides with the 'looking' event. However these two clauses are in separate intonational unit, unlike the standard framing verb *mam* 'say', which often occurs in the same intonational unit as its accompanying quote.

---

9 This example is sourced from one of the sets of responses to the "Family Problems" picture task, as discussed in San Roque et al. (2012) and Barth and Evans (2017a,b).
10 Most of these are two-word coverb + inflecting verb expressions of the kind exemplified in (7).
11 The Ngarinyin dictionary of Coate and Elkin (1974), based on Coate's fieldwork during 1946–1947 and 1963–1972, includes approximately 200 entries for speech-act verbs, most of which were not in common use by the time of Alan Rumsey's first fieldwork on Ngarinyin in 1975–1976 or Stef Spronck's in 2008–2010. Those entries are usefully brought together in a list by Spronck (2015: 365–388) – along with an account of why it proved difficult for Spronck to use Coate and Elkin (1974) as an elicitation strategy with his Ngarinyin language consultants. Many of the entries compiled by Spronck are alternative inflected forms of a single verb (e.g., *birrimenangga* 'they said to him', *budmangga* 'they tell him'), but the list includes at least 50 distinct items for which is not the case (cf. Spronck 2015: 112, Table 4.3)

Murrinhpatha

(10) *Ngamninthadharrpu,* '*Ngarra wangu Wulmithin?*'
we.two.asked where direction Old.Mission
The two of us asked, 'Which way to Old Mission?' [1981_CS1–03A_GM]

(11) a. *Bere kardu ka pumemmirlbirl warda*
well people KA they.looked.around then
Well, the people looked around then.

b. '*Ya nukunu ka Walamuma ngarra?*'
hey him KA blue-tongue.lizard where
'Hey where has the Blue-tongue Lizard Man gone?'[CS1-012-A]

Murrinhpatha quotation can also be accomplished by mentioning the speaker before or after the quote, but leaving the 'say' predicate unexpressed (12).

Murrinhpatha

(12) '*Bere thathpirr kura makura thathpirr*', *nukunu Walamuma yu.*
well really water no.water really he blue.tongue YU
'Well there's really no water left', (said) the Blue-tongue Lizard Man.

A similar type of quotation framing has been noted in Bunuba, though in that language the construction requires ergative marking on the speaker, as in (13).

Bunuba (Rumsey 2010: 1662)

(13) *niy-ingga* '*ngay nga bula nyarna*'
he-ERG not eat FUT:1SG:go much
He (said) 'I won't eat much'.

3.2.4 Signalling transitions from one voice to another

The fourth dimension of difference has to do with how transitions from one voice to another are signalled (if at all). This includes both the question of switches from the narrator to the voice of one of the characters, and also the signalling of switches between one character and another.

Prosody. There is often a distinctive upward pitch reset at the beginning of a quoted passage and a fall at the end of it, (cf. Gårding 1983; Touati 1987); Ladd (1996: 279) calls this "declination reset", which he defines as "the upward modification of the pitch range at the beginning of a new stretch of declination, and 'final lowering', the corresponding downward modification of the pitch range at the end". A pitch trace of two Dalabon examples shows the upward pitch excursion coming into a quoted passage in (14) (and note also the use of *ngale!* 'Hey!' at the start of the quote), and the downward pitch coming into the quotative verb *kahyininj* 'he said' in (15).

Dalabon (Ross 2011: 267–268)

(14) *wawurdngan . . .   kahbong   'ngale!   ngahboniyan'*
     my.brother   he.went   hey!   I.will.go
     'My brother went off, "Hey! I'll go (to the graveyard)' (JW How Djorli . . .)

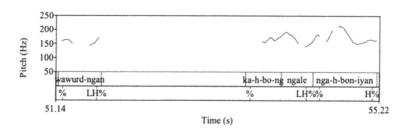

(pitch trace for 14 from Ross 2011: 267–268)

(15) *'kûrhrdûh   kanihdja/   yarranarrinjkah'*   *kahyininj*
     This.way   there   to.where.we.met.up   he.said
     'Yeah, it should be about here where we met up' he said. (Mimih and Naworneng)

Person shifts. A common cue for switches of voice involves shifts in person. We have already seen an example of shift from third person ('He felt terrible') to first person 'I have to go back (home)' in (9). We have also seen, in (8), shifts from the second person in quoted speech ('Where are you going?') to the third person in the framing verb ('He said to him'). In longer passages the latching of second person in questions to first persons in the following answers can help establish changes of character. On the other hand, continuation of the first person can indicate that the same person is talking, while switches from the first to the third person signal a switch to the narrator's voice. We can see these principles at work in the following Dalabon passage, from the same reported conversation as in (8). Between (16a) and (16b), between (16b) and (16c), and between (16e) and (16f), the speech passes back and forth between two characters (the hunter, Naworneng, returning laden with hunted animals, and the Mimih who is planning to lure him back to an ambush with his fellow Mimih spirits), whereas between (16c) and (16d) the persistence of first person subject indicates that the same character is speaking; finally, as the person value moves to third person in (16h) this signals the switch to the voice of the narrator.

Dalabon (Evans 2017: 28)

(16) a. *'Marrûhmah djahbon?'*
       Where.to   you.are.going
       'Where are you going?'

   b. *'Ngey walûngkûn, kardû=kih djahbidorrûngh*
      I   myself   maybe   you.have.someone.with.you
      wanjhma nûnda djahmarnûngoy'
      since   you're.burning.off
      'I'm all on my own, but you must've got someone with you, (since) you're burning off (the country, as you go along)?'

   c. *'Yakkû nûnh bah ngey walûngkûn ngahboninj ngahdjabibkang'*
      no   here   but   I   alone   I.was.going I.was.trying.to.burn
      'No, I'm on my own here, I've just been going along on my own trying to burn off.'

   d. *'Nga-h-kakku-komngurlka-ng kerninjhbi djukerre*
      I.made.a.lot.of.smoke   whatsit   female.wallaroo
      barrk'   *ka-h-yini-nj.*
      male.wallaroo   He.said
      'No, I'm on my own here, I've just been going along on my own trying to burn off, hunting wallaroos.'

   e. *'Yoh, mah njing? Kardûkih djahbidorrûngh?'*
      yeah well   you   maybe   You.have.someone.with.you
      'Where are you going?'

   f. *'Yakkû ngey ngahbiydih'*
      no   I   I.have.nobody.with.me
      'No, there's no-one with me.'

g. *'Ngahdjabobon*   *walûngkûn'*   *kahyininj*
I'm.just.going.around   alone   he.said
'I'm just going around on my own.' he said.

h. *kehyangnarrinj*
they.talked.to.each.other
They talked together.

Similarly, in lines (h) and (i) of text (1) in Wurla, the switch between first and second person categories in a question-answer sequence (where the subject of (h) becomes the object in (i)) makes it easy to recognise the change of speaker between those lines even in the absence of explicit framing.

    Stereotyped uses of interjections to introduce speech. Quoted speech is in many instances represented by commencing with an interjection, which helps to signal a shift from the relatively dispassionate perspective of the narrator to a more engaged reenactment of a character. This can be seen in lines (c, f, j) of the Wurla example (1) above, and *ngale!* 'hey!' in Dalabon examples (14) and (17).

Dalabon

(17) a. *kahdjanjerrhyerrûhyerrudjminj*   *njerrhwodnan*
He.came.back..with.the.body   Body.throws
He came on back with the body and threw it down.

b. *'ngale!*   *Djarrakih* *kanh* *ngûrrahwangarrebun* *mah!*
Hey   This.one   this   we.part.cook.it   let's
Hey let's part-cook it on this side first!

c. *kenbo* *wangarreno* *ngûrrahmarneyerrudjmang'*
then   cooked.part We'll.take.it.back.for.her
Then we'll take back the cooked part (to the camp) for her (the Emu).'
(Greedy Emu story)

The interjectional signal is typically deployed in concert with prosodic signalling as described above. In some languages this strategy is very frequent; for example, in Murrinhpatha a high proportion of quoted speech utterances are framed with an initial interjection *Aa!*, as in the following example where a speaker is narrating the silent comedy of a Mr Bean sketch:

Murrinhpatha

(18) a. *kardu   ngala   ku   bamkardu*
      person   big   white.person   he.sees
      The supervisor sees that he's too big (for the water-slide).

    b. *wurda*
      no
      No (he can't make it).

    c. *'aa   ngurduwurldenu'*
      ah   I'll.go.back.again
      'Ah, I need to go back!' (Mr Bean) says/thinks.

    d. *'aa',   mamna   'thunguwuy   warda   nhinhi   yu'*
      ah   he.said.to.him   you.go.out   now   you   YU
      'Ah', (the supervisor) tells him, 'Get out of there you!' (20110821GMMK-203)

3.2.5 Use of language or dialect choice to convey different characters

Multilingualism is widespread in traditional Australian culture (Brandl and Walsh 1982; Elwell 1982; Merlan 1981; Rumsey 2018; Sutton 1997). Accomplished story-tellers regularly make use of this in narrative, often getting characters to speak in different languages or dialects (as appropriate to where they come from). This may take the form of the narrator using one variety, while the characters use another, or, more radically, of different characters each speaking their own variety. For the great Russian literary theorist Bakhtin (1981: 262), "the novel can be defined as a diversity of social speech types (sometimes even a diversity of languages) and a diversity of individual voices, artistically organised" (Bakhtin 1981: 262). But what Bakhtin said about the novel – a large-scale written form – could apply equally to the oral narratives in many Australian groups. Evans (2011) gives examples which range from switches between the narrator using one variety (Kuninjku) and the characters in his story using another (Kunwinjku), both being dialects of the Bininj Kunwok (also spelled Bininj Gun-wok) dialect chain, to examples where the narrator and one character speak one variety while another character speaks a different variety (e.g., the narrator, and the "sister" character, speak Lardil while her brother Thuwathu the rainbow serpent speaks Yangkaal), to cases where the narrator uses one or more languages to advance the story line, while the characters each speak their own language, different from the primary language of the narration, though the narrator may follow these quotations with explanatory translations into the main language of the narrative.

Excerpt (19) is an example from a text by Charlie Wardaga that uses (his version of) English,[12] and two other languages, Marrku and Ilgar (one per character) for the quoted passages. Note that Marrku and Ilgar, though spoken by neighbouring groups on Croker Island and surrounding areas, are at best distantly related. Line (a) frames the dialogue, in English ('one man said . . .'), lines (b)–(h) report the speech of a Marrku-speaking man (the traditional custodian of a site – this reports an ancient incident where a careless visitor from another tribe had broken a stick at this sacred site, triggering a cyclone), and then the speech passes in (i) to a Garig-speaking man's response, acknowledging, in Garig what the Marrku custodian had said. Lines (j–k), in English, again frame the dialogue, then the Garig-speaking man continues, in lines (l–n), putting the blame for the infringement on his countrymen. Finally (within this except), in line (o) the Marrku-speaking custodian takes up the dialogue again, emphasising the damage done by the cyclone.

Multilingual passage in English, Marrku and Garig

(19) a. *one man he said* — English

b. *'Iyi, mukungurnu, ngurnu minyiwu ngurnu jang.* — Marrku
Yes that.there that he.struck.it that dreaming
He came on back with the body and threw it down.

c. *jang miyiwuwu* — Marrku
Dreaming he.struck.it.over.there
He struck the dreaming site way over there.

d. *muku makalany ngurnu marruyaj* — Marrku
that it.appeared that rainbow
That Rainbow Serpent appeared.

e. *yeah, miyiwuwu* — Marrku
Yeah He.struck.it.there
'Yes, he struck it (the dreaming site).'

12 In other parts of this text, not shown here, the narrator's portions are sometimes reinforced by the regional lingua franca Kunwinjku for the main narrative. See Evans (2011) for the full text.

f. *imin killim, he kill that ah, antbed or something, stone,*   English
   He hit it, he struck that termite mound or something, (with) a stone.

g. *'ya,   ngurnu mika ... mukungurn miyiwu   ngurnu*   Marrku
   Yeah that   [hesit.]   that.there he.struck.it that
   Yes, there he ... struck it.

h. *ngurnu jang   makalany, makalany   ngurnu*   Marrku
   that   dreaming it.appeared it.appeared that
   marruyaj, iyi'
   rainbow   yes
   'And that dreaming creature appeared, the Rainbow Serpent appeared, yes.'

i. *'Yangbalwura rakabara'*   Garig
   oh.I.say   like.that
   'Oh, I say, so that's what happened.'

j. *he said, that Garig man.*   English

k. *Yeah, he talking one another.*   English
   Yeah, they were talking to one another.

l. *'Yaa, yiharlu ngabi raka yiharlu nganami   raka*   Garig
   Well not   me   that not   I.would.do that
   'Well, it wasn't me, I wouldn't do that.

m. *Rakabara ngabi ka   ngabi arrarrkbi angmurnduruny*   Garig
   like.that my   that my   people   they.defiled.the.place
   aniwung
   they.hit.it
   That was my countrymen who defiled that place, they struck it'.

n. *Wularrud aniwung   raka kuyak.'*   Garig
   before   they.hit.it that place
   They struck that dangerous place.'

o. *Ee!   Mukungurn durrumarni.'*   Ngan, ngan,*   Marrku
   Hey! that.there   flattened.landscape I.say I.say
   'durrumarni   ka.'
   flattened.landscape emphasis
   Hey, look at all the flattened landscape. I say . . . I say . . . flattened landscape'

3.2.6 Use of triangular kin terms to index speaker and addressee

Many Australian languages have "triangular" or "trirelational terms" with meanings like 'the one who is my wife and your sister-in-law'.[13] In some of the examples of quoted speech in our corpus, this is harnessed to the listener's presumed knowledge of how characters relate to each other, in a way that provides clues about who is saying what.

In the Bininj Kunwok (Kuninjku dialect) story told by Mick Kubarkku about the antics of a naughty young novice-initiate, part of the narrative (see Evans 2003: 695 for the full example) goes as follows (translating, with the triangular kin terms in italics followed by their meanings in square brackets): "Hey!" he woke her, "that one *nadjumuwarre* [the one who is your brother and and my brother-in-law] is coming now, you (women) sleep together (for safety from his antics). It's not my fault, it's because of that novice (brother) of yours" he woke her. "Novice, you go (and sleep somewhere else), the two of us are sleeping here, me and *ngalyabokwarr* [the one who is my wife and your sister]". "Oh, I better go and sleep somewhere else then".

The lack of any overt framing or identification of speakers and addressees throughout this passage does not stop it being crystal-clear who is talking to whom, in particular the switch of the married man's speech to being addressed to his wife in the first part (indexed by using *nadjumuwarre* to refer to the naughty novice brother of his wife), to addressing the naughty novice himself in the second part (indexed by using *ngalyabokwarr* to refer to the sister of his addressee, who is the speaker's wife). What is fascinating here is that the clarity about who is addressing whom is established not by overtly identifying the speaker or addressee, but by positioning them with respect to a third referent identified by a triangular kin term.

3.2.7 Signalling voices: Overview

We have described a range of methods that provide clues about whose voice is being represented in the unfolding narrative. These include switches of person, prosody, interjections signalling the start of speech, question-and-answer sequences, and switches of language. Audiences use these clues to work out when

---

13 See Garde (2013) for a magisterially detailed account of how triangular kinterms work in Bininj Kunwok.

the voice in a story is that of the narrator, and when it is a character, and if the latter, which character, and whether it is speech-out-loud or some inner speech or feeling that is being represented. Further clues can come from employing general principles of reasoning, as will be exemplified in §3.3.2.

However, these interpretive decisions are not always clear-cut – there is often a lot of uncertainty about many of these decisions. This makes listening to such stories an interpretive challenge in many cases, and the same applies to any attempt to translate them into English (e.g., as part of a published text collection), since in addition to the risk of an inappropriate interpretation there is the additional issue of imposing a single reading on an original which may have been deliberately ambiguous. In the next section we look in more detail at a couple of texts to illustrate how such interpretive principles are applied, and how they sometimes leave unresolved problems of interpretation.

3.3 Problems of interpretation

3.3.1 Who is saying what?

Quoted speech can be used as a narrative device for introducing and individuating protagonists. As we will see below, the quotative introduction of protagonists is largely indicated by the configuration of personal pronouns (or pronominal marking on verbs), which implies the presence of certain protagonists, rather than directly describing them in primary speech. However Aboriginal narrators apparently do not always do this in a comprehensive way – there may be residual ambiguities about how many protagonists are involved, and who is saying what.

We illustrate this with the first part of a Murrinhpatha narrative (20), told by Alanga Nganbe. The complete story illustrates principles of successful cooperation, by describing a group of boys hunting peewee birds together; we here focus on the opening passage in which protagonists are introduced.[14] Alanga introduces the protagonists using a combination of primary and quoted speech. None of the quotes in this entire narrative use framing verbs (see §3.4). The primary speech techniques are familiar from say, European children's stories, where

---

14 The story was recorded by Chester Street in the 1980s, and more recently transcribed and translated by Nguvudirr Jeremiah Tunmuck and John Mansfield. The recording is archived at https://catalog.paradisec.org.au/collections/CS1

indefinite person reference is often used (e.g., "a big bad wolf . . ."). But Alanga uses person reference in combination with quotation of the protagonists, and at times, dispenses altogether with person reference and relies purely on quotation. In the initial scene-setting, line (a) provides a primary speech introduction to the protagonists, who are at this point a non-individuated group, "some boys". The noun phrase *kardu kigay* 'boys', can be interpreted as indefinite, i.e., new to the listener.[15] In lines (d, e) the narrator switches to quotation of the boys, which is not indicated by any framing verb, but rather by the interjection *ya!* The quotation in line (e) uses first-inclusive pronominal marking on the verb, which accordingly does not individuate any particular boy. This quotation could be the voice of some non-specific boy, or it could be something that they all say and agree upon, or perhaps even a shared understanding they reach without speaking at all

Murrinhpatha

(20) a. *Bere* **kardu** **kigay** *pirrinedhaneme* *ngarra* *mulurn* *thay*
well person boy they.were.sitting at shade tree
yidi.
bush.apple
Well **(some) boys** were sitting in the shade of the bush apple tree.

   b. *ku* *kalampitpit* *nu* *pirrinemardamardadhaneme* *purni*
animal peewee for they.were.waiting sitting
They were waiting for peewee birds,

   c. *thengay* *wanku* *purnengkadhukthaneme*
slingshot with they.were.together
they all had slingshots.

   d. '*Ya* *ku* *kalampitpit* *maku* *ya?*'
hey animal peewee no.animal hey
'Hey! There aren't any peewees!'

   e. '*Kanhi* *da* *pimardamardaneme.*'
here place let's.wait.boys
'Let's wait here.'

---

15 By contrast, a definite reference might add a determiner, *kardu kigay nhini* 'those young men'.

The action really starts in line (f), with both the arrival of some peewee birds, and the individuation of one boy (Boy A) who sees them. Boy A's course of action is revealed in line (i) by a return to quoted speech. Again this is unframed, so there is no explicit reference to who is speaking, but a vocative pronominal *peneme* 'you lot!' indicates that one protagonist is now speaking individually, addressing the rest of the group. This individuated protagonist is by implication Boy A. Line (j) is again quoted speech, but the pronominal form here is first-person-inclusive, so it is unclear if this again represents the whole group speaking as one, or Boy A speaking on behalf of the group.

f. *Bere* **kardu numi ka** *bampunkardu ku* *kalampitpit terert*
   well   person one   KA   he.saw.them   animal peewee   lots
   punnibarlbarldha
   they.were.flying
   Then **one boy** saw a lot of peewees come flying,

g. *I* *ngarra thay karnmurrirn parnawup*
   and   at   tree   woollybutt   they.landed
   and land in a woollybutt tree.

h. *i* *ngamere ka pepe parnawup ngarra kura yuwudha*
   and   some   KA   below they.landed   at   water it.was.lying
   And some of them landed down below where the water lay.

i. '**Peneme,** *derrk* pineme!'
   you.lot   wait   boys.let's.sit
   'Hey **you lot**, let's sit quietly!

j. '*Ku* *maku* *nukun* *kuru*-**nhentha**-*rdurrnukunneme.*'
   animal no.animal risk   it.go-**from.us**-depart
   The birds might escape **from us (incl)**.'

Lines (k) and (l) present Boy A's intended course of action, again in unframed speech, with 1SG pronouns indicating that he is now speaking (or thinking) as an individual. But in line (m) another individuated protagonist is introduced, and this time, the introduction is made purely via quotation. The 2SG pronoun and the contradiction of the previous statement suggest that this is a new individual protagonist, a dissenting Boy B who rejects Boy A's proposal. Alternatively, this could be a return to the group speaking as a whole, together agreeing that Boy A is too small to hit the peewee. This same voice (be it Boy B or the whole group) then introduces another individual protagonist, the grown-up Boy C, who will carry the next stage of the action.

k.   '*Ngay*   warra   *ngadha*   ya   *ngurrurrathawathmannemenu*   *i*
        I   first   just   YA   I.will.creep   and
        bardenu   *ku*   *numi.*'
        I.will.hit   animal   one
        'I will just try to creep up slowly on them, and **I'll** hit one bird.'

l.   '*Ku*   *ngay*   *ka*   *pangu*   *kem*   *bardenu*   *yu.*'
        animal   I   KA   there   it.sits   I.will.hit   YU
        'I'll hit that bird sitting there.'

m. '*Awu,*   **nhinhi ka**   *wurda*   *wa*   **Nhinhi ka**   *kardu*   *wakal*   *wa!*
        no   you KA   not   WA   you KA   person   small   WA
        'No not **you**! **You're** just a child!'

n.   *Nukunu*   *nimin*   *kardu*   *ngarra*   *ngala*   *ku*   *banherdenemenu*   *yu.*'
        him   instead   person   that   big   animal   he.will.hit.for.us   YU
        'It should be **him, the one who is grown up,** who will hit the bird for us.'

o.   *Bere*   *nhini*   *thangunu*   *ka*   *kardu*   *ngarra*   *ngala*   *ka*
        well   he   from   KA   person   that   big KA
        wurrinithawathmantha   *warda*
        he.crept   then
        Then the biggest boy crept up quietly

p.   *ngarra*   *ku*   *kalampitpit*   *terert*   *nu*   *pirrinidha.*
        where   animal   peewee   all   to   they.were.sitting
        to where all the peewees were sitting.

The narrative fragment above, (20), shows that familiar primary speech devices are used to introduce and distinguish protagonists, but these work in concert with quoted speech, in which protagonists and their intentions are delineated. Much of the information about protagonists is carried by the pronominal configurations in these quotes. But there are also points when it is not clear exactly how many protagonists are individuated, or who says what. This is particularly the case where first-inclusive pronouns are used; by their nature these represent all actors as a group, and do not specify individual speakers/actors. It is also unclear, at lines (k) and (j), whether a second individual protagonist is being introduced, or whether this is non-individuated groupspeak. It appears that these details are left unclear because they don't matter to the story: the main theme of the story (further expanded in the part not shown) is group cooperation, and we only need to track a couple of individuals.

3.3.2 What is being framed? Speech or thought?

In §3.2.3 we discussed the presence and frequent use in many Australian languages of a single verb to frame speech, thought, feeling and perception.[16] To illustrate the issues of interpretation that arise from this, we return to the story excerpted in text (1), as told in Wurla by Campbell Ellenbrae, about a white "bushman" man named Harry. The story starts out as follows:[17]

Wurla

(21) a. *bijroy-walu   yarrij   awanwalu,   jina   marlngarri*
      Fitzroy-from   move.down   3M:fall:PRS:PROX   3M-that   white person
      He is coming came from Fitzroy, that white man.

   b. *marlngarri   jirri   yaminggi   bayala   mumarn*
      white person   3M-that.one   downstream   follow   3N$_w$ <3SG:take:PRS
      muna   bijroy   muna
      3N$_w$:that   Fitzroy   3N$_w$:that
      That white man is following the Fitzroy downstream.

   c. *mardu urra-ngarri, nangun garra*
      walk   3M:go:PRS   night   maybe
      He walks, maybe at night.

   d. *mardu urrenggerri-nya   ubuguma   bardi*
      walk   3M:go:PST:DUR-DIST   (place.name)   arrive
      He kept walking until he got to Oobagooma

   e. *'a   munda   munda   ngurre-yali*
      Oh   3M:this   3N$_m$:this   1SG-FUT:be-indeed
      'Oh, I'll stay right here'

   f. *munda   munda'   ama*
      3N$_m$:this   3N$_m$:this   3M:do:PRS
      Here's the place' he says/thinks.

---

16 This is true of many languages around the world. For examples see Reesink (1993) regarding Papuan languages, Larson (1978) regarding the Aguaruna language of Northern Peru, and Streeck (2002) regarding some varieties of modern English.
17 For a link to the sound file for excerpt (21) see ◀) https://www.degruyter.com/document/isbn/9783110789836/html

g. *ngala-gude-ngarri   munda   mara   andon*
   meat-COM-CHAR   3N_m:this see   3PL<3SG:act.on:PRS
   He sees that there is plenty of game there.

h. *'arri anja   gajin bunda   ngara   bunda'   ama*
   o.k. what like   PL-this tree.honey 3PL-this 3M:do:PRS
   `O.k., what's this, sugarbag?' he says/thinks.

i. *ngara   bunda   dorra enyerri   murla urruma*
   tree.honey PL-this chop   3M:be:PST:DUR taste 3M:do:PRS
   He was cutting sugarbag[18] and tasted it.

j. *'aw burraninyangarri bunda'   ama*
   oh   3PL-good-CHAR   3PL-this 3M:do:PRS
   'Oh, this is good' he says/thinks.

k. *birringarri-nga   muminjal erre*
   3PL:that.one-only   eat   3M:be:PRS
   That's all that he eats.

The multifunctional Wurla framing verb *ma* occurs three times in this excerpt, at the end of lines (f), (h) and (j), always with the third person singular masculine prefix *a-*, agreeing with its grammatical subject *marlngarri* 'white man'. As indicated in the translation, in all three cases the verb does not explicitly indicate whether the words it frames were spoken or only thought. From the fact that the man is walking all by himself, probably at night, it seems likely that they were not spoken aloud. This is an example of what we have referred to in §3.2.6 as the application of "general principles of reasoning" to arrive at more and less likely ways of interpreting quotations in the narrative. A further, formal criterion that is relevant here, as discussed in §3.2.3, is that none of these three instances of the framing verb *ama* includes a reference to an addressee. But the absence of such addressee marking does not explicitly indicate that the framed material is unspoken thought – only that it might be. Here again, as in §3.3.1, the uncertainty is of little consequence: what matters is that the protagonist Harry had those thoughts, regardless of whether or not he spoke them to himself aloud.

Next the narrator Campbell describes how Harry had provisioned himself out in the bush with yams, goanna, emu, turkey and long-neck turtle, and then tells

---

18 'Sugarbag' refers to the honey made by any of Australia's several species of native bees. Some of them nest in the ground and some in trees. The ones referred to in this story nest in hollow trees. The honey is harvested by chopping a hole in the tree as does Harry in this story.

us how he (Campbell) and his fellow stockmen first came across Harry. They were mustering cattle and heard someone chopping wood. The story continues:

l. *'burruru   nana   dorra-yali   birrina'*
3PL:human 3M:over.there chop-indeed 3NSG:be:PRS:PAUC
nyadanganyina
1PL:EXCL:put:RR:PRS:PAUC
'They're chopping over there' we say to each other.

m. *'gadug gadug gadug umbirriyon*
cut   cut   cut   3M<3PL:act.on.PRS
'They're[19] chop, chop, chopping it.

n. *ngara'*
sugarbag
Sugarbag

o. *li   nganya,   burrurungarri*
look 1SG:go:PST   man
I looked and saw a man.

p. *'dupula biya'   ngumera*
red   must.be 1SG:do:PST
'It must be a red (i.e. white) man', I said.

q. *'a   burruru   burruru, a   marlngarri, marlngarri*
look 1SG:go:PST   man   oh   a white fella, a white fella
nyadanganyina
1PL:EXCL:put:RR:PRS:PAUC
'Oh a man, a man! A white fella' we say to each other.

The quotations in lines (l) and (q) are explicitly framed as speech, not by the use of an addressee-marking pronominal suffix as discussed above, but the use of a distinct framing verb *angayi* which means 'say to each other'.[20] In line (p),

---

19 As in the previous line, the verb here has a plural subject: although, as it turns it out there was only one man doing all the chopping, it presumably sounded like more. Or perhaps the plural is being used as an indeterminate number category here, as in English "would whoever left their rubbish in my room please come and take it away".

20 In Wurla as in the closely-related Ngarinyin language, the ordinary framing verb *ma* cannot be used to mean 'say to each other'. In that function it is replaced in Wurla by the verb *angayi*, and in Ngarinyin by the (presumably cognate) verb *iningayi*, which is a reflexive/reciprocal-marked the framing verb *ma* (with past-indicative suffix *ra*) could in principle mean either 'said' or 'thought', but the latter reading is strongly suggested by the fact that, unlike this line, most of the lines of quoted speech in Campbell's text are introduced by an interjection, as discussed in §3.2.4 and exemplified in text (1), lines (c), (f), and (j). This tendency is also exemplified by line (q) above, which begins with *a* 'oh'. But in that line we know in any case that the framed material is speech, from the use of the framing verb *angayi* as discussed above.

After realizing that the chopping was being done by a white man to gather sugarbag, Campbell and his mates approach him and find to their relief that he is someone whom Campbell recognises – Harry. Harry gives them a generous supply of sugarbag as narrated in text excerpt (1). Campbell gives Harry five tins of tobacco in return and says to him:

r. 'orait,   *mara* *nyuno*   *wana* *di'*
    all.right   see   2SG<SG.SBJ:FUT:act.on   when   then
    'All right, when am I going to see you?'

Harry replies:

s. *gunyalgalu*   *mara*   *nyunon*   *ah*   *munda*   *manjan*
    whereabout   see   2SG<SG.SBJ:act.on:PRS   um   there   hill
    ganda   *jog*   *winyangarri*
    that   big   3N_w:over.there
    'I'll see you on that big hill over there.

t. *ngiyala-yali*   *mindi'*   *amara,*   *'yawe*   *mindi'*
    1SG:home-indeed   3N_m:that.one   3M:do:PST   upstream   3N_m:that.one
    That's my home', he said, 'further upstream there.'

Campbell's next line is:

u. *'yaw,*   *a*   *biya*   *mara* *on.guwe*   *nana'*
    yes   oh   ought.to.be   see   3M<1SG:IRR:act.on:PST   3N_m:over.there
    ngurrumera   *ngin*   *gana*
    3M:do:PST   1SG   then
    'Yes, but why haven't I seen him there?' I said/thought.

---

form of the verb *ininga* 'put' (Rumsey 1982: 103–105). So in its speech-framing function, this verb (always with non-singular subject) in its most literal sense means 'put to each other'.

Again, the framing verb *ma* here (in 1SG PAST form *ngurrumera*) could in principle be interpreted as either 'said' or 'thought'. But there are three reasons for preferring the latter interpretation. One is that that is how Campbell himself translated the line when we were working through this text and recording in 1976 – as something like "I thought to myself". That is not completely decisive, as we cannot be sure that his audience would have taken it that way. A second clue is that the object of the verb 'see' (*marra on.guwe*) is not second person 'you' but third person masculine 'him'. It is clear from the next few lines of the story that the mental or verbal event referred in line u took place when Campbell and Harry were still present to each other, so if the question in that line were spoken aloud we would expect its grammatical object to be 2SG, i.e. 'why haven't I seen *you* there?' The fact that it is 3SG 'why haven't I seen *him* there' strongly suggests that it was a question the Campbell thought to himself without putting to Harry.

A third, equally strong clue is what Campbell said next, which was:

v. *ni   muna   bulug   murrumura*
    mind $3N_m$:that search $3N_m$:do:PST
    I thought about that but I couldn't understand it.

Taken in combination with line (u), line (v) exemplifies the kind of two-clause framing construction discussed in §3.2.3 and illustrated there by (7) from Ngarinyin (using a reduplicated form of the same coverb as in line (v), *ni* 'think'. As in (7), the verb *ma* in one of the clauses (in this case the first one, in line (t)) frames the quotation, while the coverb *ni* in the other clause specifies that the quotation represents thought rather than speech.

In this section, drawing on examples from a single story told in Wurla, we have exemplified some of the kinds of formal markers and contextual clues on which listeners base their judgements about whether quotations within the narrative are to be understood as speech vs thought, or as indeterminate between the two. The factors considered included: 1) presence or absence of an explicit addressee, 2) the framing verb used, 3) person shift, 4) whether or not the framing clause was accompanied by a clause with a verb of thinking, and 5) general principles of reasoning. The judgements based on these criteria are sometimes clearcut, but often only presumptive. Even when they are, it seldom if ever interferes with the flow of the story, but does demand close attention from the audience in order to pick up on the relevant cues.

3.3.3 Indeterminacy between quotation and primary speech

In our examples of quotation so far, although it has sometimes been impossible to be certain about what character to attribute them to, it has generally been easy to identify them *as* quotations, as distinct from the primary speech of the narrator. We now move to some examples where that is not the case. The first example comes from a passage in a story in Kayardild (South Wellesley Islands, Queensland) told by Alison Dundaman in 1987, about a creature called Nyinyaaki, which is also the name of the place on Bentinck Island that she is talking about. We won't put in any quotation marks, to illustrate the nature of the problem. If you want to listen to the original of this story you can find a link to the audio at file at the address shown below;[21] if you do this now you might find that the intonation helps you work out which parts are quoted speech.

Kayardild

(22) a. *Nyinyaaki. Dathina   ngalawanda   dulk,   Kungarr,   Kungarra*
          Nyinyaaki   that   our(PL.EXCL) country Kungarra Kungarra
          ngalawanda   dulk.
          our(PL.EXCL)   country
          Nyinyaaki. That's our country, Kungarra. Kungarra is our country.

      b. *Dabarr-i   wirdi-ja   niya   Nyinyaaki,   walmu.*
          tree-LOC   live-PRS   he   Nyinyaaki   up.high
          In a tree he lives, Nyinyaaki, high up.

      c. *Kamburij,   kamburija   ni.*
          speaks   speaks   he
          He speaks, he speaks.

      d. *Danda   jinaa   yarbuda   kamburij?*
          Here   where   animal   speaks
          Where's there an animal talking around here?

      e. *Kurrinangku   ngakulda   yarbuthu!*
          Can.t.see   we.inclusive   animal
          We can't see an animal!

---

21 For a link to the sound file for excerpt (22) see ◄)) https://www.degruyter.com/document/isbn/9783110789836/html

f. *Dathinmaanda dangkaa dathinmaanda yarbud, dathinmaanda*
   from.there   fellow   from.there   animal   from.there
   wurand, niya yarbud.
   creature he   animal
   A fellow from here, that animal is the creature for this place, he's the
   animal.

What's going on here? Who is talking in (d)? Is it the person (whoever it is) mentioned in line (c), so that we would translate lines (c) and (d) as '(Someone) says:
"Where's there an animal talking around here?"'? But then, actually, *kamburija*
can mean 'call, make a sound appropriate to a particular species' (e.g., call out,
or even croak, of a frog), so that (c) could actually also mean 'it's calling out' or
'something is calling out' rather than '(s)he speaks'. So maybe the translation
should be 'it (the Nyinyaaki creature) makes a noise. "Where's there an animal
talking around here?" (says someone)'. Continuing on, are lines (d) and (e) from
the same speaker 'Where's there an animal talking around here? We can't see an
animal!' or are they a little mini-dialogue: A: 'Where's there an animal?' B: '(What
do you mean,) we can't see an animal?' And what about line (f)? Is that something
one of the reported characters says, or is that the narrator talking, the person who
knows about what Nyinyaaki is, and they are giving us the real story on why the
people in the dialogue are puzzled?[22]

Another example of narrator-character indeterminacy can be seen in text
excerpt (3) as discussed in §3.2.2. The first line of the excerpt is translated in
context as '(He) came back home (to Mornington Island)'. As shown in the free
translation of the next line (line (3b)), there are two plausible interpretations:
'(his) blood really poured out', or an unframed quotation 'hey, I've got blood
pouring out of me!'. In other words, it is uncertain whether line (3b) is to be attributed to the narrator in the act of telling the story or to the one of the characters
whose actions he is narrating.

Again, as is true of narrative quotation more generally, the kind of narrator-character indeterminacy exemplified by lines (22f) and (3b) is by no means
unique to spoken narratives from indigenous Australia. Text excerpt (23) exemplifies the same sort of indeterminacy from written fiction – again from Tim Winton's (2013) novel *Eyrie*. It comes at a point when Keely's friend Gemma has just

---

22 At the beginning of line (f) there may be an almost imperceptible interjection o, not included
in the transcription because it is so faint and may not even be there. But if it is indeed there, it
would nudge the interpretation of (f) towards being an answer by another character: 'Oh, (he's)
a fellow from there.'

told him of her intention to hire a hitman to kill a man who has been harassing her and her grandson.

English (Winton 2013: 383)

(23) a. He [Keely] took her arm, led her out to the deck. Slid the door to behind them. She shrugged him away, scowling.

b. Gemma. Paying someone else. What're you talking about?

c. You gonna stop em? You're a fuckin' softcock, mate.

d. Well thanks a lot. But Keely knew she was right. All he'd done was make it worse. He'd indulged himself, thinking he was so bloody clever.

From the indentation of line (d) (and on other contextual grounds) we know that Gemma is no longer the speaker. But who is? Keely? He would seem to be the most likely speaker (or thinker) of the words "well thanks a lot", in response to Gemma's insult. But if so, then we would normally expect the following sentence – "but Keely knew she was right" – to begin a new indented line, since those words are clearly the narrator's (cf. what happens lines (c) and (i) of text excerpt (2)). Another plausible way of the hearing the words "well thanks a lot" is as those of the narrator, in sympathy with his character Keely, or as the words of both Keely *and* the narrator[23] – another instance of what Bakhtin (1981) called "heteroglossic" or "double voiced" speech.

3.4 Some quantitative considerations

In order to provide a rough indication of the extent to which quotation is used by story tellers in Australian languages, and what kinds of it are used, we have examined texts various narrative genres in each of the languages discussed in this chapter and counted the number of words within each them which are in framed and unframed quotation. For comparative purposes we have done the same kind of count for one chapter from the novel by Australian author Tim Winton that is

---

23 This interpretation is consistent with the fact that the man who has been harassing Gemma – Clappy – is referred to by the narrator from Keely's point of view as "the bastard": "Clappy trapped [Keely's] free hand, forced his head back so hard his neck felt it would tear free of his shoulders, and all he could do was to clamp the bastard's forearm to keep from choking" (Winton 2013: 420–421).

discussed in §3.1 and §3.3.3, and another published English-language narrative text in another genre: a personal memoir by US author J. D. Vance. The results are shown in Table 3.1. Several points stand out:

(a) quoted speech, framed or not, forms a substantial part of the narrative across the texts we examine: in 5 out of 8 of the Australian sample (and the Winton passage) it exceeds 30%;

(b) for the two of the three Australian languages with more than one text (and for English), there are inter-text differences in whether framed or unframed quotations are preferred. At least for the Bininj Kunwok case this appears to reflect speaker style rather than genre, since the proportions are reversed despite both being traditional stories;

(c) the range of values for both types is not notably distinct between our Australian and English samples, except that it is only among our Australian languages that we find texts where all quotations are unframed (Murrinhpatha, Alanga, and Kayardild, Alison Dundaman).

Table 3.1: Incidence of framed and unframed quotation in selected narratives in our target languages.

Language	Narrative Genre	Total length of text (words)	Total amount of text in quotation	Amount of text in framed quotation	Amount of text in un-framed quotation
Wurla	Personal reminiscence by Campbell Ellenbrae	1167	37%	33%	4%
Ngarinyin	Traditional dreamtime story by Wati Ngedu	404	6%	3%	3%
Ngarinyin	Traditional dreamtime story told by Dagi Ellenbrae	376	33%	17%	16%
Murrinhpatha	Traditional dreamtime story told by Albert Munar	1036	13%	9%	4%
Murrinhpatha	Children's story told by Alanga	288	41%	0%	41%
Bininj Kunwok (Kune dialect)	Traditional story told by Lena Yarinkura (Evans 2003: 683–690)	455	33%	24%	9%
Bininj Kunwok (Kuninjku dialect)	Traditional story told by Mick Kubarkku (Evans 2003: 691–703)	724	32%	4%	28%
Kayardild	Traditional story / site description, Nyinyaaki, by Alison Dundaman (Evans 1995: 602–606)	182	13%	0%	13%

Table 3.1 (continued)

Language	Narrative Genre	Total length of text (words)	Total amount of text in quotation	Amount of text in framed quotation	Amount of text in un-framed quotation
English	Chapter from a novel by Australian author Tim Winton (2013: 256–259)	587	42%	9%	33%
English	Excerpt from a memoir by US author J. D. Vance (2016: 153–155)	832	11%	8%	3%

3.5 Conclusions

In this chapter we have explored the forms and some of the main uses of quotation in spoken narrative genres in Australian Aboriginal languages. We have distinguished between "framed" quotation, where an utterance or thought is explicitly attributed to another speaker or speech situation besides the one in which it is being presented, and "unframed" quotation, in which there is no explicit attribution to such a displaced source, but various kinds of contextual cues for inferring it. Regarding the material that is framed, we have shown that in Australian languages it is common to have a single verb for either speech or thought, with no explicit indication of which it is.

For framed quotation we have detailed the grammatical means by which it is framed, and its source identified. For unframed quotation we have discussed the kinds of contextual cues that are used, and usually make it possible for listeners to recognise the quotation as such, to identify its source, and to discern whether the framed material is speech or thought. These criteria include prosody, interjections, switches of grammatical person, switches of language, presence or absence of an explicit addressee, and shared understandings about the nature of human interaction and the wider world in which it takes place. Those understandings range from very general ones – such as the nature of question-answer sequences (§3.1, §3.2.4) – to culturally very specific ones such as the conversational entailments of trirelational kin classification (§3.2.6), a phenomenon which as far as we know is unique to Australia (Garde 2014; Merlan 1989) and part of Amazonia (Coelho de Souza 2020; Lea 2004).

But while these criteria usually suffice to clear up the kinds of uncertainties summarized above, this is by no means always the case. In §3.3.1 we discussed examples from a Murrinhpatha text where it was impossible to determine exactly which of the characters was speaking, or what combination of them. In §3.3.2, we discussed a Wurla text where it sometimes remained uncertain whether the framed material was to be taken as speech or thought. In §3.3.3, drawing on an example from Kayardild, we discussed a more fundamental kind of indeterminacy, about whether a given line in the text was to be taken as a quotation from one of the characters or as the speech of the narrator commenting on the events in the narrative.

In order to assess the extent to which the phenomena summarized above are particular to spoken narratives in Indigenous Australian languages, we analysed an excerpt from a very different narrative genre – a novel in English, by Australian author Tim Winton. As shown in §3.1–3.3, and quantified in §3.4, both the Indigenous Australian spoken texts and the written English one make frequent use of quotation – usually both framed and unframed. Our quantitative study also included another excerpt of English-language written narrative of a different genre – a personal memoir – and spoken narratives of various genres in five Indigenous Australian languages. Quotation was used in all of our samples, albeit at widely varying rates, and ratios of framed to unframed quotation. The differences in all those respects appear to reflect the stylistic preferences of individual speakers/writers, rather than differences between languages, genres or written vs spoken medium. But as we have shown, there are important differences between the written English and spoken Indigenous genres in *how* quotation is framed, and in how unframed quotation is disambiguated, e.g., through indentation in the written genres vs intonation and quote-initial interjections in the spoken Indigenous ones.

A feature that we found in both the Indigenous Australian narratives and the Winton novel was the Bakhtinian phenomenon of "heteroglossia". In the Kayardild text discussed in §3.3.3 this was exemplified by an indeterminacy between quotation and primary authorial speech. There was a close parallel in the Winton text excerpt discussed in §3.3.3, where the potential double voicing between the narrator's speech and that of a character was suggested by an absence of indentation where it would otherwise have been expected. Heteroglossia of a different sort in Indigenous narrative was illustrated in text excerpt (18) in §3.2.4, where presumptive change of speaker across unframed quotations was associated with change of the language spoken. When Bakhtin defined the novel partly in terms of its "diversity of social speech types" and added (in parentheses) "sometimes even a diversity of languages" (Bakhtin 1981: 262), he could have had no idea of the extent to which the narrative traditions of Aboriginal Australia, as one of the most multilingual language ecologies in the world, display that definitional feature of the novel. Examples like those discussed here are a valuable corrective to the Eurocentric bias in Bakhtin's work, drawing our attention to the heteroglossic mastery – including the harnessing of multilingualism to narrative – which is displayed in the oral cultures of Indigenous Australia.

Having compared and contrasted our results regarding quotation in Indigenous Australian narrative traditions with its forms and uses in the modern Western novel, we will end by asking, among traditions of spoken narrative around the world, what if anything is distinctive about the forms and uses of quotation in Indigenous Australian ones? Our short answer to that question is: it is difficult to say based on the available evidence. We do know that some of the features we have described are quite common around the world. One of them, at least in non-European languages, is the use of a single framing verb to mean 'say', 'think', 'feel' and a range of other meanings (Spronck and Casartelli 2021). Another is the use of intonation to mark changes of speaker (Kvavik 1986; Klewitz and Couper-Kuhlen 1999). For other features such the use of quote-initial interjections and trirelational kin terms further research would be needed to determine whether they are found elsewhere. What we have described here is a cluster of such features which are common across Indigenous Australia. We hope our results will stimulate other studies of the uses of quotation and other kinds of reported speech in spoken narrative elsewhere in the world, on the basis of which it will be possible to determine more precisely what is most distinctive to the Australian genres that we have described.

Abbreviations

1	first person
2	second person
3	third person
3M	third person singular masculine
$3N_m$	third person singular m-class neuter
$3N_w$	third person singular w-class neuter
CHAR	characterised by
DIST	distal
ERG	ergative
EXCL	exclusive
FUT	future
IO	indirect object
IRR	irrealis
LOC	locative
OBJ	object
PAUC	paucal

PL	plural
PRS	present
Q	question
R	realis
REDUP	reduplication
RR	reflexive/reciprocal
SBJ	subject
SG	singular
SUB	subordinate clause marker
-	clearly segmentable morpheme boundary
:	morpheme boundary that is not clearly segmentable in surface form

References

Aikhenvald, Alexandra Y. 2011a. Speech reports: A cross-linguistic perspective. In Alexandra Y. Aikhenvald & R. M. W. Dixon (eds.), *Language at large: Essays on syntax and semantics*, 290–326. Leiden: Brill.

Aikhenvald, Alexandra Y. 2011b. Semi-direct speech in typological perspective. In Alexandra Y. Aikhenvald & R. M. W. Dixon (eds.), *Language at large: Essays on syntax and semantics*, 327–366. Leiden: Brill.

Bakhtin, Mikhail M. 1981. *The dialogic imagination*. Austin: University of Texas Press.

Barth, Danielle & Nicholas Evans (eds.). 2017a. *The Social Cognition Parallax Interview Corpus (SCOPIC)*. (Language Documentation and Conservation Special Publication 12). Honolulu: University of Hawai'i Press. http://hdl.handle.net/10125/24739

Barth, Danielle & Nicholas Evans. 2017b. *The Social Cognition Parallax Corpus (SCOPIC): Design and overview*. In Danielle Barth & Nicholas Evans (eds.), *The Social Cognition Parallax Interview Corpus (SCOPIC)*, 1–21. (Language Documentation and Conservation Special Publication 12). Honolulu: University of Hawai'i Press.

Brandl, Maria M. & Michael Walsh. 1982. Speakers of many tongues: Toward understanding multilingualism among Aboriginal Australians. *International Journal of the Sociology of Language* 36. 71–81.

Coate, Howard H. J. & A. P. Elkin. 1974. *Ngarinjin-English dictionary*. Sydney: Oceania Publications.

Coelho de Souza, Marcela S. 2020. Porque o parentesco é sempre triádico. In Maxwell Miranda, Águeda Aparecida da Cruz Borges, Áurea Cavalcante Santana & Suseile Andrade Sousa (eds.), *Línguas e culturas Macro-Jê. Saberes entrecruzados*, 193–220. Barra do Garças: Ceddeli.

Elwell, Vanessa. 1982. Some social factors affecting multilingualism among Aboriginal Australians: A case study of Maningrida. *International Journal of the Sociology of Language* 36. 83–103.

Evans, Nicholas. 1995. *A grammar of Kayardild*. Berlin: Mouton de Gruyter.

Evans, Nicholas. 2003. *Bininj Gun-wok: A pan-dialectal grammar of Mayali, Kunwinjku and Kune*, 2 vols. Canberra: Pacific Linguistics.

Evans, Nicholas. 2011. A tale of many tongues: Documenting polyglot narrative in North Australian oral traditions. In Brett Baker, Ilana Mushin, Mark Harvey & Rod Gardner (eds.), *Indigenous language and social identity: Papers in honour of Michael Walsh*, 291–314. Canberra: Pacific Linguistics.

Evans, Nicholas. 2013. Some problems in the typology of quotation: A canonical approach. In Dunstan Brown, Marina Chumakina & Greville G. Corbett (eds.), *Canonical morphology and syntax*, 66–98. Oxford: Oxford University Press.

Evans, Nicholas. 2017. Social cognition in Dalabon. In Danielle Barth & Nicholas Evans (eds.), *The Social Cognition Parallax Interview Corpus (SCOPIC)*, 22–84. (Language Documentation and Conservation Special Publication 12). Honolulu: University of Hawai'i Press.

Garde, Murray. 2013. *Culture, interaction and person reference in an Australian language*. Amsterdam/Philadelphia: John Benjamins.

Gårding, Eva. 1983. A generative model of intonation. In Anne Cutler & D. Robert Ladd (eds.), *Prosody: Models and measurements*, 11–25. Berlin/Heidelberg: Springer.

Hasegawa, Yoko. 2005. *Elementary Japanese*, vol. 1. Tokyo: Tuttle Publishing.

Klewitz, Gabriele & Elizabeth Couper-Kuhlen. 1999. Quote-unquote? The role of prosody in the contextualization of reported speech sequences. *Pragmatics* 9(4). 459–485.

Kraveck, Karen H. 1986. Characteristics of direct and reported speech prosody: Evidence from Spanish. In Flourian Coulmas (eds.), *Direct and indirect speech*, 333–360. Berlin: Mouton de Gruyter.

Ladd, Robert D. 1996. *Intonational phonology*. Cambridge: Cambridge University Press.

Larson, Mildred L. 1978. *The functions of reported speech in discourse*. Arlington, TX: Summer Institute of Linguistics/University of Texas.

Lea, Vanessa. 1986. *Nomes e nekrets Kayapó. Uma concepção de riqueza*. Rio de Janeiro: Universidade Federal de Rio de Janeiro dissertation.

Lea, Vanessa. 2004. Aguçando o entendimento dos termos triádicos Mẽbêngôkre via os aborígenes australianos. Dialogando com Merlan e outros. *LIAMES: Línguas Indígenas Americanas* 4(1). 29–42.

Mathis, Terrie & George Yule. 1994. Zero quotatives. *Discourse Processes* 18(1). 63–76.

McGregor, William B. 2002. *Verb classification in Australian languages*. Berlin: Mouton de Gruyter

McGregor, William B. 2019. Reported speech as a dedicated grammatical domain – and why defenestration should not be thrown out the window. *Linguistic Typology* 23(1). 207–219.

McGregor, William B. 2021. Thought complements in Australian languages. *Language Sciences* 86:101398. https://doi.org/10.1016/j.langsci.2021.101398.

Merlan, Francesca. 1981. Land, language and social identity in Aboriginal Australia. *Mankind* 13. 133–148

Merlan, Francesca. 1989. Jawoyn relationship terms: Interactional dimensions of Australian kin classification. *Anthropological Linguistics* 31(3/4). 227–263.

Reesink, Ger P. 1993. "Inner speech" in Papuan languages. *Language and Linguistics in Melanesia* 24. 217–225.

Ross, Bella. 2011. Grammar and prosody in Dalabon and Kayardild. Melbourne: University of Melbourne dissertation.

Rumsey, Alan 1982. *An intra-sentence grammar of Ungarinjin, north-western Australia*. Canberra: Pacific Linguistics.

Rumsey, Alan. 2000. Bunuba. In Barry Blake & R. M. W. Dixon (eds.), *The handbook of Australian languages*, vol. 5, 34–152. Oxford/Melbourne: Oxford University Press.

Rumsey, Alan. 2010. 'Optional' ergativity and the framing of reported speech. *Lingua* 120. 1652–1676.

Rumsey, Alan. 2018. The sociocultural dynamics of indigenous multilingualism in northwestern Australia. *Language & Communication* 62(Part B). 91–101.

San Roque, Lila, Alan Rumsey, Lauren Gawne, Stef Spronck, Darja Hoenigman, Alice Carroll, Julia Miller & Nicholas Evans. 2012. Getting the story straight: Language fieldwork using a narrative problem-solving task. *Language Documentation and Conservation* 6. 134–173.

Saxton, Lesley. 1998. Complement clauses in Dogrib. In Leanne Hinton & Pamela Munro (eds), *Studies in American Indian languages: Description and theory*, 204–211. Berkeley/Los Angeles: University of California Press.

Schauber, Ellen. 1979. *The syntax and semantics of questions in Navajo*. New York: Garland.

Spronck, Stef. 2016. *Reported speech in Ungarinyin: Grammar and social cognition in a language of the Kimberley region, Western Australia*. Canberra: Australian National University dissertation.

Spronck, Stef & Tatiana Nikitina. 2019. Reported speech forms a dedicated syntactic domain: Typological arguments and observations. *Linguistic Typology* 23(1). 119–159.

Spronck, Stef & Daniela E. Casartelli, Daniela E. 2021. In a manner of speaking: How reported speech may have shaped grammar. *Frontiers in Communication* 6:624486. https://doi.org/10.3389/fcomm.2021.624486.

Sutton, Peter. 1997. Materialism, sacred myth and pluralism: Competing theories of the origin of Australian languages. In Francesca Merlan, John Morton & Alan Rumsey (eds.), *Scholar and sceptic: Australian Aboriginal studies in honour of L. R. Hiatt*, 211–242. Canberra: Aboriginal Studies Press.

Streeck, Jürgen. 2002. Grammars, words, and embodied meanings: On the uses and evolution of so and like. *Journal of Communication* 52(3). 581–596.

Talmy, Leonard. 1985. Lexicalization patterns: Semantic structure in lexical forms. In Timothy Shopen (ed.), *Language typology and syntactic description*, vol. 3, *Grammatical categories and the lexicon*, 58–149. Cambridge: Cambridge University Press.

Touati, Paul. 1987. *Structures prosodiques du suédois et du français. Profils temporels et configurations tonales.* (Travaux de l'Institut de Linguistique de Lund 21). Lund: Lund University Press.

Vance, J. D. 2016. *Hillbilly elegy: A memoir of a family and culture in crisis*. London: Harper Collins.

Wiesemann, Ursula. 1990. A model for the study of reported speech in African languages. *Journal of West African Languages* 20(2). 75–80.

Winton, Tim. 2013. *Eyrie*. Melbourne/Sydney: Penguin Random House Australia.

Zuckerman, Charles. 2021. Figure composition. *Signs and Society* 9(3). 263–299.

Alexandra Y. Aikhenvald

4 A medial clause does it all: Coherence, continuity, and addressee involvement in Manambu

Telling a story in Manambu, a Papuan language from the Sepik region of New Guinea, involves extensive clause chains. Within a clause chain, a series of events is expressed with a sequence of dependent, or medial, clauses leading up to a main, typically "final" clause. This is a common feature of Papuan languages. Completive medial clauses stand out as being most versatile. They are employed in recapitulating linkage – serving as a transition between the two clause chains and expressing thematic continuity between the episodes in the linked clause chains. When used non-canonically – on their own and at the end of truncated clause chains – they contribute to coherence and continuity of narratives, and to conversational interactions. Non-canonical medial clauses signal continuity, addressee involvement, and invite a turn-take in conversation. Clause chaining and medial clauses are all but absent from messages on Facebook and social media in Manambu.

4.1 Preamble: What is a clause chain

Telling a story – or reporting a string of related events – in Manambu involves clause chains. Within a clause chain, a sequence of subevents will be expressed with a sequence of dependent, or medial, clauses leading up to a main, typically "final" clause. This is a common feature of Papuan languages.

Clause chains have two major properties (Sarvasy and Aikhenvald forthcoming offer an up-to-date cross-linguistic survey of clause chaining).

First, a clause chain consists of one or more medial (non-final) clauses combined with one final clause. The final clause bears the full specification for tense, aspect, mood, reality status, and subject and other participants. A medial clause

Acknowledgements: I am grateful to R. M. W. Dixon for his incisive comments and inspiration. Special thanks go to the late Pauline Yuaneng Luma Laki and my Manambu family for sharing their remarkable language with me.

Alexandra Y. Aikhenvald, Jawun Research Centre, Central Queensland University

https://doi.org/10.1515/9783110789836-004

contains a special marker of dependency. The predicate of a medial clause is typically marked for:
(a) tense relative with regard to the final clause;
(b) same-subject or different subject with regard to the following medial clause or to the final clause;
(c) subject reference, typically for clauses marked for "different subject". (In some languages, such as Hua, Yagaria, Amele, and Yalaku, a medial clause can be marked for imperative mood; at present, we will abstract ourselves from these rarities).

The clause within which switch reference is marked is referred to as "marking clause"; and the clause (main or dependent) which determines switch reference as "reference clause" (following the conventions in Haiman and Munro 1983).

Second, the syntactic relationship between clauses within a chain is dependent, but clauses within the chain are not embedded within each other.

Clause chains always have to be distinguished from serial verb constructions which never contain markers of syntactic dependency. These constitute a defining feature of clause chains (further discussion is in Aikhenvald 2018: 124–138).

The final clause can be considered the main clause, since it carries the full set of specifications for clausal categories (such as tense, aspect, mood, modality, evidentiality, and also person). Following Dixon's (2009) definition, the final clause is the focal clause, and medial clauses can be considered supporting clauses.

Organizing clauses into clause chains is a means of packaging information and structuring an event. In a straightforward, canonical situation, the final, focal clause will carry the main event line (see Dixon 2009; and also Longacre 1983: 14–17). Non-main clauses, or supporting clauses, will carry the supporting line and add backgrounded, or explanatory, information (see also Guérin and Aiton 2019: 27; Watters 2009: 99–100 on Kham, and Post 2009: 77 on Galo). Medial clauses are used in bridging constructions, connecting sentences within a narrative. They then serve to highlight continuity or discontinuity between events (see Guérin and Aiton 2019; Aikhenvald 2009, 2019 on the definitional and discourse-related properties of bridging constructions).

A medial clause may occur on its own, with a special pragmatic or semantic effect (an analysis of such non-canonical medial clauses is in Sarvasy 2015 for Nungon and a few other Papuan languages; and also Watters 2009: 99–100 for Kham, a Tibeto-Burman language). Alternatively, a medial clause may follow the final clause, creating a special effect, making the narrative flow and keeping the listener on track (see Sarvasy 2015; and also Aikhenvald 2009, 2008: 455, 493). The focus of this paper is on one subtype of medial clauses in Manambu which stands apart from the rest in its frequency and in the gamut of its non-canonical uses.

In §4.2, we start with background information on Manambu and an overview of clause chains and medial clauses in the language. In §4.3, we turn to a brief survey of recapitulating linkage. Summary linkage between clause chains and within them is the topic of §4.4. Non-canonical uses of medial clauses and their effects in marking continuity in discourse and listeners involvement are discussed in §4.5. The final section offers a summary.

4.2 The Manambu language: A backdrop

Manambu is spoken by c. 3,000 people in five villages (Avatip, Yawabak, Malu, Apaːn and Yuanab (Yambon)) in the East Sepik Province of Papua New Guinea, plus expatriate communities in Port Moresby and in Wewak. Other languages of the Ndu family are Iatmul, Boiken varieties, the Wosera-Abelam dialect continuum, Gala (or Swakap) and Yalaku.

Manambu has a large phonological system (by the Ndu standards: Appendix 1). The language is predominantly suffixing (two prefixes and several dozen suffixes), with productive verb compounding and single-word verb serialization. Grammatical relations are expressed through cases on nouns (see Appendix 2) and also through cross-referencing on a fully inflected verb. Final or fully inflected verbs can have:

A. One cross-referencing position: the subject (transitive subject A or intransitive subject S, abbreviated as A/S) (if there is no other constituent more topical than the subject), or

B. Two cross-referencing positions: the subject A/S and almost any other constituent (O, Addressee, Location, Time, etc.) if more topical than the subject.

Uninflected verbs do not take any person-number cross-referencing markers; they include desiderative and purposive modalities and a few aspectual forms.

A member of any word class can occupy the predicate slot within a main clause. Within a main clause, a non-verb takes a special set of nominal predicative cross-referencing enclitics. Within a non-main clause, a non-verb or an uninflected verb will have to occur with the multifunctional support verb te- 'be, become; have'.

Any constituent (including the predicate) can be put in a focus construction, roughly translated as 'this is what it is . . .'. This is achieved by attaching nominal predicative cross-referencing enclitics to it. There may be more than one focussed constituent in one clause. Focus constructions do not occur in medial clauses. Constituent order in main clauses tends to be verb final, but is not exclusively so. In contrast, constituent order in non-main clauses of all types is verb-final.

A further feature of the language – and the one most relevant to us here – is extensive clause-chaining with numerous markers of switch-reference (see also Aikhenvald 2008, 2009). Other means of clause-linking in Manambu include conjoined dependent clauses and clauses with heterosemous case markers as linkers. These stand apart from clause chains in their semantics and co-occurrence with each other and clause chains (as do relative clauses).

The meanings and the marking of medial clauses are summarised in Table 4.1. As expected, the subject acquires overt marking only in those clauses where it is different from that in the subsequent, reference clause (following the principles formulated in Haiman and Munro 1983; see also Roberts 1997, 2017).

Table 4.1: Medial clauses in Manambu: meanings and markers.

MARKING	SWITCH-REFERENCE	SEMANTICS	SUBJECT MARKING IN MARKING CLAUSE
1. -n	n/a	simultaneous; manner	no
2a. -ku	SS	(i) temporal completive 'after' (ii) reason	no
2b. -k	DS		yes
3. -ta:y	SS	cotemporaneous	no
4. -taka	SS	immediate sequence	no
5. -keb	DS	as soon as: a brief temporal overlap	yes
6. -ta:y-keb	SS		no

The average number of medial clauses per sentence is two or three (about 60% of the narrative corpus); sequences with up to six clauses have been attested. A medial clause marked for switch-reference can be postposed to the main or "final" clause (see §4.4.2). Only one clause within a long sequence of medial clauses can occur in the "wrong" place – and with a discourse effect which we discuss in §4.4.2.[1]

---

1 My corpus of Manambu contains over 35 hours of transcribed stories of various genres and conversations, and fieldnotes (from participant-observation-based work). I started working on Manambu in 1995. The bulk of the corpus was collected during four lengthy periods of fieldwork in Avatip and surrounding villages in 2001–2016. This corpus is being constantly expanded by on-going interaction with speakers of Manambu. The orthographic conventions here follow Aikhenvald (2008), a comprehensive grammar of the language.

General properties of medial clauses are (Aikhenvald 2009: 122):
- verb-final constituent order stricter than in main clauses;
- only verbs can be heads of predicate of a medial clause;
- a non-verb heading the predicate will have to occur with a support verb within a complex predicate;
- all medial clauses are negated with the suffix *-ma:r-* 'dependent clause negator' (in contrast to main clauses which are negated with various particles, depending on tense, mood, and modality).

The strict differentiation between same-subject versus different-subject may be occasionally overridden by same topic versus different topic. In other words, a same-subject marker may also serve to indicate topic continuity within a clause chain (even if the overt subjects are different: see Aikhenvald 2008: 531–533, resonating with Reesink 1983).

The completive medial clause (2a: *-ku* SS / 2b: *-k* DS) is highly versatile. This is the most frequent type of medial clause (found in over 90% of the corpus). It stands apart from other medial clauses in that a constituent within it can be questioned, without questioning a constituent in the main clause. Its many functions in narratives and in conversations are the topic of this paper.

4.3 What is a medial clause good for?

Packaging information into clause chains helps organise different subevents included in the chain and prioritise them. Typically, backgrounded information, additional comments, or "asides", appear within medial clauses. The main, or the focal, clause presents the main story line. The medial clause will contain supporting, or backgrounded, information.

An example is in (1), from a story about a revolt of women against men. The main story line can be traced through the main ("final" and fully inflected) clauses (their predicates are in italics). There is an intonation rise and a brief pause after each medial clause (typical for all non-main clauses), and a falling intonation at the end of the chain. Boundaries between medial clauses are shown with /. A final (or "reference") clause is set off with //.

(1) [*Leplep yaku-le-k*]_{MDC} /,
     swing   throw-3fem.sg-COMPL.DS
     'After she (one of the women) had swung (her leg),

[a-di   ta:kw   yu-ku]_{MDC}/,
that-pl   woman   go-COMPL.SS
those women having gone,

[kep-a   kwarbam   laki   ke-kwa-dana]_{MC}//
only-LK   bush+LOC   ginger   eat-HAB-3pl
(they) *ate* just ginger in the bushland

[laki   gepi-ba-k]_{MDC}/   [ke-ta:y]_{MDC}/
ginger   be.sick-1pl-COMPL.DS   eat-COTEMP.SS
ginger, as when we are sick, (they) having been eating (it),

[yi-sewul-yak-yi-sewul-yake-dana]_{MC}//
go-turn-**fully**-go-turn-**fully**-3pl
they *transformed fully* (into ginger plants).'

The completive medial clause has a number of further functions. It takes part in recapitulating linkage. The function of recapitulating linkage is to indicate continuity within the main story line, while at the same time showing that the story-line is moving ahead. Recapitulating linkage invoves partial or full repetition of the last, or "final" clause of a preceding chain as the first ("medial") clause of the following chain (see further examples and details in Aikhenvald 2019; an Appendix there outlines the main terminological issues used by previous authors, include "head-tail", "tail-head", "backgrounding repetition", and "recapitulation"; see also Dixon 2009: 8 and Guérin and Aiton 2019: 4).

The repeated verbs within recapitulating linkage in (2) are in bold throughout this chapter. Rising intonation after the repeated verb in the recapitulating medial clause is typical of a dependent clause. There is a pause after it, indicated with a comma. The final verb of the preceding clause in (2a) forms one intonation unit with the verb in the recapitulating clause in (2b) (this is indicated with //). The same applies to (2b) and (2c).

(2) a. [day-a-di   ñan-ugw   du-a-ñanugw-a-deka   tabati   **te-di**]_{MC}//
        they-LK-PL   child-PL   man-LK-child-LK-ONLY   ten   be/have-3pl
        'They had their only male children, ten.'

   b. [**Te-ku**]_{RECAP.CL}/,
        be/have-COMPL.SS

        [day-a   amæy   kwasa   ñan   **ta:l**]_{MC}//
        they-LK-fem.sg   mother   small.fem.sg   child   be/have+3fem.sg
        'Having had (the children), their mother had a little girl.'

c.   [*Te-le-k*]_{RECAP.CL}/
be/have-3fem.sg-COMPL.DS

[*asa:y   ata   wa-de-di*]_{MC} //
father   thus   say-3masc.sg.past.A-3pl.O
'After she had (a little girl), father said to them (the children) thus . . .'

The recapitulating clause consists of just the verb, and does not include any overt arguments. In this way, it can be considered a reduced, or a minimal, clause. (This is in contrast to other languages, where a recapitulating clause may include some if not all arguments from the main clause, e.g. Ma Manda, a Huon-Finisterre language from Morobe province in Papua New Guinea: Pennington 2016: 490, or a linker, as in Tariana, an Arawak language from Brazil: Aikhenvald 2019).

A recapitulating clause always occurs sentence-initially. In contrast to other clauses containing medial clause markers, it always has a fixed position. Even if the, main, reference, clause is not verb-final, just the verb gets repeated, and the intervening material is skipped. This is what we see in (3). The subject of the reference clause is postposed to the predicate, as a reactivated topic of this stretch of the narrative.

(3) [*adiya*   ***re-na-di***   *a-di*   *Suruali*]_{MC}//,
     DIST.DEM.REACT.TOP.PL   stay-ACT.FOC-3pl   DIST.DEM-pl   Suruali
     [***re-da-k***]_{RECAP.CL}/,   [*katela-le-k*]_{MDC}/,   [*kaw*
     stay-3pl-COMPL.DS   dawn-3fem.sg-COMPL.DS   batalion
     waku-d-el]_{MC}//
     go.out-3masc.sg-3fem.sg
     'They stayed, those Suruali, they having stayed, after it had dawned, the batalion (of the Manambu) went out (at that time).'

Using Stenzel's (2016: 437) words, recapitulating linkage works like "a spotlight in an unfolding theatrical production, directing the audience's attention to specific scenes on the stage". Recapitulating linkage serves as a transition between the two clause chains, expressing thematic continuity between the episodes in the linked clause chains.

We now turn to the non-canonical uses of the completive medial clause in Manambu.

4.4 Non-canonical uses of the completive medial clause

The non-canonical uses of the polyfunctional completive medial clause go along two lines (a general discussion is in Sarvasy 2015). The medial clause can be used as an independent clause on its own (without the main clause) – §4.4.1. Or it can occur in a non-medial position, postposed to the main clause – §4.4.2.

4.4.1 A medial clause on its own

A completive medial clause occurs on its own, without a main or a final clause following it, in the following circumstances. These can be described as instances of "desubordination" of dependent clauses whereby a dependent clause acquires the status of a main clause (see Aikhenvald 2010, 2016 on this term). Free-standing, or desubordinated, medial clauses are different from those instances where the main final clause is omitted but is fully retrievable from the context. In the instances A–C within this section a final clause cannot be supplied: each instance represents an independent clause used on its own, notwithstanding the fact that its predicate bears medial clause marking (see also Aikhenvald 2008: 505).

A. Addressee-oriented commands

A completive same-subject medial clause can be used in abrupt and oftentimes stern commands, to be followed up immediately (see Aikhenvald 2008: 594–595, 2016: 658).

They are typically addressed to a child, or to a peer. (4) was a stern and annoyed command to a child to get dressed immediately:

(4) *Wapwi   kusu-ku!*
     clothes   put.on-COMPLETIVE.SS
     'Put your clothes on!' (Lit. 'Having put your clothes on!')

This was pronounced with a sharp rise at the end, typical of imperatives. Note that the command in (4) consists just of a medial clause on its own, with no imperative main clause. The command meaning is understood. The completive meaning of the clause in (4) imparts somewhat peremptory overtones to the command: this is reminiscent of the meaning of urgency, brusqueness and abruptness of commands cast in perfective aspect across a number of languages (Aikhenvald 2010: 127–129; see Aikhenvald 2010: 275–279, for a survey of free-standing dependent clauses as directives; see also Stirling 1998, for a different effect of desubordinated *if* clauses as commands and requests in English).

A similar form can be addressed to one's peers, requesting and presupposing immediate compliance. A group of women sat down for a meal; (5) was a command for the audience (including the speaker) to pray before eating.

(5) *Mel*   *kuse-ku!*
     eye   close-COMPLETIVE.SS
     'Let's pray.' (Lit. 'Having closed eye.')

Such commands are almost exclusively used by women addressing children, or other women in a peer group – that is, to someone one can easily ask to comply. A free-standing same subject completive clause – addressed to a child or a junior person – can be used as a negative command. (6) was shouted by a mother to her teenage daughter, accusing her of being too lazy and urging her to change her ways. The completive clause on its own does not contain a negator. Its prohibitive meaning is understood within the context.

(6) *Les*   *yi-ku!*
     lazy   go-COMPLETIVE.SS
     'Stop being lazy!' (Lit. 'Having been lazy!')

The girl did not obey. The mother continued, using another completive medial clause on its own, with peremptory intonation typical for a stern command.

(7) *wiya:r*   *vara-ku!*
     house+ALLATIVE   come-COMPLETIVE.SS
     'Return home!' (Lit. 'Having returned home!')

Different subject completive clauses are never used as command strategies of any sort. This is in contrast to a number of other Papuan languages, including Nungon, a Papuan language from Morobe province (Sarvasy 2015), Mauwake (Berghäll 2010), a Papuan language from the Madang province, or Usan, from the PNG Highlands (Reesink 1987: 87, 307–309).

Free-standing same-subject medial clauses in Nungon are used as commands from parent to child. A comparison between a same-subject and different-subject free-standing medial clause in Nungon reveals a difference in illocutionary force: the same-subject form "seems to be brusquer and more urgent than the different subject medial form" (Sarvasy 2015: 679). This is consistent with the illocutionary force of free-standing same-subject medial clauses in Manambu: they presuppose addressee's immediate reaction and compliance.

Later in this section, we will see how this fits in with the general pattern of non-canonical use of the medial clause.

B. A free-standing content interrogative 'where from?'

Asking a question 'where from' involves a complex clause with the questioned constituent in a medial clause – 'where she having been you brought her' in (8), and 'where having been he comes' in (9). The question word 'where' is in bold.

(8) [***ake-m***   te-le-k]$_{MDC}$/   [*karya-mena*]$_{MC}$//
     where-LOC   be/have-3fem.sg-COMPL.DS   bring-2masc.sg+3fem.sg
     '(Oh, (what) a beautiful woman), where did you bring her from?' (Lit. 'After she had been staying where, did you bring her?')

(9) [***ake-m***   te-ku]$_{MDC}$/   [*ya-na-d*]$_{MC}$//
     where-LOC   be/have-COMPL.SS   come-ACT.FOC-3masc.sg
     'Where is he coming from?' (Lit. 'Where having stayed he has come?')

A frequent way of asking 'where are you coming from or bringing something from' is a free-standing medial completive clause with question intonation, as shown in (10).

(10) ***ake-m***   te-ku
      where-LOC   be/have-COMPL.SS
      'Where (are you) from?' (Lit. 'Having stayed where?')

This content interrogative is always directed just to the addressee (and accompanied by an eye-gaze). No constituent or any other material can be included, and the clause in (10) is pronounced as one intonation unit. Such questions are directed at the addreessee(s). I hypothesize that at some point in time this will grammaticalize into an additional content question marker, 'where from', with an interactional overtone.

C. Resultative meaning: Inviting the audience to join in

Medial completed clauses marked for same subject are often used on their own with a completive, or resultative, meaning. A speaker came into our house, sat down and said (11). This had the falling intonation of a main clause.

(11) *marketam   kami   yapi-ku*
      market   fish   buy-COMPL.SS
      'I have bought fish at the market.' (Lit. 'Having bought fish at the market'; same subject.)

This was of interest to everyone, and there followed a vivid discussion of how difficult it was to obtain fish, during the dry season. Same-subject marking on the independent medial clause wth resultative meaning implies that the same participants will be involved in the action, and the situation, the clause described.

On another occasion, another speaker was showing us a shell she has sewn onto her daughter's dress, in lieu of a button.

(12) *batten-a-yai   ata   tepe-taka-ku*
      button-LINKER-SUBST   then   sew-put-COMPL.SS
      'I have sewn it on in place of button.' (Lit. 'Having sewn it on in place of a button.')

This was said within the context of discussing the qualities of the sewing machine and mending clothes. Manambu does not have a dedicated resultative form, so a free-standing medial clause fills this gap – not unlike the way in which a free-standing medial clause is used in Nungon, to express perfect or completive meaning (Sarvasy 2015: 688). In all the instances, the sentence was accompanied by an eye-gaze, inviting the interlocutors to join in.

The resultative use of the completive medial clause on its own in Manambu differs from Nungon, in two respects.

First, only same-subject completive medial clauses occur in this meaning in Manambu. In contrast, Nungon employs different-subject clauses in similar contexts.

Secondly, a same-subject completive medial clause used on its own in its resultative meaning is limited to conversational contexts (and does not occur in planned narratives). This is in contrast to Nungon, where no such restriction applies. It appears that the function of the free-standing clause is not just to express the result of an action: it is a means of inviting, or inciting, the audience and the addressee to join in. This is similar to the way in which free-standing same-subject medial clauses are used to express commands requiring addressee's compliance (in A) and the addressee's involvement in questions 'where from' (in B).

In each instance in Manambu, a same-subject completive clause on its own involves participation of the addressee(s).

4.4.2 A sentence-final medial clause

Manambu has a tendency towards verb-final order. About 20% of sentences within the corpus contain a constituent postposed to the final verb within a main clause. A medial clause may follow the final, or main, clause, under the following circumstances.

I Clarification and elaboration

The post-verbal position tends to be reserved for constituents – noun phrases, adverbial modifiers, and medial clauses – which provide supplementary information and clarification. Such information may be new and unexpected, or it can provide a further background comment (some examples are in Aikhenvald 2008: 536–538). This is reminiscent of numerous Papuan languages, where putting a medial clause after the final clause is used as a means of clarification (see examples in Sarvasy 2015: 684).

Example (13) comes from a story about two sisters who had been mistreated by their paternal uncle. The uncle understands this and says (13) to the girl's brother (for whom the fact that the girl is angry is also no news).

(13) [le [le-ke se kwa:l-a tamiya:b]$_{REL.CL}$/
she she-OBL+fem.sg sleep stay+3fem.sg-LK area+LK+TERM
kwa:l aka]$_{MC}$// [wuna:k
stay+3fem.sg DIST.DEM.REACT.TOP.fem.sg I+LK+DAT
warsama-ku]$_{MDC}$/
be.angry-COMPL.SS
'She is in the place where she sleeps, having got angry with me.'

The medial clause 'having got angry with me' is postposed to the main clause, as a reminder and a clarification why the girl wouldn't come out and greet her relative.

II Leading to a new episode

A postposed medial clause may contain new and additional information serving as a lead to the next sentence and the next episode in a narrative. This is reminiscent of Berghäll's (2010: 302) account of postposed medial clauses in Mauwake, a Papuan language from Madang Province. There, a medial clause can undergo right dislocation as a means of 'giving prominence to the dislocated clause', which then leads to something important. Ending a sentence with a medial clause may imply that futher, related events are expected to follow – see Franklin (1983: 47) on Kewa, and Reesink (1987: 87) on Usan (further similar examples are discussed in Sarvasy 2015: 682).

Example (14) comes from a narrative about a practical joke a group of men played on their mate Wulabikaman: they put a man disguised as a woman into his mosquito net. Wulabikaman comes back from work when it is already dark, and thinks he has got a woman in his net – to the mirth of his companions. The medial completive clause at the end of the chain (marked for different subject) postposed to the main clause specifies that the action is taking place at the end of an afternoon. Example (14) also contains an instance of recapitulating linkage, similar to (2) (the repeated material is in bold: see other examples in §4.3). This device serves to indicate cohesion between two adjacent clause-chains.

(14) [*Ku-sula-taka-da-k*]_{MDC}/,   [*aleb* **ra:l**]_{MC}//.
get-inside-put-3pl-COMPL.DS   there sit+3fem.sg
'After they put (the man disguised as a woman) (into the mosquito net), she sat there.'

[**Re-le-k**]_{RECAP.CL}/   [*de ada*   *yawib*
sit-3fem.sg-COMPL.DS he   DIST.DEM.REACT.TOP.masc.sg   work.TERM
te-ku]_{MDC}/
be-COMPL.SS
'She having sat there, he (Wulabikaman) having been at work,

[*ata ya:d*]_{MC}//,
then come+3masc.sg
(he) came then,

[*grab kuse-le-k*]_{MDC}/.
afternoon finish-3fem.sg-COMPL.DS
afternoon having finished.'

This leads to the next part of the story: Wulabikaman mistakes the man in his mosquito net for a woman because it is getting dark (as it happens at the end of the afternoon) and he cannot see properly. The additional information ('afternoon having finished') offers a lead into Wulabikaman's further actions – that is, his failure to distinguish a man from a woman in the dark.

III Completed action presupposing continuation

A medial same subject clause postposed to the final clause and containing the same verb as that in the final clause marks completed action. This action creates a background for the next subevent.

An example of this phenomenon is in (15), from the same story as (14). The man disguised as a woman got up and ran away; the man who had played the practical joke on Wulabikaman ran away. In the second line of the example this is phrased as 'ran away having run away'. The use of the completive same-subject medial clause after the final, inflected verb emphasizes the completion of 'running away'. (Wulabikaman stayed back and didn't sleep, thinking of how he could get his own back.)

(15) [de   a-de   du   ada
      he   DIST.DEM-masc.sg   man   REACT.TOP.DIST.DEM.masc.sg
      rase-ku]_{MDC}/
      get.up-COMPL.SS
      'That man (disguised as a woman) having got up,

      {[**tabu-waku-d**]_{MC}//   [**tabu-waku-ku**]}_{MDC}/.
      run-go.out-3masc.sg   run-go.out-COMPL.SS
      ran out completely (lit. ran out having run out).'

The two instances of the repeated verb form one intonation unit (captured by curly brackets {} and bolded). There is a pause after the medial clause with the repeated verb. That this is not an instance of recapitulating linkage is indicated by
(a) sentence final intonation after the sentence-final medial clause with the repeated verb (*tabu-waku-ku*) and
(b) the same-subject marking on the repeated verb; note that the subject of the next clause is different.

A repeated same subject medial clause at the end of a sentence never occurs at the end of a narrative. It signals that one thing is completed and something – and often something dramatic and linked to the preceding event – is to follow.

IV Addressee involvement and turn-take in conversations

Repeating the verb of a final clause cast as a same subject medial completive clause is very frequent in conversations, and especially so with speech reports. Similar to what we saw in (15), the completive clause forms one intonation unit with the preceding final clause. An example is in (16), a part of a dialogue recounted by a speaker within a conversation (further examples are in Aikhenvald 2008: 455, 493).

(16) a. [*le   ata   wa-l-ek*]ₘ_DC/
          she   then   say-3fem.sg-COMPL.DS
          'She then having said,

      b. [*wa:l   ja-kna-d,   yi-tukwa*]ₛₚ.ᵣₑₚ
          rain   fall-fut-3masc.sg   go-PROH
          it will rain, don't go

      c. [[*wa:l   je   ma:*]ₛₚ.ᵣₑₚ
          rain   fall.NEG   NEG
          It won't rain,

      d. {**wa-tua**}ₘ_C//   [**wa-ku**}]ₘ_DC/
          say-1sgA/S+3fem.sgO   say-COMPL.SS
          I said.' (Lit. 'I said having said.')

Sequences of a fully inflected verb *wa-* 'say, speak' followed by the completive same subject medial form of the same verb – pronounced as one intonation unit – have sentence final intonation. They are always used at the end of a speaker's turn. They are usually accompanied with an eye-gaze by the speaker to the interlocutors, as a means of inviting them to contribute: "this is what I said, over to you to say what you have to say now".

Similar to free-standing commands (A in §4.4.1), a free-standing content interrogative (under B in §4.4.1) and resultative free-standing medial clauses with resultative meaning (under C in §4.4.1), the same-subject completive medial clause sentence presupposes and invites addressee involvement.

The addressee will obviously be a different subject than the speaker. The use of the same-subject form is reminiscent of same-topic continuity – one of the principles of switch-reference in Manambu (along the lines of Reesink 1983 and de Sousa 2006, among others).

We can recall, from §4.3 (example (1)), that medial clauses typically include backgrounded events. In examples like the one in (16), the repeated medial clause backgrounds what the previous speaker has said, as they offer their turn to their interlocutor, inviting them to follow on.

The instances in III and in IV have two features in common.

Firstly, both involve reduced same subject medial clauses, as no further specifications or participants can be included in the medial clause. Secondly, in both cases sentences end in a completive medial clause – but something has to follow.

This is reminiscent of the phenomenon of grammaticalized, or conventionalised, incompleteness. In many languages, a dependent clause can be used on its own to achieve a special performative effect. For instance, a mild directive in English can be cast as an *if-* clause without a main clause (see, for instance, Stirling 1998 for Australian English, Ford and Thompson 1986: 365 for American English, and Quirk et al. 1985: §11.38, §11.41 for British English, and Lombardi Vallauri 2004: 210–211 for instances in other languages, including Finnish and Japanese). An incomplete utterance can come to be associated with lesser force of a command or a request, leaving the 'implicature "hanging in the air" (see Brown and Levinson 1987: 227; and further examples and discussion in Aikhenvald 2010: 275–279). The effect of what looks like an incomplete sentence – ending in a medial clause in Manambu – is an implicit implicature of something else to come, and an invitation for the addressee to join and to continue what has been left for them to continue.

4.5 To conclude: The medial clause does it all

Clause-chaining in Manambu does many jobs. It is crucial for organizing a narrative by backgrounding actions or states outside the main event line with a clause chain. Completive medial clauses – the most frequent type – stand out as being most versatile.

First, they are employed in recapitulating linkage serving as a transition between the two clause chains and expressing thematic continuity between the episodes in the linked clause chains – §4.3, example (2).

Secondly, they can be used non-canonically – on their own and within truncated clause chains at the end of a chain. They then contribute to coherence and continuity of narratives and to conversational interactions. Non-canonical medial clauses signal continuity, addressee involvement, and invite a turn-take in conversation.

These functions of the completive medial clause are summarised in Figure 4.1.

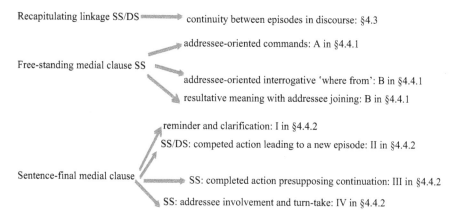

Recapitulating linkage SS/DS ⟹ continuity between episodes in discourse: §4.3

Free-standing medial clause SS
→ addressee-oriented commands: A in §4.4.1
→ addressee-oriented interrogative 'where from': B in §4.4.1
→ resultative meaning with addressee joining: B in §4.4.1

Sentence-final medial clause
→ reminder and clarification: I in §4.4.2
→ SS/DS: competed action leading to a new episode: II in §4.4.2
⟹ SS: completed action presupposing continuation: III in §4.4.2
→ SS: addressee involvement and turn-take: IV in §4.4.2

Figure 4.1: The medial clause does it all.

To reiterate: a major function of clause chaining is to provide discourse continuity, coherence, and breaks in the right place. And the medial clause – in its many guises – does it all. The same-subject clause is the most versatile. As a reduced clause – with no other participants or constituents – is the glue that keeps the story going, and the interlocutor alert.

A brief post-scriptum. The introduction of new means of communication – writing, internet, and social media – results in creating new genres, and new linguistic means for their expression. Short sentences with little if any chaining are a feature of new genres – messages on social media such as Facebook and on WhatsApp, and also personal letters. Reduced clauses addressed throughout this paper do not tend to occur in any of these, possibly, under the impact of Tok Pisin and English, the two national languages whose influence is tangible in the evolution of the written language and communication via social media.

Abbreviations

1	first person
2	second person
3	third person
A	transitive subject
ACT.FOC	action focus
ALL	allative
COMIT	comitative case
COMP	comparative
COMPL.DS	completive medial clause marked for different subject

COMPL.SS	completive medial clause marked for same subject
COMPL.VB	completive verb
COTEMP.SS	cotemporaneous medial clause marked for same subject
DAT	dative
DEM.DIST	distal demonstrative
du	dual
EMPH	emphatic
fem	feminine
FUT	future
FUT/IRR	future/irrealis
HAB	habitual
IMPV	imperative
LK	linker
LOC	locative
masc	masculine
MDC	medial clause
MC	main clause
NEG	negative
O	object
OBL	oblique marker
pl	plural
PROH	prohibitive
PROX.DEM	proximal demonstrative
REACT.TOP.DIST.DEM	reactivated topic distal demonstrative
REACT.TOP.PROX.DEM	reactivated topic proximal demonstrative
RECAP.CL	recapitulating clause
REL.CL	relative clause
S	intransitive subject
SEQ	sequential
sg	singular
SP.REP	speech report
SUBJ	subject
SUBST	substitutive case
TERM	terminative case

Appendix 1: The phonological system of Manambu

Table 4.2: Consonant phonemes in Manambu.

	bilabial	labiodent	apico-dental	apico-alveolar	post-alveolar	lamino-palatal	dorso-velar	glottal
voiceless non-labialized stops	p		t				k	
voiceless labialized stops	p^w						k^w	
voiced non-labialized stops	b [^{m}b]		d [^{n}d]				g [^{n}g]	
voiced labialized stops	b^w[$^{m}b^w$]						g^w[$^{n}g^w$]	
voiced fricative		v						
voiceless fricatives				s				h
voiced affricate					j			
lateral			l					
trilled rhotic			r					
nasals	m		n			$ñ$		
glides	w					y		

Table 4.3: Vowel phonemes in Manambu.

	Short vowels			Long vowels		
	front	central	back	front	central	back
high	i		u	i:		u
middle		e				
low	æ	a		æ:		a:

Appendix 2: Cases in Manambu

- A/S case: formally unmarked
- O case -*Vm*: for personal pronouns, and definite participants which are completely involved in the action (DOM)
- Locative case -*Vm*: location and a constituent completely involved in the action
- Dative/aversive 'for fear of' -*Vk*

- Allative/instrumental -*Vr*
- Comitative/perlative 'along, throughout' -*wa*
- Terminative 'until the very point' -*Vb*
- Two transportative cases -*say* and -*sap* 'by means of transport, or any object' (a bit like the instrumental)
- Substitutive case -*yaey* 'instead of; for something (in exchange)'.

References

Aikhenvald, Alexandra Y. 2008. *The Manambu language of East Sepik, Papua New Guinea.* Oxford: Oxford University Press.

Aikhenvald, Alexandra Y. 2009. Semantics of clause linking in Manambu. In R. M. W. Dixon & Alexandra Y. Aikhenvald (eds.), *The semantics of clause linking: A cross-linguistic typology*, 118–144. Oxford: Oxford University Press.

Aikhenvald, Alexandra Y. 2010. *Imperatives and commands.* Oxford: Oxford University Press.

Aikhenvald, Alexandra Y. 2015. Distance, direction, and relevance: How to choose and to use a demonstrative in Manambu. *Anthropological Linguistics* 57. 1–45.

Aikhenvald, Alexandra Y. 2016. Imperatives and commands in Manambu. *Oceanic Linguistics* 55. 634–668.

Aikhenvald, Alexandra Y. 2018. *Serial verbs.* Oxford: Oxford University Press.

Aikhenvald, Alexandra Y. 2019. Bridging constructions in Tariana. *International Journal of American Linguistics* 85. 455–496.

Berghäll, Liisa. 2010. *Mauwake reference grammar.* Helsinki: University of Helsinki dissertation.

Brown, Penelope & Stephen C. Levinson. 1987. *Politeness: Some universals in language usage.* Cambridge: Cambridge University Press.

Cruse, Alan. 2006. *A glossary of semantics and pragmatics.* Edinburgh: Edinburgh University Press.

Dixon, R. M. W. 2009. The semantics of clause linking in typological perspective. In R. M. W. Dixon & Alexandra Y. Aikhenvald (eds.), *The semantics of clause linking: A cross-linguistic typology*, 1–55. Oxford: Oxford University Press.

Ford, C. E. & S. A. Thompson. 1986. Conditionals in discourse: A text-based study from English. In E. C. Traugott, ter Meulen, J., S. Reilly & C. A. Ferguson (eds.), *On conditionals*, 353–372. Cambridge: Cambridge University Press.

Franklin, Karl J. 1983. Some features of interclausal reference in Kewa. In John Haiman & Pamela Munro (eds.), *Switch-reference and universal grammar*, 39–49. Amsterdam: John Benjamins.

Guérin, Valérie & Grant Aiton. 2019. Bridging constructions in typological perspective. In Valérie Guérin & Grant Aiton (eds.), *Bridging constructions*, 1–43. Berlin: Language Science Press.

Haiman, John & Pamela Munro. 1983. Introduction. In John Haiman & Pamela Munro (eds.), *Switch-reference and universal grammar*, ix-xv. Amsterdam: John Benjamins.

Lombardi Vallauri, Edoardo 2004. Grammaticalization of syntactic incompleteness: Free conditionals in Italian and other languages. *SKY Journal of Linguistics* 17. 189–215.

Longacre, Robert E. 1983. Switch-reference systems in two distinct linguistic areas: Wojokeso (Papua New Guinea) and Guanano (Northern South America). In John Haiman & Pamela Munro (eds.), *Switch-reference and universal grammar*, 185–207. Amsterdam: John Benjamins.

Overall, Simon E. 2017. *A grammar of Aguaruna (Iniá Chicham)*. Berlin: De Gruyter Mouton.

Pennington, Ryan. 2016. *A grammar of Ma Manda, a Papuan language of New Guinea.* Munich: Lincom Europa.

Post, Mark W. 2009. The semantics of clause linking in Galo. In R. M. W. Dixon & Alexandra Y. Aikhenvald (eds.), *The semantics of clause linking: A cross-linguistic typology*, 74–95. Oxford: Oxford University Press.

Reesink, Ger P. 1983. Switch reference and topicality hierarchies. *Studies in Language* 7. 215–246.

Reesink, Ger P. 1987. *Structures and their functions in Usan*. Amsterdam: John Benjamins.

Roberts, John. 1997. Switch-reference in Papua New Guinea: A preliminary survey. In Andrew P. Pawley (ed.), *Papers in Papuan Linguistics* 3, 101–241. Canberra: Pacific Linguistics.

Roberts, John. 2017. A typology of switch reference. In Alexandra Y. Aikhenvald & R. M. W. Dixon (eds.), *The Cambridge handbook of linguistic typology*, 538–573. Cambridge: Cambridge University Press.

Quirk, R., S. Greenbaum, G. Leech & J. Svartvik. 1985. *A comprehensive grammar of the English language*. London: Longman.

Sarvasy, Hannah. 2015. Breaking the clause chains: Non-canonical medial clauses in Nungon. *Studies in Language* 39. 664–696.

Sarvasy, Hannah & Alexandra Y. Aikhenvald. Forthcoming. Clause chaining: An overview and analytic framework. In Hannah Sarvasy & Alexandra Y. Aikhenvald (eds.), *Clause chaining in the world's languages*. Oxford: Oxford University Press.

de Sousa, Hilário. 2006. What is switch-reference? From the viewpoint of the young people's switch-reference system in Menggwa Dla. *Te Reo* 49. 39–71.

Stenzel, Kristine. 2016. More on switch-reference in Kotiria (Wanano, East Tukano). In Rik van Gijn & Jeremy Hammond (eds.), *Switch reference 2.0*, 425–452. Amsterdam/Philadelphia: John Benjamins.

Stirling, Leslie. 1998. Isolated *if*-clauses in Australian English. In Peter Collins & David A. Lee (eds.), *The clause in English: In honour of Rodney Huddleston*, 273–294. Amsterdam: John Benjamins.

de Vries, Lourens. 1993. *Forms and functions in Kombai, an Awyu language of Irian Jaya.* Camberra: Pacific Linguistics.

de Vries, Lourens. 2006. Areal pragmatics of New Guinea: Thematization, distribution and recapitulative linkage in Papuan narratives. *Journal of Pragmatics* 38. 811–826.

Watters, David. 2009. The semantics of clause linking in Kham. In R. M. W. Dixon & Alexandra Y. Aikhenvald (eds.), *The semantics of clause linking: A cross-linguistic typology*, 96–117. Oxford: Oxford University Press.

Robert L. Bradshaw

5 Contact-induced clause-linking changes in Doromu-Koki: New genres, new strategies

In today's world rapid social changes are accompanied by particular patterns of language change. The Doromu-Koki language of Papua New Guinea has for many years borrowed vocabulary and structures from the Hiri Motu and English languages of wider communication. But with the advent of new communication technologies these borrowings (and code-switches) are becoming more entrenched, and with these come changes to the grammar of the language, giving rise to new genres. These phenomena centre round clause-linking as a cohesive discourse device. As people adapt to new phenomena so do language speakers.

5.1 Introduction

Borrowings are a frequent outcome of extensive language contact between speakers. The Doromu-Koki language of Papua New Guinea (PNG) has been greatly affected by its interaction with two of the three national languages, Hiri Motu (Oceanic) and English. More recently the use of Hiri Motu in modern PNG society has decreased while the use of English has increased (albeit alongside substantial impact from the more widely used national language, Tok Pisin). Today, English is regularly used as the language of government and education, and also increasingly in organised religious activities; it has replaced Hiri Motu in many domains (e.g., as lingua franca). However, the impact of Hiri Motu (and English) remains evident in Doromu-Koki, not only in the numerous borrowed lexical items (approximately 7% from Hiri Motu), which includes many conjunctions, but also in some borrowed forms, grammatical patterns (e.g., calques) and means of organising discourse.

The aim of this paper is to examine Doromu-Koki clause-linking strategies and how they are changing due to the influence of language contact, and how new means of communication are leading to the emergence of new genres. The issue of how cohesion is maintained in these new genres is of particular relevance.

Robert L. Bradshaw, James Cook University

https://doi.org/10.1515/9783110789836-005

Doromu-Koki is a Papuan (Manubaran, Southeast; cf. Eberhard, Simons, and Fennig 2021; Pawley 2005: 94; Wurm 1982: 163–164, 1975: 614 and Dutton 1970: 882) language of Central Province, PNG, comprised of approximately 2,000 speakers speaking three dialects: Koki, Kokila and Korigo (Bradshaw 2008).[1] The language community is located approximately 80 kilometres east-southeast of the capital, Port Moresby, as shown in Figures 5.1–5.3.

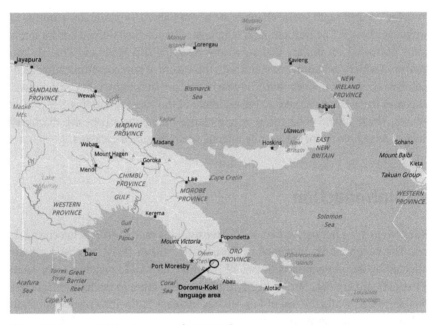

Figure 5.1: Doromu-Koki language area (QGIS 2020).

---

1 The corpus, collected over a period of almost 20 years, includes narratives (autobiographical, legends), correspondence (letters), drama, songs and digital media (mobile and Facebook Messenger texts and Facebook status group and personal posts) from over 100 individuals. Approximately 70% of the speakers are male and 30% female, of various ages and backgrounds. The majority are Koki dialect speakers, while some are Kokila or Korigo dialect speakers. Over 100 pages of texts are written or transcribed; transcribed audio recordings amount to over five hours. Included are copious annotated written and audio Scripture translation. Data were primarily collected in the Koki dialect village of Kasonomu; some limited data were collected from the villages of Amuraika, Mamanu and Oduika, and Doromu-Koki settlements in the capital, Port Moresby. **Bold** in examples indicates the morpheme under discussion or highlights topicalised or foregrounded material in the free translation, unless indicated otherwise.

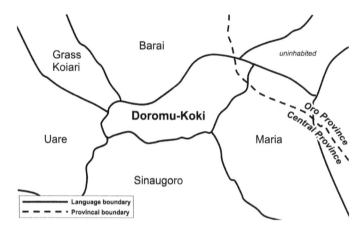

Figure 5.2: Neighbouring languages (SIL-PNG).

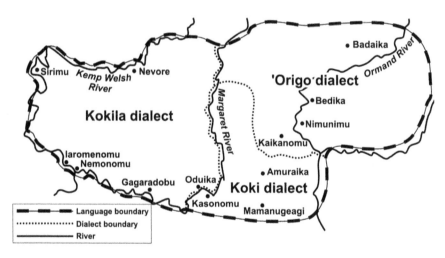

Figure 5.3: Doromu-Koki dialects (SIL-PNG).

The national language, Hiri Motu (currently having 120,000 L2 speakers; Eberhard, Simons and Fennig 2021), has also been identified as Police Motu. This language developed from the (Pure/True) Motu language spoken along the Central Province coast around the capital Port Moresby (cf. Central Province [SIL International; last accessed 12 July 2022]). The Motu language[2] continues

---

2 Spoken by approximately 39,000 people (Eberhard, Simons, and Fennig 2021). Note that both these figures for Hiri Motu and Pure Motu are rather dated.

to be spoken in its original village areas. During the Australian colonial period, Police Motu was used on patrols as a lingua franca in the south-eastern portion of the island of New Guinea, then known as Papua. Pre-independence (1975), the area was under first British rule and then later Australian administration.[3]

While use of Hiri Motu has declined in the provinces where it was originally spoken (Central and Gulf – cf. Central Province and Gulf Province [SIL International; last accessed 12 July 2022]), it continues to be perceived as a unifying language for inhabitants of these provinces. Otherwise, it has been replaced by English in most domains, and Tok Pisin, the lingua franca of the much more populous New Guinea region, continues to make great inroads into the south-east region. This is especially true in the capital, Port Moresby, which has seen a great influx of highlanders and other New Guinea region peoples. Inhabitants of the south-eastern region have resisted Tok Pisin usage, as a further means of solidarity, in order to distinguish themselves from those migrating from New Guinea regions (e.g., particularly the Highlands). Their success, however, other than merely slowing down its advance, is doubtful. Since the beginning of colonialism in the south-eastern region (as a protectorate in 1884), English has dominated in governmental and educational spheres, and continues to be the second language of choice amongst people in the region. But as migration continues it may lose that dominance.

As recently as 17 years ago, approximately 50% of the Doromu-Koki population was considered semi-literate in Hiri Motu and a quarter literate in their own language (Bradshaw 2004: 14); those percentages appear to have decreased. At that time, English literacy rates (60%) were higher than those of Hiri Motu (30%); most likely, those have remained unchanged.

Switch-reference (SR) marking is a common clause-chaining strategy amongst most Papuan languages. SR acts as a means of tracking participants throughout a discourse. In Doromu-Koki this strategy appears to be decreasing in frequency of use in some newer genres, while use of conjunctions now appears to be favoured. At the expense of the original clause-chaining techniques, there appears to be a potential cause-effect relationship between Hiri Motu influence and the expansion of conjunctions as a clause-linking technique in discourse.

---

3 Many name changes have taken place over the years. The former Irian (West) Jaya province is now called Papua and the eastern half of the island of New Guinea has been known as Papua New Guinea (or PNG) since independence in 1975. The north-eastern portion (German New Guinea, then later the Australian mandated Territory of New Guinea) was known as New Guinea and the western portion as Irian Jaya, part of Dutch New Guinea (and later Indonesia).

Discussion will focus on this switch-reference system (§5.2) and recapitulating linkage and summary bridging linkage discourse strategies (§5.3), which are based on the switch-reference system. Discussion of conjunctions (§5.4) will follow. Investigation into what types of lexical items and grammatical patterns have been borrowed into the language from Hiri Motu (§5.5) will also be included. Lastly, discussion will take into account the impact of new genres and media of communication on the techniques of clause-linking and the expression of narrative cohesion (§5.6).

5.2 Switch-reference

Doromu-Koki non-final (or medial) verbs may take switch-reference marking. In this way, their function is to link clauses in temporal relations. When the subject is the same between clauses, only same subject (SS) switch-reference marking is indicated on the dependent verb; the tense-aspect-mood (TAM) marking is then reserved for the final verb. When the subjects are different (DS), then TAM marking corresponding to the first clause subject is indicated on the first clause non-final verb while the different subject of the second clause carries its own TAM marking (cf. Roberts 1997, 2017: 538). The four Doromu-Koki switch-reference suffixes are indicated in Table 5.1 (Bradshaw 2022: 276).

Table 5.1: Non-final verb switch-reference marking.

Type	Subtype		Different subject
Switch-reference and TAM	Sequential	(Mood) Tense	-ma
	Simultaneous	(Mood) Tense	-ri
			Same subject
Switch-reference	**Sequential**		-si
	Simultaneous		-gasa

Each of these is exemplified on the marked (cf. Roberts 1997, 2017) [medial, i.e., non-final] verbs; i.e., the same subject markers -*si* (sequential) in (1) and -*gasa*[4] (simultaneous) and (2), and the two different subject markers -*ma* (sequential) and -*ri* (simultaneous) in (3).

---

4 Note: in example (2) -*gasa* is realised in its rapid speech form -*ga*.

(1) *Nai*   *baba*   [*kero* *re-si*]$_{MV}$ *kimo=ka*   *kimo=ka*
    1SG.POSS father   turn do-SEQ.SS carefully=also carefully=also
    kami   *na*   *ni-yo . . .*
    so.then 1SG say-3SG.PAST
    '[My father]$_i$ turned around, so then [he]$_i$ carefully and quietly said to
    me . . .' [1.07]

(2) [*Mina* *totona* *bona* *aura* *yafuyafu* *buni* *moi-ga*]$_{SC}$
    this   for   and   wind breeze   good get-SIM.SS
    [*amei-da*   *dada*]$_{SC}$, [*nai*   *rautu* *bi* *ura* *rei-da*]$_{FC}$.
    stay-1SG.PRES because 1SG.POSS village TOP like do-1SG.PRES
    'Because of this and the nice breeze that [I]$_i$ get while living (there), [I]$_i$ like
    my village.' [5.02]

Due to the use of switch-reference, *ini nono* 'his mother' in the final clause of (3)
is not necessary, but included for pragmatic effect.

(3) [*Rautu* *oki-yafa-ri*]$_{DC1}$ [*na* *ya* *ini*   *nono*   *sina*
    village arrive-1PL.PAST-SIM.DS 1SG DSM 3.POSS mother story
    nioteimar-aka-ma]$_{DC2}$ [*ini*   *nono*   *sena*   *gubuyo* *re-yo*]$_{IC1}$
    tell-1SG.PAST-SEQ.DS 3.POSS mother already anger do-3SG.PAST
    'When we arrived in the village I told the story to his mother and his mother
    was already angry' [3.09]

Based on an analysis of a corpus of 80 texts, *-gasa* 'simultaneous same subject' is
the least frequently used. The relative frequency percentages for each of the four
markers are indicated in Table 5.2 (Bradshaw 2022: 378). The marker *-si* 'sequential same subject' is more frequently used than all the other markers combined.
The same relative frequency applies across genres. The highest instances of *-si*
'sequential same subject' are found in narratives and legends.[5] The highest use of
-ri 'simultaneous different subject' and *-gasa* 'simultaneous same subject' is also
found in legends. Together these may suggest a modern trend toward less use of
non-final verb switch-reference marking. That is, switch-reference use is much
less common in conversations and quite rarely observed in letters, notes, social
media and songs. As newly introduced genres, these present a plausible example
of contact-induced change, having most likely been influenced by English.

---

5 This may be an explanation for grammaticalisation of the frequently used *-si* marked verb
re- 'do'.

Table 5.2: Frequency and context for use of switch-reference markings.

SR marking	Relative frequency	Frequency in first SR marked clause	Context
-si 'SEQ.SS'	58.6%	50.0%	(DC/IC) ___DC/IC
-ri 'SIM.DS'	17.1%	23.3%	(DC/IC) ___DC/IC
-ma 'SEQ.DS'	13.1%	12.8%	(DC/IC) ___DC/IC
-ga(sa) 'SIM.SS'	11.2%	14.0%	(DC) ___DC/IC

The most commonly occurring switch-reference marker, -si 'sequential same subject', has also been prominently observed in contact-induced grammaticalisation. These forms are seen in Table 5.3.

Table 5.3: Grammaticalised forms involving -si 'sequential same subject'.

Components	Gloss(es)	Derived forms	Gloss(es)
beika + re-si	what + do-SEQ.SS	beika resi	'why'
gokai + re-si	how + do-SEQ.SS	gokai resi	'how, why'
mina + re-si	this + do-SEQ.SS	mina resi	'therefore'

The first form, *beika resi* 'why' is conceivably derived from the Hiri Motu *dahaka badina, dahaka dainai or dahaka totona* (what because/in order to) 'why' (Dutton and Voorhoeve 1974: 188, 190, 204), while the third form, *mina resi* 'therefore' may be derived from *unai dainai* (that because) 'therefore' (Dutton and Voorhoeve 1974: 190, 205; *The Dictionary and grammar of Hiri Motu* 1976: 40). It is not clear, however, how the second form, *gokai resi* 'how, why' was derived, but the relationship between the forms is evident. The conjunction *mina resi* 'therefore' presents an instance of a demonstrative plus some other elements forming a conjunction (cf. Kuteva et al. 2019: 135), while the other two are instances of an interrogative plus another element forming another interrogative.

Either a dependent or an independent clause can precede non-final verb clauses with any switch-reference marking except -gasa 'simultaneous same subject'. Only an optional dependent clause may precede a 'simultaneous same subject' marked clause; this marking begins the sequence of actions. Either a dependent or an independent clause may follow any other non-final verb clauses. Dependent clauses do not occur independently.

Most sentences consist of one switch-reference marked (non-final) clause and one final verb clause. The longest observed clause-chain has three SR-marked clauses preceding the final verb clause, occurring about half as frequently as two-SR clauses + final verb.

5.3 Recapitulative and summary bridging linkage

Recapitulative linkage (cf. Chapter 4, §4.3, Aikhenvald, this volume) restates an action; one clause concludes with a verb form while the next commences with the same verb form to slow down the progression of the story (cf. Aikhenvald 2019: 461), focussing on the currently relevant event. Recapitulative linkage is uncommon in Doromu-Koki, in comparison to other Papuan languages; it may typically occur once or not at all in a stretch of discourse. When recapitulative linkage does occur, it takes various forms: i) copy of the previous verb form (4), ii) another form of the same verb (5–6) or iii) with inclusion of limited arguments preceding the recapitulated verb form (7–8) (cf. Guérin 2019; Aikhenvald 2019; Bradshaw 2022: 393).

(4)   ...***bo-yafa.***   ***Bo-yafa-ma*** ...
    ... go-1PL.PAST   go-1PL.PAST-SEQ.DS
    '... we went. We went and then ...' [1.04–05]

In (5), same subject is marked on the complex non-final verb, with TAM marking indicated on the final verb. The context for these sentences is a hunting trip, in which the 'going' was particularly relevant: traversing the bush, over mountains and across rivers and streams.

(5)   ... *Airadi*   ***bo-yafa***].   [***Bo***   *re-si*]$_{\text{CL1}}$ [*ema*   *oki-si*]$_{\text{CL2}}$
    ... (name)   go-1PL.PAST   go   do-SEQ.SS   river.mouth   arrive-SEQ.SS
    [*omuna*   *keu*   *ri-yafa*]$_{\text{CL3}}$.
    mountain   ascend   make-1PL.PAST
    '... we went on to Airadi. Going there, then we arrived at the river mouth and ascended the mountain.' [4.09–10]

In (6), the first instance of the verb *bo-* 'go' is in the imperative and the second as a medial verb indicates simultaneous same subject.

(6)   ... ***bo-nadi***] ...   [***bo-ga***]$_{\text{CL1}}$ [*ve-gam-afa-ri*]$_{\text{CL2}}$ [[*dona*
    ... go-1PL.IMP   go-SIM.SS   see-PAST.IMPERV-1PL.PAST-SIM.DS   pig
    anuka   maka]$_{\text{o}}$ *ve-gam-afa*]$_{\text{CL3}}$ ...
    print   only   see-PAST.IMPERV-1PL.PAST
    '... let's go ... We went and when we were looking, we were just seeing pig tracks ...' [4.06–07]

In (7), the writer includes the oblique NP to further specify his destination.

(7) . . . *sufa* **di-yaka.**   **Gagani** *di-yaka-ma* . . .
      . . . bush go-1SG.PAST place   go-1SG.PAST-SEQ.DS
      '. . . I went to the bush. I went to the place (there) and then . . .' [2.01–02]

In (8), all the individual items being carried have been identified together in the second clause as *dinaga* 'load'.

(8) . . . [*nai*   *viro, vabara bona baiya*]$_o$ **moi-***da*]$_{CL1}$.   [[**Nai**
      . . . 1SG.POSS axe light and bush.knife get-1SG.PRES   1SG.POSS
      mina dinaga]$_o$ **moi-***si*]$_{CL1}$ . . .
      this load   get-SEQ.SS
      '. . . I take my axe, matches (lit. light) and bush knife. I take my load and then
      . . .' [21.02–03]

Recapitulative linkage is used to provide discourse continuity, primarily as a cohesion device or means of indicating emphasis (cf. Guérin and Aiton 2019: 29).

Similar recapitulative linkage has also been observed in the neighbouring Fuyug (Bradshaw 2007), Korafe (Farr 1999: 204), Ömie (Austing and Austing 1977: 61) and Uare (Kikkawa 1993: 165) Papuan languages.

Summary bridging linkage (SBL), which uses the non-final verb *re-si* 'do-SEQ.SS', is more common in Doromu-Koki. It is also a common feature in the Korafe (Farr 1999: 204) and Manambu (Aikhenvald 2008: 463–464) Papuan languages (cf. Guérin and Aiton 2019: 32–33). Summary bridging linkage requires agreement between the subject of the previous and following clauses. However, agreement in tense is not always required (12), as would be the situation with use of the SR marking -*si* 'sequential same subject'. An action occurring in the first clause is reiterated by the use of *resi* (do-SEQ.SS) 'SBL' prior to introduction of the subsequent event. Its use is exemplified in (9–10). There is always agreement between clauses linked by SBL.

(9) . . . [*na* *ve-gasa*]$_{CL1}$ [*ame-gam-o*]$_{CL2}$.   [*Resi*]$_{CL1}$ [*koro=ri*
      . . . 1SG see-SIM.SS   stay-PAST.IMPERV-3SG.PAST SBL   border=at
      vare-yo-ri]$_{CL2}$ . . .
      sleep-3SG.PAST-SIM.DS
      '. . . he sat looking at me. And doing so, when he was sleeping . . .' [3.03–04]

Summary bridging linkage is limited to one occurrence per sentence. It may begin a sentence, referring to the final clause of the previous sentence, and thus serve to link sentences as well as clauses in a discourse. The previous clause is backgrounded by means of summary bridging linkage (10).

(10) ... [ini   *nono*   *sena*   *gubuyo*   re-yo]_{CL1},   [***resi***]_{CL2} [*na*
      ... 3.POSS mother   already   anger   do-3SG.PAST   SBL   1SG
      nikaite-yo   *aruma*   *yaku* *aki*   *re-yo*   *ba*   *de*]_{CL3}
      ask-3SG.PAST   snake   DSM   bite   do-3SG.PAST   or   NEG
      '... his mother was already angry, and doing so, she asked me if the snake
      had bitten (him)' [38.27]

An analogous construction is found in the Ma Manda Papuan language (Morobe, PNG), as a type of verbal ellipsis (Pennington 2018: 474, 502); without it a new sentence would be required (i.e., instead using the recapitulation strategy) as in ... *gubuyo re-yo*. **Gubuyo re**-*si* ... (anger do-3SG.PAST anger do-3SG.PAST-SEQ.SS) '... (she) got angry. (She) got angry and ...' (cf. (3) above). The repetitive nature of the recapitulation strategy naturally slows the discourse, while summary bridge linkage provides a simplified reduced transition. The *resi* 'SBL' construction behaves similarly to additive coordinating conjunctions. It occurs in legend and conversation genres. Summary bridging linkage does not co-occur in the same clause with any discourse markers other than the topic marker *bi* (11).

(11) ... [*oure-si*   *bi*]_{SC} [*ini*   *rata*   *ogau*   *ni-do*]_{SC},
      ... be.first-SEQ.SS   TOP   3.POSS   stem   appear   become-3SG.PRES
      [***resi*** *bi*]_{SC} [*ini*   *imu*   *mamo*   *meko*   *vare-do*]_{FC}.
      SBL   TOP   3.POSS   blossom   and.then   fruit   sleep-3SG.PRES
      'first its stem/blade appears, and doing so, then/at once it blossoms and
      bears (lit. sleeps) fruit/grain.' (*Sei di Uka Ago Ruaka* [God's New Covenant]
      2017: 83:4.28)

Since variation in tense (and person) between the preceding and following clauses occurs, as previously mentioned and seen in (12), it may be considered a grammaticalised form, no longer segmentable for speakers and semantically bleached. In that case, the summary bridging linkage form *resi* would then be considered the conjunction 'and so' (cf. also its use in forms in Table 5.3).

(12) [[*Nai*   *tobaini* *bi*]$_A$ [*Samarai* *amiye* *yokoi*]$_o$ *me-yo*]$_{CL1}$
      1SG.POSS   sister   TOP   (name)   person one   marry-3SG.PAST
      [*resi*   [*Alotau*   *=ri*]$_{OBL}$ *ame-dedi*]$_{CL2}$.
      and.so   (name)   =at   stay-3PL.PRES
      'My sister had married a Samarai man and so they were (lit. are) living in
      Alotau.' [11.03]

The discourse function of SBL in Doromu-Koki is to indicate discourse discontinuity, that is, one chunk is finished (now moved to background), and then another one begins. Recapitulative linkage is used, though infrequently, in social media texts, while SBL is not used at all. This may be due to the relative brevity of these genres, in which the majority of background information is implied, being shared between the speaker and listener, or to the influence of the language of wider communication.

5.4 Conjunctions

The coordinating conjunctions found in Doromu-Koki are displayed in Table 5.4 (Bradshaw 2022: 247) and the subordinating conjunctions in Table 5.5 (Bradshaw 2022: 251).[6] Of particular relevance are forms which have been borrowed from Hiri Motu [indicated by (HM)], all having corresponding autochthonous forms.[7] These conjunctions are highlighted by contrastive examples following each relevant table.

Table 5.4: Coordinating conjunctions.

Additive		Alternative	
ma	'and'	*ba*	'or, and'
bona (HM)	'and'	*o* (HM)	'or'
=ka	'also, too, in addition to, and, as well as'	**Contrastive**	
kumo	'and/even (then)'	*idu*	'but, yet, nevertheless, even though'
ma(mo) (HM?)[8]	'(and) even/then, until'	*to* (HM)	'but'
kami(ni)	'(and) then'		

---

6 Clauses can be linked by all the forms, while only *ma/bona* 'and' and *o* 'or' can also link NPs.
7 Cf. Chamacoco (Zamucoan, Paraguay; Ciucci 2021: 111–134), which has borrowed other similar word classes' lexical items – see also Table 5.6, for example word classes which have borrowed terms (cf. also Haig 2001 and Matras 1998).
8 From *maoro(maoro)* 'at once, immediately' (Dutton and Voorhoeve 1974: 199; Wurm and Harris 1963: 53).

Nearly all the coordinating conjunctions have corresponding autochthonous and borrowed terms, which incidentally can occur in the same sentence (in different clauses, having the same or slightly different meanings), as with *kamini* 'and then' and *mamo* 'and then' (13). (Cf. also *mamo* in 11 above.) The additive conjunction *kamini* 'at once, (and) even/then, until' is discontinuous in nature, similar to the summary bridging linkage *resi* 'and so'; they could conceivably be used interchangeably.

(13) [*Naike   mini*]_{FC} [***mamo   dona mina nei   de-si*]_{SC},
      1SG.REFL here   and.then pig   this go.down come-SEQ.SS
      [***kamini   beuka ni-si*]_{SC}   [*yai   re-yo*]_{FC},   [*mo
      and.then   grunt   say-SEQ.SS   knock.down   do-3SG.PAST   and
      na=ka   esika amute-si]_{SC} [*kimo   ame-na   bi   de*]_{FC}.
      1SG= also pain   feel-SEQ.SS   carefully stay-NOMZ TOP   NEG
      'I myself (was) right there, and then the pig went down and came, and then grunted and knocked (me) down, and then I felt pain and carefully/quickly didn't remain (there).' [1.16]

While the additive coordinating conjunction *ma* (14) has traditionally been considered autochthonous, since it is a very short form it is difficult to prove if it might instead be a loan (cf. Dutton and Voorhoeve 1974: 199).

(14) [*O   Magdalene bi   toga   esiroka ni-do*]_{FC}   [*idu ina bi
      oh   (name)   TOP   always   cough   say-1SG.PRES but   3   TOP
      buni]_{SC} ***ma*** [*dubu   nai   usa yokoi ya ni-da   bi* . . .
      good   and   brother 1SG.POSS ask one   2   say-1SG.PRES TOP
      [*vare-fo*]_{IC}.
      sleep-2PL.PO.IMP
      O, Magdalene is always coughing, but she is well and brother my one petition to you is . . . Goodbye.' [24.03]

In (14) *ma* 'and' conjoins clauses, but it is also used to join NPs (15). This conjunction is the one most frequently observed in newer genres.

(15) *Nono,   baba   **ma**   mida~mida amei-nu   re-yadi.*
      mother   father   and   child~PL   stay-STAT do-3PL.PAST
      'Mothers, fathers and children sat down.' (Bradshaw 2021: 159)

Similarly, the borrowed additive coordinating conjunction *bona* is also used to coordinate clauses (16) and NPs (2).

(16) [de   *meki*   *re-gam-afa*]   **bona** [boi omuna
      NEG   chase.away   do-PAST.IMPERV-1PL.PAST and   go   mountain
      iruruka   *re-yafa*]
      climb.up   do-1PL.PAST
      'we weren't chasing (it) and we went and climbed up the mountain' [4.07]

The borrowed contrastive coordinating conjunction *to* 'but' (17) is used in the same manner as the autochthonous *idu* 'but' (14).

(17) [na   nikaite-yo   [[aruma yaku aki re-yo]_FC   ba   [de]_FC]_SC]_FC,
      1SG   ask-3SG.PAST   snake   DSM   bite do-3SG.PAST   or   NEG
      [**to**   na   yaku   ni-yaka   bi   [de   aki   re-yo]_FC4]_FC5
      but   1SG   DSM   say-1SG.PAST TOP   NEG   bite do-3SG.PAST
      'she asked me if the snake had bitten (him) or not, but I told (her) that it did not bite (him)' [3.09]

The autochthonous alternative coordinating conjunction *ba* 'or' (17), is also used identically to the borrowed *o* 'or' (18), linking supporting as well as conjoining NPs.

(18) [*Goina* *sana=ri*   *nai*   *ne*   *yaku* *dona* *kono=ri*   *vei-da*]_SC
      which   place=at   1SG.POSS eye   DSM   pig   ground=on   see-1SG.PRES
      o   [vi   o   uka   yabo   odoro=ri   neide-da-ri*
      or   possum.species or   possum tree   above=in   hear-1SG.PRES-SIM.DS
      bi]_SC,   [*are*   *re-si*]_SC   [*veifaite-na*   *siko*   *re-si*]_SC
      top   stand   do-SEQ.SS   perceive-NOMZ   first   do-SEQ.SS
      [*mokei-da*]_FC.
      think-1SG.PRES
      'In whatever place my eyes see a pig on the ground **or** when I hear one possum or another up in the trees, I stand and first sense/perceive (it), and then I think (about it).' [21.07]

There are only two borrowed subordinating conjunctions, *bema* 'if' and *badina* 'because', as indicated by (HM) in Table 5.5.

Table 5.5: Subordinating conjunctions (according to position).

Cause-effect		Result-reason		Conditional	
ye	'so, and'	*adina*	'because'	*vonisi*	'if, even though'
ine[9]	'so, because'	*badina* (HM)	'because'	*bema* (HM)	'if'
rofu	'so that'			**Negative consequence**	
dada	'so (that), because'			*baebu*	'lest, possibly, otherwise'
mina	'therefore, for this reason,			*baeko*	'might, maybe, probably,
dada/resi	because'				possibly, perhaps'

The autochthonous contingent subordinating conjunction *vonisi* 'if, even though' occurs supporting clause (SC) final (19) while the borrowed *bema* occurs SC initial (20).

(19) *Ye   mina   muye-yo   amiye, rumana **vonisi** bi,   ini*
      and this   die-3SG.PAST person man   if   TOP   3.POSS

      obu,   muye-yo   meda gutuna rafe-na   de   yava=ri
      widow die-3SG.PAST day   from   wash-NOMZ NEG house=in

      ame-do ...
      stay-3SG.PRES

      'And this dead person, if a man, from the day of his death, his widow remains in the house unwashed ...' [54]

The subordinating conjunction *bema* 'if' is borrowed from Hiri Motu, and behaves as it would in the source language (cf. Wurm and Harris 1963: 38; Curnow 2001); that is, it precedes the condition (20). As a borrowing, it is less commonly used, dependent on the whim of the speaker.

(20) [*Ye   **bema** dona vei-da-ri*   *bi*]$_{SC}$ [*ora   yaku*
       and if   pig   see-1SG.PRES-SIM.DS TOP   spear DSM

      you-si]$_{SC}$ [*imi-da-ma*]$_{SC}$ [*muye-do*]$_{FC}$, [*mirona=ri Geresi*
      throw-SEQ.SS   pierce-1SG.PRES-SEQ.DS die-3SG.PRES   there=at   (name)

      rautu   di-da]$_{FC}$.
      village go-1SG.PRES

      'And if/when I see a pig, I throw (my) spear and pierce (it) and it dies; I go there to Geresi village.' [21.08]

---

9 This form is possibly borrowed from Hiri Motu *ine(i)*, a variant of *inai* 'this'. One supporting clue is that it was never used in the Doromu-Koki New Testament translation (*Sei di Uka Ago Ruaka* [God's New Covenant] 2017), as words that were perceived as 'borrowed' and having an autochthonous corresponding form (e.g., *bona* 'and' and *to* 'but') were avoided.

The autochthonous result-reason subordinating conjunction *dada* 'because' (21) is also used similarly to the borrowed term *badina* 'because' (22). (The form *adina* 'because' may be a variant of *badina*.) The subordinating conjunction *dada* 'so' occurs clause finally (unlike in its cause-effect use), while *adina* and *badina* 'because' occur clause initially (as is the case in Hiri Motu; cf. Wurm and Harris 1963: 38).

(21) [*Nai   uka   esika re-yo*]_{FC}   [***adina***   *fidi   re-na*
      1SG.POSS stomach pain   do-3SG.PAST   because shoot do-NOMZ
      *dona   to   moi vegu ri-gika   **dada**]*_{SC}.
      pig   but   get life make-CON   because
      'My heart was in pain because of shooting the pig or letting it live.' [2.13]

(22) [[*Nai   rautu   bi*]_O *ura rei-da*]_{CL1},   [***badina*** *ne~ne re-gasa*]_{CL2}
      1SG.POSS village top   like do-1SG.PRES   because go~PL do-SIM.SS
      [*gagani   vei-da*]_{CL3}.
      place   see-1SG.PRES
      'I like my village, because when I'm going around I see the view (lit. place(s)).' [5.01]

These borrowed terms (20), (22) function in much the same way as the autochthonous terms (21). In some instances they are used together, e.g., borrowed *mamo* 'and then' and autochthonous *kamini* 'and then' in (13). Their use corresponds to the source language function, and some are involved in potential loss of clause chains (i.e., *ma/bona* in particular).

5.5 Borrowings

Lexical borrowings span all open word classes, and the occasional closed classes (conjunctions, locatives, postpositions and adverbs) as well (cf. Bradshaw 2021); 14% of nouns are borrowed; 72.6% of borrowings are nouns.

A closed class like conjunctions (and also postpositions) contains numerous borrowed terms. A selection organised by word class (open classes above the middle line and closed below) is found in Table 5.6; there are no borrowed function words or words found in other classes than those listed here.

Table 5.6: A selection of Hiri Motu lexical borrowings.

Word class	Term	Gloss	Original term	Gloss	Reference
Noun	*vanagi*	'boat'	*vanagi*	'canoe'	Dutton and Voorhoeve (1974: 205)
Complex verb	*abitore re-*	'borrow'	*abitorehai*	'borrow'	Dutton and Voorhoeve (1974: 245)
Adjective	*buruka*	'elderly'	*buruka*	'(to be) old'	Dutton and Voorhoeve (1974: 189)
Verb	*diba*	'know'	*diba*	'know, understand, knowledge'	Dutton and Voorhoeve (1974: 190)
Conjunction	*ine*	'so'	*inai*	'this'	Dutton and Voorhoeve (1974: 196)
Locative	*iseni*	'up over there'	*iniseni*	'here'	Dutton and Voorhoeve (1974: 212)
Postposition	*neganai*	'during'	*neganai*	'(at the time) when'	Dutton and Voorhoeve (1974: 201)
Adverb	*vorovoro*	'excessively (noisy)'	*vorovoro*	'revolver, pistol'	*The Dictionary and grammar of Hiri Motu* (1976: 41)

A speaker frequently uses an autochthonous form in one utterance and a borrowed form in another, as they both have identical meaning (e.g., *edini* vs *nakimi* [Dutton and Voorhoeve 1974: 200], both meaning 'brother/sister-in-law'; cf. conjunctions in §5.4, Tables 5.4 and 5.5: *ma/bona* 'and', *ba/o* 'or', *idu/to* 'but' and *vonisi/bema* 'if').

In addition to these lexical borrowings, a small number of grammatical constructions (Table 5.7) also occur. Usually at least one element (indicated in **bold**) is used in a construction conceivably derived from Hiri Motu.

Table 5.7: Hiri Motu borrowed grammatical constructions.

Form	Gloss	Constituents					
beikadinare	'when'	*beika*	'what'	+	*dina*	'day' (ʜᴍ)	+ *ri* 'on'
gokai	'how'	*goina*	'which'	+	*makai*	'likewise'	
mina dada	'therefore'	*mina*	'this'	+	*dada*	'so'	

The first form, *beikadinare* 'when', is assumed to be derived from the Hiri Motu *edana neganai* (which time) 'when' (Dutton and Voorhoeve 1974: 191, 201). The second, *gokai* 'how', is similar to *edana bamona* (which like) 'how' (Dutton and Voorhoeve 1974: 188, 191) and the third, *mina dada* 'therefore', is most likely derived from *inai dainai* (this because) 'therefore' (Dutton and Voorhoeve 1974: 196, 190; *The Dictionary and grammar of Hiri Motu* 1976: 78).

9.5% of lexical entries (Bradshaw 2021) are of Hiri Motu origin, whilst total borrowed terms constitute 11.8% (i.e., 80.3% of all borrowings are of Hiri Motu origin, Bradshaw 2022: 507).

5.6 The impact of new media and new genres on clause-linking

A proliferation of text messages and social media posts are seen today through the extensive use of mobile phones. Many of these digital messages are written in Doromu-Koki, with differences from spoken speech and more formally written genres, such as personal stories or handwritten notes. One particularly notice-able feature is the high use of code-switching, as well as borrowing. Most often these code-switches are in English, likely triggered by a desire to express concepts new to Doromu-Koki culture. Lexical acculturation, common to many languages in which there are no corresponding autochthonous terms, may be a significant issue. The decreased use of switch-reference marking, in favour of conjunctions, may also be due to English influence. Some details of each of these types of phe-nomena follow.

Contrary to most, example (23) begins with English then switches to Dor-omu-Koki and then back to English, presumably because the source of the writer's information was broadcast in English. The trigger (cf. Gumperz 1982 and Clyne 1987) for the code-switch to Doromu-Koki is emotional, while the trigger for the code-switch into English is the social media abbreviation LOL. In line d. the writer includes some Tok Pisin . . . *go lo bus! Super fit ya mi tok* (go to bush super fit already 1SG say) '. . . go into the bush! I say really nice', most likely to impress readers, otherwise Tok Pisin is avoided. After the Tok Pisin aside, the text contin-ues and remains in English throughout the remainder. (All the examples in this section are from new social media.)

(23) a. *Did you guys see the Kokorogoro   houses on TV? Irie.doka* (sic).
                          (PLACE.NAME)   sorrow
      'Did you guys see the Kokorogoro houses on TV? (So) sorry.'

b. *Aura   tora   meda   remanu   ameo,   mo* (HM) *yava*
   wind   big   day   three   stay.3SG.PAST   at.once   house
   ibounai (HM)   *no*   *niadi.*
   all   bad   become.3PL.PAST
   'There were big winds for three days, and at once all the houses were destroyed.'

c. *Sau   vene   ni-gam-aka,   mi   nai   rautu* . . .
   odour   people   say-PAST.IMPERV-1SG.PAST   this   1SG.POSS   village
   LOL . . .
   well at least the neares (sic) *to it.*
   'I say highlanders (lit. 'smelly people'), my village . . . Laughing out loud . . . well at least the nearest to it.'

d. *After that.* . . . . *Leg*[10] *fire go lo bus! Super fit ya   mi   tok.*
                      let   to bush   yeah   1SG   talk
   'After that. . . . Let the fire go into the bush! I say really nice.'

e. *We need a road. We need bridges over the rivers so kids stop drowing* (sic) *in em.*

f. *We need that bloody airstrip. Tora   vene   should stop their*
                                  big   people
   politics and work together for the benefit of all! The smell of a mine coming soon? Well we have to be united so all of Doromu-Koki benefit and not just the companies and the government . . . . *Just thinking out loud.*

   'We need that bloody airstrip. The elders should stop their politics and work together for the benefit of all! The smell of a mine coming soon? Well we have to be united so all of Doromu-Koki benefit and not just the companies and the government . . . . Just thinking out loud.' [26.01–06]

In (24), three common lexical Hiri Motu borrowings are used; the first, *varavara* 'relative' is used in the compound noun *varavara vene* 'relatives', a regular feature of all genres. Again, the writer has switched to English to conclude the discourse, conceivably because it is easier to do so, e.g., AutoCorrect features can make writing in a language not known to the computer software more difficult in all these newer media.

---

10 From English *let's.*

(24) *Meda buni nai varavara* (HM) *vene; dia sina beika*
day good 1SG.POSS relative people NEG word what
buni to (HM)*; sivoni vene yaku ni-dedi kana*
good but white.skin people DSM say-3PL.PRES like
HAPPY VALENTINES (sic) *ia ibounai* (HM) *rofu.*
2 all to
over to the expects, did I say it properly . . . lol . . . lovely day to all..

'Good day to my relatives; not a good saying but; like white people say HAPPY
VALENTINE'S to everyone . . . over to the experts, did I say it properly...LOL..
lovely day to all..' [28.01]

A loss of switch-reference is only observed in (23b), incorporating the Hiri
Motu conjunction *mo* 'at once' rather than using the standard *-ma* 'sequential different subject' as . . . *ame-yo-**ma** yava ibonai* . . . '. . . stayed (were) and
then . . .'. This strategy is relatively common, as seen in (25); a string of three
finally inflected verbs (indicated in bold) occur, rather than the expected SR
marked non-final verbs *ve-**si** neide-**si** ada re-yafa* (see-SEQ.SS hear-SEQ.SS happiness do-1PL.PAST) 'we saw and heard and rejoiced' or *ve-**gasa** neide-**gasa**
ada re-yafa* (see-SIM.SS hear-SIM.SS happiness do-1PL.PAST) 'when we saw and
heard we rejoiced'. Presumably this is a calque of the English 'saw and heard….'
Clause chains are short in these newly emergent genres, with usually only one
non-main clause. (In general, the highest percentage regularly contains two
clauses; cf. Bradshaw 2022: 363.)

(25) *Gua Papua.New.Guinea bi lagani 45 years independence*
now papua new guinea TOP year
*moi-yo bi ruika **ve-yafa**, **neide-yafa** ma*
get-3SG.PAST TOP right.away see-1PL.PAST hear-1PL.PAST and
***ada re-yafa** mini.*
happiness do-1PL.PAST here
'Today Papua New Guinea has attained 45 years of independence, which
we have just seen, heard and are rejoicing in.' [126b]

Further along in the same message, the writer includes SR (26). In the second
clause of (26a) *-gasa* 'simultaneous same subject' (simplified in rapid speech to
-ga) is used, rather than a temporal constituent, such as the borrowed *neganai*
'during/when'.

(26) a. [*Ye   una   Doromu-Kokila bi   Governor yaku mina   ago*
and.so 1PL   (name)   TOP   DSM   this   word
ni-do   bi]$_{CL1}$ [*una imitai   re-**ga**   ame-do*
say-3SG.PRES TOP   1PL continue do-SIM.SS stay-3SG.PRES
mini,]$_{CL2}$ [*badina   Doromu-Kokila bi   mina   feta (in the basket)*
here   because   (name)   TOP   this   basket
ide=ri]$_{CL3}$.
inside=in
'So this word that the governor says to us Doromu-Kokila (people)
continues on (lit. when continuing it stays) with us, because Doromu-
Kokila is in the basket.'

In clause 1 (26b), *-si* 'sequential same subject' occurs again, where *moi-**do** ma
ago ni-do* (get-3SG-PRES word say-3SG-PRES) 'got and said' could instead have been
used. (This occurred in the next line.) SR marking continues to be maintained
to bind predicates more closely together, while non-SR use tends to give more
emphasis to each individual action.

(26) b. [*Ye Governor yaku   beika   yaduka   moi-**si**   ago*
SO   DSM   what   dream   get-SEQ.SS   word
ni-do   bi   neide-sifa]$_{CL1}$ [*ma   ve-sifa   mini*]$_{CL2}$, [*ye*
say-3SG.PRES TOP   hear-1PL.PRES   and   see-1PL.PRES here   so
uniye   bi   gokai   re-gifa]$_{CL3}$ [*ma   mina   ni-do*
1PL.REFL TOP   how   do-1PL.FUT   and   this   say-3SG.PRES
ago   di   ona (good benefits) buni   mina   duduka
word   GEN liquid   good   this   drink
re-bi-gifa]$_{CL4}$?
do-FUT.IMPERV-1PL.FUT
'So the vision that the governor has and speaks of we listen to and we
see, so how will we partake of the benefits of this word that he says?'
[126f–g]

In the following message (27), the writer only uses SR marking in one instance
(*bou ri-si* 'cover and'), suggesting that SR clause-chaining is waning in these new
genres, under the influence of English. (In fact, these seem more like translations
from English.) When switch-reference marking is used, it indicates a closer relationship between the clauses.

(27) *Baba   Sei,   mina   ari=ri   i   vava   yaku   una   **biri**   **ri***
      father god   this   day=on   2.POSS   power   DSM   1PL   close   make
      ***ma**   una   bou   ri-si   i   dava   yaku   una   rafei   ma.*
      and   1PL   cover make-SEQ.SS   2.POSS   blood   DSM   1PL   wash   give
      'Father God, on this day close us in with your power and cover us and wash
      us in your blood.'

      *Uni   no   koitei   **maku**   **ma**   uni   moke-na   moi*
      1PL.POSS   bad   wash   throw.away   and   1PL   think-NOMZ   get
      rorobo   ri.
      straight   make
      'Forgive our sin and make our thinking righteous (lit. straight).'

      I   vima   kikifa   yaku   una   ourefeide-yaine   ari   neinei.
      2.POSS   spirit   holy   DSM   1PL   lead-3SG.IMP   day   every
      'May your Holy Spirit lead us every day.' [125]

Yet another writer, in the following text message (28) does make use of SR marking.
However, as one with whom I have closely worked, it could be motivated from a
desire to maintain greater formality, though conceivably the speaker interpreted
this more as a unit. The non-SR use *moi-gida ma di ne-gida* (get-1SG.FUT and go
go.down-1SG-FUT) 'I will get . . . and I will go down' would convey greater separation and distinction between the actions.

(28) *Dubu   agiya   debado   PMV   moi-si   di*
      brother   tomorrow   (place.name)   get-SEQ.SS   go
      ne-gida   ma   vakoi   dairi-gifa,   vare-vo . . .
      go.down-1SG.FUT   and   together return-1SG.FUT   sleep-2SG.PO.IMP
      'Brother, tomorrow I will get a PMV (Public Motor Vehicle) at Debadogoro
      and go down and we'll return to the village together, goodbye . . .' [36]

Recapitulative and summary bridging linkage are completely absent in these
newer types of discourse. They have been replaced by other strategies, specifically less SR use with heightened use of conjunctions between final verbs.

5.7 Envoi

Various clause-linking strategies in the Doromu-Koki language have been inves-
tigated, including clause-chaining switch-reference (§5.2), recapitulative and

summary bridging linkage (§5.3) and conjunctions (§5.4). The first two are common in Papuan languages. Particular to Doromu-Koki is its concomitant use of conjunctions along with these other strategies. Due to the prolific borrowings for Hiri Motu (§5.5), several conjunctions have corresponding autochthonous and borrowed terms with no differences in meaning. These are regularly used interchangeably.

While Hiri Motu borrowings have been considered a threat to the vitality of the language, they have still become thoroughly entrenched. New media and new genres (§5.6) have been created through the medium of digital communication (Barasa 2010: 2); the language is 'evolving parallel grammatical structures' (Aikhenvald 2013: 3), following a more English (and Hiri Motu-like) non-SR clause linking pattern, but still allowing for SR marking when it is more advantageous. Recapitulative linkage has been replaced with reduced clauses with less frequent SR marking, for maintaining continuity, and elimination of SBL in favour of final-verb + conjunction + final-verb clause-linking to highlight discontinuity in a discourse. The language is adapting to its new environment through the creation of new (e.g., social media) genres, having new linguistic means of expression (i.e., less non-final verbs).

Abbreviations

1	first person
2	second person
3	third person
A	transitive subject
CL	clause
CON	conative
DC	dependent clause
DS	different subject
DSM	differential subject marker
FC	focal clause
FUT	future
GEN	genitive
HM	Hiri Motu
IC	independent clause
IMP	imperative
IMPERV	imperfective
L2	second language
LOL	laughing out loud
MV	medial (non-final) verb
NEG	negative
NOMZ	nominaliser

NP	noun phrase
O	object
OBL	oblique argument
PAST	past
PL	plural
PMV	public motor vehicle
PNG	Papua New Guinea
PO	polite
POSS	possessive
PRES	present
REFL	reflexive
SBL	summary bridging linkage
SC	supporting clause
SEQ	sequential
SG	singular
SIL	Summer Institute of Linguistics
SIM	simultaneous
SR	switch-reference
SS	same subject
STAT	stative, stationary
TAM	tense-aspect-mood
TOP	topic marker

References

Aikhenvald, Alexandra Y. 2008. *The Manambu language of East Sepik, Papua New Guinea.* Oxford: Oxford University Press.

Aikhenvald, Alexandra Y. 2013. Multilingual fieldwork, and emergent grammars. In Thera Crane, Oana David, Donna Fenton, Hannah J. Haynie, Shira Katseff, Russell Lee-Goldman, Ruth Rouvier & Dominic Yu. (eds.), *Proceedings of the Thirty-Third Annual Meeting of the Berkeley Linguistics Society, 9–11 February 2007: General Session and Parasession on Multilingualism and Fieldwork*, 3–17. Berkeley: Berkeley Linguistics Society.

Aikhenvald, Alexandra Y. 2019. Bridging linkage in Tariana, an Arawak language from northwest Amazonia. *International Journal of American Linguistics* 85(4). 455–442.

Austing, John F. & June Austing. 1977. *Semantics of Ömie discourse* (Language Data, Asian-Pacific 11). Ukarumpa: SIL-PNG.

Barasa, Sandra Nekesa. 2010. *Language, mobile phones and internet: A study of SMS texting, email, IM and SNS chants in computer mediated communication (CMC) in Kenya.* Utrecht: Landelijke Ondersoekschool Taalwetenshap (LOT).

Bradshaw, Robert L. 2004. *Sociolinguistics and literacy study – Doromu-Koki language.* Ukarumpa: SIL-PNG. Ms.

Bradshaw, Robert L. 2007. Fuyug Grammar Sketch. *Data papers on Papua New Guinea languages* 53. Ukarumpa: SIL-PNG.

Bradshaw, Robert L. 2008. *Doromu-Koki dialect survey report.* Ukarumpa: SIL-PNG. Ms.

Bradshaw, Robert L. 2021. *Doromu-Koki – English Dictionary* (Languages of the World 77). Munich: Lincom.

Bradshaw, Robert L. 2022. *A grammar of Doromu-Koki: A Papuan language of Papua New Guinea*. Cairns: James Cook University dissertation.

Ciucci, Luca 2021. The hispanization of Chamacoco syntax. In Alexandra Y. Aikhenvald & Péter Maitz (eds.), Language contact and emerging languages. A special section of *Italian Journal of Linguistics* 32(2). 111–134.

Clyne, Michael. 1987. Constraints on code switching: How universal are they? *Linguistics* 25. 739–764.

Curnow, Timothy J. 2001. What language features can be 'borrowed'? In Alexandra Y. Aikhenvald & R. M. W. Dixon (eds.), *Areal diffusion and genetic inheritance: Problems in comparative linguistics*, 412–436. Oxford: Oxford University Press.

The dictionary and grammar of Hiri Motu. 1976. Port Moresby: The Papua New Guinea Government Office of Information.

Dutton, Thomas E. 1970. *Languages of the Rigo area of the Central District* (Pacific Linguistics C-13: 879–983). Canberra: Australian National University.

Dutton, Thomas E. & Clemens L. Voorhoeve. 1974. *Beginning Hiri Motu* (Pacific Linguistics D-24: 185–257). Canberra: Australian National University.

Eberhard, David M., Gary F. Simons & Charles D. Fennig (eds.). 2021. *Ethnologue: Languages of the Pacific*, 24th edn. Dallas: SIL International. http://www.ethnologue.com.

Farr, Cynthia J. M. 1999. *The interface between syntax and discourse in Korafe, a Papuan language of Papua New Guinea* (Pacific Linguistics C148). Canberra: Australian National University.

Guérin, Valérie (ed.). 2019. *Bridging constructions* (Studies in Diversity Linguistics 24). Berlin: Language Science Press.

Guérin, Valérie & Grant Aiton. 2019. Bridging constructions in typological perspective. In Valérie Guérin (ed.), *Bridging constructions* (Studies in Diversity Linguistics 24), 1–44. Berlin: Language Science Press.

Gumperz, John J. 1982. *Discourse strategies* (Studies in Interactional Sociolinguistics 1). Cambridge: Cambridge University Press.

Haig, Geoffrey. 2001. Linguistics diffusion in present-day East Anatolia: From top to bottom. In Alexandra Y. Aikhenvald & R. M. W. Dixon (eds.), *Areal diffusion and genetic inheritance: Problems in comparative linguistics*, 195–224. Oxford: Oxford University Press.

Kikkawa, Keiko. 1993. *Kware grammar essentials*. Ukarumpa: SIL-PNG. Ms.

Kuteva, Tania, Bernd Heine, Bo Hong, Haiping Long, Heiko Narrog & Seongha Rhee. 2019. *World lexicon of grammaticalization*, 2nd edn. Cambridge: Cambridge University Press.

Matras, Yaron. 1998. Utterance modifiers and universals of grammatical borrowing. *Linguistics* 36(2). 281–331.

Pawley, Andrew. 2005. The chequered career of the Trans New Guinea hypothesis: Recent research and its implications. In Andrew Pawley, Robert Attenborough, Jack Golson & Robin Hide (eds.), *Papuan pasts: Cultural, linguistic and biological histories of Papuan speaking peoples* (Pacific Linguistics 572), 67–107. Canberra: Australian National University.

Pennington, Ryan. 2018. *A grammar of Ma Manda: A Papuan language of Morobe Province, Papua New Guinea*. Munich: Lincom.

QGIS 3.12.3. 2020. Boston: Free Software Foundation, Inc.

Roberts, John R. 1997. Switch-reference in Papua New Guinea: A preliminary survey. In Andrew Pawley (ed.), *Papers in linguistics* 3 (Pacific Linguistics A-97), 101–241. Canberra: Australian National University.

Roberts, John R. 2017. A typology of switch reference. In Alexandra Y. Aikhenvald & R. M. W Dixon (eds.), *The Cambridge handbook of linguistic typology*, 538–573. Cambridge: Cambridge University Press.

Sei di Uka Ago Ruaka [God's New Covenant]. 2017. Orlando: Wycliffe Bible Translators, Inc.

Wurm, Stephen A. (ed.). 1975. *New Guinea area languages and language study*, vol. 2, *Papuan languages and the New Guinea linguistic scene* (Pacific linguistics C-38). Canberra: Australian National University.

Wurm, Stephen A. 1982. *Papuan languages of Oceania*. Tübingen: Gunter Narr Verlag.

Wurm, Stephen A. & J. B. Harris. 1963. *Police Motu: An introduction to the trade language of Papua (New Guinea) for anthropologists and other fieldworkers* (Pacific linguistics B-1). Canberra: Australian National University.

Hannah S. Sarvasy

6 Verbatim narrative prompting to children in Nungon

Verbatim prompting is a widespread practice among speakers of the Papuan language Nungon. When Nungon-speaking mothers and children participated in longitudinal studies of child language development, some mothers frequently exhibited verbatim narrative prompting, through which they "fed" the children personal experience narratives to repeat, from the children's perspectives. Verbatim narrative prompting sequences can last for up to six or more minutes, with children dutifully repeating each prompt. The duration and constituency of prompts shows a high degree of consistency across two mothers with minimal literacy and who lack formal education. Nungon verbatim narrative prompting also reveals that individual clauses in clause chains are psychologically salient units, and further showcases adult speakers' ability to maintain impeccable switch-reference marking, even when children's repetitions intervene between clauses in clause chains.

6.1 Background on the Nungon language and the study

One of the central questions of speech planning concerns the amount of language that a speaker plans at a time. In some contexts, English speakers have been shown to plan speech incrementally, phrases or individual words at a time, although there is robust evidence that English speakers can also plan a single clause fully in advance, before beginning to speak; by the end of that clause, the

Acknowledgments: Deep thanks to Nungon speakers Stanly Girip, Yongwenwen Hessy, James Jio, Lyn Ögate, and Nathalyne Ögate for running the Nungon longitudinal studies and for their hard work transcribing the child-caregiver conversations. Thanks to Arisen's and Daren's families for participating faithfully and cheerfully in the studies. Thanks to Alexandra Y. Aikhenvald, Robert Bradshaw, Luca Ciucci, Pat Clancy, Nico Nassenstein, and Pema Wangdi, and the audience at the International Workshop on Language Production, for helpful comments. Funding was received from the Australian Research Council (grants CE140100041 and DE180101609). The child speech study was approved by the Australian National University Human Ethics Committee.

Hannah S. Sarvasy, University of Western Sydney

https://doi.org/10.1515/9783110789836-006

speakers are likely beginning to plan their next clause (see summary in Sarvasy et al. 2022). Evidence for the scope of planning has been gathered from various types of data: highly controlled and, one could also say, contrived, experiments (Smith and Wheeldon 1999, *inter alia*); short samples of uncontrolled, natural speech (Ford and Holmes 1978); and at least one corpus of natural conversation (Pawley and Snyder 2000). Studies of speech planning scope have targeted phenomena like placement of disfluencies, locations of pauses, and timing before and during speech. Chafe (1992, 2015, *inter alia*) proposed that intonation units – prosodically-defined swatches of speech – are important cues to the ways speakers process language.

One problem for at least some of this literature is that most psycholinguists now agree that speech planning occurs on different levels. For instance, a speaker likely has in mind the overall event structure of an entire narrative before beginning, but has not yet planned out the syntactic structures with which the story will be told, nor the phonological or lexical characteristics of the exact words.

Into this realm, enter parent-child verbatim prompting of narratives in the Nungon language of Papua New Guinea (Finisterre-Huon; 1,000 speakers; Sarvasy 2017a), where an adult may plan speech twice as far in advance, measured in time, to allow for a child's repetitions. Adult Nungon speakers are known to "feed" each other speech, telling their peers what to say to a third party (the feeding metaphor comes from Sarvasy 2017a: 571–572). This verbatim prompting can continue for multiple turns in certain contexts, with the prompter, person A, supplying an appropriately-worded utterance (the "prompt") to the speaker, person B, who then obediently repeats A's utterance verbatim (the "repetition") to person C, who may well have clearly heard A saying it the first time. I have never observed B demurring and declining to repeat the prompt, even when all must be aware that C clearly heard A the first time: the point seems to be for B to say it. I will use the term "verbatim prompting" to emphasize the difference here from cues or prods (sometimes also called prompts) along the lines of English *Now, what do you say . . . ?* to get a child to say *thank you*.

Verbatim prompting is such a widely occurring phenomenon in the Nungon speech community that there is a verbal expression describing just this: *ok yi-* 'to repeat after someone' (Sarvasy 2017a: 571; this appears to be an adjunct+verb construction, see Pawley and Hammarström 2017: 92–93, but neither component – adjunct *ok* or verb *yi-* – can be glossed separately, so this is still conjectural). Indeed, nowadays, when much of my own communication with Nungon speakers is by phone, there are often pauses in which I can hear a third person telling my interlocutor what to say to me. On a field trip in mid-2019, I observed long-time female assistant Lyn Ögate telling James Jio – another longtime assistant, and also a respected community leader – what to say on the phone to another community member. When a person B is speaking to a person C who has relatively high status due to their position in the community or because they are an important outsider, B seems more likely to be fed speech by others listening to the conversation, apparently to ensure that B says the right things. Women often feed men speech; there does not seem to be shame or loss-of-face entailed in having someone else feed one speech in front of an outsider or important person. I have only observed this adult verbatim prompting in conversational, not narrative, contexts.

The most extended Nungon verbatim prompting sessions I have encountered occurred in parent-child recording sessions as part of longitudinal studies of child language acquisition (2015–2017; 2019). In the Nungon studies, I observed a tendency for parents, especially mothers, to feed personal experience narratives to children. Mothers would feed the child entire narratives to be repeated, bit by bit, verbatim, for the benefit of the recording device. Such exchanges – or repetition drills – could last for several minutes at a time, with the child patiently and obediently repeating every prompt. These narratives are fed from the child's perspective (they often involve the mothers themselves, but these are described as "my mother", in the third person), and invariably describe relatively recent experiences of the children themselves, such as particular trips to particular farm plots, or trips to particular waterfalls for bathing. Prompting of individual utterances has long been recognized in parent-child interactions (especially from Schieffelin and Ochs 1986a, and studies in Schieffelin and Ochs 1986b), including for the Papuan language Kaluli (Schieffelin 1985, 1990). Likewise, parent-child co-construction of narratives has been well-studied (recent references in Kelly et al. 2020). But I am not aware of accounts of extended narrative prompting sequences, directed at either children or adults, in other languages.

The phenomenon of verbatim narrative prompting in Nungon raises several questions: when someone without formal education who is semi-literate or illiterate feeds someone else a story to repeat back, where do they choose to break up the story? What size speech units do they proffer, and what can this tell us about the cognitive processes associated with speech planning, and with language processing in general?

Before delving into this, some preliminary notes on the Nungon language and discourse structure are in order; more detailed discussion is in Sarvasy (2017a). Nungon is primarily agglutinating, with some fusion. Constituent order is generally verb-final. Nouns bear minimal inflectional morphology; verbs can either occur marked for tense or reality status and subject person/number, with object person/number also obligatorily marked on some transitive verbs, or they can take various non-finite forms that lack tense marking and, in some cases, subject person/number marking. Predicates can include multiple verbs; such multi-verb predicates are similar to serial verb constructions (Sarvasy 2021a,b).

Like Japanese, Korean, Turkish, and many other Papuan languages (see Sarvasy and Aikhenvald, forthcoming; Sarvasy 2022, forthcoming), Nungon is a clause chaining language. Clause chains in Nungon are sequences of "medial" clauses with verbal predicates that are under-specified for tense and mood, and marked for switch-reference, followed by a single "final" clause with a fully-specified verbal predicate. In the Papuanist tradition, the special verbal inflections used in medial clauses are called "medial"; verbs so inflected are called "medial verbs", and those types of inflected verbs that can occur in final clauses – and as independent, non-chained clauses elsewhere – are called "final verbs". Switch-reference marking indicates whether the grammatical subject of the next clause will be exactly co-referential with the current grammatical subject. Nungon clause chains are closely associated with tense-iconic, or narrative, discourse organization (Sarvasy 2022). Clause chains occur predictably in narratives and in any discourse describing sequences of related events and actions, but they are fewer, shorter, and less predictably distributed in thematically organized Nungon monologues than in procedural texts and narratives (Sarvasy 2022; and see Farr 1999 on the same for Korafe). From age three, children learning Nungon produce many more clause chains than coordinated or subordinated final clauses (Sarvasy 2020). A short sample Nungon clause chain, spoken by the child Towet Oe's father to Towet Oe when she was three years, four months (notated as 3;4), is in (1):

(1) *Ongo-ng-a,* *yamuk guo-ng* *ga-mo-ng-a*   *imon*
go-DEP-MV.SS water bathe-DEP 2SG.O-give-DEP-MV.SS lice
doop-dangka-mok.
3NSG.O.kill-NF.DU-1DU
'Going on, bathing you in water, the two of us will kill lice.' (TO's father to TO, 3;4)

The father and daughter were looking at a photograph of the Towet village men's hut next to the Yapem waterfall. Earlier, the father suggested jokingly that the two of them go there and sing and dance traditional songs together. Then, seeing rain, he suggested in (1) that they go there, but instead bathe, then kill the child's head lice. In this three-clause chain, both medial verbs are marked for same-subject (SS). While it might be strange at first to understand why the subject argument of 'bathe you' (a benefactive construction: literally 'bathe (and) give you'; see Sarvasy 2017a: 513–516) is still first person dual (that is, the child is included among those giving the bath, and also indicated as the one being bathed), this is unsurprising given the child-directed nature of the conversation. In colloquial English, this

(3) Mother: *Ongo-ng-a,*
              go-DEP-MV
              'Going,

     Arisen: *ongo-nga,*

     Mother: *mö-ng-a,*
              fall-DEP-MV
              falling,

     Arisen: *mö-ng-a,*

     Mother: *net-do-k.*
              1SG.O.beat-RP-3SG
              it hurt me.' [Less literally: 'I hurt myself by falling.']

     Arisen   *net-do-k.*

(4) Mother: *Ni-in-a,*
              1.O-DS.3SG-MV
              'It having hurt me,

     Arisen: *ni-in-a,*

     Mother: *ur-in=don,*
              cry-LOC=RESTR
              crying,

     Arisen: *ur-in=don,*

     Mother: *dök-no=dek*   *e-e-ya,*
              piggyback-3SG.POSS=LOC be-DS.1SG-MV
              I being on her back,

     Arisen: *dök-no=dek   e-e-ya,*

     Mother: *to-ng-a,*
              SG.O.take-DEP-MV
              (she) taking (me),

     Arisen: *to-ng-a,*

     Mother: *Sapmangga   ongo-go-k.*
              Sapmangga   go-RP-3SG
              she went to Sapmangga.'

     Arisen: *Sapmangga   ongo-go-k.*

(5) Mother: *Sapmangga   ongo-ng-a,*
      Sapmangga   go-DEP-MV
      'Having gone to Sapmangga,
   (no repetition by Arisen)

   Mother: *maraseng   na-m-un-a,*
      medicine   1SG.O-give-DS.3SG-MV
      she giving me medicine,

   Arisen: *malaseng   na-m-un-a,*
   (rhotic produced as lateral)

   Mother: *öö-ng   ep-bo-mok.*
      ascend-DEP   come-RP-1DU
      we two came back up.'

(6) Mother: *Yo-i,   mak na   maraseng   honggir-un-a*
      say-IMP.2SG   mother-1SG.POSS   medicine   grab-DS.3SG-MV
      ep-bo-mok,   yo-i.
      come-RP-1DU   say-IMP.2SG
      'Say it: my mother having grabbed medicine (at the Sapmangga
      health station), the two of us came, say it.'

   Arisen: *mak-na   maraseng honggir-un-a ep-bo-mok.*

(7) Mother: *E-ng-a,*
      come-DEP-MV
      'Coming,

   Arisen: *e-ng-a,*

   Mother: *Mag-ot   duo-go-mok.*
      mother-COMIT   sleep-RP-1DU
      we two slept with Mother.'

   Arisen: *Mag-ot   duo-go-mok.* (Arisen 4;0, 14:24–14:54)

One of the startling things about the sequence in (3–7) is that Arisen's mother maintains switch-reference marking impeccably, despite the halting nature of storytelling-while-prompting, and the child's repetitions' intervening between her own prompts. That is, when she uses SS marking on the predicate of clause A, the subject in clause B accordingly has the same reference as that of clause A, and when her clause A has DS marking, the subject in clause B differs in reference from that of clause A. This shows that when Arisen's mother produces a medial clause as prompt, she must already know at least the subject (and probably the predicate as well) of the next clause she will prompt. Thus, she likely plans at least two clauses at a time, despite knowing that the child's speech will precede the second of each pair of two clauses. Similar planning scope was demonstrated for adult Nungon speakers telling clause chains without prompting by Sarvasy et al. (2022). In that study, where eye-tracking results implied planning of approximately two clauses at a time, Nungon speakers' "gaze-voice span" (Griffin and Bock 2000), the timing between visual fixation on an object and oral production of a linguistic reference to it, was three times the usual amount known for English speakers (three seconds in Nungon versus one second in English), implying that Nungon speakers may plan clause chains farther ahead than English speakers generally plan. Verbatim narrative prompting could push the timing of that planning to twice as long, since the child's repetitions intervene between parental utterances, although verbatim narrative prompting is a different type of task than typically used to measure the eye-voice span. In any case, verbatim narrative prompting is undoubtedly more cognitively demanding than monologual storytelling, since Arisen's mother must hold the second clause of each pair in her mind while simultaneously monitoring the accuracy of the child's repetition of the first clause.

At what level is all this planning done? Arisen's mother's first clause must be planned at the concrete morphosyntactic level, such that correct switch-reference markers are applied to the verb, but could the second clause of each pair be envisioned more vaguely, as just a notion of whether or not the actor in the first clause will act again, but no specific morphosyntactic plan?

Cases where the conceptual actor does not correspond to the grammatical subject supply evidence that two-clause planning proceeds at the morphosyntactic/grammatical level, not just at a rougher, conceptual level. The end of the prompt in (3) and the beginning of the prompt in (4) involve the expression of the experiencer of 'hurt' as the grammatical object. In this sequence, the child falls and gets hurt, then cries and rides on her mother's back. Throughout these events, the child herself continues to be topical and the only character of interest, but the grammar requires different-subject marking within the sequence, because 'hurt' indexes the experiencer (the child) as a grammatical object, not subject, while the predicate of the second prompt in (4), 'be', indexes the experiencer (again, the child) as a grammatical subject, not object. Of course, there is no object or actor 'it' in 'it having hurt me'; the child was hurt through falling. The mother must seemingly be attuned to morphosyntax, then, to be able to correctly apply different-subject marking to 'it having hurt me'.

If the Nungon-speaking mothers here indeed plan two clauses at a time at the morphosyntactic level, their mental processes must be very different from those of speakers of English, which does not have switch-reference marking. Speech planning in English can be incremental (Ferreira and Swets 2002), such that a speaker could presumably produce a prompt A, and begin to plan her next prompt, B, either while she were producing prompt A, or perhaps even while the child were producing the repetition of A. But when the Nungon-speaking mothers produce a medial clause in prompt A, the very form of that medial clause makes a promise about the following prompt, B (whether the subject will be co-referential). Impressively, both mothers follow through on these switch-reference marking promises in the vast majority of cases in the data here: they are able to hold them in their minds even with the child's intervening repetitions.

At least in the first several months of recordings, these two mother-child pairings (Arisen and her mother, and Daren and his mother) were somewhat more inclined to engage in narrative prompting sequences than the other four parent-child groups in this cohort (studied from 2015 through 2017). This could be due to various factors. Arisen and Daren were the oldest of the five children studied in this period. In contrast, the two youngest children of the group were probably not yet advanced enough (in verbal and/or cognitive development) for most of the study period to go along with such extended verbatim repetition drills. Although the middle child was probably linguistically able to keep up with such prompting, he might have been disinclined to conform to it, or developmentally lacking in the necessary patience. Further, the mother of the middle child was younger and had had more formal education than the other four mothers: she might have had a slightly different conception of the aims of the project – perhaps comprehending the target as spontaneous, unprompted speech from the child – or more readily complied with the researchers' requests to not do verbatim prompting. Alternatively, she might have simply used a different interactive style with her child, due to her youth, education, or personality, and their dyad might have been less used to verbatim prompting than the older two.

From the transcriptions of these two sessions, when Arisen was four years old, and Daren was three years, nine months, I extracted two stretches of verbatim narrative prompting. (There were additional verbatim narrative prompting stretches in these sessions that are not considered here; in fact, the majority of Arisen's session was taken up by these.) These two excerpts involve sustained verbatim prompting by the mother and repetitions by the child. The stretch in Daren's session involves four different narratives that are prompted consecutively, without another intervening type of conversation; the stretch in Arisen's session involves three different narratives, also consecutive.

In general, there is very little divergence by mother or child from the narrative in these sequences – there are few asides or interruptions. Once a mother has begun feeding the child the storyline, she almost never stops feeding content to ask the child questions, nor, generally, is the child asked mid-way through to take over the storytelling him- or herself. In one instance in Arisen's session (not included in the stretch analyzed here), the child herself asks to take over storytelling, saying, *nn yo-wa, öö yo-i!* 'IJ say-IMP.1SG, yes say-IMP.2SG': 'mm, let me say (it), do say yes!' (see Sarvasy 2017b on 'say yes!' as a child-like way of cajoling by Nungon children and adults alike). The mother acquiesces, saying simply, *yo-i!* 'say-IMP.2SG': 'say (it)!', then ceasing to prompt, and only occasionally asking content questions for the remainder of the narrative. Occasionally, a mother repeats her own prompt, usually when the child's repetition is inaudible or unintelligible. (These self-repetitions are not included in the counts analyzed here.) It is clear that the mothers do not require truly verbatim repetition by the child; the child's omission of a word here or there, or even occasional paraphrasing, do not generally trigger a repetition of the original prompt by the mother. The length in seconds of each stretch of prompting, number of prompts in them, and ratio of seconds to prompts are in Table 6.1.

Table 6.1: Summary of verbatim narrative prompting sequences studied.

	Duration of prompting stretch	No. of mother's prompts	Average time between mother's prompt onsets
Daren's mother A	59 seconds	19	3.10 seconds
Daren's mother B	154 seconds	49	3.14 seconds
Daren's mother C	61 seconds	20	3.05 seconds
Daren's mother D	75 seconds	20	3.75 seconds
Arisen's mother A	154 seconds	51	3.01 seconds
Arisen's mother B	147 seconds	40	3.86 seconds
Arisen's mother C	94 seconds	29	3.24 seconds

As seen in Table 6.1, the overall rhythm of the prompting sequence is remarkably similar across the seven stretches of discourse: the duration of the stretch of prompting divided by the number of prompts is always between 3.01 and 3.86 (this can be thought of as the average seconds between the onsets of the mother's prompts). This reflects that overall, the mothers prompt in consistent-sized snatches of speech, and the feed-repeat pattern has a regularity to it. The children usually repeat satisfactorily without marked delays, and the mothers feed the speech confidently and without major disfluencies or self-corrections. This in turn indicates that the children are already well-accustomed to this type of task.

It is further remarkable that the total duration of each stretch of prompt-ing is 349 seconds (Daren's mother) and 395 seconds (Arisen's mother). As with their swift and in-time repetitions, the children's patient continued repetition for such long periods and so many utterances at a time would seem to stem, in part, from their familiarity with the practice of verbatim prompting. In the rest of this section, I will discuss the size and character of prompts in terms of linguistic con-stituency and clausehood.

In both mothers' speech, prompts regularly comprise: individual NPs, with or without grammatical relation-marking enclitics; single medial clauses (as seen in examples 3, 4, 5, and 7); single final clauses (as seen at the ends of examples 3, 4, 5, and 7); two medial clauses; or a medial clause and a final clause (as in example 6). In just two instances does a prompt contain a sequence of more than two chained clauses: these are both three-medial-clause sequences within longer clause chains. Table 6.2 shows the linguistic types of all prompts.

Table 6.2: Constituency of all prompts in the four verbatim prompting sequences.

Whole clauses	single medial clause of a clause chain	82
	final clause of a clause chain	38
	2-clause chain (two medial clauses, or one medial clause and one final clause)	26
	3-medial-clause sequence	2
	non-chained final clause	24
	final clause marked by subordinator =ma	6
	relative clause alone (without matrix clause)	2
Predicates alone (some arguments fed separately)	partial medial clause	3
	partial final clause	1
NPs alone	NP argument	18
	NP in list	22
	partial NP	2
Other	adverb	1

Over half of prompts (120 of 227) are single clauses within clause chains, as in all the prompts in examples (3), (5), and (7). Of these, there are twice as many prompts that are single medial clauses within clause chains as single final clauses within clause chains – which makes sense, since clause chains have only one final clause, but can have more than one medial clause. There are relatively few (24 of 227) prompts that comprise independent, non-chained final clauses; the Nungon preference for clause chains in narratives (Sarvasy 2022) is evident here. Beyond this, there is a clear tendency for both mothers to break a narrative (comprising mostly strings of clause chains) into clauses. That is, the individual clause within a clause chain – often comprising just a medial verb – is a prosodically, and perhaps psychologically, salient unit.

Of all 117 medial clauses, including those produced alone and those produced with other medial or final clauses in a single prompt, 31 are different-subject (DS) marked, and 86 are same-subject (SS) marked. These proportions fall within the 10–40% DS range attested in Nungon child-directed speech more generally (Sarvasy 2020). Across all medial clauses, I noted only two instances of possible switch-reference mismatches: change in subject that are not heralded in advance by DS marking on the previous medial clause. It is possible that where these appear in the transcription, the medial clause that is apparently wrongly marked is actually produced with falling, final intonation, hence actually functions as a sentence-final clause, disconnected from the following one (a "non-canonical medial clause": Sarvasy 2015). The scarcity of such mismatched switch-reference markings is impressive, given that natural speech should be rife with false starts, self-corrections, and other disfluencies. This is further evidence that Nungon switch-reference marking does strictly track grammatical subjects, regardless, in general, of subjects' animacy type, predicate control, topicality, and other attributes that have been said in other Papuan languages to make for differential application of switch-reference marking (Reesink 1983).

When a medial clause and a final clause, or two medial clauses, are produced in the same prompt, this is sometimes clearly motivated by the tight temporal relationship between the actions the two clauses describe. One example is at the end of the stretch in (8–9), from Daren's session. The clause chain before (8) ended with a clause describing that Daren was searching for his chicken. Example (8) thus begins with a bridging clause, 'searching . . .':

(8) Mother: *Dawi-ng-a,*
            search.for-DEP-MV
            'Searching for it,

     Daren: *dawi-ng-a,*

     Mother: *honggir-a,*
            grab-MV
            grabbing it,

     Daren: *honggir-a,*

     Mother: *k-e-ng*   *tuo-ng*   *hi-wa-ya,*
            SG.O-come-DEP   tie.up.to.post-DEP   put-DS.1SG-MV
            I bringing and tying it up and putting it (in place),

Daren: *k-e-ng tuo-ng hi-wa-ya,*

Mother: Sairasi=hon hap=po,
          Sairasi=GEN dog=FOC
          it was Sairasi's dog who,

Daren: *Sairas=ton hap=po,*

Mother: *hara   yi-i-wa-k   i-no-hi.*
          almost   3.O-bite-NP-3SG   3SG.O-tell-IMP.2SG
          almost bit it, tell him.'

Daren: *hara yi-i-wa-k.*

(9) Mother: *Mama-na=ho   wan   oo-ng-a*
               mama-1SG.POSS=FOC   quick.TP   descend-DEP-MV
               honggir-e-k   i-no-hi.
               grab-NP-3SG   3SG.O-tell-IMP.2SG
               'It was my mama who, descending quickly, grabbed it, tell him.'

     Daren: *mama-na=ho oo-ng-a wan honggir-e-k.* (Daren 3;9, 2:37–2:51)

Here, the relationship between the 'descending' in the medial clause and 'grabbed it' in the final clause in the last prompt in (9) is explicitly described as 'quick', perhaps motivating their inclusion together in a single prompt. Example (8) shows a transitive subject NP serving as a prompt on its own; this could be motivated by discourse structure (introduction of a new actor), but alternatively could simply reflect the need to minimize extra-long prompts.

Individual NPs are also often prompts on their own when they are members of a list. Indeed, the prosody of Nungon clause chains has been described as similar to that used in listing NPs (Sarvasy 2015). Impressionistically, list intonation is characterized by flat or slightly rising pitch and sustaining of the last syllable. Example (10), from Daren and his mother, includes three prompts that comprise NPs:

(10) Mother: *I-mo-nga,*
                3SG.O-give-DEP-MV
                'Giving it to him,

      Daren: *imo-ng-a,*

      Mother: *tanak   söbeng   morö,*
                food   saucepan   large
                a large saucepan of food,

Daren:	*tanak söbeng morö,*		

Mother:	*ho-ng-a*	*ger-a*	*tamba*	*to-ng-a,*
	cook-DEP-MV	ladle.out-MV	divide.up	do-DEP-MV
	cooking (it), ladling (it) out, dividing (it) up,			

Daren:	*ho-ng-a ger-a tamba to-nga,*		

Mother:	*a*	*Keisa*	*nan-no=ha,*
	HES	Keisa	father-3SG.POSS=BEN
	ah, for Keisa's father,		

Daren:	*Keisa nan-no=ha,*	

Mother:	*Döminik*	*nan-no=ha,*
	Döminik	father-3SG.POSS=BEN
	for Döminik's father,	

Daren:	*Döminik nan-no=ha,*	

Mother:	*hatdek*	*yo-mo-wa-t*	*i-no-hi.*
	much	3NSG.O-give-NP.SG-1SG	3SG.O-tell-IMP.2SG
	tell him, I gave them a lot.'		

Daren:	*hatdek yo-mo-wat.* 2_12 (Daren 3;9, 1:58–2:12)	

It is noteworthy that the analyzed data does not include any instances where a single prompt includes multiple NPs (as in a list of NPs, or multiple arguments of a verb) but no predicate. That is, if an NP is to be included in a prompt without its associated verb, it generally occurs alone in this sample, not with other NPs.

Unmodified nouns (NPs comprising a single grammatical or phonological word) are also attested as entire prompts in their own right; sometimes these occur in lists, too (*pauk* 'sweet potato' is a prompt, followed by *inowak* 'cassava', as another prompt: a two-item list of crops planted in one farming excursion).

As would be expected based on their analysis by Sarvasy (2017a) as clitics, grammatical relation-marking enclitics are almost never separated from their hosts in the prompting: there is just one example of this, shown in (11–12), from Daren's mother, describing the distribution of wood. This excerpt also shows an aside from the mother, directing the child to move his hand down with a non-canonical medial clause:

(11) Mother: *Mait nan-no=ha*   *höan*   *hi-t*
                 Mait father-3SG.POSS=BEN group put-NP.1SG
                 i-no-hi.
                 3SG.O-tell-IMP.2SG
                 'I put a pile for Mait's father, tell him.'

      Daren: *Mait nan-no=ha höan hi-wa-t.*

(12) Mother: *Obu-ya*   *k-oo-nga*   *ya-a-k;*   *numa,*
                 hand-2SG.POSS SG.O.descend-DEP-MV say-PRES-3SG who
                 Sek   *nan-nit=ta,*
                 Sek   father-ASSOC.PL=BEN
                 'He says, taking your hand down! Who, for Sek and his father,

      Daren: *Sek.*

      Mother: *Sek*   *nan-nit*   *agep* *yo-i.*
                 Sek   father-ASSOC.PL firm say-IMP.2SG
                 Sek and his father, say it loudly.'

      Daren: *Sek nan-nit.*

      Mother: *=ta*   *höan* *hi-t*   *yo-i.*
                 =BEN group put-NP.1SG say-IMP.2SG
                 'For (them), I put a group, say.'

      Daren: *höan hi-t.* (Daren 3;9, 0:32–0:49)

In the last prompt of (12), Daren's mother provides the benefactive enclitic for the NP she directed Daren to produce in the preceding prompt; that NP was missing the enclitic, because it was in turn a correction to Daren's previous repetition, where he mis-produced the NP, omitting mention of Sek's father. This seems to confirm that enclitics, unlike inflectional suffixes, are somewhat separable from their hosts in the minds of speakers.

There are no clear differences between the two mothers in the overall length of prompts, nor type of constituents chosen to fill the prompts. The mothers do show at least one difference in storytelling styles in these excerpts: use of bridging clauses (Guérin 2019) at the beginning of a new clause chain. There are 16 bridging clauses in the sample here, including those in (3–5), (7), and (8); of these, all but two were produced by Arisen's mother.

The mothers rarely seem to over-estimate their children's abilities to retain and repeat prompts by using overly long or complex prompts. There is, however, at least one instance of this in the current dataset, from Daren's mother. In this case, shown in (13–15), she first prompts with a particularly complex two-clause chain, in which two arguments in the medial clause are modified by elements marked with the subordinator and modifying marker =*ma*. Daren fails to repeat it, so the mother breaks up and rephrases the original prompt until he has approximated its content, and then she elaborates on it.

(13) Mother: *Owi-na*   *Worin=ma=ha*   *songgöm*
                grandmother-1SG.POSS   Worin=SPEC=BEN   corn
                yit-no   *nungon hi-wa-t=ma yoo-ng-a*
                seed-3SG.POSS what   put-NP.SG-1SG=REL   NSG.O.take-DEP-MV.SS
                ongo-rang-ka-morok   i-no-hi.
                go-PROB.DU-NF-2/3DU   3SG.O-tell-IMP.2SG
                'Tell her, taking the corn seeds and whatnot that I set aside for my grandmother of Worin (village), the two of them will go.'

(14) Mother: *I-no-hi*   *oro.*
                3SG.O-tell-IMP.2SG   well
                'Tell her, okay.'

(15) Daren: *Owi-na.*
               grandmother-1SG.POSS
               'My grandmother.'

      Mother: *Worin=ma=ha.*
               Worin=SPEC=BEN
               'Of Worin.'

      Daren: *Worin=ma=ha*   *yoo-ng-a*   *ongo-wang-ka-k.*
               Worin=SPEC=BEN   NSG.O.take-DEP-MV.SS   go-PROB.SG-NF-3SG
               'Of Worin, taking them for (her), she will go.'

      Mother: *Songgöm*   *yit*   *hi-t=ma.*
               corn   seed   put-NP.1SG=REL
               'The corn seeds that I put.'

      Daren: *Songgöm*   *hi-t=ma.*
               corn   put-NP.1SG=REL
               'The corn that I put.'

Mother:	*Au*	*yoo-ng-a*	*Worin*	*ongo-rang-ka-morok,*
	other	NSG.O.take-DEP-MV.SS	Worin	go-PROB.DU-NF-2/3DU
	i-no-hi.			
	3SG.O-tell-IMP.2SG			
	'Taking some, the two of them will go to Worin, tell her.'			

Daren:	*Au*	*to-ng-a*	*Worin*	*ongo-rang-ka-morok.*
	other	SG.O.take-DEP-MV.SS	Worin	go-PROB.DU-NF-2/3DU
	'Taking another, the two of them will go to Worin.'			

Mother:	*Au*	*naga=ha*	*mö-wang-ka-t.*
	other	PRO.1SG.EMPH=BEN	plant-PROB.SG-NF-1SG
	'Others, I will plant for myself.'		

Daren:	*Au*	*naga=ha*	*mö-wang-ka-t.*
	other	PRO.1SG.EMPH=BEN	plant-PROB.SG-NF-1SG
	'Others, I will plant for myself.' (Daren, age 3;9, 33:47–34:05)		

In the third turn in (15), Daren is able to supply some of the material he originally heard from his mother in (13), without her repeating it all again.

6.3 Concluding summary

Verbatim prompting is widespread in Nungon discourse, and may be directed at adults or children. In longitudinal studies of Nungon language development, extended stretches of verbatim prompting to children, lasting up to six minutes or more, are evident; these stretches involve "feeding" the child a narrative, clause by clause, or, in some instances, with other constituents as prompts. While verbatim prompting in general is widespread, it is unclear whether verbatim narrative prompting is also a common practice, or whether it arose in the Nungon child language longitudinal studies because of parents' understanding of the aims of those studies (possibly: to get the children to "tell stories"). It is possible that the verbatim narrative prompting sequences that are so prevalent in these studies are actually not prevalent, or are even non-existent, in the speech community at large.

Regardless of how natural verbatim narrative prompting is in the greater community, this case study has shown that two Nungon-speaking mothers without formal schooling and with limited literacy use very similar-sized prompts in this type of interaction, with similar timing. There are always about three seconds, on average, between onsets of the mothers' prompts (encompassing prompt A by the mother, and repetition A' by the child, before the mother produces prompt

B). As with Nungon narratives and tense-iconically-organized Nungon discourse in general (Sarvasy 2022), these verbatim narrative prompting sequences involve mostly clause chains, along with some non-chained final clauses. The children comply readily with verbatim prompting of narratives for extended stretches, which I take as indication of their familiarity with (or socialization into: Schieffelin and Ochs 1986) this kind of interaction.

Of all types of constituent that can comprise a prompt, single medial clauses are the most prevalent, followed by final clauses in clause chains, two-clause sequences in clause chains, non-chained final clauses, and individual NPs. Constituent size, and duration in seconds of each prompt, is probably determined in part by the mothers' perception of the children's developmental stages, and their ability to repeat. The younger child, Daren, was unable to repeat back the prompt in (13), so his mother reissued it in smaller chunks. Because the mothers do not have formal schooling and are minimally literate, the regularity with which they divide narratives into smaller linguistic units cannot be attributed to book learning. It probably reflects a mixture of speech community practices and unconscious motivations from mental processing of Nungon prosody and syntax.

It is unclear, as yet, how far ahead mothers plan their speech when they engage in verbatim narrative prompting. They must have an overall idea of the events in the narrative before beginning. At the phonological/prosodic and morphosyntactic level, they clearly need to begin to plan at some point how much material to include in each prompt, and what will come after that prompt. The impressive maintenance of switch-reference relations that accord with grammatical rules, even in cases where the notional subject differs from the grammatical subject, as in (4), may be a clue to advance planning at the morphosyntactic level of at least two clauses at a time (as found by Sarvasy et al. 2022).

This has been, to my knowledge, the first case study of such verbatim narrative prompting in any language, to children or adults. In speech communities like this one, the widespread practice of verbatim prompting would seem to present a ready tool for further probing of speech planning, and language processing in general.

Abbreviations

1SG, 2PL, etc.	person/number
BEN	benefactive
COMIT	comitative
DEP	dependent
DS	different-subject
DU	dual

EMPH	emphatic
FOC	focus
GEN	genitive
HES	hesitation
IMP	immediate imperative
LOC	locative
MV	medial verb
NF	near future
NP	near past
NSG	nonsingular (> 1)
O	object
PL	plural (> 2)
POSS	possessive
PROB	probable
REL	relativizer
RESTR	restrictive
RP	remote past
SG	singular
SPEC	specifier
SS	same-subject
TOP	topic
TP	Tok Pisin

References

Chafe, Wallace. 1992. Intonation units and prominences in English natural discourse. In Cynthia McLemore & Mark Liberman (eds.), *Proceedings of the IRCS Workshop on Prosody in Natural Speech, August 5–12, 1992*, 41–52. Philadelphia: University of Pennsylvania.

Chafe, Wallace. 2015. Constraining and guiding the flow of discourse. In Deborah Tannen, Heidi E. Hamilton & Deborah Schiffrin (eds.), *The handbook of discourse analysis*, 2nd edn., 391–405. New York: Wiley.

Farr, Cynthia. 1999. *The interface between syntax and discourse in Korafe, a Papuan language of New Guinea.* Canberra: Pacific Linguistics.

Ferreira, Fernanda & Benjamin Swets. 2005. The production and comprehension of resumptive pronouns in relative clause "island" contexts. In Anne Cutler (ed.), *Twenty-first century psycholinguistics: Four cornerstones*, 263–278. Mahwah, New Jersey: Lawrence Earlbaum and Associates.

Ford, Marilyn & Virgina M. Holmes. 1978. Planning units in sentence production. *Cognition* 6. 35–53.

Griffin, Zenzi M. & Kathryn Bock. 2000. What the eyes say about speaking. *Psychological Science* 11(4). 274–279.

Guérin, Valérie (ed.). 2019. *Bridging constructions.* Berlin: Language Science Press.

Kelly, Kimberley R., Grace Ocular, Jennifer Zamudio & Jesus Plascencia. 2020. "But what about the beginning?" Young children's independent narrative structure and how mothers promote chronological coherence during narrative conversations. *Narrative Inquiry* 32(2). 424–451.

Pawley, Andrew & Frances H. Snyder. 2000. The one-clause-at-a-time hypothesis. In Heidi Riggenbach (ed.), *Perspectives on fluency*, 163–199. University of Michigan Press.

Pawley, Andrew & Harald Hammarström. 2017. The Trans New Guinea family. In Bill Palmer (ed.), *The languages and linguistics of the New Guinea area: A comprehensive guide*, 21–196. Berlin/Boston: De Gruyter Mouton.

Reesink, Ger. 1983. Switch reference and topicality hierarchies. *Studies in Language* 7. 215–246.

Sarvasy, Hannah. 2015. Breaking the clause chains: Non-canonical medial clauses in Nungon. *Studies in Language* 39(3). 664–696.

Sarvasy, Hannah S. 2017a. *A grammar of Nungon: A Papuan language of northeast New Guinea*. Leiden: Brill.

Sarvasy, Hannah S. 2017b. Imperatives and commands in Nungon. In Alexandra Y. Aikhenvald & R. M. W. Dixon (eds.), *Commands*, 224–-249. Oxford: Oxford University Press.

Sarvasy, Hannah S. 2020. Acquisition of clause chaining in Nungon. *Frontiers in Psychology* 11:1456. doi: 10.3389/fpsyg.2020.01456

Sarvasy, Hannah S. 2021a. Acquisition of multi-verb predicates in Nungon. *First Language* 41(4). 478–503.

Sarvasy, Hannah S. 2021b. On the acquisition of complex predicates: Introduction to the special issue. *First Language* 41(4). 369–375.

Sarvasy, Hannah S. 2022. Quantifying clause chains in Nungon texts. *Studies in Language* 46(1). 161–200.

Sarvasy, Hannah S. Forthcoming. Clause chains in Papuan languages. In Nicholas Evans & Sebastian Fedden (eds.), *Oxford guide to Papuan languages*. Oxford: Oxford University Press.

Sarvasy, Hannah S. & Alexandra Y. Aikhenvald (eds.). Forthcoming. *Clause chains in the world's languages*. Oxford: Oxford University Press.

Sarvasy, Hannah S., Adam Milton Morgan, Jenny Yu, Victor S. Ferreira & Shota Momma. 2022. Cross-clause planning in Nungon, Papua New Guinea: Evidence from eye-tracking. *Memory and Cognition* 50. 1–22.

Schieffelin, Bambi B. 1985. The acquisition of Kaluli. In Dan I. Slobin (ed.), *The crosslinguistic study of language acquisition*, vol. 1, 525–593. Hillsdale: Erlbaum.

Schieffelin, Bambi B. 1990. *The give and take of everyday life: Language socialization of Kaluli children*. Cambridge: Cambridge University Press.

Schieffelin, Bambi B. & Eleanor Ochs. 1986a. Language socialization. *Annual Review of Anthropology* 15(1). 163–191.

Schieffelin, Bambi B. & Eleanor Ochs. 1986b. *Language socialization across cultures*. Cambridge: Cambridge University Press.

Smith, Mark & Linda Wheeldon. 1999. High level processing scope in spoken sentence production. *Cognition* 73. 205–246.

Pema Wangdi
7 Adjoining clauses in Brokpa narratives

This chapter investigates ways and means of linking clauses in Brokpa narratives. We follow the semantic approach of clause linking put forward in Dixon (2009, 2010: 133–137) and Aikhenvald (2009, 2015: 261–263). Clause chaining, nominalization, and apposition are the main syntactic devices used for achieving various semantic types of clause linking. Brokpa makes use of various grammatical and lexical resources to link clauses within discourse organization. They include suffixes, case enclitics, relator nouns, and a host of conjunctions. The clause linking morphemes apply either directly to the predicate head, or to the nominalized verb stem. Generally, there is a direct correspondence between the syntactic Dependent clause and the semantic Supporting clause, and between the syntactic Main clause and the semantic Focal clause. However, there are instances in which the syntactic clause types (Dependent, Main) and the semantic clause types (Supporting, Focal) do not coincide. The data for this study is drawn from oral narratives, historical accounts, and participant observation.

7.1 Introduction

Brokpa is a Central Bodish (Tibetic) language of the Tibeto-Burman (Trans-Himalayan) language family spoken by approximately 5,000 people in Eastern Bhutan and in Northeast India. Brokpa is one of the nineteen native languages of Bhutan. Dzongkha is the national language of Bhutan. Brokpa is spoken in direct contact with Dakpa and Tshangla. Tshangla also serves as a lingua franca of Bhutan, especially in Eastern Bhutan where Brokpa is spoken.

Brokpa has two register tones, high and low, which are lexically contrastive on words with certain onset series. The language has large open word classes of nouns, verbs, and adjectives, and a semi-open class of adverbs. The language has at least eleven closed classes which have distinct grammatical properties and occupy different functional slots within a clause. Grammatical categories that are typically associated with nouns include case, number, definiteness, and evaluative morphology; and those grammatical categories typically associated with verbs include polarity, aspect, modality, and knowledge. There are four categories of knowledge namely egophoricity, evidentiality, mirativity, and epistemic

Pema Wangdi, Jawun Research Centre, Central Queensland University

https://doi.org/10.1515/9783110789836-007

modality. Evidentiality is further divided into direct, inferred, reported, and factual evidentiality.

This description of clause linking in Brokpa is based on seven months of immersion fieldwork in 2018 as well as two brief spans of fieldwork in 2004 and 2014. The aim of this chapter is to examine the different grammatical resources and techniques used to specify various semantic relations between clauses in the Brokpa narratives. It focuses on how sequences of events are connected, and clauses combined in stories and conversations in this Tibeto-Burman language. Section 7.2 presents the internal structure of clause and predicate; §7.3 briefly discusses the main syntactic devices used for linking clauses; §7.4 deals with the grammatical resources that Brokpa employ to represent various semantic relations between clauses. The chapter ends with a brief conclusion in §7.5.

7.2 An outline of the grammatical structure of Brokpa

A sentence in Brokpa typically consists of several clauses that are linked using a variety of grammatical resources and techniques described in §§7.3–7.4. A simple sentence can be formed by a clause on its own. The predicate is the essential element of a clause. Much of the grammatical information in Brokpa is coded in the predicate. Therefore, it is important to understand the internal structures of clause and predicate before embarking on the varieties of clause linkage in this language.

Clause structure: The preferred constituent order is predicate-final, in both main and dependent clauses. Typically, it is A-O-TPR and S-IPR, where A = transitive subject, O = transitive object, TPR = transitive predicate, S = intransitive subject, and IPR = intransitive predicate.

Predicate structure: The predicate structure of a main clause consists of the head, followed by optional modal auxiliaries, aspectual suffixes, grammaticalized markers of knowledge (egophoricity, evidentiality, mirativity), and an optional clause-final marker. The head of the predicate can be a simple verb root or a complex predicate formed by "lexical compounding" type of noun incorporation (see Aikhenvald 2007; Mithun 1984, 2009 on types of compounding) or a serial verb construction.

Brokpa uses a system of cases to mark its core and peripheral arguments, and further employs postpositional relator nouns to mark spatial and temporal peripheral arguments. The case-marking system prototypically works in terms of an absolutive-ergative scheme. S and O are marked in the same way with zero case for absolutive, and A is marked differently by ergative case. Copula subject and copula complement are zero-marked like S and O, and unlike A.

7.3 The syntax of clause linking in Brokpa

The main syntactic devices employed for linking clauses in Brokpa include clause chaining and nominalization.

7.3.1 Clause chain

A clause chain can involve a dependent clause, also referred to as medial clause, and a main clause. Sometimes, there can be a number of dependent clauses in a clause chain. There are two markers, the ablative case marker =næ and the suffix -zin, attached directly to the verb stem of the dependent clauses in a chain. The marker =næ typically marks what Hopper and Thompson (1980: 280) referred to as, 'sequential events' as in (1a). In contrast, the marker -zin codes 'simultaneous events' (see Givón 2001: 29; Thompson, Longacre, and Hwang 2007 on 'simultaneous events'), also referred to as 'temporal overlap' (see, for example, Longacre 2007), as in (1b):

(1) a. *[nor   me-gin=ba?=kʰe]*A   *[nor   yo-gan=ba?=la]*E
         cattle NEG.EXIST-NOMZ:AGTV=PL=ERG cattle EXIST-NOMZ=PL=DAT
         *[kʰaize]*o   *kʰer=**næ**]*DC *te*   *[kʰa=la   dʑin=**næ**]*DC *den*
         salad.greens take=SEQ   part mouth=LOC give=SEQ   PART
         *[go=la   pʰur=**næ**]*DC *[gya-go-kʰu-na]*MC
         head=LOC rub=SEQ   do-OBLIG-FUT.IMPERV-FACT
         'People without cattle take salad greens, put it into the mouths of those who have cattle, and rub their heads with it.[1]'

---

1 Square brackets are used to indicate the boundaries of a clause within a sentence such as 'main clause' [....] MC and 'focal clause' [...] FC. They are also used to indicate the boundaries of a syntactic constituent within a clause such as transitive subject [...] A and 'extended argument' [....] E

b. *[ʔazi=daŋ* ʐaŋzen ɲí ɲám *dʰo-**zin**]*DC
elder.sister=CNTV brother.in.law two with live-SIM
[ʔazi=daŋ ʐaŋzen ɲí=kʰi pʰrugu sum
elder.sister=CNTV brother.in.law two=GEN child three
*re-ti-na]*MC
become-PERV-FACT
'While I was living together with my elder sister and brother-in-law, their children increased to three.'

The three dependent clauses (1a), all marked by =næ, share the same subject argument, and the events described by the dependent clauses happen in the given order.

In (1b), the dependent clause and the main clause involve different subject arguments. The events described by the dependent clause and the main clause in (1b) are simultaneous: during the narrator's stay with his elder sister and brother-in-law, the number of their children increased to three.

There is a strong probability that simultaneous events – marked by the suffix -zin – will involve different subjects, and the sequential events – marked by =næ – have the same subject. In fact, the dependent clauses marked with -zin almost always tend to have a different subject from the main clause.

However, the marker =næ can either occur in the same subject or in different subject constructions, although in most instances it is the former. In other words, not all dependent medial clauses are switch-reference sensitive, and it is instructive to mention that Brokpa has no clear switch-reference system synchronically.

7.3.2 Nominalization

In Brokpa, nominalized predicate forms a key structural framework for clause linking. Consider:

(2) a. *ta=ye* kʰo *pʰü+taŋ-ŋai*
horse=ERG 3SG.MASC push+send-NOMZ
'The horse threw him.'

b. *ta=ye* kʰo *pʰü+taŋ-na..*
horse=ERG 3SG.MASC push+SEND-COND
'If the horse throws him . . . .'

c. *ta=ye* kʰo *pʰü+taŋ-ŋai=daŋ* . . .
horse=ERG 3SG.MASC push+send-NOMZ=CNTV
'After/as soon as the horse threw him . . . .'

The predicate of the clause (2a) is in a nominalized form. In (2b), the slot of the nominalizer is filled by a clause linker; as a matter of fact, a dependent clause in a clause chain is formed like this by replacing the nominalizer by either the sequential or the simultaneous marker. In (2c) a clause linker is attached to the nominalized predicate.

Brokpa uses suffixes, case enclitics, relator nouns (or simply 'relators'), connectives, grammaticalized conjunctions, and adverbs to link clauses. These clause linkers apply either directly to the verb stem of a dependent clause, as in (2b), or to the nominalized verb stem, as in (2c). The clause linkage of a nominalized clause, as in (2a), can be achieved by apposition without any clause linker.

7.4 The semantics of clause linking in Brokpa

The present description of the grammar of clause linking in Brokpa essentially follows the semantic approach put forward in Dixon (2009, 2010: 133–37) and Aikhenvald (2009, 2015: 261–263). Other literature on this topic including Givón (2001: 327–85), Longacre (2007), Thompson, Longacre, and Hwang (2007) are also consulted.

A distinction between Focal clause and Supporting clause can be drawn for most clause linking types in Brokpa.

In most clause linkage types, there is a direct correspondence between the syntactic Dependent clause and the semantic Supporting clause and between the syntactic Main clause and the semantic Focal clause. However, there are also instances in which the syntactic clause types (Dependent, Main) and the semantic clause types (Supporting, Focal) do not coincide.

Table 7.1 provides an overview of clause linking strategies in Brokpa.

Table 7.1: An overview of clause linking constructions in Brokpa.

SEMANTIC TYPE	SUBTYPE	MARKER	MEANING	MARKS
TEMPORAL	Temporal succession	=næ	'and (then)'	SC (DC)
	Relative time	-zin	'while'	SC (DC)
		=la	'at the time of'	SC (DC)
		=daŋ	'after'/'as soon as'	SC (DC)
		gaŋ/ɕuŋ (=la)	'while'/'during'	SC (DC)
		kap(su) (=la)	'while'/ 'during'	SC (DC)
		sumke/sakai (=la)	'until'	SC (DC)

Table 7.1 (continued)

SEMANTIC TYPE	SUBTYPE	MARKER	MEANING	MARKS
		ʔuntɕin	'before'	SC (DC)
CONDITIONAL	Conditional	-na	'if'	SC (DC)
	Concessive conditional	-na=ye	'even if'	SC (DC)
CONSEQUENCE	Cause	-soŋ	'because'	SC (DC)
		=di=la	'because'	SC (DC)
		ʔo-soŋ=di=la	'because of that'	FC (MC)
		tɕi se-na	'(why) because'	SC (MC)
		=ge	'because, since'	SC (DC)
	Result	ten=næ	'since'/ 'due to'	SC (MC)
		ʐor=næ	'as a result'	SC (MC))
		ʔoti=la ten=næ	'for that reason'	FC (MC)
	Purpose	don(da)=la	'in order to'	FC (DC)
POSSIBLE CONSEQUENCE	Possible consequence	ʔo man	'or else'	SC (MC)
		má-Pred-na	'NEG-PRED-COND'	FC (DC)
ADDITION	Unordered addition	=daŋ	'and'	n/a
		apposition		n/a
		apposition		n/a
	Same-event addition	matsʰæ	'not only ~ but'	FC (DC)
		=næ	'and (so)'	FC (DC)
		tse=la	'in addition to'	FC (DC)
	Elaboration	apposition	n/a	MC, MC
	Contrast	ɕin(tari)	'but'	SC (MC)
		yin-ne=ye	'even then'	FC (MC)
		matakpa(læ)	'although' / 'otherwise'	SC
ALTERNATIVES	Disjunction	yaŋman(a)	'if not'	n/a
		yaŋna(n)	'or else'	n/a
		nam	'or'	n/a
	Rejection	tsʰama(=la)	'instead of'	SC (DC)
		man ~ yin	'NEG.COP ~ COP'	SC (MC), FC (MC)

Table 7.1 (continued)

SEMANTIC TYPE	SUBTYPE	MARKER	MEANING	MARKS
		apposition	n/a	
	Suggestion	=læ	'rather than'	SC (DC)
MANNER	**Real manner**	ʔotɕins(-gyan)	'as like that'	FC (MC)
		ʔoḍou	'like that'	FC (MC)
	Hypothetical manner	-ḍou	'like'/'as if'	SC (DC)

As can be seen in Table 7.1, Brokpa makes use of different grammatical means to specify different semantic relations between clauses. Unordered addition, apart from that shown by the morpheme =daŋ, Elaboration, and one type of Rejection linkage is shown by apposition. All other linkage types are shown by one or more of the clause linkers given in Table 7.1. The following sections deal with all clause linkage types summarized in Table 7.1.

7.4.1 Temporal

This section discusses temporal clause linking (§7.4.1.1) and conditional clause linking (§7.4.1.3) in Brokpa. Temporal clauses that link up with a main clause include temporal succession and relative time. Conditional linking covers possible conditional, counterfactual conditional, and concessive conditional.

7.4.1.1 Temporal succession

Brokpa shows temporal succession by the sequential clause chaining marked with the enclitic =næ 'and (then)' on the dependent clause. Note that this marker =næ can also mean 'after' or 'by', and can be used for marking other clause linking types. The sequential =næ marking temporal succession is found in (3):

(3)   *[tɕʰaŋ*   *palaŋ=tɕiʔ*   *kʰer=**næ**]*DC:SC   *[kʰi=ge*
     alcoholic.drink   wooden.container=INDEF   take-ABL.SEQ   2PL=ERG
     poŋpoŋ=ɕiʔ   *ḍi-go-pʰi]*MC:FC
     talk=INDEF   ask-OBLIG-PERV
     'You take a wooden container of alcoholic drink, **and (then)** you ask.'
     Lit. 'Take a wooden container of alcoholic drink, **and then** you must ask one talk.'

In (3), the marker =*næ* on the Dependent clause indicates temporal sequence. Therefore, the Dependent clause is the Supporting clause and the Main clause Focal. The actions described by the two clauses will happen in that order, an instance of iconic motivation.

7.4.1.2 Relative time

Brokpa utilizes a number of grammatical resources for showing Relative time clause linkage. Dixon (2009: 10) points out two parameters in relative time clause linkage: (1) whether the reference is to a point in time or to a longer duration of time, and (2) whether the time in the supporting clause is past, present, or future relative to the time in the focal clause.

(i) Length of time linkage 'while'

There are three ways of showing a length of time linkage 'while' in Brokpa: 1) by the simultaneous clause chain with the suffix -*zin* ~ -*sin* attaching directly to the verb stem of a dependent clause; 2) by the continuous suffix -*doŋ* ~ -*toŋ* or -*rim* attached directly to verb stem of the dependent clause obligatorily followed by one of the three synonymous relators *gaŋ*, *ɕuŋ*, *kap(su)* all meaning 'while, during, at the time of'; and 3) by those same three relators – *gaŋ*, *ɕuŋ*, *kap(su)* – applying to a nominalized dependent clause.

First, the simultaneous clause chain in which the suffix -*zin* is attached directly to the verb stem of the dependent clause shows a length of time linkage 'while'. Consider:

(4) a. [*zopʰu   muzu gaŋyu   tʰün   taŋ-**zin**]DC:SC
        morning   other all   prayer   do-SIM
        [*ŋa ɲas naŋ=la   buŋbuŋ-gyan   ɲa:+dʰæ]MC:FC
        1SG bed   RELAT:INSD=LOC   comfortable-ADV   sleep+stay:PERV
        '**While** all others were doing prayer in the morning, I slept like a log in the bed.'

    b. [*te   lam+go=næ   yoŋ-**zin**]DC:SC [te   ŋa=raŋ   mwoi=kʰe
        PART   path+head=ABL   come-SIM   PART 1SG=EMPH   wife=ERG
        *lap-soŋ . . .]MC:FC
        say-PERV.DIRECT
        '**While** coming onto the path, my wife said . . . .'

In both (4a) and (4b), the Dependent clause marked by the suffix -*zin* directly on the verb stem is the Supporting clause and the Main clause ending in the perfective verb stem *d^{h}æ* is the Focal clause; the event described by the Dependent clause puts the event of the Main clause in a temporal perspective. In both examples, there is a temporal overlap between the Supporting clause and the Focal clause.

Secondly, a length of time linkage 'while' is shown by the continuous suffix -*doŋ* ~ -*toŋ* or -*rim* applying directly to the verb stem within the Dependent clause followed by one of the three synonymous relators *gaŋ*, *ɕuŋ*, *kap(su)*, all meaning 'while, during, at the time of'. Consider:

(5) a. *[k^{h}yö petɕ^{h}a lap-***toŋ*** **gaŋ=la**]*DC:SC *[mwoi tsaː=næ=se*
         2SG book study-CONT RELAT:OCN=LOC wife search=SEQ=QUOT
         *... ma-ɖik-pa=se]*MC:FC
         ..NEG-be.ok-MIR=QUOT
         '[My mother] said: "You have found a wife **while** studying. That is not ok."'

     b. *[ŋa petɕ^{h}a lap-***rim*** **ɕuŋ=la**]*DC:SC *[ŋa*
         1SG book study-CONT RELAT:AROUND=LOC 1SG
         *k^{h}yo=daŋ ɲambu ɖik-pi-soŋ]*MC:FC ...
         2SG=COM together arrange-PERV-BECAUSE
         'Because I have married (stayed with) you **while** I am studying ....'

The continuous suffixes -*doŋ* or -*rim* attach directly to the verb of a Supporting clause followed by the relator *gaŋ* or *ɕuŋ*, as in (5a) and (5b). In contrast, the relator *kapsu* applies to a nominalized clause optionally followed by the genitive marker. The genitive marker is used with the nominalized Supporting clause when it is followed by a relator.

Thirdly, a length of time linkage 'while' can be shown by one of the above relators: *gaŋ*, *ɕuŋ*, *kap(su)* all with the meaning of 'while, during, at the time of', without the preceding continuous suffixes, but the predicate of the Dependent clause has to be then nominalized, as in (6). The relators may be optionally followed by the locative case =*la*, as in (6):

(6) *[ʔun=la raŋ d^{h}o-bi=gi **kapsu=la**]*DC:SC .... *[l̩apsaŋ*
     before=LOC self stay-NOMZ=GEN RELAT:OCN=LOC smoke.offering
     *gæpa=di=raŋ taŋ-yo]*MC:FC
     detailed=DEF=EMPH do-EXIST.EGO
     '**While** I was living there, we used to perform the detailed Smoke Offering (prayer).'

The relator *kapsu* in (6) can be replaced by the relator *gaŋ* or *ɕuŋ* with no difference in meaning.

Note that a length of time linkage 'while' can be shown by another relator *riŋ* 'during, when'. This morpheme applies to a nominalized Dependent clause and can replace the relator *gaŋ*, *ɕuŋ* or *kap(su)* in the above examples without any difference in meaning.

(ii) Length of time linkage 'until'

A length of time linkage 'until' can be shown either by the relator *sumke ~ sumbe* or the relator *sakai*, both with a lative meaning 'until'. There is an equivalent relator *tsʰuntsʰon* 'until' in Dzongkha which is also used in Brokpa. With NPs, these two relators have both spatial and temporal locational sense and with clauses it marks a length of time linkage. As with other relators, these relators may also be optionally followed by the locative case. Consider:

(7) a. *[ʔot   má-soː   **sumke**]*DC:SC *[den   doŋbe=gi*
         DEM   NEG-supplicate   RELAT:UNTIL   PART   face=GEN
         *ɕoː=di=su   ʔoɖou   pʰan-ma-ɲæn-ni]*MC:FC
         pustule=DEF=PL   like.that   help-NEG-listen-PERV
         'Not **until** that prayer is performed, will the pustules on the face heal.'
         Lit. 'Until that is supplicated, the face's pustules will refuse to heal.'

     b. *[tsam   yo-ti=di   ʔuntɕin tuŋ-ma-zin²   **sakai**=la]*DC:SC
         how.much EXIST-NOMZ=DEF   before   drink-NEG-FINISH RELAT:UNTIL=LOC
         ... *[temre=di=su   tsi-zin-ni]*MC:FC
         ...celebration=DEF=PL   observe-finish-PERV
         'Not **until** all the drinks have been finished . . . . . will the celebrations be finished.'

The Dependent clauses marked by the relator *sumke* in (7a) and *sakai* in (7b) are Supporting clauses because they specify the end point of a period of time, referring to a prolonged action. The Main clauses in the same sentences above are Focal clauses as they describe an event or state extending in time with respect to the time specified by the Dependent clauses.

---

2 Note that the *zin* occurring as the minor verb in a serial verb construction in both the dependent clause and in the main clause is a lexical verb 'to finish', which is homophonous with the simultaneous marker *-zin*.

(iii) Point in time linkage 'when'

A point in time linkage 'when' can be shown by the locative case marker =la applied to a dependent clause which is nominalized. This is a very typical Tibeto-Burman feature (Aikhenvald 2011; Watters 2009). When used as a case marker with NPs, the enclitic =la has a spatial or temporal locational sense, but as a clause linker it marks relative time as in:

(8) [*ʔou=daŋ*   *bom*   *ɲí=ye*   *kʰyim=la*   *dok-pʰi=ʑiʔ=la*]DC:SC
     boy=CNTV   girl   two=EMPH   house=LOC   arrive-NOMZ=INDEF=LOC.WHEN
     [*pʰama*   *ʑi*   *zom=næ*   *tʰatɕæ*]MC:FC
     parent   four   meet=SEQ   decide:PERV
     'The four parents meet and decide **when** the groom and the bride arrive at home.'

In example (8), the nominalized Dependent clause marked by the locative enclitic =la is the Supporting clause as it indicates a temporal perspective. The second clause is the Focal clause because it describes an event with respect to the temporal perspective provided by the Supporting clause.

(iv) Point in time linkage 'after'

A point in time linkage 'after' or 'as soon as' can be shown by the enclitic =daŋ attached to the nominalized Dependent clause. Consider:

(9) [*ʔaʑi=di*   *ɲén+ɖik-pi=daŋ*]DC:SC   [*numo=baʔ*
     elder.sister=DEF   marriage+arrange-NOMZ=CNTV   younger.sister=PL
     lekyaŋ=ge   *tʰoŋ-ɲai*]MC:FC
     natural=INST   see-NOMZ.BECAUSE
     '**After/as soon as** the elder sister is married, (her husband) will naturally see her younger sisters.'

In (9), the Dependent clause marked by =daŋ is the Supporting clause and Main clause the Focal clause because the action expressed by the Main clause (seeing younger sisters) will take place only after the event or situation expressed by the Dependent clause (marrying off the elder sister). The marker =daŋ shows that the event of the Supporting clause is in an immediate past with reference to the Focal clause.

(v) Point in time linkage 'before'

A point in time linkage related to 'before' can be shown by the adverb *ʔuntɕin* 'before' on the Dependent clause, which is nominalized, as in (10):

(10)   *[kyespʰo=baʔ=la*   *tɕʰaŋ*   *má-luk-pi*   **ʔuntɕin**=di=la]*DC:SC
      man=PL=DAT   alcohol NEG-pour-NOMZ before=DEF=LOC
      [ʔama.dʑomo=gi *ʐuk-sa=di*   *ʐuk+tan*   *tin+ʐak-pi*
      Ama Jomo=GEN sit.HON-NOMZ:LOC=DEF sit.HON+mat lay+keep-NOMZ
      ʔuntɕʰoʔ=di=la *tɕʰaŋ*   *penza=ʑiʔ* *ʔo=la*   *kaŋ-go-kʰu-na]*MC:FC
      front=DEF=LOC alcohol cup=INDEF DEM=LOC fill-OBLIG-FUT.IMPERV-FACT
      '**Before** pouring drinks for the menfolk, they must fill a wooden cup with liquor in front of the sitting-mat for Ama Jomo.'

Note that *ʔuntɕin* may be followed by the marker of definiteness =*di* and/or the locative =*la*, and the preceding nominalized Supporting clause may take genitive marking. However, all these accompanying grammatical elements are optional and the 'before' linkage can simply be shown by the adverb *ʔuntɕin*.

The adverb *ʔuntɕin* marks a Supporting clause expressing an event in the future, as in (10). In the same vein, a Supporting clause expressing an event in the past can be shown by the adverb *tɕʰiti* 'after', also optionally followed by the locative =*la*.

7.4.1.3 Conditional

Dixon (2009: 16) distinguishes two varieties of conditional linking: Possible conditional and Counterfactual conditional clause linking. Brokpa uses the conditional marker -*na*, attached directly to the verb stem of the Dependent clause, for both varieties of Conditional linking. Consider:

(11) a. *[padar=ge*   *dʰaŋ-**na**]*DC.SC   *[padar=ye*   *dʑin]*MC.FC
         heroic.sash=INST be.sufficient-COND heroic.sash=EMPH give.IMP
         'If there are enough scarves (lit. Heroic Sashes), give the scarves.'

     b. *[zomo=la*   *tæ-**na**]*DC.SC *[lúʔ=la*   *ma-dʰaŋ]*MC.FC
         cross.bred.yak=DAT see:PERV-COND sheep=DAT NEG-be.sufficient
         'If cross-bred yaks are taken care of, sheep could not.'
         Lit. 'If cross-bred yaks were seen, not enough for sheep.'

Sentence (11a) is an example of Possible conditional linkage where the Dependent clause corresponds to the Supporting clause and the Main clause to the Focal clause. The action of giving the scarves, described by the Focal clause, will take place only if there are adequate numbers of it, the condition set out in the Supporting clause.

Sentence (11b) gives a Counterfactual conditional reading. Because the cross-bred yaks have to be looked after (the condition set out by the Supporting clause), the sheep could not be looked after (the result described by the Focal clause). In (11b) too, the Dependent clause coincides with the Supporting clause and the Main clause with the Focal clause. If the cross-bred yaks did not have to be looked after, then the event described by the Focal clause – that of looking after the sheep – could happen, which is a Counterfactual condition.

Concessive conditional 'even if'
Further, if a Supporting clause marked by the conditional -*na* is followed by the emphatic marker =*ye*, it has a sense of 'concessive conditional' similar to 'even if' in English (see Thompson, Longacre, and Hwang 2007). This type of Conditional linkage refers to what Longacre (2007) describes as a 'frustrated implication'. This type of Conditional linkage, that is the conditional clause followed by the emphatic =*ye*, shows that the result described by the Focal clause will be contrary to expectation or one of, in Longacre's (2007) words, 'frustrated contingency'. Consider:

(12) [kʰa+tan-ɖou=ẓiʔ   bru+ga-**na=ye**]DC:SC   [tɕʰæ   pʰok-ki-yona]MC:FC
     outer.mat-SIMI=INDEF   fall.off+go-COND=EMPH   fine   hit-IMPERV-FACT
     '**Even if** an outer mat falls off, we have to pay fines.'

Sentence (12) is from a procedural text about a pilgrimage trip. The speaker says that even a minor thing as a mat falling off a horse (the concessive condition described by the Supporting clause) will lead to the owner of that horse paying a fine to the other pilgrimage members (the result described by the Focal clause), which is one of a frustrated contingency.

Furthermore, a Concessive conditional linkage in Brokpa can involve both positive and negative condition within the same Supporting clause followed by the emphatic marker. This kind of Concessive conditional linkage shows that the expected result described by the Focal clause will not eventuate and, if it did, it will be against expectation. Consider:

(13) [*muzu=e   lap-**na**   ma-lap-**na**=ye*]DC:SC [*kʰoŋ=ge   den*
    other=ERG   tell-COND   NEG-tell-COND=EMPH   3PL=ERG   PART
    norze=ta   ter-mí-tʰob-tuŋ]MC:FC
    cattle.gift=FOC   give-NEG-ABIL-INFER
    'Even if they requested it of them, they cannot give the gift of cattle.'

Generally, someone would be expected to give something if requested, but as can be seen in (13), the Focal clause refers to a negative result.

The conditional marker -*na* (see §7.4.1.3) appears to have grammaticalized from the copula *na*, and therefore it is homophonous with the grammaticalized factual knowledge marker -*na* as well as with the rarely occurring locative =*na*. The conditional marker always occurs with a dependent clause and the factual -*na* with a Main clause, following TAM morphology. The locative =*na* will apply to a peripheral NP if it occurs.

The grammaticalization of the conditional clause linker from a copula is found in other languages such as Hmong (Nathan White, p.c.) and Chinese (see Yip and Rimmington 2004). The Chinese copula *shì* forms part of the connector *yàoshì* used for introducing subordinate clauses with the meaning of 'if' (Yip and Rimmington 2004: 256).

7.4.2 Consequence

There are three kinds of Consequence linking: Cause, Result, and Purpose. In all these varieties, the Focal clause describes the consequence even though the clause linker may be associated either with the Supporting clause or with the Focal clause.

7.4.2.1 Cause

There are several ways of showing Cause linkage in Brokpa. One is by adding the morpheme -*soŋ* 'because' to the nominalized verb stem which is the predicate of the Supporting clause. Consider:

(14) a. [*numo=baʔ   lækyaŋ=ge   tʰoŋ-ŋai-**soŋ***]SC   [*te   tɕiktɕik=ke*
       younger.sister=PL   definite=INST   see-NOMZ-BECAUSE   PART   one.one=ERG
       den   numo=baʔ=kʰe=ye   den   ʔaʑi=gi
       PART   younger.sister=PL=ERG=EMPH   PART   elder.sister=GEN

makpa=la   *sem+ɕor]*FC
husband=DAT   mind+lose
'**Because** the younger sisters will definitely be seen, so the younger sisters also fall in love with their elder sister's husband.'

b. *[ŋa=raŋ*   *tʰimpʰu*   *dok=næ=raŋ*   *lo*   *sumtɕu-zam*
   1SG=REFL.EMPH Thimphu arrive=ABL.SEQ=EMPH year thirty-APPROX
   *ga-li-**soŋ**]*SC   *[te*   *ŋa=raŋ=ge*   *ɖan+ʑeː-duʔ]*FC
   go-NOMZ-BECAUSE PART 1SG=REFL.EMPH=ERG memory+forget-DIRECT
   '**Because** about thirty years have passed since arriving in Thimphu, I have forgotten (that).'

In both (14a) and (14b), the Focal clause describes what ensues as a direct consequence of the event or state described by the Supporting clause.

Note that the morpheme *-soŋ* also marks direct evidential perfective aspect, and it is homophonous with the imperative form of the verb *ɖo* 'to go'. As an aspect marker, *-soŋ* applies directly to the verb stem of the main clause.

A Cause linkage is also shown by adding the dative/locative case *=la* to the Supporting nominalized clause. The nominalized Supporting clause may be marked for definiteness. The dative *=la* also applies to NPs and marks a Recipient semantic role in extended argument function (E) or mark spatial peripheral arguments. With clauses, the dative/locative *=la* mark Cause linkage with a meaning 'because' or 'for':

(15) *[kʰyo=ge* *ʔotɕin*   *lap-náŋ-ŋai=di=**la**]*SC   *[násmeti*
     2SG=ERG like.that say-give.HON-NOMZ=DEF=DAT very.much
     *kaɖintɕʰe-soŋ]*FC
     be.grateful-PERV.DIRECT
     '**Because** you have spoken like that, I felt immensely grateful.'

Furthermore, Brokpa has a frequently used sentential conjunction *ʔo-soŋ=di=la* (dem-because=def=dat) 'because (of that)', 'due to that', which is formed by a reduced form of the demonstrative *ʔoti*, the aspect marker/clause linker *-soŋ*, the definiteness marker *=di* followed by the dative/locative *=la*.[3] This demonstrative-derived sentence conjunction introduces the Focal clause of a Cause linking:

---

3 Sometimes, this clause linker occurs without the demonstrative as *-soŋ=di=la* following the predicate of the dependent clause.

(16) *[dʰuŋ-tɕʰok-pi   tɕo-pʰi=gi   lamluk ʔoɖou=ʑiʔ   duŋ]*sc
      beat-PERM-NOMZ   make-NOMZ=GEN   system like.that=INDEF   COP.PERV
      [ʔo-soŋ=di=la   te   ŋa   zapta   maŋbu=ʑiʔ
      dem-BECAUSE=DEF=DAT   PART 1SG beating many=INDEF
      *da   kʰoŋ=ge   ʔotɕins   taŋ]*FC
      PART 3PL=ERG   like.that do:PERV
      'There was a system in which beating was allowed, **because** of that they
      gave me too much beating.'

This type of Cause linking involves two main clauses, but semantically the first
clause shows a cause or reason; therefore, the first clause is the Supporting
clause, and the second clause shows result or purpose and is the Focal clause.

Finally, Cause linkage in Brokpa can be shown by stating the Focal clause
first and then introducing the Supporting clause using a reported speech construction. The reported speech construction in a clause linking function is formed
by the interrogative word followed by the generic verb *se* 'to say'[4] and the conditional -*na*, as in *tɕi se-na* (what say-cond) '(why) because', '(lit. if told what).
Consider:

(17) *[ŋa   tsʰokpa=i   naŋ=la   ʑu-ma-ɲæn]*FC   *[tɕi*
      1SG committee=GEN   RELAT:INSD=LOC tell.HON-NEG-be.able what
      ***se-na   gaŋtʰaŋ=ge=raŋ   ... má-suŋ-pʰi]*SC**
      say-COND everybody=ERG=EMPH ... NEG-say.HON-PERV
      'I could not speak in the committee, **because** nobody said anything.'

The verb 'say' is used in 'quotative complex' constructions with a range of grammaticalized functions in neighbouring Tibeto-Burman languages such as Newari,
Sherpa, Jirel, Magar, Methei, and Adi, and is supposed to be an areal feature due
to Indic influence (Saxena 1988). But Brokpa has two forms of the verb 'say', *se*
and *lap*, and both forms have several grammaticalized functions including those
as quotatives and conjunctions, even though Brokpa is not geographically contiguous with Indic languages. Cause linkage is just one example of it.

Cause linkage achieved by grammaticalized speech verb occurring with a
question word, as in (17), involves two main clauses. Semantically, the first clause
is the Focal clause describing the consequence, and the second is the Supporting

---

4 The quotative enclitic =*se* has grammaticalized from the verb *se* ~ *ze* 'say'. The use of *se* as a
verb is found only in restricted circumstances such as in this one where it takes the conditional
marker -*na*.

clause which states reason or cause. The use of the speech verb in causal linkage is reminiscent of a common Tibeto-Burman pattern described by Saxena (1988).

Furthermore, a Cause linkage in Brokpa can be shown by the ergative/instrumental case marker *=ge*, attached directly to the verb root or to the nominalized verb in the supporting clause, as in (18):

(18) *ŋi*   *pʰama=di=su*   *yin-ne=ye*   *lona*   *ya=la*
    1PL   parent=DEF=PL   COP.EGO-CNSV=EMPH   age   up=ALL
    *ga-li=**ge***   *te*   *laika=ye*   *gya-mi-tʰob-ba*
    go-NOMZ=INST   PART   work=EMPH   do-NEG-ABIL-MIR
    'Because we, the parents have got old, we are also not able to work.'

The ergative/instrumental case showing Cause linkage can be attested in closely related languages such as Classical Tibetan and Dzongka; it is also reported for other Tibeto-Burman languages such as Kham (see Watters 2009: 21).

7.4.2.2 Result

Result linkage is shown by three clause linkers: (1) *ten=næ* 'due to, since, because'; (2) *ʐor=næ* roughly meaning 'as a result'; and (3) *ʔo(ti)=la ten(=næ)* 'for that reason'. The marker *ten=næ* is a combination of the grammaticalized verb *ten* meaning 'to depend/rely on' plus the ablative/sequential *=næ*, but the verb has undergone decategorialization (see among others, Brinton and Traugott 2005: 25–26; Hopper and Traugott 2003: 106–114 for discussions on 'decategorialization'). Similarly, *ʐor* is a relator roughly meaning 'sake' or 'purpose'. All these phrases, despite consisting of several morphemes, effectively function as conjunctive elements at the intra-sentence as well as inter-sentence levels.

In a Result linkage, the Supporting clause is nominalized and preposed to the Focal clause. (1) and (2) mark the Supporting clause while (3) introduces the Focal clause.

Examples of Result linkage shown by the grammaticalized conjunction *ten=næ* include:

(19) *[me+ɽa*   *tɕʰuŋku=ʑiʔ*   *lán+ga-li*   ***ten=næ]***SC   *[te*
    fire+burn   small=INDEF   rise+go-NOMZ   rely.on=ABL   PART
    Merak=se   *ʔotɕis*   *lap-to]*FC
    Merak=QUOT   like.this   say-FINAL
    '**Since** a small fire broke out there, it is called 'Merak' (lit. fire-burning).'

Sentence (19) is regarding the etymology of the place name 'Merak'. The Focal clause, 'It is called Merak', is as a result of what is described by the Supporting clause, the outbreak of a small fire.

In the same vein, the phrase *ʐor=næ* marks Supporting nominalized clause which may be followed by the genitive marker. This relator typically occurs with peripheral NPs, but it appears as a clause-linking marker in spontaneous conversation rather than in planned narratives. The relator *ʐor* can also occur with the dative/locative *=la*. When *ʐor* takes the locative *=la* it shows a Purpose linking, and when it is followed by the ablative/sequential marker it shows a Result linking.

Examples of *ʐor=næ* marking Result linking include:

(20) *pʰrugu=baʔ   ɲén+gyak-pi=gi   ʐor=næ]*SC   *[ŋe=raŋ*
      child=PL   marriage+do-NOMZ=GEN RELAT:sake=ABL 1PL=EMPH
      *mí   pʰoʔ]*FC
      person   hit
      'We are related **as a result of** our children marrying.'

In (20), what is described by the Focal clause is the natural result of that described by the Supporting clause. The fact that the referents of the first person plural pronoun are related is the natural consequence of their children marrying each other.

The phrase *ʔo(ti)=la ten(=næ)* 'for that reason' or 'for this reason', introduces the Focal clause in a result linkage. The same examples (19a) above can be repeated to show the shifting in marking of Result linkage from the Supporting clause to the Focal clause:

(21) *[me+ɽa   tɕʰuŋku=ʑiʔ láŋ+ga-li]*SC *[ʔoti=la   ten=næ   te*
      fire+burn   small=INDEF rise+go-NOMZ DEM=LOC rely.on=ABL PART
      *Meraʔ=se   ʔotɕis   lap-to]*FC
      Merak=QUOT like.this say-FINAL
      'A small fire broke out, **for that reason** it is called 'Merak' (lit. fire-burning).'

Note that there is a slight difference in the reading of the sentence in (19) where the marker of the Result linkage is *ten=næ* on the Supporting clause, as compared to (21) where the Result linkage is achieved by *ʔo(ti)=la ten(=næ)* in the Focal clause. In this type of Result linkage where the Supporting clause is nominalized and preposed to the Focal clause which is introduced by a grammaticalized conjunction, the nominalized Supporting clause can also be an independent clause syntactically.

It is quite clear that if the demonstrative is involved in deriving a clause linker in Brokpa, that clause linker will be associated with the Focal clause with an ana-phoric reference to the preceding Supporting clause. For example, the relator with ablative *ʐor=næ*, which otherwise marks Supporting clause in a Result linkage as in (20) above, can be preceded by the demonstrative *ʔoti* optionally fol-lowed by the genitive marker and the resulting phrase *ʔoti=gi ʐor=næ* (dem=gen relat:sake=abl) 'due to that' can mark the Resulting linkage. However, when the demonstrative is involved, this marker of the Result linkage will be associated with the Focal clause and not with the Supporting clause.

7.4.2.3 Purpose

Purpose linkage in Brokpa is shown by the marker *don(da)=la* 'for the sake of' or 'in order to'. This marker of Purpose linkage is a combination of the relator *don(da)* which has a sense of 'meaning' or 'purpose' followed by the dative/loc-ative *=la*. As a relator, *don(da)* marks a benefactive peripheral argument. As a marker of Purpose linkage, *don(da)=la* applies to the nominalized Dependent clause which may optionally be followed by the genitive marker. Consider:

(22) *kʰoŋ=raŋ*   *ɲí*   [*ɲén+gya-mi=gi*   **don=la**]DC:FC
      3PL=REFL.EMPH   two   marriage+do-NOMZ=GEN   RELAT:PURPOSE=DAT
      [*bro+tɕʰi-ti*]MC:SC
      escape+go-PERV
      'The two of them eloped in order to marry/for the sake of marrying.'

In a Purpose linkage, the Supporting clause describes what was done to make sure that the event or state of the Focal clause should take place, along the lines of Dixon (2009). Based on this, the Dependent clause is the Focal clause and the Main clause the semantic Supporting clause in Brokpa.

In (22), the Main clause is the Supporting clause and the Dependent clause Focal; the Main clause shows what was done volitionally to make the event, that of marrying, happen which is described by the Dependent clause.

7.4.3 Possible consequence

Brokpa has two techniques for showing Possible consequence linkage. One is by placing the Focal clause first in the positive imperative mood and then introducing the Supporting clause with the demonstrative *ʔo* followed by the negative copula *man*. These two syntactic elements function as an introducer of the Supporting clause of a Possible consequence linkage with a meaning 'or else, otherwise'. Consider:

(23) *[diriŋ* *kʰyo* *ŋa=i* *kʰyim=la* *ɲaː+dʰo]*FC
today 2SG 1SG=GEN house=LOC sleep+stay.IMP
[ʔo ***man*** *ŋa* *sem-mi-gaː]*SC
DEM NEG.COP 1SG mind-NEG-be.happy
'You sleep in my house today, **or else** I will not be happy.'

Like in a Purpose linkage, the Focal clause precedes the Supporting clause in a Possible consequence linkage. However, syntactically, both the clauses – Supporting and Focal – in a Possible consequence linkage involving this technique have the same status, that of a Main clause. It goes without saying that an imperative clause can be a main clause in a biclausal linking or a sentence involving multiple clauses, and it can stand alone as a complete sentence. When an imperative clause stands as a complete sentence, it is typically accompanied by a rising intonation pattern. However, semantically, in a Possible consequence linkage, the imperative clause is the Focal clause – describing what is to be done or not done – followed by the Supporting clause – describing a possible consequence – which is introduced by the demonstrative and the negative copula. In (23), 'You sleep in my house today' is the semantic Focal clause and 'I will not be happy' is the possible consequence. Note that in (23), the Supporting clause is negative and the Focal clause positive. It does not have to be always like this. The Supporting clause can also be positive and the Focal clause negative in a Possible consequence linkage.

The other technique for showing Possible consequence is to negate the predicate of the Supporting clause followed by the conditional marker. In other words, this technique of showing a Possible consequence is by negating a Conditional clause. Consider:

(24) *[ʔoti* *lænse=ʑiʔ* ***ma-lap-na]*DC:FC** *[mo=ye* *sem+ɕi-ro]*MC:SC
DEM reply=INDEF NEG-say-COND 3SG.FEM=EMPH mind+die-FINAL
'If we don't give a reply, she will also be disheartened.'

In (24), the first clause 'If we don't give a reply' is the semantic Focal clause as it describes what is to be done and the second clause 'She will also be disheartened' is the Supporting clause showing the possible consequence. Similar to (23) above, the Focal clause precedes the Supporting clause, but, in contrast to (23), the semantic Focal clause is a syntactic Dependent clause in (24), and a subordinate one at that, with the conditional -na as a marker of subordination. This kind of technique – employing a negative Conditional clause to achieve a Possible consequence linkage – is reported for Galo, a Tibeto-Burman language of the Tani branch (see Post 2009).

7.4.4 Addition

An Addition linkage is one in which it is not in any other clause linking relation including Temporal, Condition, Consequence, Possible consequence, Alternative, or Manner (Dixon 2009). Dixon mentions four subtypes of Addition linkage: Unordered addition, Same-event addition, Elaboration, and Contrast. Brokpa has ways and means for showing all the subtypes. Some subtypes may utilize the same morphemes used for achieving other linkage types, but it will be the instance of a single form with different functions.

7.4.4.1 Unordered addition

Brokpa has two ways of showing Unordered addition linkage: apposition and using the polyfunctional morpheme =daŋ. Strictly speaking, Unordered addition is effectively handled by apposition of clauses, as in:

(25) [lala   zomo   názi+gya-go-ro]MC   [lala   zaŋ
     some   cross.bred.yak herder+do-OBLIG-FINAL   some   yak
     názi+gya-go-ro]MC   [lala=ni   lúʔ   ta-go-ro]MC   [lala=ni
     herder+do-OBLIG-FINAL   some=TOP   sheep see-OBLIG-FINAL   some=TOP
     te   da   pʰaltsʰul   korgya+ɖo-go-ro]MC
     PART   PART   here.there   grain.collection+go-OBLIG-FINAL
     'Some have to herd the cross-bred yaks, some have to herd the yaks, some
     have to go around for grain collection.'

In (25), four independent clauses describing distinct events, but all relating to a typical lifestyle of a Brokpa family, occur in apposition without any marker. All four clauses are of equal status. Each clause can stand independently as a sentence. The order of these clauses can be interchanged without impacting the overall meaning of all the clauses put together. Temporal sequence is not important and therefore not stated. The events described by those clauses in (25) usually take place simultaneously if there are enough sons and/or daughters in a Brokpa family. If not, those events can happen in either order.

As shown in §7.4.1.2, the morpheme =*daŋ* coordinates NPs with a meaning of 'and', functions as a comitative case marker and also shows Relative time linkage meaning 'as soon as' or 'immediately after'. The morpheme =*daŋ* also joins complement clauses which is outside the scope of this paper. The morpheme =*daŋ* marking Unordered addition clause linkage with its 'and' meaning is not quite clear. Unordered addition linkage shown by =*daŋ* is extremely rare in my corpus. Consider:

(26) *kʰoŋ=ge tsuk-pi=**daŋ***   *ŋa=ye*   *tsuk-ku*
       3PL=ERG   put.in-PERV=CNTV   1SG=EMPH   put.in-FUT.IMPERV
       'They have put it in **and** I will also put it in.'

In (26), two independent clauses are conjoined by the enclitic =*daŋ* which is cliticizable to the first clause. Semantically, there is no Supporting versus Focal clause distinction in an Unordered addition.

7.4.4.2 Same-event addition

Same-event addition linkage in Brokpa can be shown by one of the following ways: utilizing the connective *mátsʰæ* which approximately means 'not only ~ but' in English, by *tse=la* 'in addition', 'besides', 'on top of', which is the relator *tse* 'tip' followed by the locative marker =*la*, and the ablative marker =*næ* 'and (so)' which also marks Temporal succession (§7.4.1.1).

All these markers occur with the Focal clause which precedes the Supporting clause, which inversely correspond to the syntactic Main clause and the Dependent clause. That is, the syntactic Dependent clause is the semantic Focal clause, and the syntactic Main clause the semantic Supporting clause.

The connective *mátsʰæ* follows a nominalized Dependent, semantically Focal, clause which may or may not be followed by the genitive marker:

(27) *[ʔot   mí   ḍo-mi   me-ti=gi   **mátsʰæ]**DC:FC*
       DEM   person go-NOMZ   NEG.EXIST-NOMZ=GEN not.only.but
       [...] [tʰakpa=tɕiʔ=næ zuŋ-ti=ran   ya=te   kʰer-ma
       [...] rope=INDEF=ABL   start-NOMZ=EMPH   up=ALL   take-MIR.IMPERV

*me-ti-na]*MC:SC
NEG.EXIST-NOMZ-FACT
'**Not only** are those people not allowed to go, **but** also they cannot take (anything) up there starting from a rope.'

In (27), the Supporting clause is the Main clause as it describes an aspect of the event which follows from that described by the Focal clause, which is the Dependent clause.

In the same vein, the marker =næ can be used in a non-temporal sense to mark a Same-event addition in a clause-chaining construction:

(28)   *[kʰyo=daŋ   pʰræ=**næ**]*DC.FC   *[sem+ga:-soŋ]*MC:SC
      2SG=COM   meet=SEQ   mind+be.happy-PERV.DIRECT
      'I met you **and (so)** I am happy.'

In a Same-event addition shown by the morphological sequential marker =næ in a clause chain also, the syntactic Main clause is the semantic Supporting clause and the Dependent clause the Supporting clause. In (28), the state described by the Main clause (the speaker being happy) depends on the event described by the Dependent clause (his meeting with the hearer). Hence, there is no direct correspondence between the syntactic Dependent and Main clauses and the semantic Supporting and Focal clauses here.

Furthermore, Same-event addition can be shown by the relator *tse* obligatorily followed by the locative =*la*. The resulting form *tse=la* meaning 'in addition to', 'moreover' applies to the nominalized Focal clause which is stated before the Supporting clause:

(29)   *[bomo=ye   den   laika   dukʰur   kʰyakpo   yo-ti=gi*
      girl=EMPH   PART   work   hardworking   resolute   EXIST.EGO-NOMZ=GEN
      ***tse=la]*FC   *[kyaptɕʰokpu   tuʔ]*SC
      RELAT:tip=LOC   good.looking   EXIST.DIRECT
      'The girl is also good-looking **in addition to** being hard-working.'
      Lit. 'The girl, on top of being hardworking, is good-looking.'

Example (29) contains two existential clauses. The first clause, which is nominalized followed by the genitive, describes the main quality (state) of the girl, therefore the semantic Focal clause. The second existential clause with the subject shown via zero anaphora describes an additional quality of the girl which follows from that described by the Focal clause, and therefore it is the Supporting clause.

7.4.4.3 Elaboration

Elaboration addition in Brokpa is achieved by apposition of two main clauses, just like one of the strategies for showing Unordered addition (§7.4.4.1). Consider:

(30) *[ʔoyi   teŋ=la   den   tsʰoʔ*   *lúk=næ   te   gaŋyu*
     up.there RELAT:surf=LOC PART   food.offering serve=SEQ PART all
     tsʰoʔ   *za-gi-yona]*MC:SC   *[tsʰoʔ*   *ʑæ=næ   tɕʰaŋ*
     food.offering eat-IMPERV-FACT   food.offering eat=SEQ   liquor
     *tuŋ=næ   de=næ   tɕinam   gya-gi-yona]*MC:FC
     drink=SEQ DEM=ABL other.things do-IMPERV-FACT
     'We serve the food offerings and eat up there, we eat food offerings, drink liquors, and then we do other things.'

The second clause – the semantic Focal clause – provides an elaboration on what was already provided by the first clause. Although both the clauses in (30) can stand alone as an independent clause, the first clause is the Supporting clause because it provides only a limited information, that of eating the food offerings up there. The second clause is the Focal clause because it provides all the details or the fuller information.

In this type of construction, that is showing Elaboration addition by apposition, the first clause (Supporting clause) is typically accompanied by a non-sentence final intonation. There is no pause between the two clauses in an Elaboration addition, as would normally be expected between two independent sentences.

7.4.4.4 Contrast

There are three markers for Contrast linkage, *ɕin(tari)* 'but'/'although'/'however', *yin-ne(=ye)* 'even then'/'however', and *matakpa(læ)*/*matokpa* 'although'/'otherwise'. Syntactically, Contrast linkage in Brokpa typically involves two independent clauses. Semantically, the second clause is the Focal clause as the information provided by it contrasts with that of the first. The marker *ɕin(tari)* marks the Supporting clause in a Contrast linkage. Consider:

(31) a. *[teː+ta=di=la   wok+taŋ-gu   sam   ɕintari]*SC
       pick+see=DEF=LOC throw.away+send-FUT.IMPERV think:PERV but
       [da   ŋa   saŋ   pʰa=la   te   pʰon   me-ti
       PART 1SG tomorrow there=ALL PART phone NEG.EXIST-NOMZ

> sam   den   *ẓak-pi]*FC
> think PART   leave-PERV
> 'When I picked up I thought of throwing it away, **but** I thought I won't
> have a phone from tomorrow, I kept it.'

b. *[láp sam-kʰu*   *çin]*SC *[ŋa=ye   láp-ma-ɲæn-pʰi   dʰæ-ti]*FC
   tell think-FUT.IMPERV   but   1SG=EMPH tell-NEG-listen-PERV stay-PERV
   'Although I would like to tell (him), I also could not tell (him).'

In both (31a) and (31b), the information provided by the Focal clause contrasts
with that of the Supporting clause. In other words, the Supporting clause provides one piece of information, and the Focal provides another piece of information which is quite the opposite.

The second marker of Contrast linkage *yin-ne(=ye)* 'even then', 'however' is
composed of the relational copula verb *yin* followed by the concessive suffix *-ne*
and optionally followed by the emphatic *=ye*. This grammaticalized marker of
Contrast in Brokpa is the same as the Contrastive marker <yin na'ang> in Classical Tibetan, which means 'even though', 'but', 'however', 'although', depending
on context. The Contrast marker <yin na'ang> in Classical Tibetan is also formed
by the copula <yin>, the concessive <na> and the emphatic <yang>, just like in
Brokpa.

In Brokpa, *yin-ne=ye* introduces a Focal clause, as in (32):

(32) ... *[paŋkʰep=daŋ kʰada=di zin+ga-soŋ]*SC   *[te   **yin-ne=ye***
     ... apron=CNTV   scarf=DEF finish+go-PERV.DIRECT PART COP-CNSV=EMPH
     *da   kʰi=la   diriŋ kamtɕʰa=ẓi? den da   pʰuː+taŋ-go-ro]*FC
     PART 2PL=DAT   today dry.gift=INDEF PART PART give.HON+send-OBLIG-FINAL
     'We ran out of aprons and scarves, **even then** we will offer you a dry gift
     (cash).'

Example (32) consists of two independent clauses, the second one introduced by
yin-ne=ye. The first clause provides one piece of information, about the running
out of the stock of aprons and scarves. The second clause introduces another
piece of information, that of providing 'dry gift' which is a cash payment in lieu
of the aprons and scarves, considered an important wedding gift in the Brokpa
culture. The information of the second clause contrasts with that of the first.

Sometimes the marker *-çin(tari)* and *yin-ne(ye)* can co-occur in a Contrast
linkage, with the former marking the Supporting clause and the latter Focal clause:

(33) [wái ʔot ŋi=ta ma-bo ɕintari]SC [yin-ne=ye
INTJ DEM 1PL=FOC NEG-invite.PERV but COP-CNSV=EMPH:even.then
ɲéŋŋepʰ pʰambutsʰa yin ŋi ɖo-go-ɦoŋ]FC
kith.kin parent.child COP.EGO 1PL do-OBLIG-POTEN
'Oops, we are not invited, even then we must go as we are all family members
and relatives.'

When both ɕin(tari) and yin-ne=ye co-occur, there can be a pause in between
them. This shows that ɕin(tari) is associated with the preceding Supporting
clause and yin-ne=ye with the following Focal clause.
     Examples of matakpal(æ) marking Contrast linkage include:

(34) [ʔunla yin-na te baŋɕuŋ=se]SC [matakpal(æ)
before COP.EGO-COND PART cane.basket=QUOT although
da diriŋ+saŋ-ɖou tʰali=se lap-pʰi ʔoɖou minuŋ]FC
PART today+tomorrow-SIMI plate=QUOT say-NOMZ like.this NEG.EXIST
'(If it is) in the olden days, **although** there was a so-called 'cane basket',
there was no such things as 'plate' like nowadays.'

The Focal clause, introduced by the morpheme matakpal(æ), contrasts with the
preceding Supporting clause in (34).

7.4.5 Alternatives

Alternatives clause linking includes Disjunction, Rejection, and Suggestion. All
three varieties have distinct grammatical markers and techniques. Supporting
versus Focal clause distinction applies only to Rejection and Suggestion clause
linking types. A Disjunction clause linking involves two or more clauses which
are all independent and there is no Supporting clause versus Focal clause distinction.

7.4.5.1 Disjunction

Dixon (2009: 31) mentions two types of Disjunction linkage:
open disjunction: X or Y (but there is a small chance that neither may hold);
closed disjunction: X or Y (with no further alternative possible).

An open disjunction in Brokpa is shown by the connective *yaŋman(a)* 'if not (lit. if it is not again)' or *yaŋna(n)* 'or else (lit. if not again really)', and the closed disjunction by the connective *nam* meaning 'or' or 'whether'.

A Disjunction linkage involves clauses with equal status without a Supporting versus Focal clause distinction in Brokpa as is the case cross-linguistically (Dixon 2009). In an open disjunction, both clauses can be nominalized or can be inflected for TAM and knowledge categories. The second clause, describing the second alternative, is introduced by one of the open disjunction markers. There can be more than two alternatives in a Disjunction linkage. Consider:

(35) *de=næ*   *goto=gi*   *ŋám*   *ton-tɕuʔ*   **yaŋman** *kyi=yi*
      DEM=ABL   rooster=GEN sound take.out-CAUS or.else   dog=GEN
      ŋám   *ton-tɕuʔ*   **yaŋman** *buŋbu=i*   *ŋám*   *ton-tɕuʔ*
      sound take.out-CAUS or.else   donkey=GEN   sound take.out-CAUS
      'After that, make them produce a rooster's sound, **or else** make them produce a dog's sound, **or else** make them produce a donkey's sound.'

Example (35) contains three syntactically independent clauses, each clause realized by a causative construction. The second and the third clauses describing Disjunctive alternatives are introduced by the grammaticalized conjunction *yaŋman(a)*.

In the same vein, two or more clauses of equal status can be linked by the connective *yaŋna(n)* showing open disjunction, as in:

(36) *kʰoŋ=raŋ=baʔ=ti*   *tʰoŋ-ri-lá=ʑiʔ*   *dʑuŋ-yoduŋ*   **yaŋnan**
      3PL=REFL=PL=DEF see-NOMZ-SIMI=INDEF occur-EXIST.INFER or
      tʰoŋ-ri   *dʑuŋ-meduŋ*
      see-NOMZ occur-NEG.EXIST.INFER
      'They might have seen each other, **or** they may not have seen each other.'

In (36) there are two clauses, one positive polarity and the other negative, introduced by the Disjunctive conjunction *yaŋnan*. Note that the negative clause is also an independent clause with its subject argument omitted under identity.

A closed disjunction is shown by the connective *nam* meaning 'or' or 'whether'. As a Disjunctive conjunction, *nam* joins two or more clauses of equal status and shows a closed disjunction, as in (37):

(37)   ... *goŋgo=næ*   *tsʰu=la*   *den*   *yuː*   *námoŋ*   *tsʰu=la*
       ... threshold=ABL   this.side=ALL   PART   village   edge   this.side=ALL
       kʰyoŋ-go-ti   *nam*   *yuː*   *bar*   *tsʰu=la*
       bring-OBLIG-NOMZ   or   village   middle   this.side=ALL
       kʰyoŋ-go-ti   *nam* ...
       bring-OBLIG-NOMZ   or ...
       'Whether they have to bring it from the house (threshold) on this side to the
       edge of village **or** they have to bring it to the middle of the village **or** . . . .'

This technique of showing closed disjunction in Brokpa is an "exclusive closed
disjunction: (either) X or Y but not both" (Dixon 2009: 31).

7.4.5.2 Rejection

Rejection alternative in Brokpa can be shown by using the grammaticalized conjunction *tsʰama* 'instead of'. Rejection alternative linkage can also be shown
simply by apposition.

The connective *tsʰama* may be optionally followed by the dative/locative
marker =*la*.

Used as a marker of Rejection alternative, *tsʰama(=la)* applies to the Supporting clause which is syntactically a nominalized Dependent clause. The Supporting clause may be optionally followed by the genitive marker. The genitive marker
appears between a clause linker such as a relator and the preceding clause if the
predicate of that clause is realized by nominalization. However, the genitive
marking in this kind of construction is not obligatory:

(38)   [*ŋa=e*   *kʰo*   *rup+laŋ-tɕuk-pi(=gi)*   ***tsʰama(=la)***]DC:SC
       1SG=ERG   3SG.MASC   anger+arise-CAUS-NOMZ(=GEN)   instead.of
       [*gæ+ɕor-tɕuk-pi*]MC:FC
       laugh+let.out-CAUS-PERV
       '**Instead of** making him angry, I made him laugh.'

Example (38) involves two clauses with a shared A argument and O argument, but
a Rejection alternative construction can also involve two clauses with different
core arguments.

The same sentence (38) can be used with the rejection conjunction *mani*, but
the nominalizer of the Supporting clause changes from -*pi* to the instrumental
nominalizer -*ma*, also marking mirativity, as in:

(39) [*ŋa=e* *kʰo* *rup+laŋ-tɕuk-ma* ***mani*]DC:SC
 1SG=ERG 3SG.MASC anger+arise-CAUS-NOMZ:INST instead.of
 [*gæ+ɕor-tɕuk-pi*]MC:FC
 laugh+let.out-CAUS-PERV
 'Instead of making him angry, I made him laugh.'

Furthermore, Rejection alternative can be shown by the egophoric copula *yin* and its negative counterpart *man*. In this type, the negative copula *man* applies to the Supporting clause which is nominalized and the copula *yin* applies to the Focal clause, also nominalized. Syntactically, the two clauses have equal status:

(40) [*ŋi=gi* *tɕʰaŋ* *rin* *dega* *dʑin-ni* ***man*=s]MC:SC
 1PL=GEN alcohol value free give-NOMZ NEG.COP.EGO=ASSERT
 [*rup* *dʑin-ni* ***yin*=s]MC:FC
 money give-NOMZ cop.ego=assert
 'Our alcohol was not given for free, we have paid money.'

In (40), the speaker rejects the fact that the alcohol was given for free in the Supporting clause and then he mentions that he has paid money for it.

In addition, Rejection alternative can be effectively handled by apposition. Instead of using the grammaticalized conjunction *tsʰama* which involves a Dependent (non-main) versus Main clause structure, as in (38), a Rejection alternative indicated by apposition involves two syntactically independent clauses, as in:

(41) [*ʔotɕins* *petɕʰa* *má-tæ-pʰi* *ma-dʰo=s*]MC:SC [*da*
 like.this book NEG-see-NOMZ NEG-stay.IMP=assert PART
 petɕʰa=ta *petɕʰa* *kʰaʔ+tɕʰe-gu-na=s*]MC:FC
 book=TOP book importance+be.big-FUT.IMPERV-FACT=ASSERT
 'Don't stay like this without studying, education (book) really will be important.'

In (41), the addressee not studying (as expressed by the Supporting clause) is rejected in favour of education (what is described by the Focal clause) indicating that the addressee should study instead of wasting their time.

In (41), the Supporting clause expressing what is rejected is in the negative imperative, and the Focal clause expressing what is to be done in place of rejection is in the declarative. But a Rejection alternative can be in apposition with the Supporting clause in the negative imperative while the Focal clause is positive, as in:

(42) [kʰyo tɕʰaŋ   **má-tʰuŋ**]MC:SC [dʑa   **tʰuŋ**]MC:FC
     2SG   alcohol NEG-drink.IMP   tea   drink.IMP
     'You don't drink alcohol, (you) drink tea.'

In (42), Rejection alternative is achieved by an apposition of two main clauses. The first clause, the Supporting clause, expresses a negative command (negative imperative) and the second clause, the Focal clause, a positive command (positive imperative). The drinking of alcohol described by the Supporting clause is rejected in favour of drinking tea described by the Focal clause.

7.4.5.3 Suggestion

A suggestion alternative is shown by the ablative case marker =læ which is used as a mark of comparison in comparative constructions. In a Suggestion alternative linking, the marker =læ is added to the Supporting clause which is typically nominalized, as in:

(43) [riŋgo   tɕæ-ta=**læ**]SC [den miŋgo   tɕæ-ti=gi   gaː]FC
     mountain.head cut-MIR=ABL PART person.head cut-NOMZ=GEN be.happy
     'It will be easier cutting off a person's head rather than cutting off a moun-
     taintop.'
     Lit. 'It will be happy cutting off human head than mountain head.'

In (43), the marker =læ is added to the nominalized Supporting clause. The cutting off a mountain head (what is described by the Supporting clause) is recommended to be discarded in favour of cutting off a person head (what is described by the Focal clause).

7.4.6 Manner

Dixon (2009: 35) distinguishes two subtypes of Manner clause linking, Real and Hypothetical. In this language Real manner (§7.4.6.1) is shown by demonstrative adverbs and/or adverbial suffix. Hypothetical manner (§7.4.6.2) is shown by two suffixes, with roughly the same semantic contribution, applied to the nominalized predicate of the Focal clause.

7.4.6.1 Real

Brokpa indicates Real manner by using the demonstrative adverb *?otɕins* 'like this' to introduce the Focal clause. This demonstrative adverb describes the manner of doing something. The Supporting clause describes the manner, and the Focal clause describes an action done in the manner described by the Supporting clause. The Supporting clause may be marked by the tag *mo*, as in (44a). Alternatively, the Supporting clause may be marked by the grammaticalized adverbial suffix *-gyan(æ)*, as in (44b), or the Supporting clause may be marked simply by the sequential marker *=næ* , as in (44c):

(44) a. [*tɕʰaŋ   den   botol   ridum   ka:-ɦoŋ   mó*]SC
          alcohol PART bottle full   impose-POTEN TAG
          [*ha:p   ka:-ɦoŋ   mó*]SC [*?otɕins-gyan   ka:=næ*]FC . . .
          half   impose-POTEN TAG   like.that   impose=SEQ
          'Whether they impose a full bottle or impose a half bottle of alcohol, that is what they impose.'

      b. [*tɕʰatsʰaŋ   ɖi   me-ti-gyan*]SC   [*den   ?otɕins-gyan*
          complete   taints NEG.EXIST-NOMZ-ADV PART like.that-ADV
          ɖadi+gya-go-pʰi-na]FC
          preparation+do-OBLIG-PERV-FACT
          'Without there being any taints, like that we prepare.'

      c. [[*pʰama=i   ɖinlam   dʐor-mi-dʐor   [mík   tsum=næ*]ADV.CL.SC
          parent=GEN gratitude pay.off-NEG-pay.off eye   close=SEQ
          ?otɕins   takpa   ta-ma-yona]]FC
          like.that   sign   see-MIR-FACT
          'We see signs of how we can repay the parents' gratitude, by closing our eyes.'
          Lit. 'By closing eyes, like that we see signs of how we can repay the parents' gratitude.'

Note that this adverbial suffix *-gyan* is originally a combination of the light verb *gya* 'to do' plus the ablative marker *=næ*, but in this function it has become semantically bleached and functions as an adverbial suffix with a meaning 'as' or 'like'. Note that Brokpa uses the suffix *-gyan* to derive adverbs from nouns and adjectives. When *-gyan* is added to the manner adverbial *?otɕins*, there is an addition of adverbial meaning to the effect 'as like that'.

   Syntactically, example (44a) involves all non-Main clauses, and (44b) and (44c) a dependent adverbial clause and a Main clause, respectively. The manner adverbial clause in (44c) is attached to the Main clause using the sequential marker =næ on the Dependent clause and the adverb ʔotçins to introduce the Main clause. It shows that the dependent clauses in a sequential clause chain can also be reinterpreted as manner adverbial clauses. Semantically, in all these examples, the Main clause is the Focal clause because it describes how an action is done in the manner described by the preceding clause(s).

Brokpa has two other derived adverbs ʔoɖou and ʔozum, both having the same meaning as ʔotçins 'like this/that'. These two adverbs – ʔoɖou and ʔozum – are formed by adding the suffix -ɖou and -zum both meaning 'like', 'as if' to the demonstrative root ʔo. Note that ʔotçins is non-segmentable whereas ʔoɖou and ʔozum are, with the etymology of both the components being transparent.

Interestingly, the suffix -ɖou and -zum, on their own, mark Hypothetical manner by attaching to the Supporting clause, and after lexicalization with the demonstrative mark Real manner by introducing the Focal clause, as in:

(45) [doŋbo=i loksu=la çoː re=næ]DC:SC [ʔoɖou maŋbo
     face=GEN side=LOC pustules become=SEQ like.that many
     yoŋ-gi-yona]MC:FC
     come-IMPERV-FACT
     'Many things happen like pustules erupting on the face.'
     Lit. 'Pustules erupt on your face; like that many things happen.'

Further note that there are other syntactic markers which can be used for showing Real manner in Brokpa. They include tʰiː 'in accordance with', tun 'comply with' or 'in keeping with' which can be heard in everyday speech. In addition, two Classical Tibetan loanwords tar 'like', 'as', 'similar to' and ʑin(du) also meaning 'like', 'as', 'similar to' are heard marking Real manner clause linkage in formal register. All these markers apply to the Supporting clause which precedes the Focal clause in a Real manner clause linkage.

7.4.6.2 Hypothetical

Brokpa shows Hypothetical manner with the marker -ɖou or -zum both meaning 'like', 'as if'. With lexemes, these two morphemes function as non-word-class-changing derivational suffixes with meanings including 'same', 'like', 'somewhat', 'approximately', etc. As a clause linker, both -ɖou and -zum apply to a nominalized predicate and are glossed 'similative':

(46) [*ŋa=raŋ=raŋ*   *yin-ni-ḍou*]DC:SC   [*ŋa=raŋ=raŋ*   *ɕe:-pʰi-ḍou*]DC:SC
      1SG=REFL=EMPH   COP.EGO-NOMZ-SIMI   1SG-REFL=EMPH   know-NOMZ-SIMI
      [*ŋa=raŋ=raŋ*   *tʰoŋ-ŋai-ḍou*]DC:SC   [*ʑui-ḍo-ro*   *ʔa*   *sam*]MC:FC
      1SG=REFL=EMPH   see-NOMZ-SIMI   say.HON-go-FINAL   INTJ   think.PERV
      'I thought I might end up talking **as if** I myself was the only one, **as if** I
      myself was the one who knows everything, **as if** I myself was the one who
      has seen everything.'

In (46), there are three supporting clauses all marked by the suffix *-ḍou* and then
the Focal clause, also the syntactic Main clause. The Focal clause portrays an
activity of what the Speaker might say and all the preceding Supporting clauses
describe what the speaker might appear like, but it isn't. Note that the marker
-ḍou in all the slots in (46) can be replaced by *-zum* with no difference in meaning.
The marker *-ḍou* can also mark Hypothetical manner involving two existential
clauses, attaching to the first which is a semantic Supporting clause, as in:

(47) *yu:=di*   *mí+kæ*   *kyi+kæ*   *me-ti-ḍou*   *ma-gau*
      village=DEF   person+noise   dog+noise   NEG.EXIST-NOMZ-SIMI   NEG-happy
      toŋhaŋhaŋ   *tu?*
      empty   EXIST.DIRECT
      'The village is empty **as if** there are no humans or dogs.'

Further, the two markers *-ḍou* and *-zum* occur with the demonstrative *ʔo* and the
resulting forms *ʔoḍou* and *ʔozum* function like a lexicalized word both meaning
'like this/that' marking Real manner just like *ʔotɕins*, also with the same meaning
'like this/that'.

7.5 Conclusion

Brokpa uses various markers to show different kinds of clause linkages. The grammatical markers associated with different clause linking constructions almost
always apply to the dependent clauses. We have seen that some case markers
and relators which mark NPs also occur with predicates and function as clause
linkers.

    Table 7.2 gives a comparison of the functions of case markers and relators, or
both, with NPs and with clauses.

Table 7.2: Versatile case markers and relators with clause-linking functions in Brokpa.

FORM	WITH NPs	WITH CLAUSES
=næ	Spatial/temporal location 'away from'	Temporal succession 'and (then)', 'after'
=læ	Spatial/temporal location 'from'	Suggestion 'rather than'
=la	Spatial location 'at' (locative)	Point in time 'when'
	Recipient 'to' (dative)	Cause linkage 'because'
=daŋ	Comitative/associative 'with'	Relative time 'as soon as'
		Unordered addition 'and'
sumke/sakai	Spatial/temporal location 'until'	Length of time 'until'
gaŋ/ɕuŋ/kap(su)	Temporal location 'during'	Length of time 'while'
tse=la	Spatial location 'on'	Same-event addition 'in addition to'
donda=la	Beneficiary 'for the sake of'	Purpose 'in order to'

The case markers apply either directly to the verb stem or to the nominalized verb stem within a dependent clause. The relators are separate phonological words but are associated with the dependent clauses.

The sentential conjunctions derived from demonstratives, copulas, and verbs typically introduce the Focal clause, just like adverbs. A clause linkage shown by apposition involves two independent clauses, either nominalized or with TAM morphology and/or the markers of knowledge distinction.

For the most part, the syntactic Dependent clause coincides with the semantic Supporting clause and the syntactic Main clause with the semantic Focal clause in a biclausal linking; however, there is no such direct correspondence when the Focal clause precedes the Supporting clause. This is because, as noted earlier, sentences in Brokpa typically end with a Main clause.

Abbreviations

1	first person
2	second person
3	third person
A	transitive subject
ABIL	abilitative modality
ABL	ablative
ADV	adverb(ial)
AGTV	agentive (nominalization)

ALL	allative
APPROX	approximative
AROUND	around (relator)
ASSERT	assertive
CAUS	causative
CL	classifier
CNSV	concessive
CNTV	connective
COM	comitative
COND	conditional
CONT	continuous
COP	copula
DAT	dative
DC	dependent clause
DEF	definite
DEM	demonstrative
DIRECT	direct (or visual) evidential
E	extended argument
EGO	egophoric
EMPH	emphasis
ERG	ergative
EXIST	existential verb
FACT	factual (knowledge distinction)
FC	focal clause
FEM	feminine
FINAL	clause-final marker
FOC	focus
FUT	future
GEN	genitive
HEAD	head NP or argument
HON	honorific
IMP	imperative
IMPERV	imperfective
INDEF	indefinite
INFER	inferred
INSD	inside (relator)
INST	instrumental
INTJ	interjection
LOC	locative case
MASC	masculine
MC	main clause
MIR	mirative
NEG	negation
NOMZ	nominalizer
O	transitive object
OBLIG	modality of obligation
OCN	occasion (relator)

PART	particle
PERM	permission (modality)
PERV	perfective
PL	plural
POTEN	potential modality
PRED	predicative
QUOT	quotative
REFL	reflexive
RELAT	relator
SC	supporting clause
SELF	self-pronoun
SEQ	sequential
SG	singular
SIM	simultaneous
SIMI	similative
SURF	surface (relator)
TAG	tag (question)
TIP	tip (relator)
TOP	topic
UNTIL	until (relator)

References

Aikhenvald, Alexandra Y. 2007. Typological distinctions in word-formation. In Timothy Shopen (ed.), *Language typology and syntactic description*, vol. 3, 1–65. Cambridge: Cambridge University Press.

Aikhenvald, Alexandra Y. 2009. Semantics and grammar in clause linking. In R. M. W. Dixon & Alexandra Y. Aikhenvald (eds.), *The semantics of clause linking: A cross-linguistic typology*, 380–402. Oxford: Oxford University Press.

Aikhenvald, Alexandra Y. 2011. Versatile cases. In Alexandra Y. Aikhenvald & R. M. W. Dixon (eds.), *Language at large: Essays on syntax and semantics*, 3–43. Leiden: Brill.

Aikhenvald, Alexandra Y. 2015. *The art of grammar: A practical guide*. Oxford: Oxford University Press.

Brinton, Laurel J. & Elizabeth Closs Traugott. 2005. *Lexicalization and language change*. Cambridge: Cambridge University Press.

Dixon, R. M. W. 2009. The semantics of clause linking in typological perspective. In R. M. W. Dixon & Alexandra Y. Aikhenvald (eds.), *The semantics of clause linking: A Cross-linguistic typology*, 1–55. Oxford: Oxford University Press.

Dixon, R. M. W. 2010. *Basic linguistic theory*, vol. 1, *Methodology*. Oxford: Oxford University Press.

Givón, Talmy. 2001. *Syntax: A functional-typological introduction*, vol. 2. Amsterdam/ Philadelphia: John Benjamins.

Hopper, Paul J. & Sandra Thompson. 1980. Transitivity in grammar and discourse. *Language* 56. 251–299.

Hopper, Paul J. & Elizabeth Closs Traugott. 2003. *Grammaticalization*, 2nd edition. Cambridge: Cambridge University Press.
Longacre, Robert E. 2007. Sentences as combinations of clauses. In Timothy Shopen (eds.), *Language typology and syntactic description*, vol. 2, 372–420. Cambridge: Cambridge University Press.
Mithun, Marianne. 1984. The evolution of noun incorporation. *Language* 60. 847–894.
Mithun, Marianne. 2009. Compounding and incorporation. In Sergio Scalise & Irene Vogel (eds.), *Compounding*. Amsterdam/Philadelphia: John Benjamins.
Post, Mark W. 2009. The semantics of clause linking in Galo. In R. M. W. Dixon & Alexandra Y. Aikhenvald (eds.), *The semantics of clause linking: A cross-linguistic typology*, 74–95. Oxford: Oxford University Press.
Saxena, Anju. 1988. On syntactic convergence: The case of the verb "say" in Tibeto-Burman. *Berkeley Linguistics Society Proceedings* 14. 375–88.
Thompson, Sandra A., Robert E. Longacre & Shin Ja J. Hwang 2007. Adverbial clauses. In Timothy Shopen (ed.), *Language typology and syntactic description*, vol. 2, 237–300. Cambridge: Cambridge University Press.
Watters, David E. 2009. The semantics of clause linking in Kham. In R. M. W. Dixon & Alexandra Y. Aikhenvald (eds.), *The semantics of clause linking: A cross-linguistic typology*, 96–117. Oxford: Oxford University Press.
Yip, Po-Ching & Don Rimmington. 2004. *Chinese: A comprehensive grammar*. London: Routledge.

Christoph Holz

8 Discourse functions of 'visible' and 'nonvisible' demonstratives in Tiang (New Ireland) and in a cross-linguistic perspective

The present chapter examines the use of demonstratives in discourse as a refer-ent-tracking and clause-linking device. The crucial question is how the visibility value of a demonstrative influences its discourse functions. The investigation starts with an evaluation of the demonstrative system of Tiang, an Oceanic lan-guage of Papua New Guinea. Tiang has a set of six demonstrative forms, which indicate distance and visibility of referents in an exophoric setting. In their endo-phoric function, the different forms correlate with different discourse functions. The following tendencies are observed in Tiang: 'Visible' demonstratives tend to be exophoric, and 'nonvisible' forms tend to be endophoric. The 'nonvisible' forms are the preferred choice for anaphors, while cataphors tend to be expressed by 'visible' demonstratives. A sample of 22 languages was examined for the use of demonstratives and most were found to follow the same tendencies as described for Tiang.

8.1 Demonstratives in the discourse

Demonstratives are grammatical words that are characterised by specific syntac-tic, pragmatic and semantic functions. They deictically point towards an entity within the speech situation and help keep track of entities within the discourse. Their most notable feature is the distinction of distance of a referent from the deictic centre, with all languages having at least two deictically contrastive demonstratives: a proximal form for an entity near the deictic centre and a distal form for an entity away from the deictic centre (Diessel 1999: 2). Other semantic features of demonstratives may include temporal location, height, stance and vis-ibility of an entity (Dixon 2010: 239).

Demonstratives fall into two large categories, commonly referred to as "exo-phoric" and "endophoric". In their exophoric use, demonstratives point deicti-

Christoph Holz, Jawun Research Centre, Central Queensland University

https://doi.org/10.1515/9783110789836-008

cally to a referent in the actual speech situation. "Endophoric" is the umbrella term for all other discourse-related demonstrative uses (Diessel 1999: 93). Endophoric use, most importantly, incorporates anaphoric and cataphoric reference. Anaphors track back a previously mentioned entity, while cataphors point towards an entity that will be mentioned later in the discourse. There are two types of anaphors and cataphors: "substitution" anaphors and cataphors substitute or refer to a noun phrase, and "textual" anaphors and cataphors refer to a clause, sentence or whole stretch of text (Dixon 2010: 248–249). Other endophoric functions are identification and recognition of a referent, introduction of new information, discourse organisation, as well as emotional attitude, personal interest and familiarity towards a referent (Dixon 2010: 238, 245).

The presence of demonstratives does not only relate to keeping track of referents. As Diessel (1999: 98) puts it, "[t]he use of anaphoric demonstratives after first mention is a common strategy to establish major discourse participants in the universe of discourse". However, they can also "indicate that the antecedent is not the referent that the hearer would expect in this context" and "are used when reference tracking is somewhat problematic" (Diessel 1999: 99).

Related to the type of textual anaphors and cataphors, demonstratives link events in the discourse. They may act alone as connectives or conjunctions between two clauses (Aikhenvald 2015a: 275). When in predicate position, an anaphoric demonstrative may take the meaning 'to do thus' to sum up the previous section of a text, known as "summary linkage", or accompany the repeated lexical verb from the previous clause, a strategy called "mixed linkage" (Guérin and Aiton 2019: 4). In addition, they may become speech formulae that signal the beginning or ending of a story (Aikhenvald 2015a: 280).

Because of their diverse discourse functions, demonstratives often have close ties to various other word classes. Demonstratives are a common source of third-person pronouns and articles (Greenberg 1985: 282). Diessel and Breunesse (2020: 308) mention eight types of clause-linking morphemes that frequently derive from demonstratives: relative pronouns, linking and nominalising articles, quotative markers, complementisers, conjunctive adverbs, adverbial subordinate conjunctions, correlatives and topic markers. Kuteva et al. (2019: 136, 140) also describe demonstratives as a source of the copula, fillers and focus markers.

The deictic features of demonstratives in many languages correlate with their discourse functions. It is often reported that distal demonstratives are the natural candidates for anaphoric reference, whereas proximal forms are chosen to express cataphors (Greenberg 1985: 282, 284, Cleary-Kemp 2007: 335, Dixon 2010: 250, König 2020: 23). Other studies, conversely, highlight the anaphoric potential of medial (Anderson and Keenan 1985: 287) and proximal demonstratives (Himmelmann 1996: 226). The distance degree of demonstratives also has an impact on other discourse functions: Himmelmann (1996: 235) describes the use of the distal category as typical for recognitional use, hesitations and false starts. Furthermore, positive feelings towards a referent may be associated with nearer distance categories, and negative feelings with more distant forms (Dixon 2010: 245, Næss, Margetts and Treis 2020: 11; see Zandvoort 1975: 148 on the context sensitivity of English demonstratives).

What these studies have in common is a focus on the influence of the distance category of a demonstrative on its use within discourse. In contrast, this study focuses on a largely neglected feature of demonstratives: visibility. Data comes from the demonstrative system of Tiang, an Austronesian language of the Oceanic branch spoken on Djaul Island in the northwest of New Ireland Province, Papua New Guinea.[1] Like many other Oceanic languages (Lynch, Ross and Crowley 2011: 38), Tiang has a three-way contrast in distance. In addition, demonstratives in the language specify whether the referent is visible or not.

Tiang is a nominative–accusative language. Core arguments are marked by constituent order (SV, AVO), whereas case marking is absent. Peripheral arguments are marked by prepositions. Tiang shares many features with other Oceanic languages. Similar features include: the presence of serial verb constructions, the differentiation between first-person inclusive and exclusive, alienable and inalienable possession, pronominal possessive enclitics, and pronoun elaboration constructions. Nouns and pronouns may have four number values: SINGULAR, DUAL, PAUCAL and PLURAL. Intransitive verbs are generally derived from transitive verbs by reduplication. A handful of verbs also undergo triplication to express cessative aspect.

We will start with an overview of the morphological and syntactic behaviour of Tiang demonstratives (Section 8.2). Their exophoric and endophoric functions are discussed in Sections 8.3 and 8.4, respectively. Section 8.5 deals with how the genre of a text correlates with the choice of demonstratives for a certain discourse function. A preliminary summary of the Tiang demonstratives (Section 8.6) is followed by a cross-linguistic comparison of the discourse functions of visible and nonvisible demonstratives in 22 languages in Section 8.7.

---

1 Tiang examples appear in IPA. Allophonic variations: /i, u/ > [j, w] in diphthongs and triphthongs; /r/ > [d] often at the beginning of a word and after certain consonants; /riɨ/ > [dʑɨ]. The study is based on approximately three hours of transcribed audio recordings plus additional handwritten notes collected on Djaul between February and October 2019. For more information, see Holz (forthcoming).

8.2 Structure and syntax of Tiang demonstratives

Tiang has six basic demonstratives (Table 8.1). Each demonstrative consists of three morpheme slots. The first slot is reserved for the optional demonstrative formative ɔ- with its allomorph o-, in actual speech often reduced to [ə]. This formative has no apparent function, and its presence or absence does not affect the meaning. The likelihood of its presence, however, corresponds to the distance value of the demonstrative, with ɔ-/o- being most frequently found on proximal demonstratives, less frequently on medial demonstratives, and hardly ever on distal forms.

The second slot hosts two visibility formatives: t-/r- marks a demonstrative as 'VISIBLE', while n- marks it as 'NONVISIBLE'. The third slot reveals the distance category of the demonstrative: -o/-en is the 'PROXIMAL' root, -an means 'MEDIAL' and (-)a signals 'DISTAL'. In contrast to the aforementioned demonstrative formative ɔ-/o-, the visibility and distance formatives are obligatory categories on Tiang demonstratives. An exception is the distal root (-)a, which under special circumstances may occur on its own (see example 5b below).

Table 8.1: Basic demonstratives in Tiang.

	VISIBLE	NONVISIBLE
PROXIMAL	(o-)r-o	(ɔ/o-)n-en
MEDIAL	(ɔ-)t-an	(ɔ-)n-an
DISTAL	(ɔ-)(t-)a	(ɔ-)(n-)a

Demonstratives can occur with any kind of referent in Tiang, including human beings, animals, inanimates, locations and expressions of time (1). The relevant demonstratives appear in bold in the examples. Morpheme breakdowns for these forms will not be provided from this point on to enhance readability.

(1) ə   lɛk/   peu/   uir/   bik/   uələn   **oro**
     ART   man/   dog/   banana/   place/   moon   VIS.PROX
     'this man/dog/banana/place/month'

As illustrated in example (1), demonstratives may function as modifiers of the noun phrase head. This is not only possible with nouns as the head of a noun phrase, but also with first- (2a), second- (2b) and third-person pronouns (2c; Section 8.4.5). However, demonstratives do not modify proper names of animate referents in my corpus.

(2) a. [niɨu **na**]ₙₚ   kə   tɔkɔn ə   lɛk   i=n=ə   luntən
       1SG   NVIS.DIST   RM.PST   own   ART   man   INAL=3SG=ART   bush
       'I married a man from the bush (a spirit).'

     b. [no   **ro**   mɔ]ₙₚ ki   uin   nə   papoi   si=mai
       2SG   VIS.PROX   only   HAB   hide   PN.ART   dad   AL=1DU.EXCL
       'Only you here used to hide our Dad.'

     c. [iriai **na**]ₙₚ   mət   kauai
       3DU   NVIS.DIST   die   already
       'They are already dead.'

The same demonstrative forms may function on their own as the head of a noun phrase. This is especially common in verbless clauses, where demonstratives typically serve as the verbless clause complement (3a), or when they refer to a whole stretch of text, as in (3b), where *(o)ro* represents the instructions of how to make a garden that the speaker is about to elaborate on.

(3) a. [nə   tɨi=k]ᵥₑᵣᵦₗₑₛₛ 𝒸ₗₐᵤₛₑ ₛᵤᵦⱼₑ𝒸ₜ   [**oro**]ᵥₑᵣᵦₗₑₛₛ 𝒸ₗₐᵤₛₑ 𝒸ₒₘₚₗₑₘₑₙₜ
       PN.ART   same.sex.sibling=1SG   VIS.PROX
       'This is my same-sex sibling.'

     b. ə   səlɘn   [i=n=ə   **ro**]ₚₒₛₛₑₛₛₒᵣ ki   [laŋ **oro**]ₘₐₙₙₑᵣ
       ART   way   INAL=3SG=ART   VIS.PROX   HAB   like   VIS.PROX
       'The way of this (making a garden) is like this.'

Another syntactic function of demonstratives is as an adverbial. Example (3b) already featured an instance of the manner adverbial *laŋ (o)ro* 'like this'. Manner adverbials are generally introduced by the preposition *laŋ* 'like'. A special manner adverbial form is *laŋata* 'like that' (4a), which is the fusion of *laŋ* 'like' and *ɔta* 'VISIBLE DISTAL'. There is also the much less frequent unfused variant *laŋ (ɔ)ta*, but this has a local meaning 'like there'. Other types of adverbials are those indicating location (4b) and time or condition (4c).

(4) a. nə   təmə=riai   ə   kus   iriai   [**laŋata**]ₘₐₙₙₑᵣ
       PN.ART   father=3DU   PFV   tell   3DU   like.VIS.DIST
       'Their father told them like this.'

     b. imiai   nɨs   ua   lɘk   [**oro**]ₗₒ𝒸ₐₜᵢₒₙ?
       2DU   who   RC.PST   up   VIS.PROX
       'Who did you come here with?'

c. *semen nən ok puka,* [*tan*]_{time} *niiu ok kələpəŋ, pɔ* [...]
   if   3SG FUT fall VIS.MED 1SG FUT know   COMP
   'If he falls, then I will know that [...].'

Adverbial demonstratives generally occur in the periphery of the clause, as demonstrated in the examples above. In the imperfective aspect, however, demonstratives referring to a location may be included in the verb phrase to denote progressive aspect, in which case they cliticise to the imperfective marker *i/(i)k* (5). The demonstrative may optionally be repeated at the margins of the clause in its original position. If included in the verb phrase, the distal demonstratives generally lose their visibility formative (5b). This is the only context in which the distal root *(-)a* may appear alone. The exact conditions for the omission of the visibility formatives require further study.

(5) a. *niiu* [*oro=k*   *tin~tin*]_{VP}   (*oro*)
    1SG VIS.PROX=IPFV INTR~cook VIS.PROX
    'I am cooking here.'

   b. *nən* [*a=k*   *sɔ*]_{VP}   (*ta*)?
    3SG DIST=IPFV do.what VIS.DIST
    'What is he doing there?'

Demonstratives are often found before, and sometimes simultaneously after a relative clause. The most frequent demonstrative form to mark relative clauses is nonvisible distal *(ɔ)(n)a* (6). As relative clauses in Tiang may have, but do not need, overt marking, the use of demonstratives is optional here. The presence of a demonstrative next to a relative clause seems linked to the topicality of a referent, but more research is needed to confirm this.

(6) *ə*   *niau* (*na*),   [*e=k*   *buik* *pɛtɛn* (*na*)]_{relative clause}
   ART thing NVIS.DIST 1SG=IPFV want talk   NVIS.DIST
   'the thing that I want to say'

More than one demonstrative can occur side by side in the same noun phrase (7). The only condition is that the demonstratives have to be different, and that the second is the nonvisible distal *(ɔ)(n)a* (Section 8.4.5).

(7) [*uir*   *si=k*   **oro**   **na**]_{NP} *ə*   *mɛŋ*
   banana AL=1SG VIS.PROX NVIS.DIST PFV dry
   'My banana tree here is dry.'

Apart from the basic demonstrative forms presented here, there are other words resembling demonstratives, as well as words derived from demonstratives, which are not relevant in this chapter. More information on these words and the role of demonstratives in the noun phrase structure is provided in Holz (forthcoming).

8.3 Exophoric function of Tiang demonstratives

In their exophoric function, demonstratives serve as deictic words to indicate the spatial location of a referent in the world. Tiang demonstratives distinguish three degrees of distance: PROXIMAL 'near', MEDIAL 'mid-distant' and DISTAL 'far'. Each of these distance degrees combines with two values of visibility: VISIBLE and NONVISIBLE.

The proximal category distinguishes between *(o)ro* and *(ɔ/o)nen*. The form *(o)ro* locates a referent as nearby and visible to the speaker (8a). The form *(ɔ/o)nen* is used for near and nonvisible referents (8b). As entities close to the speaker are generally within the speaker's visual field, the nonvisible proximal form *(ɔ/o)nen* is rare in its deictic function.

(8) a. *nə*   *riŋə=k*   *kə*   *puit* *niɨu* **oro**   *Piliuə*
         PN.ART mother=1SG RM.PST find   1SG   VIS.PROX P.
         'My mother gave birth to me here in Piliua.'

   b. *ə*   *pɛn* *si=m*   **onen**   *lə* *bi*   *si=k*
         ART pen   AL=2SG NVIS.PROX in   basket AL=1SG
         'Your pen is here in my basket (and one cannot see it).'

The medial forms indicate that the referent is at mid-distance from the speaker. Often, but not always, referents marked with a medial demonstrative are associated with the addressee. The referent might be, for instance, next to or owned by the addressee. The visible medial form is *(ɔ)tan*. Example (9a) is from a story where a boy shouts down from a tree to an evil spirit that prey is coming down to the spirit; the spirit's place is visible to the boy. The nonvisible counterpart *(ɔ)nan* is used in (9b), where a father asks his two daughters whether they are pregnant; the babies in the girls' bellies cannot be seen.

(9) a. *nən* **tan**   *ik*   *ələ*   *sii*
         3SG   VIS.MED IPFV again down
         'He is coming down there (to you) again.'

b. ə   pɔpɔ **nan**   lə ku=miai   bə?
ART baby NVIS.MED   in belly=2DU INTJ
'Is there a child in your bellies, oh?'

The distal category indicates that a referent is far from the speaker and addressee. The form *(ɔ)(t)a* typically marks a referent as far from and visible to the speaker (10a), but see the discussion below. The nonvisible counterpart is *(ɔ)(n)a*, which refers to far and invisible entities (10b). Note that the latter is rarely found with a deictic meaning anymore apart from a few fixed expressions, see below.

(10) a. *no   ua   sɔ   **ta***
26SG   RC.PST do.what   VIS.DIST
'What did you do there?'

b. *nis   **na=i**   ti   pamiɲit   i=n=ə   ləmən?*
who   NVIS.DIST=IPFV stand end.of.reef INAL=3SG=ART ocean
'Who is standing there (hardly visible) at the edge of the reef towards the ocean?'

What has been noted above reflects the prototypical exophoric use of the demonstratives. In actual language use, however, their distribution is not as clear-cut, and there is a degree of interchangeability. Visible demonstrative forms are in many cases the functionally unmarked choice, no matter whether a referent is visible or not, whereas nonvisible forms more often emphasise invisibility of a referent. Place names, for instance, are always referred to with visible forms, even when they are out of sight. In this sense, visibility seems to relate to what is known and specific and seems to be linked with non-propositional evidentiality in Tiang (cf. Aikhenvald 2004: 130, Jacques 2018: 110). In some languages, sensory perception is not limited to the time of utterance but can relate to any moment in life a speaker had previously perceived a referent (Jacques 2018: 118). Interestingly, not only places that have been visited before, but any place name combines only with visible demonstratives. This could be interpreted as an extension of personal knowledge to common knowledge.

Moreover, the visibility distinction at a non-propositional level is less prominent in the distal category than in the other distance categories: the visible *(ɔ)(t)a* has already become the default distal form in exophoric contexts in contemporary Tiang regardless of visibility. A real visibility distinction in distal demonstratives is retained only in a handful of fixed expressions, such as the minimal pair *ta kɨl* 'VIS.DIST south' and *na kɨl* 'NVIS.DIST south'. The first indicates the direction from the New Ireland mainland to Djaul Island, which can be seen from the New

Ireland west coast. The latter is the direction from New Ireland to a place beyond Djaul, for instance, the New Guinea mainland, which is out of sight from New Ireland.

Even the degree of distance seems flexible to some extent, and one comes across occasional mismatches. In (11a), there are two demonstratives, *oro* and *ta*. They both refer to the location of a group around the speaker on Djaul, but the demonstratives used here have different distance values: the first is proximal, and the second is distal, even though the location and distance have not changed. This may point to a change in emotional attitude (Section 8.4.5). In (11b), a secondary school in Kokopo in East New Britain is first marked as distal by *ta*, but in the next sentence the speaker switches to medial *tan*. The motivation behind such changes is not clear, but it might be due to a shift in perspective, with the speaker travelling closer to a place in their mind or away from it (Rebekah Drew personal communication).

(11) a. *nən   ə   to-uiaŋ   si=məm   **oro**$_i$ Tiiul   **ta**$_i$*
          3SG   PFV life-small AL=1PL.EXCL VIS.PROX   Djaul   VIS.DIST
          'This is our simple life here on Djaul (there) (said while being on Djaul).'

   b. *niiu   kə   pən **ta**$_i$ Dɔn Bɔskɔ **ta**$_i$ Kɔkɔpɔ*
       1SG   RM.PST   go   VIS.DIST   D.   B.   VIS.DIST   K.
       'I went there to Don Bosco (secondary school) there in Kokopo.'

       *niiu   kə   util   ə   masat **tan**$_i$*
       1SG   RM.PST   three ART   year   VIS.MED
       'I was three years there.'

All demonstratives also express a temporal meaning when combining with nouns referring to time, for instance, *lə pət ian oro* 'at this moment (lit. in part time VIS. PROX)' or *lə ian na mii* 'in the future (lit. in time NVIS.DIST behind)'. However, the temporal use of demonstratives is in many cases endophoric rather than exophoric, as illustrated in Section 8.4.3. Other factors that contribute to the choice of a certain distance and visibility value are the discourse structure, emotional attitude of the speaker, vagueness and emphasis. These factors will be discussed in the following sections.

8.4 Endophoric functions of Tiang demonstratives

8.4.1 Substitution anaphora

Substitution anaphors trace back to a previously mentioned noun phrase. All demonstratives in Tiang may function as substitution anaphors – however, to various degrees. The visible proximal *(o)ro* (12a), the medial forms *(ɔ)tan* (12b) and *(ɔ)nan* (12c), and the visible distal *(ɔ)(t)a* (12d) are only rarely true anaphors. They rather stress the deictic value of the referent's location, while the anaphoric sense is only of a secondary nature.

(12) a. *no=k   pa   [bile,   ə   kətə,   ə   rɔlɔk]ᵢ*
        2SG=IPFV with spear ART floater.with.rope ART rattle
        'You have a spear, a floater with a rope and a coconut rattle.'

        [ə   bul   niau   oro]ᵢ   ki   kɔuɔs   kili   bil
        ART PL   thing VIS.PROX HAB jump   on   canoe
        'These things go into the canoe.'

   b. *ner   ki   pot   [ə   talat   ə   lek]ᵢ   lə   mətə=n=ə*
        3PL   HAB drill   ART four   ART hole   in   eye=3SG=ART
        bil,   i=n=[ə   lek   ɔtan]ᵢ   [. . .]
        canoe INAL=3SG=ART hole   VIS.MED
        'They drill four holes in the upper part of the canoe so that those holes [. . .].'

   c. *ə   pa   [kəs   niau   nan]ᵢ   ik   iɔ   mən*
        PFV with other thing NVIS.MED IPFV float come
        'There is something floating there (towards us).'

        [. . .]   [ə   uir]ᵢ   [nan]ᵢ
             ART banana NVIS.MED
        '[. . .] That is a banana tree.'

   d. *nən   [a]ᵢ=k   si   ti   tɔi   [ə   pɔpɔ mət ta]ᵢ*
        3SG   DIST=IPFV FOC stand touch ART baby   die   VIS.DIST
        'She is holding that dead baby.'

        [. . .]   [pɔpɔ si=m   ta]ᵢ   ə   mət   [ta]ᵢ
             baby   AL=2SG VIS.DIST PFV die   VIS.DIST
        '[. . .] Your baby there is dead.'

On the other hand, the most frequent substitution anaphors are the nonvisible proximal *(ɔ/o)nen* and the nonvisible distal *(ɔ)(n)a*. In contrast to the demonstratives in (12), *(ɔ/o)nen* and *(ɔ)(n)a* lose their deictic meaning entirely when used as anaphoric markers and may refer to any entity regardless of its visibility and distance to the speaker.

Nonvisible proximal *(ɔ/o)nen* is more of a short-distance anaphora and marks less topical referents, such as recently introduced referents at second mention, but also minor characters and inanimates in stories. In addition, it is often found in topic–comment constructions and adds a contrasting sense (13).

(13) kəs   ian   kə   pa   [uru   minminik]ᵢ₊ⱼ
      other time   RM.PST   with   DU   animal
      'Once there were two animals.'

      lɔ   [uru   minminik   ɔnen,]ᵢ₊ⱼ   [kəs]ᵢ   ki   tɔm   lə   təs,
      but   DU   animal   NVIS.PROX   other   HAB   sit   in   sea
      lɔ   [kəs]ⱼ   ki   tɔm   lə   luntən
      but   other   HAB   sit   in   bush
      'But (as for) these two animals, one lived in the sea, and the other lived in the bush.'

Nonvisible distal *(ɔ)(n)a* is by far the most frequent anaphoric marker. Unlike *(ɔ/o)nen*, it is more of a long-distance anaphora which marks the most topical referents of a story, that is, main characters after third or fourth mention and animates that are most agentive and contribute to the course of the narrative plot. Noun phrases marked with *(ɔ)(n)a* often appear in subject position, but it may also mark less topical and inanimate referents, especially when a relative clause follows or in a topic–comment construction. Example (14) is from the same story as (13). While the narrator chose proximal *ɔnen* for the second mention of the protagonists *uru minminik* 'two animals' (13), a few sentences later the narrator referred to them by means of distal *na*, once having been established as the main characters of the story (14). Table 8.2 summarises to what degree each demonstrative can act as a substitution anaphora.

(14) [ə   bus   na]ᵢ   ki   tɔm   lə   təs   [...]
      ART DUMMY   NVIS.DIST   HAB   sit   in   sea
      'The one that was living in the sea [...].'

The use of proximal *(ɔ/o)nen* for short-distance anaphors and of distal *(ɔ)(n)a* for long-distance anaphors is an iconic reinterpretation of exophoric distance to distance

Table 8.2: Substitution anaphors in Tiang.

	VISIBLE		NONVISIBLE	
PROXIMAL	(o)ro	(✓)	(ɔ/o)nen	✓
MEDIAL	(ɔ)tan	(✓)	(ɔ)nan	(✓)
DISTAL	(ɔ)(t)a	(✓)	(ɔ)(n)a	✓
	laŋata			

Notes: ✓ primary function, (✓) secondary function or rare.

in the discourse (Greenberg 1985: 285). Also note that *(ɔ)(n)a*, as mentioned earlier, hardly ever combines with the demonstrative formative *ɔ-/o-*. Such "phonetic reduction in the change from deixis to anaphora, mirrors the loss of prominence which comes with the change from making known to the mere expression of something as already known, a change from new to old information" (Greenberg 1985: 276).

8.4.2 Substitution cataphora

Substitution cataphors point to a noun phrase that will be mentioned later. Although substitution cataphors are rare in Tiang, two demonstratives have acquired this function. The default choice for expressing a substitution cataphora is visible proximal *(o)ro* (15a). The second demonstrative is the visible distal manner adverbial *laŋata* (15b). The latter is only attested once in this function. These findings are summarised in Table 8.3.

Table 8.3: Substitution cataphors in Tiang.

	VISIBLE		NONVISIBLE
PROXIMAL	(o)ro	✓	(ɔ/o)nen
MEDIAL	(ɔ)tan		(ɔ)nan
DISTAL	(ɔ)(t)a		(ɔ)(n)a
	laŋata	(✓)	

Notes: ✓ primary function, (✓) secondary function or rare.

(15) a. *məm   ə   a=saŋ   [ə   isi=n   oro,]ᵢ   [Tiiul]ᵢ*
          1PL.EXCL PFV   CAU=arrive ART name=3SG   VIS.PROX Djaul
          'We came up with this name, Djaul.'

b. *bul   aisat   i=n=ə*   *ləulə*   [*laŋata*]ᵢ
   PL   sick   INAL=3SG=ART   taro.plant   like.VIS.DIST
   'These are the diseases of the taro.'

   [*mini,   pəkə=n=ə   ləulə   ik   sat,*
   insect.sp.   leaf=3SG=ART   taro.plant   IPFV   bad
   lɔ   gəl   ləntui=n=ə   ləulə]ᵢ
   but   unhealthy   inside=3SG=ART   taro.plant
   'Taro spoiling insects, the taro leaves become bad, and disease inside
   the taro.'

8.4.3 Textual anaphora

Textual anaphors refer back to a previously mentioned clause, sentence or a
whole stretch of text. Textual anaphors often show a temporal sequencing of two
events by summarising the first event with the construction *(lə) (pət) ian* 'at that
time/moment (lit. in part time)' followed by a demonstrative. All demonstratives
except visible proximal *(o)ro* may appear in such temporal anaphoric constructions. The degree of distance of the demonstrative may reflect temporal distance
between the two events. Nonvisible proximal *(ɔ/o)nen* is the most frequent form
in this construction and generally signals that the events take place immediately
one after another (16a), whereas a medial (16b) and distal demonstrative (16c)
rather point towards a non-immediate sequence of events, that is, some time
might have passed between the events. Medial and distal demonstratives are
rare in this context. As we see in (16a), the predicate of the preceding clause may
be repeated in the new clause, yielding a similar structure to Guérin and Aiton's
(2019: 4) "mixed linkage".

(16)   a.   [*iriai   ələ   kə   iuɔŋ   kauai   [. . .]*]ᵢ
            3DU   again   RM.PST   exit   already
            'They have also already gone outside [. . .].'

            mɔt   [lə   ian   onen]ᵢ   *iriai   ə   iuɔŋ,   nə   riŋə=riai*
            and   in   time   NVIS.PROX   3DU   PFV   exit   PN.ART   mother=3DU
            ələ   ə   iuɔŋ
            again   PFV   exit
            'And at that time (when) they went outside, their mother also went
            outside.'

b. [kə   pa   ai=lik-bin   kə   saŋ   oro   lə kuriŋ [. . .]]ᵢ
RM.PST with REC=hit-big RM.PST arrive VIS.PROX in world
'There was a big war that came here to the world [. . .].'

[lə pət ian **nan**]ᵢ   kə   pa   ai=lik-bin,   [. . .]
in part time NVIS.MED RM.PST with REC=hit-big
bul Siapan kə   ia   gin
PL Japan RM.PST CONT leave
'At that moment where there was the big war, [. . .] the Japanese had to leave.'

c. [lə-uatə   i=n=ə   səkə səŋəuli pa   pətlima, sïi
in-middle INAL=3SG=ART one ten   with five   down
si=n=ə   iuai səŋəuli,]ᵢ [pət ian **ta**]ᵢ   no riŋ
AL=3SG=ART two ten   part time VIS.DIST 2SG see
ə   tamai ə   saŋ
ART marry PFV arrive
'Between (age) 15 and 20, at that time you see the marriage take place.'

By contrast, *(lə) (pət) ian (o)ro* 'this time/moment' with the visible proximal demonstrative has exophoric reference and is not attested in an endophoric context. Visible proximal *(o)ro* may, however, be used as a textual anaphora in a non-temporal setting. In (17a), it refers anaphorically to the song that the protagonist had just sung in the previous clause. *(O)ro* occurs in this function only rarely. In a similar way, the visible distal manner adverbial *laŋata* may sum up a stretch of text such as indirect speech, or even a whole story. Example (17b) is the concluding sentence of a story as a signal that the story telling is completed.

(17) a. [(*Protagonist sings a song.*)]ᵢ
tamɔ nən kə   sik   [ə   bot   **oro**]ᵢ
now 3SG RM.PST take ART sing VIS.PROX
'Now she had sung that song.'

b. [(*Narrator tells the whole story.*)]ᵢ
ə   pini ə   saŋ   mɔt   [**laŋata**]ᵢ
ART story PFV arrive finish like.VIS.DIST
'The story came to end like that.'

Apart from the abovementioned temporal construction, visible medial *(ɔ)tan* also occurs as a clause-initial temporal, conditional or manner adverbial 'then, like that' (18). This indicates that it is grammaticalising into a conjunction.

(18) [ə   uis ik   aigɔt, i=n=ə   rip   sii   lə tɔs [...],]ᵢ
ART sun IPFV ready INAL=3SG=ART drown down in sea
[*tan*]ᵢ   ə   aten,   pɔ   miui   ok   uis
VIS.MED PFV show COMP tomorrow FUT sun
'(If) the sun is about to go down over the sea [...], this shows that it will be
sunny tomorrow.'

Also nonvisible distal *(ɔ)(n)a* may occur clause-initially after the inalienable possessive preposition *i=n=ə* 'INAL=3SG=ART'. This comes with a purposive meaning 'so
that' (19). Such clause-initial instances of *(ɔ)(n)a* are not well-attested in my corpus
(but see example 24 below for a similar case of *(ɔ)(n)a* as a noun phrase head).

(19) [ner kə   a=ti   nən kili gimit,]ᵢ   i=n=[ə   *na*]ᵢ
3PL RM.PST CAU=stand 3SG on slit.drum INAL=3SG=ART NVIS.DIST
bul mini kiri əmən   ik   ŋən nən
PL   bird REP come   IPFV eat   3SG
'They put him onto a slit drum so that the birds would come to eat him.'

A summary of the textual anaphoric use of Tiang demonstratives is given in
Table 8.4. A striking difference between substitution and textual anaphors is the
frequency of nonvisible distal *(ɔ)(n)a*. Its use as a substitution anaphora is much
more frequent than its use in textual contexts. This might relate to a preference
for using *(ɔ)(n)a* only with the most topical entities, such as major characters in
a story after the third or fourth mention, that is, after becoming the established
topic for an extended stretch of discourse (cf. examples 13 and 14 above). Textual
anaphors, in turn, do not refer to a reoccurring protagonist in a story but to a
stretch of text. Such a stretch of text will in most cases only be the topic for the
following clause, for instance, as a temporal anchoring to introduce a new event
(see example 16 above). Hence, the stretch of text will not usually be a reoccurring topic for an extended stretch of discourse. As *(ɔ)(n)a* is mostly reserved for

Table 8.4: Textual anaphors in Tiang.

	VISIBLE		NONVISIBLE	
PROXIMAL	*(o)ro*	(✓)	*(ɔ/o)nen*	✓
MEDIAL	*(ɔ)tan*	✓	*(ɔ)nan*	(✓)
DISTAL	*(ɔ)(t)a*	(✓)	*(ɔ)(n)a*	(✓)
	laŋata	✓		

Notes: ✓ primary function, (✓) secondary function or rare

marking reoccurring established topics, textual anaphors are usually expressed by other, less topical demonstratives.

8.4.4 Textual cataphora

Textual cataphors point to a clause, sentence or stretch of text that will be mentioned later. Three demonstratives have been found in this function (Table 8.5). Visible proximal *(o)ro* introduces longer and important sections of a text. As such, it is a common way of explaining the main topic of a text at the very beginning. Example (20) is the first sentence of a procedural text on how to kill sharks; *ro* refers here cataphorically to the whole text that is about to follow.

Table 8.5: Textual cataphors in Tiang.

	VISIBLE		**NONVISIBLE**	
PROXIMAL	*(o)ro*	✓	*(ɔ/o)nen*	
MEDIAL	*(ɔ)tan*		*(ɔ)nan*	
DISTAL	*(ɔ)(t)a*		*(ɔ)(n)a*	(✓)
	laŋata	✓		

Notes: ✓ primary function, (✓) secondary function or rare

(20)   [**ro**]ᵢ   ə   *pini*   *i=n=ə*   *lik*   *beu*   *lə*   *tas*   [...]ᵢ
      VIS.PROX   PFV   story   INAL=3SG=ART   hit   shark   in   sea
      'This is a story about killing sharks in the sea. [...]'

The visible distal manner adverbial *laŋata* is by far the most frequent textual cataphora. In contrast to visible proximal *(o)ro* above, *laŋata* rather introduces shorter sections of a text. It is particularly common before direct and indirect speech (21). Although optional, my Tiang teachers pointed out that using *laŋata* before direct and indirect speech was good style, that is, it is developing into a quotative marker or complementiser.

(21)   *nə*   *riŋə=riai*   *ə*   *kus*   *iriai*   [*laŋata*]ᵢ
      PN.ART   mother=3DU   PFV   tell   3DU   like.VIS.DIST
      'Their mother told them like this.'

      [*ə*   *təmə=miai*   *na*   *ə*   *lɛk*   *i=n=ə*   *luntən*]ᵢ
      ART   father=2DU   NVIS.DIST   PFV   man   INAL=3SG=ART   bush
      'Your father is a man from the bush.'

Also nonvisible distal *(ɔ)(n)a* may function as a textual cataphora (22), but this is very infrequent. It seems to be an alternative to the abovementioned *laŋata*, and also introduces only shorter stretches of text. Note that the visual meaning is bleached here.

(22) nə   ore   saŋ   kili   [lɔm~lɔmɔn **na**]ᵢ
      PN.ART   cuscus   arrive   on   INTR~think   NVIS.DIST
      'The cuscus came up with this idea.'

      [bəte, ta=k   putik bɔk   lə-uətə]ᵢ
      then   1DU.INCL=IPFV   cut   break   in-middle
      'Okay, we break it in the middle.'

8.4.5 Other meanings

Some demonstratives carry additional meanings (Table 8.6). Three demonstratives occur with a recognitional meaning. A referent that has already been introduced to the discourse may later be reactivated by means of nonvisible proximal *(ɔ/o)nen*. The father in (23a) has been mentioned several times in the story and even carried the most topical substitution anaphoric marker *(ɔ)(n)a* at one point. In the course of the story, the father lost his status as the topic. When the narrator eventually started talking about this character again, he reintroduced him with *(ɔ/o)nen*, followed by an afterthought. Visible proximal *(o)ro* occurs in the same function (23b), although much less often and with a negative overtone. Note that the deictic information of *(o)ro* in (23b) is neutralised so that it may even point to referents far away and invisible in the speech situation.

Table 8.6: Other uses of Tiang demonstratives.

	VISIBLE		NONVISIBLE	
PROXIMAL	*(o)ro*	✓	*(ɔ/o)nen*	(✓)
MEDIAL	*(ɔ)tan*		*(ɔ)nan*	(✓)
DISTAL	*(ɔ)(t)a*		*(ɔ)(n)a*	✓
	laŋata			

Notes: ✓ primary function, (✓) secondary function or rare

(23) a. [ə   təmə=miai na]ᵢ   ə   lɛk   i=n=ə   luntən
          ART   father=2DU NVIS.DIST PFV   man   INAL=3SG=ART   bush
          'Your father is a man from the bush.'

     [...] *iriai* *ik*   *tɔm* *kɔkɔ* *pa*   [*nə*   *lɛk*   **onen,**]ᵢ

          3DU IPFV sit   hide with PN.ART man   NVIS.PROX

     [*nə*   *təmə=riai*]ᵢ

     PN.ART father=3DU

     '[...] They were hiding (to see) this man, their father.'

  b. *itə* *ok* *pu*   *ən*   [*ə*   *tɛn*   **oro,**]ᵢ

      1PL FUT escape about ART woman VIS.PROX

      [*nə*   *Matɔkɔmbual*]ᵢ

      PN.ART M.

      'We will escape from this woman, Matokombual (not present at speech situation).'

The most frequent recognitional demonstrative, however, is nonvisible distal *(ɔ)(n)a*, especially when followed by *mɔ* 'only'. The form *na mɔ* can be translated as 'that one, you know' and may introduce completely new referents to the discourse that might not have been mentioned yet but are common knowledge. Often an explanation follows, as in (24). It is one of the few occasions where nonvisible distal *(ɔ)(n)a* may serve as a noun phrase head (cf. example 19 above). Recognitional and substitution anaphoric use often overlaps when the speaker reminds the addressee of a referent that has been mentioned previously (Himmelmann 1996: 236–238). Hence, it does not come as a surprise that the two most important substitution anaphors, nonvisible proximal *(ɔ/o)nen* and nonvisible distal *(ɔ)(n)a*, are also the two most common recognitional demonstratives.

(24) *nii*   [*tinpɛn*   *si=miai,* *tinpɛn*   *si=miai*]ᵢ *mɔ*

      1SG paint.tin AL=2DU paint.tin AL=2DU   only

      '(The woman living in a paint tin said) I am your paint tin, just your paint tin.'

      [**na**   *mɔ,*]ᵢ [*tinpɛn*   **na**]ᵢ   *ki*   *sua*   *guguil*

      NVIS.DIST only   paint.tin NVIS.DIST HAB hang top

      'You know, that paint tin that hangs on the top (on the wall).'

Nonvisible distal *(ɔ)(n)a* also plays an important role in putting emphasis on a noun phrase, and may add a sense of contrast or focus. This is attested for noun phrases with a nominal (25a) and pronominal head (25b). Sentence (25b) also illustrates the use of nonvisible medial *(ɔ)nan* as an emphatic demonstrative, but this is the only attested instance of *(ɔ)nan* in this function. One may wonder if the speaker chose *(ɔ)nan* to imply that the information was unpredictable (hence 'NONVISIBLE') to the addressee (hence 'MEDIAL'). This use of *(ɔ)nan* has a mirative overtone (see Aikhenvald 2021: 21 for similar examples of mirative pronouns in Jukunoid and Nakh-Daghestanian languages; also see example 27 below).

(25) a. [mətə=k **na**]$_{NP}$ ə   riip
eye=1SG   NVIS.DIST   PFV   dark
'My very eyes are blind.'

b. [niiu **na**]$_{NP}$ ua   a=pik~pik   laŋ nə   təmə=miai,
1SG   NVIS.DIST   RC.PST   CAU=INTR~turn   like   PN.ART   father=2DU
lɔ   [niiu **na**]$_{NP}$ [məsələi **nan**]$_{NP}$
but   1SG   NVIS.DIST   spirit   NVIS.MED
'I turned into your father, but I am this very spirit.'

In its role as an emphatic demonstrative, (ɔ)(n)a may follow other demontratives: attested combinations are (o)ro na 'VIS.PROX NVIS.DIST' (26a), (ɔ/o)nen na 'NVIS. PROX NVIS.DIST' (26b) and (ɔ)tan na 'VIS.MED NVIS.DIST' (26c). While the first demonstrative in such a double demonstrative construction is generally deictic and exophoric, (ɔ)(n)a as the second demonstrative adds emphasis and often marks anaphoricity. Similar double demonstrative constructions are documented in Manambu (Ndu), Murui (Witotoan), Mavea (Oceanic) and Djambarrpuyŋu (Pama-Nyungan) (Aikhenvald 2015b: 27–30). In Tiang, they are not very frequent.

(26) a. [uir   si=k   **oro**   **na**]$_{NP}$ ə   mɛŋ
banana   AL=1SG   VIS.PROX   NVIS.DIST   PFV   dry
'My banana tree here is dry.'

b. [lɛk   **ɔnen**   **na,**]$_{NP}$ nən   ə   lɛk   məsələi
man   NVIS.PROX   NVIS.DIST   3SG   PFV   man   spirit
'This man, he was a spirit man.'

c. [tɛn   **tan**   **na,**]$_{NP}$ nən   ua   rərautə   mɔt   kup
woman   VIS.MED   NVIS.DIST   3SG   RC.PST   mourn   and   shout
'That woman, she was crying and shouting.'

Visible proximal (o)ro sometimes has emotional overtones of surprise or anger of the speaker (cf. the mirative use of (ɔ)nan in example 25b above). In its emotional meaning, (o)ro – much like nonvisible distal (ɔ)(n)a above – may modify a noun phrase with a nominal (27a) or pronominal (27b) head. However, it is not easy to draw the line between emotional attitude and emphasis. As in (23b) above, (o)ro loses its deictic function here and may accompany referents of any distance and visibility value.

(27) a.   *əi,*   [*ə*   *u=lek*   **oro**]_{NP}   *ua*   *bit*   *niiu?*
      INTJ   ART   DU=man   VIS.PROX   RC.PST   trick   1SG
      'Hey, did these two boys (not present at speech situation) trick me?'

    b.   [*no*   **ro**   *mɔ*]_{NP}   *ki*   *uin*   *nə*   *papoi*   *si=mai*
      2SG   VIS.PROX   only   HAB   hide   PN.ART   dad   AL=1DU.EXCL
      'Only you here used to hide our Dad.'

Nonvisible forms have a tendency towards expressing vagueness. This is particularly true for nonvisible medial *(ɔ)nan*, which may show uncertainty of the speaker. As such, it can be found in indefinite contexts or in questions (28).

(28)   [*sa*   *lɛk*   *tauən*   **ɔnan**]_{NP}   *ki*   *mən*   *ki*   *mətəi*   *kuuil*
      what   man   male   NVIS.MED   HAB   come   HAB   sleep   together
      pa   *imiai?*
      with   2DU
      'What man used to come and sleep with you?'

8.5 Demonstratives and text genres

This section investigates the correlations between the text genre and the choice of demonstratives. The focus is on four types of texts: 1) traditional narrative texts such as legends (10 texts), 2) non-traditional narrative texts such as accounts of real events, biographies and history (9 texts), 3) procedural texts (5 texts), and 4) shorter, more ritualised genres such as riddles and songs (16 texts). Spontaneous speech is excluded here, because data on this genre is very limited at this stage.

8.5.1 Traditional narrative texts

The most striking difference between traditional stories and other genres is their extremely frequent use of nonvisible distal *(ɔ)(n)a* and nonvisible proximal *(ɔ/o)nen* as substitution anaphors. This results from the fact that protagonists in traditional stories often do not have names but are called by their gender and age. To keep track of a reoccurring and topical nameless character, the narrator would in many instances add *(ɔ)(n)a* or, less frequently add *(ɔ/o)nen*, to the respective noun phrase.

No substitution cataphors occurred. Textual cataphors, in contrast, are very frequent. The most frequent textual cataphora is the visible distal manner adverbial *laŋata* to introduce direct and indirect speech, which have a particularly high occurrence rate in this genre. Visible proximal *(o)ro*, in turn, is less frequent in this function here. The preferred form for textual anaphors is nonvisible proximal *(ɔ/o)nen* and, to a lesser degree, the visible distal manner adverbial *laŋata* and nonvisible distal *(ɔ)(n)a*.

Also different to other genres, traditional stories display a more frequent use of nonvisible distal *(ɔ)(n)a* and visible proximal *(o)ro* as emotional and emphatic demonstratives. As a result, traditional stories also are the genre with the greatest diversity of double demonstratives (see example 26 above). This relates to traditional stories being a rather emotional and lively genre. Exophoric demonstratives are very frequent in direct speech, but rarely found outside of direct speech.

8.5.2 Non-traditional narrative texts

Compared to traditional texts, non-traditional stories such as biographies and narrations on real-life or historic events display fewer instances of substitution anaphors. In the cases where substitution anaphors are found, it is generally nonvisible proximal *(ɔ/o)nen* rather than nonvisible distal *(ɔ)(n)a*. The reason for the lower occurrence of substitution anaphors in this genre is that characters are usually known by name, which facilitates keeping track of the referents and makes further marking with a demonstrative unnecessary. As mentioned in Section 8.2, noun phrases with a proper name of an animate referent do not take demonstratives.

In other endophoric functions, non-traditional texts show a tendency for employing proximal and medial forms more often than do traditional texts. Substitution cataphors may be expressed by visible proximal *(o)ro*. Although textual cataphors are still commonly expressed by the visible distal manner adverbial *laŋata*, visible proximal *(o)ro* is more prominent in this function than in traditional texts. Textual cataphors fulfil a different function in non-traditional genres: rather than introducing direct or indirect speech, they more commonly introduce explanations in the style of 'it is done like this' and 'it is because of this'. The most frequent textual anaphors are nonvisible proximal *(ɔ/o)nen* and visible medial *(ɔ)tan*. This stronger reliance on proximal and medial forms in endophoric contexts seems to correspond to the more educational character of this genre. This way, the message behind a historical description or a personal life story is more immediate to the addressee than it would be with a distal demonstrative.

Emotional and emphatic use of demonstratives is almost absent in this genre, which points towards a more neutral narrative style. Double demonstratives as in (26) are rare. Recognitional *(ɔ)(n)a (mɔ)* as in (24) does occur in accounts of historical events to add explanations and clarification of certain terms. As there is not much direct speech, exophoric demonstratives occur in the narrative itself to reveal where and how far from the actual speech situation an event took place. In this context also, visible demonstratives may acquire an anaphoric function, that is, they refer back to a previously mentioned place, while retaining their deictic value.

8.5.3 Procedural texts

Like non-traditional narrative texts, procedural texts also do not feature as many nonvisible demonstratives as does the traditional genre. Nonvisible distal *(ɔ)(n)a* and nonvisible proximal *(ɔ/o)nen* are rarely substitution anaphors in procedural descriptions because of the absence of topical protagonists in this genre. Also, two visible demonstratives were found as substitution anaphors: visible proximal *(o)ro* and visible medial *(ɔ)tan*. In contrast to their behaviour in other genres, these two demonstratives do not simply refer to previously mentioned places, but instead lose their deictic meaning here and point to previously mentioned items without any deictic reference.

As in non-traditional narratives, procedural texts also exhibit instances of both substitution and textual cataphors. Textual cataphors with visible proximal *(o)ro* are particularly frequent at the beginning of a text where they function as a heading 'this is the way of doing X', although the visible distal manner adverbial *laŋata* is still the most frequent textual cataphora. Textual anaphors in most cases involve visible medial *(ɔ)tan* in temporal or conditional clauses 'when X then Y', although overall, textual anaphors are infrequent in these genres. More commonly, instructional steps in separate clauses are simply linked by the conjunctions *te* 'then' and *lə minə* 'afterwards', which gives this genre a more list-like character.

Overall, as in non-traditional narrative texts, we see a preference for visible demonstratives of a proximal and medial distance in endophoric contexts. As an educational and instructional genre, the use of visible proximal and medial demonstratives might be intended to draw the instructions closer to the address-ee's attention and make them more visual. Also, when introducing a psychologi-cal perspective, "an increasing preference for 'proximal' demonstrative anaphors is found when speakers feel more responsible themselves for the produced dis-course," due to "an assumed primordial psychological proximity between speaker and topic in the context of an addressee to which the topic (and as such, the mentioned referents) are assumed to be psychologically more distant" (Peeters, Krahmer and Maes 2020: 13–14).

The emphatic and emotional use of demonstratives is almost absent, and so are double demonstratives. This does not come as a surprise, as procedural descriptions are an educational and rather unemotional genre. Exophoric demonstratives are few in this genre.

8.5.4 Ritualised genres

The riddles and songs in my corpus contain almost no demonstratives. The few instances of demonstratives that exist are generally exophoric and of a proximal or distal degree; no medial forms occurred. Endophoric uses are basically absent, with only one instance of nonvisible proximal *(ɔ/o)nen* as a substitution anaphora. Riddles and songs are short and formulaic genres with hardly any recurrent referent that would need to be traced back in the discourse.

8.6 Summary of Tiang demonstratives

Table 8.7 summarises the exophoric and endophoric functions of Tiang demonstratives. Visible proximal *(o)ro*, visible medial *(ɔ)tan*, nonvisible medial *(ɔ)nan* and visible distal *(ɔ)(t)a* are primarily exophoric. Even when used anaphorically, their deictic information is still dominant and used to point to and locate a referent in the real world. Visible proximal *(o)ro*, however, has also developed into a cataphoric marker in both substitution and textual contexts, and may carry emotional overtones. Visible medial *(ɔ)tan* is also a frequent textual anaphora. Another exception is the fused visible distal manner adverbial *laŋata*, which has only endophoric functions; it is primarily a textual cataphora, but occasionally functions as a textual anaphora. This correlates with Diessel's (1999: 104) observation that "[m]anner demonstratives are frequently used as discourse deictics".

The most important endophoric demonstratives are nonvisible proximal *(ɔ/o)nen* and nonvisible distal *(ɔ)(n)a*, which rarely occur in exophoric contexts. They are the most frequent substitution anaphors. Proximal *(ɔ/o)nen* is also a frequent textual anaphora, and distal *(ɔ)(n)a* may express emphasis.

Contrary to what is reported for many other languages, there is no clear connection between the degree of distance and the endophoric function of a demonstrative in Tiang. Both proximal and distal forms are frequently employed in both anaphoric and cataphoric contexts. Instead, the data reveal a strong connection between the discourse function and the visibility value of a demonstrative. Two tendencies can be observed:

Table 8.7: Functions of Tiang demonstratives.

			exophoric	substitution		textual		Other
				anaphora	cataphora	anaphora	cataphora	
VIS	**PROX**	*(o)ro*	✓	(✓)	✓	(✓)	✓	✓
	MED	*(ɔ)tan*	✓	(✓)		✓		
	DIST	*(ɔ)(t)a*	✓	(✓)		(✓)		
		laŋata			(✓)	✓	✓	
NVIS	**PROX**	*(ɔ/o)nen*	(✓)	✓		✓		(✓)
	MED	*(ɔ)nan*	✓	(✓)		(✓)		(✓)
	DIST	*(ɔ)(n)a*	(✓)	✓		(✓)	(✓)	✓

Notes: ✓ primary function, (✓) secondary function or rare

Tendency 1

Visible demonstratives tend to be exophoric. Nonvisible forms tend to be endophoric.

Tendency 2

Nonvisible forms are the preferred choice for anaphors. Cataphors tend to be expressed by visible demonstratives.

The following section will demonstrate that these tendencies are not just a curiosity of Tiang. The connection between visibility and the discourse function is found in a wide array of unrelated languages in many parts of the world.

8.7 Discourse use of 'visible' and 'nonvisible' demonstratives cross-linguistically

The distinction between visible and nonvisible demonstratives is not a common feature typologically. Where it occurs, it is generally an inherited feature of related languages or an areal feature acquired through language contact. A prominent example of the latter is the Northwest Coast Sprachbund of North America (Beck 2000: 182–183). As seen in the previous section, the visibility value has a significant influence on the discourse function of demonstratives in Tiang. This section investigates this correlation in a sample of 22 languages.[2]

---

2 The discourse functions of demonstratives are notoriously understudied in many languages, which severely complicated the compilation of a balanced sample. With the help of grammati-

The data is organised in three tables: Table 8.8 lists the languages that show a strong correlation between visibility and the discourse function of demonstratives. The languages in Table 8.9 show a weaker correlation between these factors, and the ones in Table 8.10 do not show the correlation. Only such demonstratives were included that can occur in both exophoric and endophoric contexts. Purely endophoric demonstratives, such as 'ANAPHORIC' or 'CATAPHORIC' markers, are not included. Demonstratives are labelled after the terminology used by the authors, occasionally shortened to fit the dimensions of the tables.

Table 8.8 lists 13 languages. They all have in common a strong preference for nonvisible demonstratives as either the primary or the only means to express anaphors, both in a substitution and textual context. Although visible forms do sometimes occur anaphorically, they are less frequent here and often retain their original deictic meaning. Visible forms, in turn, are the preferred marker for cataphors. Nonvisible forms are not only much rarer in the latter function; in the category of substitution cataphors, they are entirely absent. If known, the most frequent demonstrative in a certain function is highlighted in bold.

Table 8.8: 'Nonvisible' as a primary anaphoric demonstrative.[3]

Language	Substitution		Textual	
	Anaphora	Cataphora	Anaphora	Cataphora
Classical K'ich'e (Mayan)	not visible			near speaker
Darma (Tibeto-Burman)	proximate; medial; (distal); **non-visible**		proximate; medial; **non-visible**	
Epena Pedee (Chocoan)	that there; **this/that invisible**		that there; this/that invisible	this here; this/that invisible

cal descriptions, personal communications and my own original analyses of published glossed texts, enough data was found to have a good understanding of demonstrative functions in the 22 languages. The findings are supplemented by data from 18 additional languages, on which data is more limited.

3 Sources: **Classical K'iche'** (Dürr 2003: 68–69, Michael Dürr personal communication); **Darma** (Willis 2007: 208, 213, 227, 537–575, Willis Oko 2015: 33–34); **Epena Pedee** (Harms 1994: 45, 62–63, 179–182); **Kham** (Watters 2004: 167, 418–441); **Khasi** (Rabel 1961: 67, 148–248); **Kunimaipa** (Geary 1985 [1977]: 32, 57, 72–73, 251–270); **Mantauran Rukai** (Zeitoun 2007: 302–303, 491–524); **Muna** (van den Berg 1989: 90–96, van den Berg 1997: 199, René van den Berg personal communication); **Sinhala** (Chandralal 2007: 8, 13–18, Kano 2000: 60, 62); **Tiang** (own data); **Ticuna** (Skilton 2019: 16, 221); **Tümpisa Shoshone** (Dayley 1989: 135–136, 448–503); **Umbeyajts** (Salminen 2016: 94–97, 157).

Table 8.8 (continued)

Language	Substitution		Textual	
	Anaphora	Cataphora	Anaphora	Cataphora
Kham (Tibeto-Burman)	(proximate); distal visible; **remote invisible**		(proximate); (distal visible); **remote invisible**	
Khasi (Austroasiatic)	this known near visible; (that near addressee); (that at distance in sight); **at distance out of sight**		this known near visible; (that near addressee); **at distance out of sight**	this known near visible
Kunimaipa (Goilalan)	(this seen); that unseen		that unseen	this seen; that unseen
Mantauran Rukai (Formosan)	(near speaker); neutral; **invisible far**		(near speaker); near hearer; neutral; invisible far	near speaker; (near hearer)
Muna (Malayo-Polynesian)	near speaker; (near hearer); away from both near; invisible	near speaker	near hearer; away from both near; invisible	near speaker
Sinhala (Indo-Aryan)	speaker-proximate; addressee-proximate; distal/visible; **distal/non-situational**		speaker-proximate; addressee-proximate; distal/visible; distal/non-situational	speaker-proximate
Tiang (Oceanic)	(visible proximal); (visible medial); (visible distal); nonvisible proximal; (nonvisible medial); **nonvisible distal**	visible proximal; (visible distal)	(visible proximal); visible medial; visible distal; nonvisible proximal; (nonvisible medial); (nonvisible distal)	visible proximal; **visible distal;** (nonvisible distal)
Ticuna (Ticuna-Yuri)	near addressee/invisible		near addressee/invisible	near speaker
Tümpisa Shoshone (Uto-Aztecan)	this right here; this here nearby; that there visible; **that there not visible;** this/that here/there		(this right here); (this here nearby); that there visible; **that there not visible**	this right here; (this here nearby); (that there not visible)
Umbeyajts (Huavean)	(proximal); medial/not visible; (distal)		medial/not visible	

Further evidence comes from nine other languages (not in Table 8.8). In Panare (Cariban) and Ute (Uto-Aztecan), nonvisible demonstratives are reported as the primary anaphoric markers (Payne and Payne 2013: 86–87, Givón 2011: 162). Other descriptions give more subtle hints about the anaphoric nature of nonvisible demonstratives. Launey (2003: 100–101) describes the nonvisible demonstrative *inere* in Palikur (Arawak) as a form that "*renvoie à quelque chose dont il a été question, mais qui n'apparaît pas ou plus dans la situation* [refers to something that is discussed but does not or not anymore appear in the speech situation]", while Green et al. (2018: 166) translate it as 'that (already mentioned)'. Similarly, the demonstrative *ñoó/ñóó* in Tezoatlán Mixtec (Otomanguean) is translated as 'that (not visible; referring to a place, a person or a thing already mentioned or known)' (Ferguson de Williams 2007: 35), and the Woleaian (Oceanic) *we* does not only mean 'that (unseen)' but also 'that we are talking about' (Sohn 1975: 83). Such translations unmistakably point to a prominent anaphoric function.

Two other languages show that nonvisible demonstratives are a source of textual anaphors. In Alacatlatzala Mixtec (Otomanguean), the adverbial *ñakán* 'therefore, so' derives from the nonvisible form *kán* 'there (not visible)' (Zylstra 2012: 74, 191). In Ulithian (Oceanic), *laa* 'near hearer' and *wee* 'away from both, invisible' are the source of several sentence adverbials (Sohn and Bender 1980 [1973]: 99).

In other languages, we find an even more deep-rooted conflation of nonvisibility and anaphoricity. Nêlêmwa (Oceanic) and Murui (Witotoan) are a case in point. Nêlêmwa has the endophoric demonstratives *eli* 'known to the speaker (anaphoric in discourse)' and *bai* 'known to the speech act participants (anaphoric in terms of common knowledge)' (Bril 2002: 277). But as the exophoric demonstratives are only used for visible referents in Nêlêmwa, the endophoric forms *eli* and *bai* must be employed to talk about invisible referents (Isabelle Bril personal communication). Murui distinguishes two types of demonstratives: 'perceivable' and 'non-perceivable'. Although all demonstratives may be anaphoric, the non-perceivable forms never have a spatial reference (Wojtylak 2017: 161, 164). Apart from that, also Lange (2017: 13) writes that in many Hindukush Indo-Aryan languages, "[t]here are indications that the invisible term is restricted to use in anaphoric contexts, or with accessible referents".

Table 8.9 shows six languages with a less dominant use of nonvisible demonstratives as anaphoric markers. Nonvisible forms still function as anaphors in these languages, but only to a lesser extent than do some of the visible counterparts. This often coincides with a general rarity of nonvisible forms in the overall language use. In Gawri (a.k.a. Kalam; Indo-Aryan), for instance, "[t]he not-visible demonstrative adjective [. . .] is not as rare as the distant demonstrative adjectives. However, it is still rare compared with the visible-nearest demonstrative adjective" (Lothers 1996: 92). Nevertheless, in the cases where the nonvisible demonstrative is documented, it is very often anaphoric (Lange 2017: 47). Visible demonstratives are again the dominant forms for cataphors in the languages of Table 8.9.

Table 8.9: 'Nonvisible' as a secondary anaphoric demonstrative.[4]

Language	Substitution		Textual	
	Anaphora	Cataphora	Anaphora	Cataphora
Crow (Siouan)	proximate near speaker; medial near addressee; (remote out of sight)		medial near addressee; distal	proximate near speaker
Gawri (Indo-Aryan)	**visible-nearest;** (visible-near); (visible-far); (visible-farthest); not-visible		visible-nearest	visible-nearest
Kokota (Oceanic)	touching; within reach; **nearby;** potentially visible; not visible		(touching); nearby	
Malecite- **Passamaquoddy** (Algonquian)	near speaker non-ABS; near addressee non-ABS; (away from both non-ABS); (near speaker ABS); (near addressee ABS); (away from both ABS)		near speaker non-ABS; **near addressee non-ABS;** near addressee ABS; away from both ABS	near speaker non-ABS
Nivkh (isolate)	**close visible/non-proximal;** invisible		non-proximal	non-proximal
West Greenlandic (Eskimo-Aleut)	this here; **that/this;** that yonder; that way down there; that down there; that way up there; that up there; that in/out there; that outside the house; that in the north; that in the south; **(that out of sight)**			that/this; (that out of sight)

There are other factors which contribute to the lower frequency of nonvisible demonstratives in these languages. In Malecite-Passamaquoddy (Algonquian), absentative demonstratives may point back to a previously mentioned referent

4 Sources: **Crow** (Graczyk 2007: 70–74, 87, Randolph Graczyk personal communication); **Gawri** (Lothers 1996: 88–92); **Kokota** (Palmer 2009: 73, 77, 395–396, Bill Palmer personal communication); **Malecite-Passamaquoddy** (Ng 2002: 151, 168, 187, 190, 219); **Nivkh** (Gruzdeva 2020: 15–18, 31, 40, 42); **West Greenlandic** (Fortescue 1984: 142–143, 254, 261–262, Berge 1997: 79).

(Ng 2002: 168). However, "[t]he absentative is used to indicate the absence of a referent which had recently been present; a former status of ownership of something; and for human referents, absentative marking is often used to indicate whether the person is alive or deceased" (Ng 2002: 15). When the absentative forms indicate only literally absent or dead people, it is clear that only the non-absentative forms have the potential of becoming the unmarked choice for anaphors. Moreover, the absentative forms are longer and hence even segmentally more marked than non-absentative forms (Ng 2002: 94).

Nivkh (isolate) has a rich demonstrative system with many different paradigms for various syntactic functions. Visibility, however, is distinguished only in a small subset of the paradigms (Gruzdeva 2020: 5), making it appear a minor category in the grammatical system of the language.

West Greenlandic (Eskimo-Aleut) has one nonvisible demonstrative *inna*, which is archaic and rarely used today (Fortescue 1984: 261). All demonstratives have special anaphoric forms. The anaphoric form for nonvisible *inna* is *taanna*. Interestingly, *taanna* also happens to be the anaphoric form of *una* 'that/this', the most frequent demonstrative in West Greenlandic (Fortescue 1984: 261–262). Due to this syncretism, the nonvisible demonstrative is arguably less archaic and rare than Fortescue (1984) suggested. One also wonders to what degree the syncretism is motivated by the anaphoric potential of the nonvisible demonstrative.

Similar patterns are found in four other languages (not in Table 8.9), for which less material is available. Although all demonstratives in Takivatan Bunun (Formosan) may be used anaphorically, their primary function is still to indicate distance and visibility. This means that "a visual singular distal demonstrative *aipa* refers to a deer being present in the distance, and its nonvisual equivalent *naipa* to it having run away. The visibility contrast and the distance contrast encoded in these demonstratives clearly represent observable situational functions. In addition, however, these demonstratives function as phoric markers" (de Busser 2017: 113).

Like Nivkh, Mangap-Mbula (Oceanic) has different sets of demonstratives, several of which can be anaphoric, but only one set features the nonvisible demonstrative *tana* (Bugenhagen 1995: 110, 156, 338). Again, the visibility distinction plays only a minor role in the language.

Two other languages where nonvisible forms only act as secondary anaphoric markers are Paiwan (Formosan) and Adzera (Oceanic). They differ from other languages in the sample in one crucial point: they distinguish visibility in terms of visible forms and visibility-neutral forms, which can be either visible or nonvisible, but they do not have truly nonvisible forms (Chang 2006: 105, Holzknecht 1986: 110). Their preference for visible forms (Chang 2006: 431–472, Holzknecht 1986: 110) is intriguing, but may be motivated by this unconventional visibility distinction.

Table 8.10 lists three languages with a visibility distinction in demonstratives, for which nonvisible demonstratives are not reported as anaphors. All anaphoric and cataphoric functions are expressed by visible demonstratives.

Table 8.10: 'Nonvisible' without any anaphoric function.[5]

Language	Substitution		Textual	
	Anaphora	**Cataphora**	**Anaphora**	**Cataphora**
Blackfoot (Algonquian)	(proximal); medial; **distal**		medial	
Pilagá (Guaicuruan)	proximal; **medial visible;** (distal visible)		proximal; medial visible	medial visible
Santali (Austroasiatic)	this; that near		that near	this

Again, several factors contribute to the scarcity of nonvisible forms in discourse. In Blackfoot (Algonquian), invisibility is indicated by the suffix -*hka* on the demonstrative. However, "the use of -*hka* is largely restricted to a few fossilized forms" (Schupbach 2013: 69). This makes it a similar case to Malecite-Passamaquoddy: invisible forms are segmentally longer and morphologically more complex than visible forms, from which they derive. This may explain why the less marked visible demonstratives are the choice for discourse use. In Pilagá (Guaicuruan), the nonvisible demonstrative *maʕa* denotes that the referent is inferred or uncertain (Payne and Vidal 2020: 153), which makes it a less suitable candidate for referent tracking. In addition, Santali (Austroasiatic) distinguishes visibility only in one special subsystem of demonstratives, which derive from visible demonstratives of another subsystem (Neukom 2001: 42–43), making it a secondary and marked category in the language.

Five other languages (not in Table 8.10) with limited data available also seem to not allow for nonvisible anaphoric demonstratives. In most cases, there are similar reasons to the ones we have seen above why nonvisible demonstratives appear less suitable as the default anaphoric form. In Malagasy (Malayo-Polynesian) and Bena Bena (Nuclear Trans New Guinea), nonvisible forms are derived from and hence are morphologically more marked than visible demonstratives (Rasoloson and Rubino 2005: 471–472, Emkow forthcoming). In Leti (Malayo-Poly-

5 Sources: **Blackfoot** (Schupbach 2013: 83–87); **Pilagá** (Payne and Vidal 2020: 166–169, 178); **Santali** (Neukom 2001: 40–45).

nesian), visibility is only a secondary category found in one subset of demonstratives (van Engelenhoven and Williams-van Klinken 2005: 759). The two nonvisible demonstratives in Iloko (a.k.a. Ilocano; Malayo-Polynesian) often encode nonexistence or death of a referent (Rubino 1997: 45, 47), similar to what we saw in Malecite-Passamaquoddy, making them unlikely candidates for anaphoric reference. Also for Hua (Nuclear Trans New Guinea), no nonvisible anaphors are reported (John Haiman, personal communication); this may be due to the existence of two exclusively anaphoric demonstratives in the language (Haiman 1980: 258), making another anaphoric demonstrative superfluous.

Altogether, we see a strong tendency towards favouring the use of nonvisible demonstratives in anaphoric contexts. In roughly three quarters of the languages of the sample, nonvisible demonstratives are reported in anaphoric function. In half of the languages of the sample, nonvisible forms are the dominant or even the only means of expressing anaphors. Nonvisible anaphors are absent in less than a quarter of the languages. Yet, all languages with an aversion to nonvisible forms show recurring patterns. Nonvisible forms are less likely to become default anaphoric markers when 1) they are morphologically more complex and segmentally longer than visible forms; 2) they have negative connotations such as implying a deceased referent; 3) demonstratives do not neutralise the distance and visibility value in anaphoric contexts; 4) they are a minor category that appears only in a few subsets of the demonstrative system; and 5) there are already exclusively anaphoric demonstratives in the language.

These findings hold for both substitution and textual anaphors, which in many cases behave quite homogenously. Anaphors generally have the widest range of possible demonstratives, and one may encounter proximal, medial and distal forms in this function. Cataphors, in turn, are almost exclusively represented by visible demonstratives, especially proximal forms. Substitution cataphors are rarely attested.

This corroborates the predictions made in the previous section on Tiang. Nonvisible forms are likely to develop into anaphoric markers, while cataphors are more commonly expressed by visible demonstratives (Tendency 2). Moreover, many languages in the sample show that nonvisible forms have a higher likelihood to occur in endophoric rather than exophoric contexts (Tendency 1). This is explicitly documented in Muna (van den Berg 1989: 90), Kham (Watters 2004: 167), Sinhala (Chandralal 2007: 6), Woleaian (Sohn 1975: 186), Murui (Wojtylak 2017: 161, 164), Nêlêmwa (Bril 2002: 277, Isabelle Bril personal communication) and Hindukush Indo-Aryan languages (Lange 2017: 13). My own corpus analyses of Darma (Willis 2007: 537–575), Khasi (Rabel 1961: 148–248), Paiwan (Chang 2006: 431–472), Rukai (Zeitoun 2007: 491–524) and Tümpisa Shoshone (Dayley 1989: 448–503) concluded with the same observation.

8.8 Discussion

Tiang demonstratives play an important role in discourse. When exophoric, they encode a referent's distance from and visibility to the speaker in the speech situation. In endophoric settings, they act as substitution and textual anaphors and cataphors to draw the attention to a certain entity in the discourse, and furthermore tell us about the emotional attitude of the speaker, or signal emphasis or uncertainty. As textual anaphors and cataphors, they may signal the beginning and ending of a narration, as well as summarise and link successive events. Distal demonstratives have a particularly high degree of grammaticalisation into clause-linking morphemes. Nonvisible distal *(ɔ)(n)a* often marks relative clauses, and the visible distal manner adverbial *laŋata* is developing into a quotative marker. Visible medial *(ɔ)tan* also has a clause-linking function as a temporal or conditional conjunction 'then'.

There is a somewhat iconic correlation between the genre of a text and the grammatical devices in use: educational genres, such as historical narrations and procedural texts, have a higher frequency of proximal and medial forms than other genres. This matches Peeters, Krahmer and Maes' (2020: 13) observation that "the proportion of use of a given demonstrative form [. . .] seems to vary strongly as a function of text or discourse genre". In their corpus, proximal forms were more frequent in scientific literature than in other genres, because the topic of an educational text is psychologically closer to the speaker than to the addressee (Peeters, Krahmer and Maes 2020: 14).

The most exciting finding is the correlation between the visibility value of demonstratives and their discourse function. Two tendencies are present in a wide array of unrelated languages:

Tendency 1
Visible demonstratives tend to be exophoric. Nonvisible forms tend to be endophoric.

Tendency 2
Nonvisible forms are the preferred choice for anaphors. Cataphors tend to be expressed by visible demonstratives.

The relationship between nonvisibility and anaphoricity can be explained by the distance and visibility of a referent in the actual speech situation. According to Lange (2017: 47), "[t]he fact that the invisible term in particular is prone to anaphoric use [in Gawri] may be explained by the fact that interlocutors are prone to talk about people that are not present at the moment, events that happened in the past or will happen in the future, and things they have seen in other locations". Also the distance of a referent to its previous mention in the discourse plays a role. In Nivkh, "[t]he immediate anaphor is located in the vicinity of its antecedent and is therefore visible to it, whereas the delayed anaphor is distant from its antecedent and hidden [i.e., invisible] from it by the text" (Gruzdeva 2020: 56). In this sense, nonvisible demonstratives can be understood as a semantic extension of distal forms, which in the literature are commonly cited as the most frequent anaphoric forms (Section 8.1). As Greenberg (1985: 282) puts it, "the distance demonstrative is easily extended to that which is absent as in narrative, or present but not visible as far distant or behind the speaker. It is therefore the natural candidate for the expression of that which was previously mentioned which will in most cases not be in the actual speech situation".

Visible demonstratives, in turn, and especially proximal forms, are the preferred choice for cataphors. Comparing cataphors with short-distance anaphors, Greenberg (1985: 284) argues that "it is the mere proximity in discourse that is involved since a demonstrative which immediately follows will probably be a nearer demonstrative also. It would seem natural immediately after an enumeration of names to refer to them by a near demonstrative". Himmelmann (1996: 221) goes even further and analyses certain cataphoric constructions as exophoric, with cataphoric demonstratives deictically pointing to the immediately following words. Mosel (2004: 172) understands proximity of cataphors as a metaphor: "what the speaker says is something he gives to the addressee. [. . .] When he refers to something he is going to talk about, he refers to what he has not given yet to the addressee, i.e. something he still has himself".

To end this chapter with the words of a Tiang storyteller, using the visible distal manner adverbial *laŋata* as a textual anaphora:

(29) *pini   si=rə   tamɔ   saŋ   mɔt   laŋata*
     story   AL=1PL.INCL   now   arrive finish like.VIS.DIST
     'Our story now comes to end like that.'

Abbreviations

1	first person
2	second person
3	third person
ABS	absentative
AL	alienable possession
ART	article

CAU	causative
COMP	complementiser
CONT	continuous
DIST	distal
DU	dual
DUMMY	anaphoric dummy noun
EXCL	exclusive
FOC	focus
FUT	future
HAB	habitual
INAL	inalienable possession
INCL	inclusive
INTJ	interjection
INTR	intransitive
IPFV	imperfective
MED	medial
NVIS	nonvisible
PFV	perfective
PL	plural
PN	personal noun
PROX	proximal
PST	past
RC	recent
REC	reciprocal
REP	repetitive
RM	remote
SG	singular
sp.	species
VIS	visible

References

Aikhenvald, Alexandra Y. 2004. *Evidentiality*. Oxford: Oxford University Press.

Aikhenvald, Alexandra Y. 2015a. *The art of grammar: A practical guide*. Oxford: Oxford University Press.

Aikhenvald, Alexandra Y. 2015b. Distance, direction, and relevance: How to choose and use a demonstrative in Manambu. *Anthropological Linguistics* 57 (1). 1–45.

Aikhenvald, Alexandra Y. 2021. *The web of knowledge: Evidentiality at the cross-roads*. Leiden: Brill.

Anderson, Stephen R. & Edward L. Keenan. 1985. Deixis. In Timothy Shopen (ed.), *Language typology and syntactic description III: Grammatical categories and the lexicon*, 259–308. Cambridge: Cambridge University Press.

Beck, David. 2000. Grammatical convergence and the genesis of diversity in the Northwest Coast Sprachbund. *Anthropological Linguistics* 42 (2). 147–213.

Berg, René van den. 1989. *A grammar of the Muna language*. Dordrecht: Foris Publications.
Berg, René van den. 1997. Spatial deixis in Muna (Sulawesi). In Gunter Senft (ed.), *Referring to space: Studies in Austronesian and Papuan languages*, 197–220. Oxford: Clarendon Press.
Berge, Anna M. S. 1997. *Topic and discourse structure in West Greenlandic agreement constructions*. Berkeley: University of California dissertation.
Bril, Isabelle. 2002. *Le nêlêmwa (Nouvele-Calédonie): Analyse syntaxique et sémantique*. Paris: Peeters.
Bugenhagen, Robert D. 1995. *A grammar of Mangap-Mbula: An Austronesian language of Papua New Guinea*. Canberra: Pacific Linguistics.
Busser, Rik de. 2017. Spatial deixis, textual cohesion, and functional differentiation in Takivatan Bunun. *Oceanic Linguistics* 56 (1). 90–122.
Chandralal, Dileep. 2007. Demonstratives and deixis in Sinhala. *Kobe papers in linguistics* 5 (1). 1–20.
Chang, Anna Hsiou-chuan. 2006. *A reference grammar of Paiwan*. Canberra: Australian National University dissertation.
Cleary-Kemp, Jessica. 2007. Universal uses of demonstratives: Evidence from four Malayo-Polynesian languages. *Oceanic Linguistics* 46 (2). 325–347.
Dayley, Jon P. 1989. *Tümpisa (Panamint) Shoshone grammar*. Berkeley: University of California Press.
Diessel, Holger. 1999. *Demonstratives: Form, function, and grammaticalization*. Amsterdam & Philadelphia: John Benjamins.
Diessel, Holger & Merlijn Breunesse. 2020. A typology of demonstrative clause linkers. In Åshild Næss, Anna Margetts & Yvonne Treis (eds.), *Demonstratives in discourse*, 305–341. Berlin: Language Science Press.
Dixon, R. M. W. 2010. *Basic linguistic theory*, vol. 2, *Grammatical topics*. Oxford: Oxford University Press.
Dürr, Michael. 2003. *Morphologie, Syntax und Textstrukturen des (Maya-)Quiché des Popol Vuh: Linguistische Beschreibung eines kolonialzeitlichen Dokuments aus dem Hochland von Guatemala*. Revised electronic edition. [http://home.snafu.de/duerr/download.html]
Emkow, Carola. forthcoming. Bena Bena. In Nicolas Evans & Sebastian Fedden (eds.), *The Oxford guide to the Papuan languages*. Oxford: Oxford University Press.
Engelenhoven, Aone van & Catharina Williams-van Klinken 2005. Tetun and Leti. In Alexander Adelaar & Nikolaus P. Himmelmann (eds.), *The Austronesian languages of Asia and Madagascar*, 735–768. Abingdon: Routledge.
Ferguson de Williams, Judith. 2007. *Gramática popular del mixteco del municipio de Tezoatlán, San Andrés Yutatío, Oaxaca*. Tlalpan: Instituto Lingüístico de Verano.
Fortescue, Michael. 1984. *West Greenlandic*. London: Croom Helm.
Geary, Elaine. 1985 [1977]. *Kunimaipa grammar: Morphophonemics to discourse*. Ukarumpa: Summer Institute of Linguistics.
Givón, Thomas. 2011. *Ute reference grammar*. Amsterdam & Philadelphia: John Benjamins.
Graczyk, Randolph. 2007. *A grammar of Crow: Apsáalooke aliláau*. Lincoln: University of Nebraska Press.
Green, Diana, Harold Green, Ivanildo Gomes, Aldiere Orlando, Nilo Martiniano, Raimunda Ioiô, João Felício, Antonia E. Romanowski, David Green, Alan Vogel, Simoni M. B. Valadares, Leni Andrade & Timotheo L. M. Correa. 2018. *Kagta iwitkekne parikwaki – parantunka: Dicionário palikur – português e vocabulário português – palikur*. Oiapoque: Associação Internacional de Linguística.

Greenberg, Joseph H. 1985. Some iconic relationships among place, time, and discourse deixis. In John Haiman (ed.), *Iconicity in syntax: Proceedings of a symposium on iconicity in syntax, Stanford, June 24–6, 1983*, 271–287. Amsterdam & Philadelphia: John Benjamins.

Gruzdeva, Ekaterina. 2020. Demonstratives in Nivkh: A semantic and pragmatic analysis. *Studia Orientalia Electronica* 8 (1). 1–60.

Guérin, Valérie & Grant Aiton. 2019. Bridging constructions in typological perspective. In Valérie Guérin (ed.), *Bridging constructions*, 1–44. Berlin: Language Science Press.

Haiman, John. 1980. *Hua: A Papuan language of the Eastern Highlands of New Guinea.* Amsterdam & Philadelphia: John Benjamins.

Harms, Phillip Lee. 1994. *Epena Pedee syntax.* Dallas: Summer Institute of Linguistics.

Himmelmann, Nikolaus P. 1996. Demonstratives in narrative discourse: A taxonomy of universal uses. In Barbara Fox (ed.), *Studies in anaphora*, 205–254. Amsterdam & Philadelphia: John Benjamins.

Holz, Christoph. forthcoming. *A comprehensive grammar of Tiang.* Cairns: Central Queensland University dissertation.

Holzknecht, Susanne. 1986. A morphology and grammar of Adzera (Amari dialect), Morobe Province, Papua New Guinea. *Papers in New Guinea Linguistics* 24. 77–166.

Jacques, Guillaume. 2018. Non-propositional evidentiality. In Alexandra Y. Aikhenvald (ed.), *The Oxford handbook of evidentiality*, 109–123. Oxford: Oxford University Press.

Kano, Mitsuru. 2000. On the usage of the medial demonstrative *o*-series in colloquial Sinhala. *Bulletin of Language Science and Humanities* 14. 57–74.

König, Ekkehard. 2020. Beyond exophoric and endophoric uses: Additional discourse functions of demonstratives. In Åshild Næss, Anna Margetts & Yvonne Treis (eds.), *Demonstratives in discourse*, 21–42. Berlin: Language Science Press.

Kuteva, Tania, Bernd Heine, Bo Hong, Haiping Long, Heiko Narrog, Seongha Rhee. 2019. *World lexicon of grammaticalisation: Second, extensively revised and updated edition.* Cambridge: Cambridge University Press.

Lange, Noa. 2017. *Distance and visibility in Gawri demonstratives.* Stockholm: Stockholm University MA thesis.

Launey, Michel. 2003. *Awna parikwaki: Introduction à la langue palikur de Guyane et de l'Amapá.* Paris: IRD Éditions.

Lothers, Michael D. 1996. *Deixis in Kalam Kohistani narrative discourse.* Arlington: University of Texas MA thesis.

Lynch, John, Malcolm Ross & Terry Crowley. 2011. *The Oceanic languages.* Abingdon: Routledge.

Mosel, Ulrike 2004. Demonstratives in Samoan. In Gunter Senft (ed.), *Deixis and demonstratives in Oceanic languages*, 141–174. Canberra: Pacific Linguistics.

Næss, Åshild, Anna Margetts & Yvonne Treis. 2020. Introduction: Demonstratives in discourse. In Åshild Næss, Anna Margetts & Yvonne Treis (eds.), *Demonstratives in discourse*, 1–20. Berlin: Language Science Press.

Neukom, Lukas. 2001. *Santali.* München: Lincom Europa.

Ng, Eve C. 2002. *Demonstrative words in the Algonquian language Passamaquoddy: A descriptive and grammaticalization analysis.* Buffalo: State University of New York dissertation.

Palmer, Bill. 2009. *Kokota grammar.* Honolulu: University of Hawai'i Press.

Payne, Thomas E. & Doris L. Payne. 2013. *A typological grammar of Panare: A Cariban language of Venezuela.* Leiden: Brill.

Payne, Doris L. & Alejandra Vidal. 2020. Pilagá determiners and demonstratives: Discourse use and grammaticalisation. In Åshild Næss, Anna Margetts & Yvonne Treis (eds.), *Demonstratives in discourse*, 149–183. Berlin: Language Science Press.

Peeters, David, Emiel Krahmer & Alfons Maes. 2020. A conceptual framework for the study of demonstrative reference. *Psychonomic Bulletin & Review*. https://doi.org/10.3758/s13423-020-01822-8

Rabel, Lili. 1961. *Khasi, a language of Assam*. Baton Rouge: Louisiana State University Press.

Rasoloson, Janie & Carl Rubino. 2005. Malagasy. In Alexander Adelaar & Nikolaus P. Himmelmann (eds.), *The Austronesian languages of Asia and Madagascar*, 456–488. Abingdon: Routledge.

Rubino, Carl R. G. 1997. *A reference grammar of Ilocano*. Santa Barbara: University of California dissertation.

Salminen, Mikko. 2016. *A grammar of Umbeyajts as spoken by the Ikojts people of San Dionisio del Mar, Oaxaca, Mexico*. Cairns: James Cook University dissertation.

Schupbach, Shannon S. 2013. *The Blackfoot demonstrative system: Function, form, and meaning*. Missoula: University of Montana MA thesis.

Skilton, Amalia E. 2019. *Spatial and non-spatial deixis in Cushillococha Ticuna*. Berkeley: University of California dissertation.

Sohn, Ho-min. 1975. *Woleaian reference grammar*. Honolulu: University of Hawai'i Press.

Sohn, Ho-min & B. W. Bender. 1980 [1973]. *A Ulithian grammar*. Canberra: Pacific Linguistics.

Watters, David E. 2004. *A grammar of Kham*. Cambridge: Cambridge University Press.

Willis, Christina M. 2007. *A descriptive grammar of Darma: An endangered Tibeto-Burman language*. Austin: University of Texas dissertation.

Willis Oko, Christina M. 2015. Deictic expressions in Darma (Almora). *Linguistics of the Tibeto-Burman Area* 38 (1). 26–65.

Wojtylak, Katarzyna I. 2017. *A grammar of Murui (Bue): A Witotoan language of Northwest Amazonia*. Cairns: James Cook University dissertation.

Zandvoort, Reinard W. 1975. *A handbook of English grammar*. London: Longman Group Limited.

Zeitoun, Elizabeth. 2007. *A grammar of Mantauran (Rukai)*. Taipei: Academia Sinica.

Zylstra, Carol F. 2012. *Gramática del Tu'un Savi (la lengua mixteca) de Alacatlatzala, Guerrero*. Tlalpan: Instituto Lingüístico de Verano.

Gwendolyn Hyslop

9 Miratives and magic: On "newness" as iconic grammar in Kurtöp narratives

Mirativity, the grammatical marking of unexpected information, is a core feature in Kurtöp grammar (Hyslop 2014, *inter alia*) and found widely throughout the Himalayas (eg DeLancey 1997, Andvik 2010, Hyslop and Tshering 2017), as well as pockets elsewhere in the world. Little is known about the development of these systems from a diachronic perspective in general, though I have outlined their diachronic pathways in Hyslop (2020, 2022). This article analyses the use of miratives in narratives in comparison to other genre types, and then situates these findings in the context of the historical development. I then propose that Kurtöp miratives iconically mark "newness" as part of their mirative package and that mirative markers, in general, are thus likely to be commonly replaced in language.

9.1 Introduction

Mirativity, the grammatical marking of unexpected information, is a core feature in Kurtöp grammar[1] (Hyslop 2011, 2017, 2018) and found widely throughout the Himalayas (e.g. DeLancey 1997; Andvik 2010; Hyslop and Tshering 2017), and elsewhere.[2] There has been some work done on the diachronic development of mirative markers. For example, Shimada and Nagano (2017) have argued that Japanese *no* 'SFP' and *koto* 'SFP' have recently acquired mirative extensions, as part of their polyfunctional

1 The fieldwork for this project has been generously supported by the Endangered Languages Documentation Project (ELDPIGS0049) and the Australian Research Council (DP140103937). A fellowship from the Alexander von Humboldt foundation afforded me the time to write this up. I am also grateful to the participants of the workshop *Celebrating Indigenous Voice: Legends and Narratives in Languages of the Tropics* for their comments and discussion; feedback and suggestions from Alexandra Aikhenvald have been particularly valuable. Joanna Bialek also kindly offered comments on an earlier version of this paper. Finally, I would like to thank Carl Bodnaruk for his assistance in formatting the manuscript and to the School of Art, Communication, and English for supporting this.
2 The validity of mirativity in Tibetan languages and as a cross-linguistic category has been widely contested as well. See, for example, Hill (2012), DeLancey (2012), Aikhenvald (2012), and other articles in the same volume.

Gwendolyn Hyslop, The University of Sydney

https://doi.org/10.1515/9783110789836-009

package, from proper nouns. Hyslop (2020) recently outlined the diachronic development of many epistemological markers, including that of some miratives.

The line of enquiry followed in this article continues in the same vein, but also bringing in a perspective from discourse at large. More specifically, this article will analyse the use of miratives in narratives in comparison to other genre types. In doing so, we will see that miratives are arguably "over-used" in narrative texts. This finding, taken together with our understanding of their recent diachronic development, will be presented as evidence for the proposed iconicity of the Kurtöp mirative itself. That is, I argue that Kurtöp mirative markers are newly grammaticalized forms that iconically mark "newness" as part of their mirative package. I further predict that, over time, the mirative markers will cease to be understood as "new", due to overuse, and new mirative markers will need to be developed in the language, should the mirative contrast continue to be maintained. In this way, we can see development of mirativity and mirative markers as perhaps involved in a euphemistic treadmill of diachronic morphology. This hypothesis about the relatively recent rise and fall of mirative markers diachronically, could be tested in other languages around the world.

This article therefore has the following structure. In §9.2 I provide background on mirativity, as a theoretical construct, and give further information about Kurtöp and the people who speak it. In §9.3 I show how and where mirativity is encoded in Kurtöp and present plausible diachronic origins for most of the forms. §9.4 presents and discusses the use of miratives in narratives, as opposed to other genres of speech. This preponderance in narratives, as opposed to other genres, is discussed in the conclusion offered in §9.5, where I argue that the recent diachronic development of the forms is part and parcel of what they mark. That is, mirativity in Kurtöp is an example of iconicity in grammar; the "new" forms in the language are used to encode "new" knowledge.

9.2 Background

9.2.1 Mirativity

Mirativity has been described as the grammatical marking of new or unexpected information. Building from work on languages of the Balkans (e.g. Aronson 1967; Friedman 1977, 1986), DeLancey (1997) is often credited with the establishment of mirativity as a valid cross-linguistic category, although in response to a debate on the topic in the previous decade, DeLancey (2012) links the first proposal for mirativity as a cross-linguistic category to Akatsuka (1985). Mirativity has been described in Tibetan and other Tibeto-Burman languages (eg Watters 2002), Athabaskan (DeLancey 1997, 2012, *inter alia*), and several other language families. Aikhenvald (2012) offers a thorough typology of the different core meanings and semantic extensions in mirativity in several languages around the world. While extensions of surprise are quite common, I will assume here that mirativity refers to the grammatical marking of new or unexpected information, commonly also conceived of as a sudden realization.

9.2.2 Kurtöp

Kurtöp is an East Bodish language spoken by approximately 10,000 speakers in Lhüntshe district, in Northeastern Bhutan, and various diaspora in Bhutan's capital of Thimphu and elsewhere in the world. East Bodish languages are a distinct grouping of Tibeto-Burman languages, that are probably closely related to Old Tibetan and modern descendants (ie Tibetic languages), in addition to being heavily influenced by them.[3] Hyslop (2017) is a recent grammar of the language.

9.2.2.1 The speakers

There has been little ethnographic study of Kurtöp speakers, with most of our knowledge coming from the small amount of work presented in Hyslop (2017) and more available in Huber (2020). According to the 2020 census data, there were 13,974 inhabitants in Lhüntshe, more than half of whom were under 40.

As outlined in Hyslop (2017), Kurtöps are by and large subsistence farmers, with each family raising cows for dairy and cultivating grains and vegetables for individual use. Dairy from cows is used primarily for making cheese and butter; their byproducts whey and buttermilk are also consumed.

Rice has become a staple grain only in recent years; previously maize, ground into small pieces called *kharang*,[4] was probably the most important, but wheat (*go*), sweet buckwheat (*cara*), millet (both finger millet, *Eleusine coracane* – called

---

3 See Hyslop (2013b, 2014, forthcoming) for further details about the historical relationship of East Bodish languages within the context of Tibeto-Burman.
4 Kurtöp are presented here using the Romanized orthography (see Hyslop 2014): The symbols correspond to the IPA as follows: <k> [k], <kh> [kʰ], <g> [g], <ng> [ŋ], <c> [c], <ch> [cʰ], <j> [ɟ], <ny> [ɲ], <tr> [ʈ], <thr> [ʈʰ], <dr> [ɖ], <t> [t̪], <th> [t̪ʰ], <d> [d̪], <p> [p], <ph> [pʰ], <b> [b], <m> [m], <ts> [ts], <tsh> [tsʰ], <sh> [ɕ], <zh> [ʑ], <s> [s], <z> [z], <l> [l], <lh> [l̥], <r> [r], <a> [ɑ], <e> [e], <i> [i], <o> [o], <u> [u], <ö> [ø], <ü> [y], <'CV> high tone on following vowel, <^> long vowel.

thre locally, and foxtail millet, *Setaria Italica* – called *ran* locally), and bitter buckwheat (*brâma*) have also been in use. Historically, taro (*byo*) and other roots were also used, though today people prefer to cultivate the grains described above instead.

Common crops are potatoes (*ki*), which grow particularly well in Shawa, green onion (*tsong*), several varieties of beans (*shepen*), eggplant (*dolom*), daikon radish (*muya*), squash (*laushar*) and, more recently, cabbage (*banda kopi* < Hindi), cauliflower (*meto kopi* < Kurtöp *meto* 'flower' + Hindi *kopi* 'cabbage'). Chiles (*banggala*) are a very important crop and they are used in several different ways. In addition to being used in its fresh, green state, chiles may be dried in the sun after turning red (*banggala kam*), dried green (*'ngokam*) or boiled and then dried, becoming white (*banggala kharti*).

Several foods are found growing in the wild, including a wide variety of mushrooms (*mu*), and fiddlehead (*zhiwa*). Fruits are citron (*kapula*), banana (*cela ~ ceya, ngala* in some dialects), guava (*'andre*), fig (*khongdi*), orange (*tshalu*), a sweet tomato that grows on trees (*'lambenda*) and various berries (*mrip*). Spices are cilantro (*wesi*), ginger (*saga*), garlic (*chacu*) and salt (*tsha*), which is used generously in nearly all cooking. People rarely drink water, but tea (*ja*) in a variety of forms (e.g. *suja* 'butter tea' *'ngâja* 'sweet tea'), whey (*shurkhu*) and buttermilk (*tarwa*) are common. Kurtöps also make alcohol out of a variety of grains, such as rice, corn, and millet. Distilled alcohol is called *zhor*. Potatoes are a common cash crop.

The official religion of the Kurtöps, like mainstream Bhutan, is Buddhism. However, also like mainstream Bhutan, many of the Buddhist practices are actually interlaced with various pre-Buddhist practices. Amongst these are the need to appease local deities and various festivals. For example, the *priu* festival, which occurs once a year in May in the village of Jasabi, appears to incorporate various non-Buddhist elements.[5] In the past, it is said that live animals used to be sacrificed as part of the festival but these days that has been discouraged. Another characteristic of the *priu* is the creation of red eggs, which are hardboiled and dyed with madder, yielding a bright red colour. Recent work by Toni Huber (Huber 2020) also identifies a cult referred to as Srid-pa'i Bon, practiced by Kurtöps and other speakers of East Bodish languages. Much of these traditions are highly endangered as most of the rituals are no longer conducted in the Kurtöp-speaking region, being replaced by mainstream Buddhism.

---

5 This festival is also associated with a text referred to as the *priu zhung*, written using 'ucen script and apparently presenting a hybrid sort of language that is mostly Chöke but mixed with some Kurtöp elements as well.

As elsewhere in Bhutan, marriage amongst the Kurtöps involves little ceremonious ritual. People become "married" once they've moved in together. In Dungkar *geok*[6] both polyandry and polygamy are practiced. In the mid 2000s, I was aware of one instance of each. In the case of the former one woman has three husbands who are brothers and in the case of the latter the husband's two wives are sisters. In this case the husband is a former monk, a status which affords him social prestige and added financial gain. Villagers report that the norm is for men to move in with their wives' families but it was not possible to obtain much data about this in practice.

A growing trend at present is for younger villagers to leave the area for education and eventually find themselves settled in the capital, marrying people from other regions in Bhutan, and speaking Dzongkha to their children. For example, in the family which has housed many researchers,[7] there were five children but none of them resided in the village, despite the fact that the youngest was only approximately ten years of age. The children were either living/studying in Thimphu or studying elsewhere.

Even in a community as small as the Kurtöp-speaking community, there are different registers of speech, depending primarily on education, time spent in the village, and exposure to Dzongkha. The highest register of Kurtöp involves a high level of Classical Tibetan (referred to as Chöke in Bhutan) and Dzongkha borrowings and is characterized by the use of the honorific particle *la* and honorific vocabulary. Interestingly, the pronunciation of these words varies significantly, depending on education and experience of the speaker. For example, front-rounded vowels are only found in the speech of the most educated speakers, or those who have grown up in Thimphu. As in Dzongkha, Hindi borrowings are also characteristic of the cool speech of the younger generation, though some words, such as *thrika* 'okay; good' appear to have filtered to all registers.

In addition to these different registers, most Kurtöp speakers are also highly multilingual. Without exception, every Kurtöp speaker I met spoke at least one other language (minimally Dzongkha or Chocangaca) in addition to Kurtöp. More common was for speakers to also be familiar with at least one or more of the following languages: Tshangla, Dzala, Bumthap, Khengkha, Tibetan, Nepali, Hindi, English.

---

6 A *geok* is a division of land within a district. For example, there are eight *geoks* within Lhüntshe district.

7 In addition to hosting the current author, this family has also hosted others conducting anthropological and linguistic research in the Kurtöp region.

9.2.2.2 The language

Like many other Tibeto-Burman languages, Kurtöp is verb-final, agglutinating, and suffixing.[8] The language uses a "pragmatic ergative" system (Hyslop 2010) though verbal arguments are often omitted altogether from discourse. Verbs are marked for tense, aspect, and epistemological categories, including evidentiality, egophoricity, and mirativity; the language seems to keep track of verbal participants through use of these forms, coupled with shared knowledge about speech-act and discourse participants.

The basic clause types, finite verb and nominalization plus copula, are illustrated in (1) and (2) below.

(1) *ngat geshang*
     ngat   *ge-shang*
     1.SG.ABS   go-PFV.EGO
     'I went.'

(2) *khit gewala wen*
     khit   *ge-pala*   *wen*
     3.SG.ABS   go-NMZ:PFV   COP
     'He went.'

The language also has a robust clause-chaining construction (described in Hyslop 2013a and Hyslop forthcoming) and also makes ample use of productive nominalization strategies that involve copulas. A simple example of a clause-chain is shown in (3):

(3) *ngat gezi zushang*
     ngat   *ge-si*   *zu-shang*
     1.SG.ABS   go-NF   eat-PFV:EGO
     'I left and ate.'

9.3 Kurtöp miratives

Mirativity is encoded in Kurtöp in perfective aspect, imperfective aspect and in each affirmative and negative existential and equational copular domain. The

---

8 The only prefix in the language is the negative marker.

forms are always portmanteau morphs, encoding mirativity along with aspect or copular functions. The discussion below builds from Hyslop (2011, 2017, 2018).

9.3.1 In form

Kurtöp mirative forms are shown in Table 9.1 below.

Table 9.1: Mirative markers in Kurtöp.

Imperfective	Perfective	Affirmative Existential Copulas	Negative Existential Copulas	Affirmative Equational Copulas	Negative Equational Copulas
-ta	-na	nâ	mutna	wenta	minta

The suffix -*ta* is used to mark mirative in imperfective contrasts, in contrast to -*taki*, which is used for non-mirative contrasts. In perfective contexts, -*na* is used to mark mirativity in contrast to egophoric -*shang*, indirect evidential -*mu*, presumptive -*para* and unmarked -*pala*. Kurtöp has at least[9] four existential copulas, in both the affirmative and negative domains. The mirative affirmative existential *nâ* contrasts with unmarked, presumptive, and dubiative forms, while mirative negative existential *mutna* contrasts with presumptive, indirect evidential and dubiative forms. The mirative copula *wenta* is also one of four affirmative equational copulas (contrasting with unmarked, presumptive, and dubiative forms).

The forms consist of obviously similar formatives *na* and *ta*; the reasons for this will be elucidated in §9.3.3.

---

9 Even after fifteen years of researching the language, surprises continue to arise. While it seems the analysis is exhaustive to date, it could be possible there are even more marginal forms in the language that have not (yet) been found. For example, amongst 900 pages of transcription an affirmative existential copula *naki* 'EXIS.NCRT' appears twice. Upon further discussion and clarification with other speakers, the copula is not limited to particular speakers or dialects or considered otherwise unusual; rather it is not just not commonly uttered. Exactly how it differs from the other affirmative existential copulas (*nâ* 'EXIS.MIR', *nawala* 'EXIS', *nawara* 'EXIS.PRES', *nakshu* 'EXIS.DBT', *naksho* 'EXIS.EMPH') is still not entirely clear. With this background, it seems plausible to assume there may be even more rare forms not yet recorded.

9.3.2 In function

Mirativity is used to mark that the speaker is reporting on information that is new, or that they did not have previously (that is, there is a lack of expectation). In imperfective contexts, miratives look like they could be third person markers, as exemplified by the data below. We see -*taki* used in a first person context in (4) and -*ta* used with a third person referent in (5).

(4) *ngat getaki*
     ngat   *ge-taki*
     1.SG.ABS   go-IPFV
     'I am going.'

(5) *khit* **geta**
     khit   *ge-ta*
     3.SG.ABS   go-IPFV:MIR
     'S/he is going.'

However, in natural speech, mirative markers can occur with first and second person while non-miratives can also occur with second and third person; such uses are quite common, depending on the extent to which the speaker has integrated the knowledge into their cognition. Below are two examples, drawn from natural speech. Example (6) was given in a self-introduction and uttered by a speaker in response to a request for him to tell a story; the speaker uses the non-mirative form because he is reporting on integrated knowledge about himself.

(6) *ngat 'Lama 'Lachung ngaktaki la*
     ngat   *'Lama* *'Lachung* *ngak-taki* *la*
     3.SG.ABS Lama 'Lachung do-IPFV   HON
     '(They) call me Lama Lachung.'

While it is relatively uncommon for the mirative imperfective to be used with first person, (7) below is one such example. This example was uttered in response to a request for the speaker to tell a story. While their own ability to tell a story (or not) was likely already known to them, the use of the mirative here enables the speaker to stop any further questioning from the interlocutors. The "sudden realization" of lack of knowledge leaves no space for the questioner to protest.

(7) *mekhanta ngaita laptorang*
    me-khan-ta   *ngai=ta*   *lap-to=rang*
    NEG-know-IPFV:MIR   1.ERG=EMPH   tell-INF=EMPH
    'I don't know at all (how) to tell (a story).'

In imperfective contexts, the mirative has a wider semantic distribution than else-where. For example, the mirative can be used regardless of whether the speaker has gained their knowledge directly (e.g. through visual evidence) or indirectly (e.g. via another person's report) or whether they have exclusive access to the information (i.e. egophoricity). In the perfective semantic space, however, the mirative is more obviously restricted to new and unexpected information. See examples (8–10) below.

(8) *palanggi jedo thilathe darnari*
    palang=gi *je=to*   *thila=the*   *dar-**na**=ri*
    bed=GEN   top=LOC thumb=DEF remain-PFV:MIR=REP
    'On the bed remained a toe (it is said).'

(9) *yala.. onga tshô thrakna wai*
    yala *onga* *tshô* *thrak-na*   *wai*
    God   child here arrive-PFV:MIR wow
    'God, this child has arrived! Wow!'

(10) *tshe khit mya thungmo mya zhiknami*
    tshe   *khit*   *mya*   *thung-mo* *mya*   *zhik-na=mi*
    DM   3.SG.ABS arrow do-CTM   arrow be.hit-PFV:MIR=TAG.EXC
    'While playing archery, he was hit by an arrow, right?'

These mirative examples can be contrasted with egophoric perfect (11) and the unmarked perfective (12) below:

(11) *Paroko yumgi ngak zonshangmi*
    Paro=ko   *yum=gi*   *ngak* *zon-shang=mi*
    Paro=LOC mother.HON=ERG do   send-PFV:EGO=TAG.EXC
    'The mother sent (me) to Paro, right?'

(12) *mê drup zatsi tshon gapoya thung zatpala*
    mê   *drup*   *zat-si*   *tshon*   *gapo=ya*   *thung* *zat-pala*
    house complete finish-NF colour PL.FOC=also do   finish-PFV
    'The house is finished; the colour has even been done.'

The mirative perfective can also be contrasted with the indirect and presumptive perfective, as shown below. The indirect evidential perfective is often used in story-telling, as shown in (13), in which the speaker is narrating a story about a lama who possesses magical powers to turn into different creatures, including a fish.

(13) *nyana trü khor gimu*
     nya=na   *trü*   *khor* *gi-mu*
     fish=LOC transform carry go-PFV:IND
     'He was transformed into a fish.'

Example (14) also comes from a narrative. In this example, the speaker is relaying the portion of the story in which a demon is coming for some siblings, and the younger sister, who was spinning thread, leaves a trail of thread behind her. After the siblings are revealed to have disappeared, the speakers highlights the possible presence of the thread in the story with the presumptive perfective marker *-para*.

(14) *da wo 'rotmanthe darwara wudi nga*
     Da   *wo*   *'rotman=the* *dar-para*   *wudi*
     Now   DEM:PROX thread=DEF remain-PFV:PRES DEM:DIST
     ngaksi
     QUOT
     '"Now that thread may have remained out there", (he) said.'

Mirativity as encoded in the copular domains is likewise semantically more narrow than mirativity in the imperfective domains. That is, mirativity is used in fewer contexts in the copular domain than in the imperfective domain. The examples of mirative copulas, shown below, also entail some surprise with their use:

(15) *wit sanji 'ngui wenta ngaksi*
     wit   *sanji*   *'ngui*   *wenta*   *ngaksi*
     2.SG.ABS buddha genuine COP.EQ.MIR QUOT
     'You are a real buddha (enlightened one) (he) said.'

(16) *net zon . . . net zon minta*
     net   *zon* *net*   *zon* *minta*
     1.PL.ABS two 1.PL.ABS two COP.EQ.MIR
     'The two of us . . . no, it wasn't the two of us.'

(17) *Hâpathe nâ*
      Hâpa=the   nâ
      Hâpa=DEF   COP.EXIS.MIR
      'He was a Hâpa (a person from Hâ).'

(18) *tshe wo Hâpaya 'namisamithe lapmal zhâya mutna*
      Tshe   wo   Hâpa=yang   'namisami=the   lap-male
      DM   DEM:PROX   Hâpa=also   very=DEF   speak-NMZ:IRR
      zhâ=yang   mutna
      what=also   COP.EXIS.MIR
      'So even this Hâpa had nothing at all to say.'

In each of (15–18), the mirative is used with speaker direct access to the knowledge and solely encoding that the knowledge is new to the speaker. Example (15),
(17) and (18), in particular, denote surprise – a sense that in addition to being
new, the information is counter to expectation. The use of the mirative in (16) is
triggered by the speaker's sudden awareness that they had incorrectly recounted
people present in an experience being relayed.

9.3.3 Diachronic development

The current synchronic mirative markers in Kurtöp are clearly recent grammati-
calizations of auxiliary verbs which have developed into suffixes. Their development is outlined in detail in Hyslop (2020, 2022) and just briefly summarised here.
    The Kurtöp clause-chaining construction, as illustrated in (3) above, has a
sub-construction for instances in which the second verb is an auxiliary. In these
cases, the non-final suffix *-si* is often deleted and the two verbs became phonologically adjacent, resulting in one serial verb construction. Two auxiliary verbs
have eventually grammaticalized into mirative suffixes in this context; *nak* 'to be
at' has become the perfective mirative marker and *tak* 'to become' has become
the imperfective mirative marker. This is summarised in Figures 9.1 and 9.2 below.

verb-si tak 'become' > verb *tak* > verb-*tak* > verb-*ta*

Figure 9.1: Proposed grammaticalization pathway of Kurtöp imperfective mirative.

verb-si nak 'be at' > verb *nak* > verb-*nak* > verb-*na*

Figure 9.2: Proposed grammaticalization pathway of Kurtöp perfective mirative.

The mirative existential copula *nâ* is also very likely to be a direct grammaticalization of *nak* 'to be at'. The source of the mirative formatives in the other copulas – *mutna, wenta, minta* is very likely to be the same auxiliaries, although there is no additional language-internal or external evidence to explain these developments. Nonetheless, even preliminary comparative work shows these copulas are also recent developments in Kurtöp.

While the source construction for Kurtöp miratives appears to be unambiguous, the precise semantic connection between the source construction and the mirative function remains to be understood. Kuteva et. al (2019) proposes that miratives come historically via reinterpretation of "adversatives", "perfects", or "inferred evidentials". Aikhenvald (2021: 33–34) proposes three potential pathways wherein mirative extensions can develop out of evidentials. The first scheme sees mirativity as resulting from a lack of first-hand information (i.e. grammatically a non-first hand evidential). In this proposal the lack of participation and control of the speaker leads to a reanalysis of an unprepared mind and thus a mirative meaning. The second scheme is also linked to a speaker's non-involvement but sees the lack of participation as a deliberate and leading to a distancing effect; the mirative extends from this semantic space. Aikhenvald's (2021) third scheme sees the mirativity resulting from a speaker's "deferred realization" of an event; that is, the speaker results an event post factum and understands the result as unexpected. More work is needed in Kurtöp to better understand which of these schemes – or a different one – best accounts for the shift in meaning that comes with the grammaticalization of the auxiliary into a mirative marker. On the surface, it would appear that the meaning of the auxiliaries *nak* 'to be at' and *tak* 'to become' would not be necessarily evidential, and so the "newness" of the semantic extension would not be intermediated by an evidential at all. However, we are currently lacking the necessary comparative data to make more concrete proposals about the meanings of the auxiliaries *nak* 'to be at' and *tak* 'to become' at earlier stages of Kurtöp and/or Proto East Bodish.

9.4 Miratives in narratives

In order to get a better understanding of how the miratives are used in narratives, as opposed to elsewhere in the language, I looked at each clause in four separate narratives and counted how many times a mirative was used, as opposed to a different finite category. Recall that there is one non-mirative imperfective, four non-mirative perfectives, and at least fourteen non-mirative copulas.

The four narratives were *Drukpa Künle and the Grandmother*, narrated by Kuenga Lhendup in 2006, *The Tiger and the Frog*, narrated by Sonam Tshering in 2008, *Kala Wangpo*, narrated by Pelden in 2006, and *Marsang* narrated by Jurme Tenzin in 2008. The narratives varied significantly in length: *Drukpa Künle and the Grandmother* had 56 finite clauses; *The Tiger and the Frog* had 63 finite clauses; *Kala Wangpo* has 298 clauses and *Marsang* is the longest with 352.

Each of these stories contain characters who possess special powers of some sort. Drukpa Künle, the protagonist of the first story, appears unannounced in a village and after some time has magically transformed an elderly lady into rays which are dispersed into heaven, save for one toe left on the bed. The *Tiger and the Frog* features a trickster frog, who manages to convince a tiger that he consumes tigers. *Kala Wangpo* is a fabled king whose wife is a demon, performing evil magical deeds on his children. In *Marsang*, a mother's lazy son eventually ventures out on his own and encounters demons as well.

Mirative proliferated these texts, with the first finite clause in both *Drukpa Künle and the Grandmother* and *Kala Wangpo* containing a mirative, as shown in (19) and (20). In both these examples we see the mirative equational copula being used at the end of a clause.

(19) *'ator mapa wo sung khepo aaa . . . neri nangpagi 'lama lam Drukpa Künle ngawalagi gangki wenta*
  'ator   mapa   wo   sung   khepo aaa ... neri
  how   originally DEM:PROX   story FOC   HES   1.PL.INCL.GEN
  nangpa=gi   'lama lam   Drukpa Künle ngak-pala=gi
  inside=GEN lama   Lama   Drukpa Künle do-NMZ:PFV=GEN
  gang=ki   wenta
  time=GEN   COP.EQ.MIR
  'This story is about how; originally, our . . ., it's during the time of our lama who was called Lama Drukpa Künle.'

(20) *dangpu wentawa . . . lungpathena jepothe nawal wenta la*
  dangpu   wenta=wa ...   lungpa=the=na   jepo=the
  in.the.past COP.EQ=TAG:EXCL country=DEF=LOC king=DEF
  nawala   wenta   la
  COP.EXIS   COP.EQ.MIR   HON
  'Once upon a time, there was a king in a country.'

Miratives were used within the first three clauses for the two narratives, also setting the tone for the introduction of the characters and place. When asked about the choice of mirative in each of these cases, speakers responded similarly, stating that the mirative "made it interesting" or was "how to tell a story".

Miratives continued to be used abundantly through the duration of the narratives. The number of miratives for each text is shown in Table 9.2 below.

Table 9.2: Summary of mirative counts in each of the four texts.

	Drukpa Künle	Tiger and Frog	Kala Wangpo	Marsang
wenta (including NMZ+COP)	28	46	119	149
nâ	1	0	1	5
minta	0	0	2	2
mutna	0	0	0	3
-ta	3	4	13	37
-na	4	0	6	5
Total Mirative	36	50	141	201
Grand total (including non-mirative)	56	63	298	352
Percent mirative	64%	79%	47%	57%

As is immediately evident, the overall percentages of miratives in the narratives is strikingly high, ranging from 47% in *Kala Wangpo* to 79% in *Tiger and Frog*. This means that for three out of four of the narratives, well over half of all finite clauses were marked with a mirative. Even allowing for some speaker variation due to style, this is an extremely large number, almost suggestive of miratives being part of the narrative style, as opposed to other styles (conversation, in particular).

9.5 Summary and conclusions

This paper has presented Kurtöp miratives, their diachronic development, and their use in narratives. Mirativity is a pervasive aspect of Kurtöp grammar, and one of several possible epistemological contrasts available in perfective, imperfective, and copular contexts. Comparative evidence shows that these mirative markers are recent grammatical innovations in the language. An examination of miratives in narratives finds them to be wildly productive, with speakers reporting their use helps make stories "interesting". I suggest there is something iconic about the use of miratives, in general. Relatively new grammar is used to encode new information. This leads to a prediction that as miratives become older in the language, they will lose their iconic status as new grammar and perhaps then also lose mirative functions, just as Skibrink (this volume) has also discovered.

The idea of an iconic motivation behind a continual renewal of mirativity could have implications for our continued understanding of language as a cognitive and communicative phenomena. Renewal cycles are not unknown in linguistics. Jespersen (1917) first pointed to renewal cycles in negation, showing how a negative adverb is first weakened, deemed "insufficient", and then strengthened, usually through the addition of a new word. Heath (1998) argues that grammatical systems tend to use new formal material in order to express older grammatical categories (see also Heath's 1997 "lost wax system of renewal"). In other words, we may perceive of at least some grammatical categories as being relatively time-stable in some languages, even when their forms are regularly replaced. Other similar phenomena may include taboo replacement in Indo-European languages. What dictates what language will have which categories, is of course a fascinating question.

Abbreviations

1	'first person'
2	'second person'
3	'third person'
ABS	'absolutive'
COP	'copula'
CTM	'co-temporal'
DEF	'definite'
DEM	'demonstrative'
DBT	'dubiative'
DIST	'distal'
EGO '	egophoric'
EMPH	'emphatic'
EQ	'equative'
ERG	'ergative'
EXC	'exclusive'
EXIS	'existential'
FOC	'focus'
GEN	'genitive'
HES	'hesitation'
HON	'honourific'

INCL	'inclusive'
IND	'indirect evidential'
INF	'infinitive'
IPFV	'imperfective'
IRR	'irrealis'
LOC	'locative'
MIR	'mirative'
N.CRT	'non-certain'
NEG	'negative'
NF	'non-final marker'
NMZ	'nominaliser'
PFV	'perfective'
PL	'plural'
PRES	'presumptive'
PROX	'proximate'
REP	'reported speech'
QUOT	'quotative'
SFP	'sentence final particle'
SG	'singular'
TAG	'tag particle'

References

Aikhenvald, Alexandra Y. 2012. The essence of mirativity. *Linguistic Typology* 16(3). 435–486.

Aikhenvald, Alexandra Y. 2021. *The web of knowledge: Evidentiality at the cross-roads*. Leiden: Brill.

Akatsuka, Noriko. 1985. Conditionals and the epistemic scale. *Language* 61. 625–639.

Andvik, Erik. 2010. *A grammar of Tshangla*. Leiden/Boston: Brill.

Aronson, Howard. 1967. The grammatical categories of the Indicative in the contemporary Bulgarian literary language. In *To honor Roman Jakobson: Essays on the occasion of his seventieth birthday, 11 October 1966*, vol. 1, 82–98. (Janua Linguarum. Series Maior 31). The Hague: Mouton.

DeLancey, Scott. 1997. Mirativity: The grammatical marking of unexpected information. *Linguistic Typology* 1. 33–52.

DeLancey, Scott. 2012. Still mirative after all these years. *Linguistic Typology* 16(3). 529–564.

Friedman, Victor. 1977. *The grammatical categories of the Macedonian Indicative*. Columbus: Slavica.

Friedman, Victor. 1986. Evidentiality in the Balkans: Bulgarian, Macedonian, and Albanian. In Wallace Chafe & Johanna Nichols (eds.), *Evidentiality: The linguistic coding of epistemology*, 168–187. (Advances in Discourse Processes 20). Norwood, N.J.: Ablex.

Heath, Jeffrey. 1997. Lost wax: Abrupt replacement of key morphemes in Australian agreement complexes. *Diachronica* 14(2). 197–232.

Heath, Jeffrey. 1998. Hermit crabs: Formal renewal of morphology by phonologically mediated affix substitution. *Language* 74(4). 728–759.

Hill, Nathan W. 2012. 'Mirativity' does not exist: Hdug in 'Lhasa' Tibetan and other suspects. *Linguistic Typology* 16(3). 389–433.

Huber, Toni. 2020. *Source of life: Revitalisation rites and bon shamans in Bhutan and the Eastern Himalayas*. Vienna: Austrian Academy of Sciences Press.

Hyslop, Gwendolyn. 2010. Kurtöp case: The pragmatic ergative and beyond. *Linguistics of the Tibeto-Burman Area* 33(1). 1–40.

Hyslop, Gwendolyn. 2011. Mirativity in Kurtöp. *Journal of South Asian Linguistics* 4(1). 43–60.

Hyslop, Gwendolyn. 2013a. The Kurtöp clause-chaining construction: Converbs, clause chains, and verb serialization. In Tim Thornes, Erik Andvik, Gwendolyn Hyslop & Joana Jansen (eds.), *Functional-historical approaches to explanation: In honor of Scott DeLancey*, 155–178. (Typological Studies in Language 103). Amsterdam/Philadelphia: John Benjamins.

Hyslop, Gwendolyn. 2013b. On the internal phylogeny of the East Bodish languages. In Gwendolyn Hyslop, Stephen Morey & Mark Post (eds.), *North East Indian Linguistics 5*, 91–109. New Delhi: Cambridge University Press/Foundation.

Hyslop, Gwendolyn. 2014. A preliminary reconstruction of East Bodish. In Nathan Hill & Thomas Owen-Smith (eds.), *Trans-Himalayan linguistics*, 155–179. Berlin: Mouton de Gruyter.

Hyslop, Gwendolyn. 2017. *A grammar of Kurtöp*. (Languages of the Greater Himalayan Region 18). Leiden: Brill.

Hyslop, Gwendolyn. 2018. On egophoricity and mirativity in Kurtöp. In Elisabeth Norcliffe, Simeon Floyd & Lila San Roque (eds.), *Egophoricity*, 109–137. Amsterdam/Philadelphia: John Benjamins.

Hyslop, Gwendolyn. 2020. Grammaticalized sources of Kurtöp verbal morphology: On the development of mirativity versus egophoricity in the Himalayas. *Studies in Language* 44(1). 132–164.

Hyslop, Gwendolyn. 2022. Kurtöp verbal morphology in the East Bodish context: A case study in ethnohistorical morphosyntax? In Mark W. Post, Stephen Morey & Toni Huber (eds.), *Ethnolinguistic prehistory of the Eastern Himalaya*. 323–362. Leiden: Brill.

Hyslop, Gwendolyn & Karma Tshering. 2017. An overview of some epistemic categories in Dzongkha. In Lauren Gawne & Nathan W. Hill (eds.), *Evidential systems of Tibetan languages*, 352–365. Berlin: Mouton de Gruyter.

Hyslop, Gwendolyn. Forthcoming. Clause-chaining in Kurtöp.

Jespersen, Otto. 1917. *Negation in English and other languages*. Copenhagen: Høst.

Kuteva, Tania, Bernd Heine, Bo Hong, Haiping Long, Heiko Narrog & Seongha Rhee. 2019. *World lexicon of grammaticalization*. 2nd edn. Cambridge: Cambridge University Press.

Shimada, Masaharu & Akiko Nagano. 2017. Miratives in Japanese: The rise of mirative markers via grammaticalization. *Journal of Historical Linguistics* 7(1–2). 213–244.

Watters, David. 2002. *A grammar of Kham*. Cambridge: Cambridge University Press.

Elena Skribnik

10 Reading Siberian folklore: Miratives, pre-mirative contexts and "Hero's Journey"

This paper discusses the use of mirative expressions in narratives, as a means of marking surprising key points, in relation to the plot patterns which lead to these points. A typical sequence of predications with specific semantics (a verb of motion plus a verb of perception – *veni, vidi*) is labelled "pre-mirative context". Such sequences correspond to important structural units of a folklore narrative within the "Hero's Journey" (Propp 1928; Campbell 2008). An investigation of corpora of folktales in several Siberian languages has shown that pre-mirative contexts lead up to the use of mirative forms in those languages which have them. Alternatively, a non-mirative form may acquire a mirative extension. The special marking can also occur in the pre-mirative sequence itself, signalizing that a surprising key point follows; the two types of marking can also be combined. Whether the type of contextual implicature within the Hero's Journey context plays a role in the emergence of grammaticalized mirativity, is a question for further research.

10.1 Introduction

This paper focuses on two perspectives in investigating folklore narratives – the structure and the development of the plot, and the linguistic devices employed. The main topic of my discussion here is the use of mirative expressions in narratives, as a means of marking surprising key points. The plot patterns which produce – or lead to – these points are a further topic. The principal notion in the discussion is "pre-mirative context", understood as a typical sequence of

Acknowledgements: I express my deep gratitude to Olga Kazakevich, who shared with me her expertise in Selkup, Ket, and Evenki grammar, as well as to Alexandra Aikhenvald for her helpful comments on an earlier version of this article. I am also grateful to Josefina Budzisch, Liliya Gorelova, Natalia Grishina and Irina Nevskaya for expert information on some morphological nuances. Mistakes are all my own.

Elena Skribnik, Ludwig Maximilian University, Munich

https://doi.org/10.1515/9783110789836-010

predications with specific semantics followed by a mirative expression. I argue that "pre-mirative context" is intrinsically linked with the notion of "Hero's Journey" in folklore studies. It reflects a typical sequence of actions representing one of the building blocks of a tale.

Mirativity is defined as a category conveying "the status of the proposition with respect to the speaker's overall knowledge structure", and "experience for which the speaker had no psychological preparation" (DeLancey 1997: 33, 35). Aikhenvald (2012: 437) lists the following mirative meanings: sudden discovery, sudden revelation or realization; surprise; unprepared mind; counter-expectation; new information. All these meanings can refer to the speaker, to the audience/addressee, or to the main character. Third person singular mirative forms in narratives express "an unexpected realization on the part of the character as told by the omniscient narrator" (Aikhenvald 2012: 442). My data support this observation.

This study is based on an investigation of corpora of folktales[1] in the following Siberian languages:
- Uralic languages: Khanty and Mansi (Finno-Ugric), Selkup (Samoyedic),
- Altaic languages: Altai-kizhi, Khakas, Shor, and Tuvan (South Siberian Turkic); Buryat (North Mongolic); Evenki (North Tungusic);
- Yenisseic languages: Ket.

As formulated in (Georg 2008: 151), "The Siberian mainstream favours exclusively suffixing (not necessarily simple) agglutinative morphology, more or less strict SOV syntax, vowel harmony, phonetically robust lexical, especially verbal, roots and <. . .> morphological transparency, paired with a great degree of morphological predictability". In contrast, Yenisseic languages are characterized by phonemic tone, and a "polysynthetic and exclusively prefixing make-up" of the verb.

Many of these languages have specialized mirative forms or mirative extensions of evidential forms (Skribnik and Aikhenvald forthcoming). Mirative expressions and forms are particularly salient in the languages of Western and Central Siberia which appear to constitute what can metaphorically be referred to as a "mirativity belt". In Ob-Ugric languages, erstwhile evidentials (grammaticalized markers of information source) have been reanalyzed into pure miratives (Skribnik 1998). Mirativity is also a prominent feature of South Siberian Turkic languages and Buryat, a North Mongolic language. Yenisseic languages, most of

---

1 The sources of my data are different folklore collections, especially the series "Folklore Monuments of the Peoples of Siberia and the Far East" (FMPS), published by the Institute of Philology, Siberian division of the Russian Academy of Sciences (Novosibirsk, Russia); folklore texts published in grammars; and annotated corpora (see the list of sources in the end).

which are extinct or close to extinction, have no evidentials. They code mirativity distinctions with particles (Vajda 2004: 90; Georg 2007: 449). In this paper, I will illustrate the common traits in the use of miratives (or the emergence of mirative readings of other forms) in the languages of this region. The question of potential contacts and convergent developments remains open due to the lack of necessary information.

This article is structured as follows. Section 10.2 introduces the two central concepts "Hero's Journey" and "pre-mirative context". Section 10.3 analyzes verbs of motion and visual perception as well as verbs of comprehension and speech as components of pre-mirative contexts. Section 10.4 focuses on possible marking types: to the right from the pre-mirative/mirative borderline, i.e. miratives and mirative extensions, and to the left of this borderline, in the last clause of a pre-mirative sequence, i.e. literally a "pre-mirative marking". The last Section 10.5, offers a summary and outlines directions for future research.

10.2 "Hero's Journey" and "pre-mirative contexts"

There has been a substantial amount of literature on the patterns of organization of folklore narratives. The work of two experts is of particular importance for the present study. One of them is the Russian folklorist Vladimir Yakovlevich Propp (1895–1970), and especially his key publication, *Morfologiya skazki*, *Morphology of the Folktale*, first published in 1928 and translated into many languages (English translation 1958 and 1968). The other one is an American specialist in comparative mythology Joseph Campbell (1904–1987), whose book *The Hero with a Thousand Faces*, first published in 1949, received world-wide recognition and introduced the concept "Hero's journey".

> A hero ventures forth from the world of common day into a region of supernatural wonder: fabulous forces are there encountered and a decisive victory is won: the hero comes back from this mysterious adventure with the power to bestow boons on his fellow man. (Campbell 2008: 24)

Campbell states that "The standard path of the mythological adventure of the hero is a magnification of the formula represented in the rites of passage: *separation – initiation – return*" (Campbell 2008: 24).

Similarly, out of thirty one narrative units, or functions, introduced by V. Propp as tools of structural analysis of folklore narratives, there are several that correspond to Campbell's notions and are important for my study. A typical structure describing the Hero's Adventure / Hero's Journey, especially in mythological narratives, commonly includes Departure (Function 11 after V. Propp: "Hero leaves home") and Return (Function 20, "Hero sets out for home").[2]

Leaving his homeland to fulfill his task and moving into the Unknown, the Hero sees many unusual things, meets Helpers and Instruments who assist him in his adventure; coming back, the Hero can meet different antagonists, e.g., False Heroes, and be confronted with unexpected changes in his home (e.g., a widespread motif of the last spark of fire in the hearth, see example 1). For a linguist, these parts of the narrative are true "birthplaces of mirativity": typical patterns of storytelling are realized through typical sequences of linguistic expressions. Such sequences usually start with a verb of motion followed by a verb of perception (the pattern captured by *veni, vidi*) and end almost invariably with one of the mirative forms. The sequences were termed "pre-mirative contexts" in (Skribnik 1999).

There are two more Proppian functions reflected in Siberian folklore, for which pre-mirative sequences are typical. First, it's Proppian Function 8 "Villainy" – "Antagonist(s) causes harm or injury to victim(s)/member of Hero's family". Such tales often start with the Hero's absence from home fulfilling everyday tasks – hunting, fishing, reindeer herding, picking berries; coming back, s/he finds one of possible subtypes of F8, for instance, "Kidnapping of a person" or "Murder", and has to deal with it. Though it is not a classic "Hero's Journey", the beginning of such a tale shows the same sequences of linguistic expressions: motion (coming back), perception, revelation.

Secondly, many tales include variations of Proppian Function 4, "Antagonist(s) makes Attempt at Reconnaissance" (often moving directly to Function 8 "Villainy"). In such cases a static protagonist usually hears someone (unexpectedly) approaching or some strange/unexpected sound. Such plots demonstrate similar pre-mirative sequences, but more of the type "sat and heard" than "went and saw".

Theoretically, such sequences in their complete form can include two further components: a verb of cognition (implying realization or interpretation of obtained information) and a verb of speech; in practice, they usually contain from one to three components. Note that such a sequence – *Veni, vidi, comprehendi, dixi: WOW!* – or its parts has been attested not only in epic narratives, but also in other types of tales in the Aarne-Thompson-Uther taxonomy (Uther 2004): animal tales, tales of magic, realistic tales, even in anecdotes and jokes (compare

---

2 For a list of Proppian functions see, e.g., https://sites.ualberta.ca/~urban/Projects/English/Content/Propp_Functions.htm, http://courses.missouristate.edu/MarkTrevorSmith/eng200Spring03/ProppStructure.htm and many more.

one of frequent openings of German anecdotes: *Kommt ein Mann zum Arzt* . . .
'A man walks into a doctor's office'). The event of the mirative clause following
the pre-mirative sequence can be compared to "The Most Reportable Event" in
Labov's theory on narrative analysis (1997).[3]

Preliminary analysis of the folklore data shows that in the clause following
such a pre-mirative sequence, in the context of the Hero's Journey, languages
which have miratives use a mirative marker. In languages which have no specialized miratives, another verb form in such a clause will acquire a mirative reading.
Some languages develop also a kind of a "pre-mirative marking" through verbal
forms or particles in the last clause of a pre-mirative sequence.

10.3 Components of pre-mirative sequences

As already mentioned, pre-mirative sequences consist of verbs of motion (§10.3.1),
verbs of perception (§10.3.2), and possibly also of cognitive verbs of comprehension and speech verbs (§10.3.3). The order of components is usually iconic.
Depending on the language, they can be presented as a sequence of juxtaposed
finite clauses or as a non-finite clause chain.[4]

10.3.1 Verbs of motion (*veni*)

This component is central for pre-mirative sequences and the most typical one.
It can also occur on its own: the arrival on the scene presupposes the automatic
perception of it. In this case native speakers often add the missing link(s) of the
pre-mirative sequence in the translation, using expressions meaning 'as it turned
out' or '(one) found/noticed/understood that'. The following examples illustrate
motion verbs on their own.

The motion is venitive in reference to locations and objects relevant for the
plot. The motion predication is presented as a non-finite temporal clause in
(1) and (2) and as an independent finite clause in (3).

---

3 "The event that is less common than any other in the narrative and has the greatest effect upon
the needs and desires of the participants in the narrative (is evaluated most strongly)" (Labov
1997: 406).
4 Note that most Siberian languages started to acquire finite coordination and subordination
via conjunctions only recently, under the influence of Russian; original native constructions use
different non-finite forms like converbs or participles/action nouns with case suffixes and postpositions as connectors.

In the clause describing the mirative event, the two Ob-Ugric languages, Khanty and Mansi, use miratives (grammaticalized from participles in finite use). In (1), the protagonist comes back home after his adventure (The Hero's Return) and finds out, to his surprise, that his aunt is on the brink of dying ("the last spark" metaphor). After that he restores her health, youth, and beauty.

(1) North Mansi (OUDB NM 1234: 226)
    joxt-me-te   *akʷ-e*   *akʷ ula sultm-e*
    arrive-PTCP.PST-POSS.3SG aunt-POSS.SG<3SG one fire spark-POSS.SG<3SG
    arəyt-am
    stay-MIR.PST[3SG]
    'When he came back, (it turned out that) there was (only) one spark of the aunt's fire left.'

In (2) the orphaned protagonist left the place where he lived with his parents to look for a wife (Hero's Journey). He came to a riverbed that had to his surprise no water in it (see example 7) and went further upstream to find the cause.

(2) North Khanty (Khanty Tales 2002: 58, transcription Sipos 2022: 606)
    imultijn ***ʃoʃ-əs,***   ***ʃoʃ-əs,***   *ij*   *texij-a*
    once   stroll-PST.3SG stroll-PST.3SG one place-LAT
    juxt-m-aɬ-n   *jelaŋ-iki*   *juxan ʃəpi*   ***uɬ-m-aɬ***
    arrive-PTCP.PST-POSS.3SG-LOC *jelaŋ*-man river   across lie-MIR.PST-3SG
    'Once he was walking, he was walking, after reaching a certain place (he found that) a giant was lying across the river.'

Samoyedic languages use evidentials with their mirative extensions. In (3) from Selkup these are an inferential and a so-called "past narrative". Example (3) is exemplifying the Proppian Function 8 "Villainy", here as a punishment for breaking a taboo. The men are on the hunt, two women are left at home with their children, and one of the women talks and laughs too loudly after sunset. As a bear/devil arrives, the other woman can flee with her baby and warn the hunters. They return home and from a distance see the first woman with her children standing outside.

(3) Selkup (INEL corpus, IF_196X_WomanAndDevil_flk)
    sukul'teːla ***tüː-q-olam-nɔː-tin.***   *Pïpa* *ira*   *na*   *inna*
    back   come-INF-BE.GOING.TO-CO-3PL bear old.man INFER up

qaj	***am-nï-t.***		*Ïja-ï:-n-tï*	*aj*	*ima-n-tï*
whether	eat-INFER-3SG.OBJ		child-PL-GEN-POSS.3SG	and	wife-GEN-POSS.3SG
olï	*po-ntï*	*ïnna*	***tokk-altï-mpa-t.***		
head	tree-ILL	up	put-TR-PST.NARR-3SG.OBJ		

'(The hunters) started to return. (As it turned out,) an old bear-man had probably eaten them (= the family members). He put onto the poles the heads of the wife and of the children' (so that from afar it would look as if they stand on the bank greeting the hunters).

Example (4), from Ket, appears to illustrate a similar point. This comes from an article on the use of a mirative particle *bīn* and is given without context. According to Vajda (2004: 90), it "portrays the narrated event as noteworthy and unexpected".

(4) Ket (Shabaev 1982: 154, phonological transcription and glossing Olga Kazakevich, personal communication October 2021)

bū	*qā*	***d[u]-i[k]-in-bes***	*bu-da*	*ke²t*	*qōt*
3SG.M/F	home	SUBJ.3SG.M-here-PST-R	3SG.M-GEN.M	man	already
bīn	*du-[i]n-qo*				
PTCL.MIR	SUBJ.3SG.M-PST-die				

'He came home: (it turned out that) his friend had died already.'

The verb of motion can be replaced by a verb denoting any action that enables perception (e.g., see (6) 'wake up') as well as by verbs of eye movement ('look around') or attention focus movement ('notice').

10.3.2 Verbs of (visual) perception (*vidi*)

Sequences of actions leading to a surprising focal point presented by a mirative expression typically contain a verb of uncontrolled perception – 'see', 'perceive', 'notice'. As already mentioned, this component can be omitted, as the Hero's arrival on the scene presupposes his ability to perceive what is happening there (see §10.3.1). In most instances, a verb of visual perception is used (also see below on verbs of auditory perception).

In the clause describing the perceived event, Ob-Ugric languages use miratives.

In (5), God created a man and a woman out of the black earth. When the devil tried to do the same, he managed to get only lizards, beetles, and frogs. Out of spite, the devil befouls the humans with spit and snot. God comes back to check on his creations.

(5) Pelym Mansi (OUDB PM 1277: 35–37)

> to:rəm jeæl-s   ʃe:məl mɔ: mort-əx   jal.   to:rəm **joxt-s**
> god   go-PST[3SG] black earth measure-INF down god   come-PST[3SG]
> **nuŋk, ʃunʃ-i**   jæləmkoləs-eæn   toɣr: taylə
> up   look-PRS[3SG] human-POSS.DU<3SG towards fully
> **lərk-əm**   taylə **sæl'l'-əm**
> clear_nose-MIR.PST[3SG] fully spit-MIR.PST[3SG]

'God went down to measure the black earth. God comes up, looks at his two humans: (to his surprise,) they are completely befouled with spit and snot.' [After that God turns the humans inside out, hiding the fluids inside.]

In (6), a witch wants to fell down the tree which the trickster has climbed. A fox offers its help and persuades her to take a nap. While she sleeps, the fox chops at a stone instead of the tree.

(6) North Mansi (OUDB NM, 1229: 108)

> anʲ e:kʷa   **no:x u:nt-əs**   sa:yrap-e   **sunsiyl-i-te**
> now old_woman up   sit-PST[3SG] axe-POSS.SG<3SG look_at-PRS-SG<3SG
> o:s   l'aŋkʷli-jəy **sa:yrlat-ima**
> again dull-TRNS   chop-MIR.PST.PASS[3SG]

'The old woman woke up (lit. sat up) and took a look (lit. takes a look) at the axe: (as it turned out,) it was blunt (lit. chopped blunt) again.'

The next example (7) precedes example (2) in the same narrative.

(7) North Khanty (Khanty Tales 2002: 58, transcription Sipos 2022: 606)

> sʲiti   **mɛn-s,   mɛn-s,   juxan-a juxt-əs,**
> in.this.way **go-PST.3SG   go-PST.3SG   river-LAT arrive-PST.3SG**
> **βan-ɬ-əɬe:**   juxan isa   sɔrm-a **pit-m-aɬ.**
> look_at-PRS-SG<3SG river totally dry-LAT become-MIR.PST-POSS.3SG

'So he was walking, he was walking, he reached a river and sees that the river has dried out.'

Note the change of tense on the perception verb in all three examples: the whole narrative as well as verbs of motion are in the past tense, but here the present tense is used. This instance of *praesens historicum* conveys "the meaning of the dramatic immediacy of an eye-witness account" (see Quirk et al. 1985: 181 about a similar non-present use of present tense in English).

Additionally, the finite perception verb in (6) and (7) carries the suffix of agreement with both the subject (3SG) and the object (in singular number, as the object marker distinguishes only number, but not person). This object marker refers to the following mirative clause ('the axe was blunted', 'the river has dried out'). Object marking of a finite verb of information processing (perception, cognition, speech) with a non-finite content clause is one of complementation strategies in many Uralic languages (see also example 14–15). Thus, the mirative clause in (6) and (7) can also be analyzed as a postposed complement clause. As evidentials/miratives in Ob-Ugric are expressed by non-finite forms (participles/action nouns) with nominal personal (possessive) marking, see (5), they can be seen as the result of "desubordination",[5] and cases like (6) and (7) as bridging contexts to (5).

In languages without dedicated mirative forms, an evidential form can acquire a mirative meaning in the context of a perception verb to express the surprise reaction of the character. The following Selkup example demonstrates mirative extension of an inferential evidential, similarly to (3).

(8) Selkup (INEL Selkup corpus, YIF_196X_Kamadzha2_flk)
     Trug   ***manče-ǯ'-la***   *urop*   ***tö-špi-ndi***
     suddenly   look-PERF-FUT[3SG]   wild_animal   come-IPFV-INFER[3SG]
     [The younger brother is thrown out from his brother's house, finds a river, catches a lot of fish, and starts to smoke it.] 'Suddenly (he) looks up: a beast is coming.' [After that he gives the beast some food, gains its trust, kills it while it sleeps, and brings his catch to his brother's family.]

The two following examples are from publications on evidentials and their mirative extensions, without previous contexts but containing a visual perception verb. In Even (Tungusic) example (9), the perfect-resultative form together with the question word *įamį* 'why' expresses the mirative meaning (Zippel 2012: 58).

(9) Even (Greed 2018: 945, Zippel 2012: 58)
     Taḓǔk   ***koje:*** *(koje:-t-tu)*   *įamį   kǫbalaŋ-ŋ-un*
     DIST:ABL   watch watch-RES-NFUT.1PL.EXCL   why   bear-ALI-POSS.1PL.INCL
     koke-če.
     die-PTCP.PRF
     'Then we look, why, the bear is dead.'

---

5 "Insubordination" (Evans 2007) / "desubordination" (Aikhenvald 2010): conventional omitting of matrix clauses, resulting in reanalysis of non-finite complement clause predicates as evidentials and miratives (see L. Campbell 1991 for Estonian reportatives, Skribnik 1998 for Mansi miratives, Nevskaya 2002 for mirative constructions in Shor etc.)

A mirative extension of the inferential evidential in Nganasan is also illustrated by an example with the *veni, vidi* sequence (10).

(10) Nganasan (Gusev 2007: 425)
*Məkiʔa **ŋarəbtu-sa kat'əmi-ʔə** kəndə-tu   ńini məkini-nti*
back   turn-CVB   see-PERF sledge-GEN.POSS.3SG on behind-POSS.3SG
ŋəmtə-baδa-ʔ   *ŋanaʔsa*
sit-INFER-3SG.REFL   man
'Turning back, (the girl) saw: (to her surprise,) there is a man sitting on the sledge behind her.'

Expression of auditory perception in comparison to visual perception has both similar and differentiating features. Verbs of hearing can be preceded not only by verbs of motion: situations are common in folklore when a static protagonist hears a strange/unexpected sound or someone (unexpected) arriving. The protagonists are usually in the tent / house, listening to what is happening outside.[6] Such situations can be part of the Hero's Departure/Hero's Return, but also of other "building blocks" of folklore narratives, like Proppian Function 4 ("Antagonist(s) makes Attempt at Reconnaissance") or Function 8 "Villainy" ("Villain(s) approaching"). The following expression is also marked as mirative or gets a mirative reading.

Thus, Ob-Ugric languages use either miratives after verbs of auditory perception (11) similarly to the visual perception, – or constructions with a participial complement clause and the matrix verb *sujt-* 'to be heard' (12).

(11) North Mansi (Mansi Tales 2015: 18)
xu:ntl-i   *me:ŋkw-ət e:kw-anəl*   ***potərta-ne:-nəl.***
hear-PRS[3SG] giant-PL   wife-POSS.PL<3SG/PL talk-MIR.PRS-POSS.3PL
[After killing three forest giants, the hero continued his journey and found a big house. As he approached it,] '(He) hears: (as it turned out,) the wives of these forest giants are talking.' [The hero learned how they plan to avenge the death of their husbands, and avoided their traps.]

---

6 Il'jina (2017) stresses two important sociocultural factors that could influence the emergence of auditives (non-visual evidentials) in Samoyed languages and in Yukaghir. First, light mobile dwellings in the tundra (conic tents covered by reindeer pelts) allow people to hear everything that happens outside without seeing it. Second, animism and shamanism presuppose communication with invisible spirits.

(12) North Mansi (Mansi Tales 2015: 8)
    akwmat **xu:ntl-i**   *wo:r* *pa:l-nəl* *xotjut*   *tat^jem* *ta:kəs^j*
    once   hear-PRS[3SG] forest side-ABL something so   strong
    xa:jt-um-e   **sujt-əs**
    run-PTCP.PST-POSS.3SG   be_heard-PST[3SG]
    [A young girl talked too loudly after sunset, breaking the taboo. She could not sleep that night.] '(She) hears something approaching very fast from the forest.' [She could not wake up her parents while the forest spirit was jumping on the roof, but she was well-behaved ever after.]

These two Mansi examples suggest once more that miratives originate from non-finite complement clauses (here a subject clause, as the matrix verb means 'to be heard') through desubordination: formally they are still participles/action nouns with possessive personal marking.

    Samoyedic languages possessing auditive (non-visual evidential) can use this form (13). Indirective evidentials with a mirative extension can also be used, as shown in (14).

(13) Selkup (INEL Selkup corpus, NEP_196X_OrphanBoyAndPanOldMan2_
    flk: 119)
    na *ija* **tül'-č'i-kunä,**   *ponä* *ima-ti*   **üŋkil-ti-mpa.**
    this guy come-PERF-AUD[3SG] outside wife-POSS.3SG hear-IPF-DUR[3SG]
    [The hero went to search for his enemies, but they arrived at his house instead. Nevertheless, he comes back in time to oppose them.] 'This guy is returning (it can be heard), his wife hears (it) from outside (to her joy).' [The battle starts and the hero wins.]

In example (13) the verb 'hear' is postposed: the narrator added it as an afterthought, explaining who learned this information and experienced the surprise. In the next example the clause order is standard and iconic:

(14) Selkup (Urmanchieva 2014: 72)
    Ütynyk **üŋkylty-mp-a-ty:**   *picy-t*   *sümy*   **ünny-nty.**
    evening hear-DUR-AOR-3SG.OBJ axe-GEN sound be_heard-INFER[3SG]
    'Towards evening (he) listens: the sound of an axe can be heard.'

In (14) the verb of auditory perception carries the object suffix (number and person of the object are not differentiated). Both the auditive and the indirective are of non-finite origin (cf. Gusev 2017). It can be seen as one more case of desubordination at work in the semantic zone of evidentiality/mirativity (more on the topic see Skribnik and Aikhenvald forthcoming).

Note that clauses denoting perceived events in perception constructions *per se* are neutral, they get mirative readings after pre-mirative sequences used in the Hero's Journey part of the tale.

10.3.3 Further components of pre-mirative contexts

Verbs of cognition/comprehension (*comprehendi*) appear relatively seldom and indicate that the following mirative value is a deferred realization:

(15) North Mansi (OUDB, NM, 1229: 85)
    jujio:wəlt **ta:ra_patt-əs-te**   **nasat^ji**   *tak^wi n^ja:wram-aγe*
    finally   get_to_know-PST-SG<3SG   PTCL.MIR own child-POSS.DU<3SG
    al-ima-y
    kill-MIR.PST.PASS-3DU
    [A cannibal witch brought the hero to her home. When she was gone, he persuaded her children to set him free and then killed them. He cooked their bodies in the kettle for the witch to eat and hid himself. When she came back, she tasted the food and called her children to join her; they did not answer.] 'Finally, she understood: her two children were murdered.'

(16) Khakas (Khakas corpus, 1.1034)
    Aniŋzar *pazox* *paxla-biz-ip,*   **sızın-ge-m:** *taniy-lar* <...>
    DEM.ALL again look-PERF-CVB feel-PST-1SG sign-PL
    xojrix-majrix *taa*   *pol-za*   *stročka-li* **paz-il-tir**
    scattered   PTCL be-CVB.COND line-ADV write-PASS-INDIR/MIR
    'Taking one more look at it, I realized: the signs, though scattered, were (actually) written in lines.'

This component of a pre-mirative sequence, often omitted, can be "reconstructed" by native speakers in translations, as in (17); the mirative reading of an indicative present form here is induced by the context and supported by the emphatic particle =*no*.

(17) Shor (Shor corpus, *Ačiqta*: 48)
    Anaŋ *mattap*   **kör-gen-im**   *ılar* *iygele* *meeni*
    then attentively look-PTCP.PST-POSS.1SG they both 1SG.ACC

askayla-p	**qatqıčaqta-š-ča-lar=no**
laugh_at-CVB	laugh-MULT-PRS-PL=PTCL

[A young boy was asked by his two elder cousins to pray to forest spirits. He did it earnestly until he noticed that they were laughing.] 'Then, as I looked attentively at them, (I realized that) they were indeed laughing derisively at me (to my surprise and shock).'

The last possible component of a pre-mirative sequence, a verb of speech (*dixi*), is usually implied. The following mirative expression is a "reported thought" more often than a "reported speech" of the protagonist, presented by the "omniscient narrator". Example (18) from an Evenki heroic epic poem is a rare case where this fact is expressed unambiguously: the narrator stresses that the hero 'talks to himself', and the speech verbs are placed not before, but after the reported speech expression.

(18) Evenki (FMPS 1: 140, transcription and glossing Olga Kazakevich, personal communication)

il-da-n=da:		*di:gidə:-duk-ki:*		*alaŋa-wi:*	
stand_up-NFUT-3SG=PTCL.FOC		up_mountain-ABL-DIR		bow-ACC.REFL.SG	
ča:wari:-hi(n)-na-n=da:		*tuliski:*	**ju:-məlčə-rə-n**		*ertiki:*
catch-INC-NFUT-3SG=PTCL.FOC		outside	go_out-MOM-NFUT-3SG		here
tartiki:	**adu:ra:-ra-n**	*so:*	*aja-ja*	*ə-čə:*	*ičə-rə*
there	look-NFUT-3SG	very	good-ACC.INDEF	NEG-PERF[3SG]	see-CNG
aja-ja		*a:čin*	*inəŋi:*	*bi-diŋə:-s*	*bo:llaga*	**gun-nə**
good-ACC.INDEF		NEG.EX	day	be-FUT-2SG	probably	say-CVB
mə:n-i-n		*do:-du:-wi:*		**sumkə:t-nə**	
REFL-EP-POSS.3SG		inside-DLOC-REFL.SG		persuade-CVB	
mə:n-ńu:n-mi		**ulgučə:-mə:t-tə-n**			
REFL-COM-REFL.SG		talk-RCPR-NFUT-3SG			

[A brother and a sister grew up alone. The brother asked why no one ever came to them. The sister answered that people could come with evil intentions. Both had bad dreams that night.] '(The brother) stood up, grasped his bow (from above), and ran out. He took a look here and there (interpreting what he saw as a bad sign). "Nothing very good is to be seen, you probably will not have a good day", so saying he talked to (lit. with) himself, persuading himself (lit. inside himself).'

The whole narrative here is in the non-future (or aorist) form in -*RA* (the choice of its consonant is conditioned by the last consonant of the stem, its vowel by the vowel harmony). The "reported speech or thought" contains the negative auxiliary *ə-čə:* with the past perfect marker *-čA* (of participial origin) which can also have evidential extension: "may also denote the recent past situations that were not witnessed by the speaker" (Nedjalkov 1997: 239). Further he states: "Forms in -rA and -chA very rarely co-occur in one sentence or in one narrative chain. If a speaker chooses one of these forms for narration (e.g. -rA) it will continue to be used throughout the narrative. If the forms co-occur then the form in -chA either denotes a pragmatically important result or expresses a situation prior to that of the main verb" (Nedjalkov 1997: 239). This "pragmatically important result" in the *veni, vidi* context additionally gets a mirative reading.

Verbs of speech usually appear if several protagonists communicate with each other, as in (19).

(19) North Mansi (OUDB NM, 1237: 96)
      te:n **la:w-e:y** **nasatʲi** *me:nki ja:ɣpi:ɣ-me:n* **o:l-əm**
      3DU say-PRS.3DU PTCL.MIR 1DU brother-POSS.SG<1DU be-MIR.PST[3SG]
      [On entering, the hero's steps split the floorboards into small pieces; judging by this, the masters of the house arrive at an astounding conclusion.] 'The two of them say: You must be our brother.'

Similarly to perception constructions, the direct speech in narratives is not necessarily mirative *per se* – and it can also include miratives independently from the context. Still, in the Hero's Journey context the mirative reading is prevailing.

10.4 Mirative and pre-mirative marking

Pre-mirative > mirative sequences in narratives are treated differently in different languages. All previous examples illustrated mirative marking in clauses presenting an unexpected event, be it a dedicated mirative form or a mirative extension. However, specific marking can be employed not only in the final, mirative part, but also in the last pre-mirative clause (possibly also in both). Thus, two connected questions arise: Which verbal forms in the language in question are selected for the mirative clause? Which verbal forms are selected for the final link in the pre-mirative sequence?

A choice of a special converb or a particle with a finite form for the final pre-mirative clause can be seen as "pre-mirative marking". It is also context-dependent, i.e. can be characterized as "pre-mirative extension" of certain mostly temporal constructions. Though specialized "mirative" converbs are rare (e.g. a converb of unusual manner in Buryat, see Skribnik 2003: 117), there exist temporal succession forms denoting an abrupt change, a succession of opposing events or states ("unexpected succession"). For instance, in Buryat the polyfunctional "terminative converb" in *-tAr* denotes not only a terminal boundary ('A until B') but also an unexpected succession ('A, but then unexpected B') or simultaneity ('During continuous A, punctiliar unexpected B') (Skribnik and Darzhaeva 2016: 171–173). In pre-mirative sequences exactly this converb usually marks verbs of motion, as in (20).

(20)   Buryat (FMPS 20: 210)
  . . . oj sooguur jaba-na   *xa.*   *Tiige-že* **jaba-tar-aa,**
  forest in   go-PRS[3SG/PL] PTCL.MOD V.DEM-CVB go-CVB.TERM-REFL
  baaxalda-taj *uulza-ba*   *xa.*
  bear-COM meet-PST[3SG/PL] PTCL.MOD
  [The trickster wanted to hide his mother from the revenge of his last victim.]
  '(They) went into the forest. While (they) were walking this way, (they) met
  (lit. with) a bear.' [The trickster fights with it.]

Verbs of visual perception in such sequences often take a complex form *-n ge-xe-de*(-POSS); it is an idiomatized combination of a general temporal form *-xA-dA* (-POSS) (PTCP.FUT-DLOC with optional possessive marking) and a periphrastic form *-n ge-* (a modal converb and the auxiliary quotative verb *ge-* 'say'). This form denotes an immediate succession, often after an action that has started but was not necessarily completed. As a final link in a pre-mirative sequence, it signals that what follows is an immediate realization of what has happened, by the protagonists:

(21)   Buryat (Buryat corpus)
  Nileed *uda-n*   *jaba-ža,* *tedener* *elhen* *dobo-joo*
  quite slow_down-CVB.MOD go-CVB they sand hill-REFL
  gatal-ba.   *Gente* **xara-n** **ge-xe-de-n',** *tee*
  cross-PST[3SG/PL] suddenly see-CVB.MOD AUX-PTCP.FUT-DLOC a_little
  urda-n'   *nogoon* *dolgito-n* *bai-ba*
  before-POSS.3SG grass sway-CVB.MOD be-PST[3SG]
  [Tired travelers move through wastelands.] 'Moving quite slowly, they
  crossed over this sandy hill. Suddenly they noticed that a little further
  on (lit. a little before them) there was grass swaying.' [They hurried their
  horses to reach it.]

Buryat has lost common Mongolic evidentials (Brosig and Skribnik 2018) and seems to be in the process of grammaticalizing a new set; there are no dedicated miratives, though some periphrastic forms demonstrate a tendency to be used with mirative extensions. Consequently, mirative meanings are co-expressed through specific converbs in the final clause of pre-mirative sequences.

South Siberian Turkic languages demonstrate different tendencies. Tuvan uses in such constructions the general temporal form *-Ar-gA* (PTCP.FUT-DAT) 'when', common to all Turkic languages of this region. In the mirative clause the same past tense form is used as in the whole narrative, the perfect/indirective in *-GAn*, also common for many Turkic languages since Middle Turkic (Johanson 2018: 514). Thus, no specialized marking is used, the mirative extension of the indirective evidential is implied by the context.

(22) Tuvan (FMPS 8: 238)

Aldïï	*oran-ga*	*bar-ïp*		*düš-keš,*	*argamčï-zïn*		*bagla-p*
below	land-DAT	descend-CVB		AUX-CVB	lasso-POSS.3SG.ACC		tie-CVB

qaaš,	**qïlašta-p**	**čoruu-r-ga,**	*mal-dïg*	*čaŋgïs*	*ulug*
AUX.CVB	march-CVB	go-PTCP.FUT-DAT	cattle-PROPR	lone	big

ak	*ög*	**tur-gan.**
white	tent	stand-INDIR[3SG]

[The hero pursues an unknown rider who killed off all animals in his hunting grounds; the traces lead to the Underworld.] 'After descending into the Underworld and tying his lasso, he goes further (and sees to his amazement): there stands alone a big white tent surrounded by cattle.'

In Shor, Khakas, and Altai-kizhi, pre-mirative sequences are closed not by regular temporal converbs, but by some specific form from several options. In Shor it is a form of the perfect participle in *-GAn* with possessive personal marking, grammaticalized as a converb (23), (see also example (17)).

(23) Shor (Shor corpus, *Mašmoruq*: 15)

Čelbegen	*anaŋ*	*kel-ip*	**kör-gen-i**	*Mašmoruq*	*payba-ya*
NAME	then	come-CVB	look-PTCP.PRF-POSS3SG	NAME	sack-DAT

irik	*töŋeš*	*tïqta-p*	*sal-a*	**per-tir,**	*pooz-u*
rotten	stump	put-CVB	put_in-CVB	give-INDIR/MIR[3SG]	self-POSS.3SG

čoyul.
NEG.EX.FOC

[A cannibal caught the hero and brought him home in a sack. When the cannibal took a nap, the hero managed to free himself. The cannibal's children sang a song about their father bringing them a rotten stump to eat.] 'Chelbegen came closer and looked into the sack: (as it turned out,) Mashmoruk had put a rotten stump into the sack, he was not in there anymore.'

Khakas and Altai-kizhi prefer the conditional converb in -*SA* in pre-mirative contexts, as in (24–25).

(24) Khakas (Khakas corpus)
  *Pıs   čügüris kil-ıp   **kör-ze-bıs**,   Sanqa-aabaj Petke-nı*
  1PL run   come-CVB look-CVB.COND-POSS.1PL NAME   NAME-ACC
  *xulaa-naŋ   tut   **sal-tïr***
  ear.POSS.3SG-ABL hold   AUX-INDIR/MIR[3SG]
  '[Hearing shouts,] We came in running and saw: Sanqa-abai holds Petke by the ear (to our surprise).'

(25) Altai-kizhi (FMPS 21: 142)
  *Tujuq   qara   d'iš-ti   **odü-p   čïq-sa**,   uč-i_baž-i*
  thick   black   forest-ACC pass-CVB AUX-CVB.COND   top-POSS.3SG
  *kör-ün-bes,   teŋeri-ge d'edi-p   qal-gan   tajga   **turu***.
  see-PASS-PTCP.NEG sky-DAT   touch-CVB AUX-PTCP.PST mountain PTCL.MIR
  [A young woman follows a witch who stole her baby. She meets supernatural obstacles on her way and helpers to get across.] 'As (she) passed through the thick black forest, (she saw to her surprise that) there stands a (huge) mountain, touching the sky, its top invisible.'

All three languages also have an indirective in -*GAn*, like Tuvan. Nevertheless, in Shor and Khakas examples (23–24) a younger indirective/mirative form in -*(p)TIr* is used. The marker goes back to a periphrastic construction with an auxiliary *tur*- 'stand' (Johanson 2018: 515). In addition to -*GAn* and -*(p)TIr* forms, Altai-kizhi has a set of dedicated mirativity markers. Diachronically they belong to different chronological layers, and synchronically they reflect differing degrees of speaker's surprise: the older the marker, the weaker the mirative effect. Similar to the renewal of negation in Jespersen's cycle, the older mirative markers were replaced by new ones expressing stronger surprise; it is an indication of communicative importance of mirativity in Altai-kizhi (Skribnik and Ozonova 2007; Skribnik and Aikhenvald forthcoming). Example (25) shows one of the newer mirative particles grammaticalized from the same auxiliary verb *tur*- 'stand'. In combination with the *SA*-converb on the verb of motion, Altai-kizhi example illustrates a case of both pre-mirative and mirative marking in a Hero's Journey sequence.

  Ket offers an example of a particle which marks a finite verb within a pre-mirative sequence. The particle *qāj* among other functions indicates that the following clause expresses "an unforeseen, unexpected event" (Kotorova and

Nefedov 2015: 268; cf. also Gajer 1971),[7] similarly to "unexpected succession" converbs in Buryat. In a pre-mirative context, it indicates that the clause following *qāi* has a mirative reading as in (26).

(26) Ket (Ket Tales 1969: 171, transcription and glossing by Olga Kazakevich, personal communication)
      qāj   *d-ik-o-[i]l-do-n*   *kī*   *hāj*   *bən*   *qajkus'*
      PTCL SUBJ.3PL.ANIM-here-TH-PST-look-SUBJ.PL this again NEG spirit
      [The younger brother caught a sable in the forest who turned out to be a *qajkus'* (forest spirit) in the form of a beautiful woman, and brought her home as his second wife. He became an extraordinary successful hunter. His envious elder brothers killed him to get the *qajkus'* for themselves, but she felt the moment of his death and fled to the Underworld. The first wife refused to join her. The brothers come and catch the woman they believe to be *qajkus'*.] 'They looked – it was not the forest spirit!' [The brothers had killed the first wife, the *qajkus'* revived her husband in the Underworld and they lived happily ever after.]

Some examples combine the particle *qāj* in the last pre-mirative clause and the mirative particle *bīn* in the following clause, so Ket, similarly to Altai-kizhi, can employ double marking in Hero's Journey sequences.

10.5 Conclusions

In this preliminary overview I have outlined some common tendencies of Siberian folklore language: there do exist sets of linguistic means that are given preference in text sequences that correspond to the important structural element of a folklore narrative – the Hero's Journey. Practically every instance of a sequence "verb of motion – verb of visual perception" (*veni, vidi*) is followed by a clause with a mirative reading, so that such a sequence seems to have a special culturally conditioned narrative and communicative function.

Linguistic marking can occur to the right of the pre-mirative/mirative borderline, and here miratives will be used, or non-mirative forms will acquire a mirative extension. The marking can also occur on the left side of this borderline through special converbs or different particles. Often the chosen converbial forms indicate

---

7 Georg (2007: 449) calls it a backgrounding, "anti-mirativity" particle, with no further explanation and no examples.

an unexpected temporal sequence or an abrupt change of situation. Such forms add to the suspense of the plot and acquire "pre-mirative" reading. Additional research is needed to find out whether the type of contextual implicature produced by the Hero's Journey context plays a role in emergence of grammaticalized mirativity. Can the Hero's Journey /*veni, vidi* sequence indeed be one of the "birthplaces of mirativity"?

Many questions are still open: which forms are preferably used in such sequences in the absence of miratives, indicative, modal, or evidential? Are they simple or periphrastic? Are particles involved? What is the role of intonation? If a language has evidentials, which semantic type will be selected and acquire mirative overtones, indirective/inferential or direct perception forms? All these are questions for the further research.

Abbreviations and glossing conventions

The glossing of the examples, with a few marginal exceptions, follows the Leipzig Glossing Rules. Morphemes written in capital letters for Altaic and Uralic languages represent the most frequently attested underlying allomorphs (suffixal consonants can be influenced by the last consonant of the stem, and vowels follow the vowel harmony rules). Personal names are glossed as NAME. In "objective conjugation" (subject-object agreement paradigm) notations like SG<3SG mean "object in singular, subject in 3rd person singular", and 3SG.OBJ means "subject in 3rd person singular, any object". Similar notation for possessive markers (POSS. SG<3SG) means "possessee in singular, possessor in 3rd person singular".

1, 2, 3	first, second, third person
ABL	ablative
ACC	accusative
ADJ	adjectivizing suffix
ADV	adverbialising suffix
ALI	alienable possession
ALL	allative
ANIM	animated
AOR	aorist
AUD	auditive
AUX	auxiliary
CNG	connegative
CO	coaffix
COM	comitative
COND	conditional

CVB	converb
D	determiner
DAT	dative
DEM	demonstrative pronoun
DIST	distal
DLOC	dative-locative
DU	dual
DUR	durative
EP	epenthetic
EXCL	exclusive
FUT	future
GEN	genitive
ILL	illative
INCL	inclusive
INDEF	indefinite
INDIR	indirective
INF	infinitive
INFER	inferentive
IPFV	imperfective
LAT	lative
LOC	locative
M	masculine
MIR.PRS	mirative present
MIR.PST	mirative past
MIR.PST.PASS	mirative past passive
MOD	modal
MOM	momentaneous
MULT	multiplicative
N	neutral
NFUT	non-future
OBJ	object, object agreement
PASS	passive
PERF	perfect; perfective
POSS	possessive
PRED	predicate
PROL	prolative
PROPR	proprietive
PRS	present
PST	past
PST.NARR	past narrative
PTCL	particle
PTCL.FOC	focal particle
PTCL.MIR	mirative particle
PTCP.FUT	future participle
PTCP.PRF	perfect participle
PTCP.PRS	present participle
PTCP.PST	past participle

R	root (of a light verb in a compound)
RCPR	reciprocal
REFL	reflexive
RES	resultative
SG	singular
SUBJ	subject, subject agreement
TERM	terminative
TH	thematic vowel
TR	transitivising suffix
TRNS	translative
V	verb

Sources

Buryat corpus: [http://web-corpora.net/BuryatCorpus] (last accessed 14 July 2022).

FMSP 1 = *Эвенкийские героические сказания. Храбрый Содани-богатырь. Всесильный богатырь Дэвэлчэн в расшитой-разукрашенной одежде.* 1990. (Памятники фольклора народов Сибири и Дальнего Востока, т. 1). [Evenki Heroic Epos. Folklore Monuments of the Peoples of Siberia and the Far East, vol.1.] Новосибирск : Наука.

FMSP 8 = *Тувинские народные сказки.* 1994. (Памятники народов Сибири и Дальнего Востока, т. 8.) [Tuvan folktales. Folklore Monuments of the Peoples of Siberia and the Far East, vol. 8.] Новосибирск: Наука.

FMSP 20 = *Бурятские народные сказки. О животных. Бытовые.* 2000. (Памятники народов Сибири и Дальнего Востока, т. 20.) [Buryat folktales. Animal tales. Realistic tales. Folklore Monuments of the Peoples of Siberia and the Far East, vol. 20.] Новосибирск: Наука.

FMSP 21 = *Алтайские народные сказки* (Памятники народов Сибири и Дальнего Востока, т. 21.) [Altai-kizhi folktales. Folklore Monuments of the Peoples of Siberia and the Far East, vol. 21.] Новосибирск: Наука. 2002.

INEL Selkup corpus = Maria Brykina, Svetlana Orlova & Beáta Wagner-Nagy. 2020. INEL Selkup Corpus. Version 1.0. Publication date 2020-06-30. Archived in Hamburger Zentrum für Sprachkorpora. http://hdl.handle.net/11022/0000-0007-E1D5-A. In Beáta Wagner-Nagy, Alexandre Arkhipov, Anne Ferger, Daniel Jettka & Timm Lehmberg (eds.), *The INEL corpora of indigenous Northern Eurasian languages.* (Last accessed 14 July 2022).

Ket Tales 1969 = *Кетский сборник. Мифология, этнография, тексты.* [Ket collection: Mythology, Ethnography, Texts.] Москва: Наука.

Khakas corpus: [https://khakas.altaica.ru/corpus] (last accessed 14 July 2022).

Mansi Tales 2015 = *Сказки, песни, загадки народа манси. Фольклорный сборник.* Сост. Кумаева М.В. [Tales, songs, riddles of Mansi people.] Ханты-Мансийск: ОУИПИР.

OUDB = Ob-Ugric Database, [http://www.babel.gwi.uni-muenchen.de] (last accessed 14 July 2022).

Shor corpus: [https://www.shoriya.uni-frankfurt.de] (last accessed 14 July 2022).

Khanty Tales 2002 = *Арєм-моньщєм еɟ ки мӑнɟ . . . Если моя сказка-песня дальше пойдёт . . .*
(*Фольклорное творчество Пелагеи Алексеевны Гришкиной из деревни Тугияны.)*
Сост. Л. Р. Хомляк. [If my song and tale goes further . . . Folklore Heritage of Pelageja
Grishkina from Tugijany village.] Ханты-Мансийск: Полиграфист.

References

Aikhenvald, Alexandra Y. 2010. *Imperatives and commands.* Oxford: Oxford University Press.
Aikhenvald, Alexandra Y. 2012. The essence of mirativity. *Linguistic Typology* 16. 435–485.
Brosig, Benjamin & Elena Skribnik. 2018. Evidentiality in Mongolic. In Alexandra Y. Aikhenvald
(ed.), *The Oxford handbook of evidentiality*, 554–579. Oxford: Oxford University Press.
Campbell, Joseph. 2008 [1949, 1968]. *The hero with a thousand faces*, 3rd edn. (Bollingen
Series XVII). Novato, California: New World Library.
Campbell, Lyle. 1991. Some grammaticalization changes in Estonian and their implications.
In Elizabeth C. Traugott & Bernd Heine (eds.), *Approaches to grammaticalization*, vol. 1,
285–299. Amsterdam: John Benjamins.
DeLancey, Scott. 1997. Mirativity: The grammatical marking of unexpected information.
Linguistic Typology 1. 33–52.
Evans, Nicholas 2007. Insubordination and its uses. In Irina Nikolaeva (ed.), *Finiteness:
Theoretical and empirical foundations*, 366–431. Oxford: Oxford University Press.
Gajer 1971 = Гайер Р. С . О различных случаях употребления и оттенках значения частицы
кай в имбатском диалекте кетского языка [Combinatorics and semantics of the particle
qai in Ket]. *Языки и топонимия Сибири*. Вып. 4. 37–46. Томск: Изд-во ТГУ.
Georg, Stefan. 2007. *A descriptive grammar of Ket (Yenisei-Ostyak)*, vol. 1, *Introduction,
phonology, morphology* (Languages of Asia 1). Folkestone: Global Oriental.
Georg, Stefan. 2008. Yenisseic languages and the Siberian Linguistic Area. In Alexander
Lubotsky, Jos Schaeken, Jeroen Wiedenhof, Rick Derksen & Sjoerd Siebinga (eds.),
Evidence and counter-evidence: Essays in honour of Frederik Kortlandt (Studies in Slavic
and General Linguistics 33), vol. 2., 151–168. Amsterdam/New York: Rodopi.
Greed, Teja. 2018. From perfect to narrative tense: The development of an evidential meaning
examined generally and in the Even language. *Studies in Language* 42(4). 923–966.
Gusev 2007 = Гусев, Валентин Ю.: Эвиденциальность в нганасанском языке [Evidentiality
in Nganasan]. В. С. Храковский (ред.) *Эвиденциальность в языках Европы и Азии*,
415–444. Санкт-Петербург: Наука.
Gusev, Valentin. 2017. On the etymology of auditive in Samoyedic. *Finnisch-Ugrische
Mitteilungen* 41. 131–151.
Il'jina 2017 = Ильина Л.А. О вероятных социокультурных детерминантах граммем
незрительной чувственной засвидетельствованности в диахронии языков Северной
Азии [Sociocultural factors determining the development of non-visual evidentials in
languages of North Asia]. *Сибирский филологический журнал* 2017(2). 159–174.
Johanson, Lars. 2018. Turkic indirectivity. In Alexandra Y. Aikhenvald (ed.), *The Oxford
Handbook of evidentiality*, 510–524. Oxford: Oxford University Press.
Kotorova, Elizaveta & Andrej Nefedov. 2015. *Comprehensive dictionary of Ket*, vol. 1 (Languages
of the World / Dictionaries 57). Munich: Lincom Europa.

Labov, William. 1997. Some further steps in narrative analysis. *Journal of narrative and life history* 7. 395–415.

Nedjalkov, Igor V. 1997. *Evenki*. London/New York: Routledge.

Nevskaya, Irina. 2002. Evidentials, miratives and indirectives in Shor. In Nurettin Demir & Fikret Turan (eds.), *Scholarly depth and accuracy: A festschrift to Lars Johanson*, 307–321. Ankara: Grafiker.

Propp 1969 [1928] = Пропп В.Я. *Морфология сказки* [Morphology of the Folktale], 2-е изд. (Исследования по фольклору и мифологии Востока 1). Москва: Главная редакция восточной литературы издательства «Наука».

Quirk, Randolph, Sidney Greenbaum, Geoffrey Leech & Jan Svartvik. 1985. *A comprehensive grammar of the English language*. London: Longman.

Shabaev 1982 = Шабаев В.Г. Использование частицы *бин* для выражения видового значения завершенности в кетском языке [The particle *bin* expressing perfectivity in Ket]. *Грамматические исследования по языкам Сибири*, 153–159. Новосибирск: Наука.

Sipos, Mária. 2022. North Khanty. In Marianne Bakró-Nady, Johanna Laakso & Elena Skribnik (eds.), *The Oxford guide to the Uralic languages*, 582–607. Oxford: Oxford University Press.

Skribnik 1998 = Скрибник Е.К. К вопросу о неочевидном наклонении в мансийском языке (структура и семантика) [Evidentials in North Mansi: Structure and semantics]. *Языки коренных народов Сибири*. Вып. 4, 197–215. Новосибирск: Изд-во СО РАН.

Skribnik, Elena. 1999. Miratives and pre-mirative contexts in West-Siberian languages. Paper presented at ALT III, Third Biennal Conference of the Association for Linguistic Typology, Amsterdam, 26–29 August, 1999.

Skribnik, Elena. 2003. Buryat. In Juha Janhunen (ed.), *The Mongolic languages*, 102–128. (Routledge language family series). London/New York: Routledge.

Skribnik, Elena & Alexandra Y. Aikhenvald. forthcoming. Evidentiality in languages of Northern Asia. In Edward Vajda & José Andrés Alonso de la Fuente (eds.), *The languages and linguistics of Northern Asia: A comprehensive guide*.

Skribnik & Darzhaeva 2016 = Скрибник Е.К., Даржаева Н.Б. *Грамматика бурятского языка. Синтаксис сложного (полипредикативного) предложения*. Т. 1. [The grammar of Buryat: Clause combining, Vol. 1.] Улан-Удэ: Изд-во БНЦ СО РАН.

Skribnik & Ozonova 2007 = Скрибник Е.К., Озонова А.А. Средства выражения засвидетельствованности и миративности в алтайском языке [Evidentiality and mirativity in Altai-kizhi]. *Эвиденциальность в языках Европы и Азии*, 519–551. Санкт-Петербург: Наука.

Urmanchieva 2014 = Урманчиева А.Ю. Эвиденциальные показатели селькупского языка. Соотношение семантики и прагматики в описании глагольных граммем [Evidential markers in Selkup]. *Вопросы языкознания* 4. 66–86.

Uther, Hans-Jörg. 2004. *The types of international folktales: A classification and bibliography. Based on the system of Antti Aarne and Stith Thompson*, vols. 1–3. (Folklore Fellows' Communications 284–286.) Helsinki: Suomalainen Tiedeakatemia.

Vajda, Edward J. 2004. *Ket*. Munich: Lincom Europa.

Zippel, Luise. 2012. *Finitheit im Ewenischen: Eine Untersuchung verbaler (In)finität unter besonderer Berücksichtigung des dialektalen Vergleichs des Perfektpartizips auf -čE*. Leipzig: Universität Leipzig MA thesis.

Francesca Merlan

11 Jawoyn trickster stories of Southern Arnhem Land

Trickster stories have been recorded world-wide, along with continuing debate about how well-defined a genre this may be. Trickster stories have not been recorded as such for Australia. This paper features two examples of what seem unproblematically to be trickster stories of southern Arnhem Land, northern Australia. The two example stories have particular characteristics which justify their inclusion within a narrative type characterized by deception and the combination of norm-breaking and norm-setting. The stories and conclusions draw out the particular kinds of meanings that story-tellers of the region foreground, and the kind of narrative devices that they use. Although these stories were probably told for the amusement of mixed audiences, they seem to have been a speciality of male narrators of southern (and perhaps wider) Arnhem Land, at least over the latter part of the last century as languages and narrative traditions of the region have come to be at risk.

11.1 Introduction

A great number of anthropologists have written about tricksters and trickster tales: Franz Boas (1914), Robert Lowie (1909, 1918), Paul Radin (1956), Edward Evan Evans-Pritchard (1967), Mary Douglas (1970), Victor Turner (1986), Claude Lévi-Strauss (1963), Thomas Beidelman (1980) – among others. A great range of linguists, educationists and other students of communication have also done so.

Michael Carroll (1981) maintains that there is a tendency in this diverse literature to overgeneralize and apply the term "trickster" to any character type that makes extensive use of deception. Beidelman (1980) also finds the category too wide and suggests that one can really best study narratives within particular systems of meaning and symbolism.

This paper features two examples of what seem unproblematically to be trickster stories of southern Arnhem Land, northern Australia. Though they seem to fall easily within a broad concept of "trickster" stories, they have particular characteristics. This paper pays attention to both kinds of criticism cited above by illustrating the way in which deception seems to be characteristic of the genre

Francesca Merlan, Australian National University

https://doi.org/10.1515/9783110789836-011

in Jawoyn, a language of southern Arnhem Land,[1] justifying its inclusion within a narrative type usually characterized by deception; and by exemplifying the particular kinds of meanings that storytellers of the region foreground. Before turning to the Jawoyn stories, this paper sets out views on the characteristics of trickster stories in general, and expression of deception.

11.2 Tricksters in the literature

A considerable focus of the scholarship on tricksterism is on the "trickster" himself. The genre features a character type who embodies its key traits.

Hynes and Doty (1993) suggest six characteristics of the trickster figure:

(1) The trickster is ambiguous and anomalous in character. No borders are sacrosanct. The figure is polyvalent, often incorporating extremes and going beyond boundaries, as Claude Lévi-Strauss observed.

(2) The trickster is a deceiver and trick-player. The trickster is the cause of disruptions and disorders; but though he plays tricks on others, he often turns out to be the one duped. Deception is practised by the trickster but often projected upon him.

This can be illustrated with a famous episode of anthropologist Paul Radin's versions of the Winnebago Trickster cycle (Radin 1956: 15–18).[2] Trickster entices a group of ducks into dancing with their eyes closed; he wrings their necks and sets them out for a nice meal for himself in a sandbar. But other animals come and eat the ducks and stick the heads and tails back in the sand. The trickster is confounded to the point that he threatens to burn with a stick those whom he had set to watch his ducks, only to find that he is mistakenly poking the stick up his own anus, part of the narrative account about why the anus has the shape it does. Trickster eventually picks up and savours some of his own intestine which has fallen on the ground after being cooked in this way. He then self-designates, saying, "Correctly am I named the Foolish One, Trickster! By their calling me

---

1 Jawoyn is a language of the Gunwinyguan language family. It was spoken, doubtless in a number of dialects, along the upper Katherine River into southern Arnhem Land. People we know today as Jawoyn lived in close association with groups of southern Arnhem Land, including those collectively designated "Mayali" (see fn. 3), and Ngalkbon. Jawoyn speakers largely migrated south and west in the nineteenth and twentieth centuries, towards developing townships, mines and pastoral properties. As they did so, there is evidence of the reduction of dialect differences towards two slightly variant standard forms. Jawoyn is no longer actively spoken.
2 Radin designates the figure "Trickster" with a capital.

thus, they have at last actually turned me into a Foolish One, a Trickster!" (Radin 1956: 18).

In other words, the narrative presents a variety of perspectives on the events. The narrator represents the main figure as duping and killing the ducks. He is then duped by those he set to watch the ducks. He becomes aware of having been duped and physically mistakes his own body for something else. He calls himself stupid, at the same time setting the context for what the anus looks like.

The African Akan gum-baby and the American Br'er Rabbit stories also involve the tables turning on a trickster figure who wants to take advantage of others but eventually gets so tangled up with the tar baby that he cannot get away, and gets thrown by Br'er Fox into the briar patch. We will see that though the Jawoyn trickster is not narrated as reflexive; he sows chaos until he is extinguished by it.

(3) The trickster is a shape-shifter – he disguises himself and morphs. The Winnebago trickster is a man but capable of becoming a woman. There are levels of awareness represented, e.g from the Winnebago cycle: "Trickster took an elk's liver and made a vulva from it. Then he took some elk's kidneys and made breasts from them. Finally he put on a woman's dress. . . . He now stood there transformed into a very pretty woman indeed. Then he let the fox have intercourse with him and make him pregnant, then the jaybird and, finally, the nit. After that he proceeded toward the village where he married the chief's son and becomes pregnant to him, giving birth to a boy". Then he becomes pregnant twice more and gives birth to two more boys (Radin 1956: 22–23). Eventually, this "chief's son's wife" is discovered to be "trickster", and all the men, especially the chief's son, are ashamed of his anomalous behaviour. Trickster runs away and goes back to his erstwhile wife and son and to other adventures.

(4) The trickster is a situation-inverter, but this often results in the establishment of what are considered contemporary norms.

(5) Trickster is a messenger-imitator of the gods, or at least transcends the ordinary in a way that is both destructive and creative. He may destroy a previous status quo and introduce a new one, moving between sacred and profane.

(6) Trickster is often lewd and an improviser, a bricoleur. Tricksters perform sexual, gastronomic, and fecal feats. These obviously were an enormous element of narrative performance, such as when Winnebago trickster is sleeping and expels huge volumes of gas with loud eruptions, temporarily driving away the foxes who want to eat the roast duck he has planted in the sand (one can just imagine the fun Winnebago narrators made out of this).

Hynes and Doty (1993) point out that the combination of these dimensions of the trickster has led to many psychological and psycho-social kinds of analyses.

Indeed, the genre is aptly characterized as expressing many aspects of the pro-
hibited and the ineffable, psychically and verbally out of ordinary bounds.

Michael Carroll (1984) writes of the combination in the trickster of culture
hero and selfish buffoon. People desire both to satisfy their wants, and they desire
an orderly life. The trickster has inordinate appetites; but also sets in place or
preserves the status quo. Approached with a psychoanalytic eye, the figure may
be seen to represent a sort of basic, common concern about organization and dis-
organization in the world, disrupting but also setting the context of norms. The
trickster is an archetype; a tension-releasing figure (Jung in Radin 1956); a culture
hero often associated with particular (usually solitary) animal types (coyote,
spider, hare, raven). Roger Abrahams (1968) has said the trickster is paradoxical
in combining so many different types of characters: jester, hero, initiate, fool.

One conclusion that regularly emerges from the analyses of "trickster" figures
is that they are polyvalent, complex and unaccountable, beyond ordinary ethics.

11.3 Just tricking: Defining tricksterism

We may define "tricksterism" as a narrative complex of character and events in
which the trickster figure does things which become understood by the audience
as beyond the knowledge of another or others within the story, in a way that
advances the story-line.

As mentioned, in many North American Indian traditions, trickster figures
tend to be named as animals (Raven, Mink, Coyote, Hare, and so on). Many have
proper names, or epithets (e.g., *Waunchu* 'the mocker', Sioux, Lame Deer and
Erdoes 1994). These figures are sometimes referred to as "old man" or "firstborn"
(Radin 1956: 57, note 67).

Tricking involves duping and deception, but it need not involve lying. Lying
would overtly involve saying something to another that the trickster knows not to
be true. Duping or deception is different in that it need not involve direction of a
speech act to another within the narrated event. But it does involve the trickster's
acting in a way that may cause the person/s with whom he is interacting to think
or act in some way that s/he would not if s/he were privy to the trickster's intentions and thoughts. Duping, in short, is or may be less directly communicative with
another (character in the narrated event) than is lying. But there are questions
around who is duped or deceived, by whom and for how long, and how this is represented in narration. What kinds of concepts help us look at these states of affairs?

First, there is a trickster. Second, there is another party or parties with whom
the trickster is interacting. Third, there is an audience who are made aware in the

telling itself of the machinations of the trickster and the responses or actions of the other with whom the trickster is dealing. As this implies, the trickster story involves a Narrative Event (Jakobson 1984) within which the narrator and audience are in direct interaction, and a Narrated Event (Fig. 11.1). The communications within the Narrated Event are those between the trickster character and those with whom trickster is interacting. The story is told in such a way that the audience understands the duplicity being enacted, although in the stories before us, the trickster's interlocutors do not.

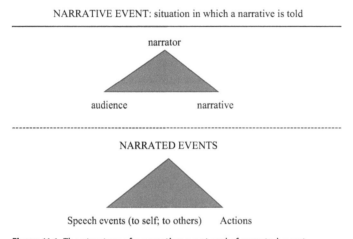

Figure 11.1: The structure of a narrative event and of narrated event.

The double framing of Narrative and Narrated Events is characteristic of storytelling generally, but what appears particular to trickster stories is the question of how the duplicity which characterizes the genre, and relatedly the special characteristics of the trickster as actor, is conveyed by the narrator to the audience through narrative style and content. This is not presented directly or explained; it is embodied in the narrative and conveyed in content and manner of expression (cf. Abrahams 1968).

11.4 Jawoyn trickster stories

The following (attached) stories were recorded (several times) over the course of my friendship and kinship with a set of men and their families of the region. The stories were part of their personal repertoires. They enjoyed them and returned to them on various occasions.

The places of residence of these men and their families had been, for the last several decades, Pine Creek and Katherine, two principal Northern Territory towns on the Stuart Highway. But their earlier years had been spent in and on the fringes of Arnhem Land; and both there, and in the towns where they later lived, their most closely associated "countrymen" were people of a background generally referred to (from a Katherine perspective) as Mayali,[3] people whose countries of origin are somewhat further north and east. Living together over decades in multilingual communities (where predominant languages were Bininj Gun-wok[4] and Jawoyn), these people shared a repertoire of story types and characters, to which these trickster stories belong.

Over the years I have known Jawoyn people (since 1976), the language has, unfortunately, ceased to be a spoken tongue. It is known only in a fragmentary manner by descendants of speakers. Bininj Gun-wok, especially in parts of Arnhem Land, remains more vital. I know from the Jawoyn men who told these stories that they shared experiences, stories and periods of residence with Mayali people over many years – hence my reference to the genre we will examine as one of southern and probably also Arnhem Land, not limited to Jawoyn-speaking people, but characteristic of them and the countrymen with whom they shared their camps and lives.

In this paper I examine some of the features of this kind of story as exemplified in the tellings of Peter Jatbula, a master raconteur. He and his close relatives, brothers and cousins, seem to have been among the most prolific exponents of aspects of southern Arnhem verbal and visual culture.[5]

With respect to the characteristics of tricksterism as set out above, we may summarize ways in which Jawoyn stories conform to them. The tricksters in the following stories are anomalous (1); they are deceivers (2), planning and carrying out things with the intention of duping others. With reference to (3) above, in the Jawoyn stories ahead, the trickster figure Najik is a shape-shifter who slips into holes, and trees. With reference to (4), trickster as disrupter but also establisher of norms: our Jawoyn stories tell how women used to hunt, but because of Najik's actions, men now hunt. With reference to (5), transcending the ordinary: the

---

3 The (multi-dialectical) language has been described by Evans (2003). From the perspective of people living in Katherine and communities to the south of Arnhem Land, these closely related speech forms are often referred to generically as "Mayali".

4 Evans (2003).

5 Peter Jatbula was born sometime in the early 1930s in Gimbat, a remote and fairly penurious cattle station in the upper-mid Northern Territory, south of Arnhem Land. The station drew to it people who originated from Arnhem Land and to the south of it, for whom the Katherine River and the Arnhem escarpment had been homelands.

Jawoyn Najik figure inaugurates both the transition from women's to men's hunting, and the sensitivity of kangaroos to smell. In relation to (6), trickster as lewd improviser and bricoleur, in the Jawoyn stories, Najik establishes current norms by farting. With respect to the role of appearance and personal characteristics of trickster, in Jawoyn stories below, one trickster figure is called Najik 'owlet nightjar', a rather surprising and menacing-looking bird. The other story concerns *na-balukgayin* 'the guardian' (a man charged with taking care of boys on their initiatory journey).

There is no single word in Jawoyn that expresses the concept generic concept "trickster"; the Jawoyn terms are specific sobriquets for these characters. *Balukgayin* is understood to be senior and is charged with a responsible role of making young men into adults. Instead of acting responsibly, he transgresses every norm of responsible and ethical behaviour.

The Jawoyn stories before us involve the narrator using content and paralinguistic expression, both with respect to *Najik* and *na-balukgayin*, to illuminate the trickster's anomalous character, and to couch his activities in particular ways.

11.4.1 Story 1: Najik, content and expressive features

Jawoyn does not mark case overtly on nominals in major subject and object clause functions. There is also no absolutely fixed subject-object order of independent nominals. From the first utterance (1), we know that the trickster, Najik, is on the lookout for women. He sees kangaroos and this is the cue for the narrator to establish a major theme of the story: women, not men, used to hunt (and that is why they are, as it turns out, cooking kangaroos).

Narrator Peter Jatbula establishes significant context in several sentences: "He just searched for women. He saw kangaroos. Women killed kangaroos then".

In listening to stories I often used to make minor comments or give signals indicating I was listening. Here I broke in briefly, causing Peter to answer my question: "Men didn't kill them, no". It is characteristic of these and much story-telling in Indigenous Australia that the narrator launches into the story without explicitly naming or identifying main characters.

In lines 8–11: Najik goes along and catches up to two people, but what sex they are is now placed in question as the narrator aligns the audience with Najik's inquisitive perspective. Najik peers at the people: "this one" is lying belly down; then they (*bu-* 3NSg) see *him*. Najik is prying, and the audience understands that he is trying to figure out the (sex of) the person lying down. But the audience narrator now knows that Najik and the other characters are aware of each other.

Lines 13–18: Najik asks a question designed to determine who they are; he addresses one as if she were a man, asking him/her "Are you and your wife by yourselves?" Najik's voice quality is nasal, odd. In voicing Najik in this way the narrator gives the audience to understand that Najik is not on the level; he is peculiar in some way. Thomas Beidelman (1980: 31), who writes about narrative traditions of East Africa, notes that trickery is often expressed through deviant speech patterns.

Yes, says the person, described by the narrator as *ngal-jaja-ngayu* 'her little sister' (*ngal-won ngal-jaja-ngayu*). This little sister says of the other person, S/he's (third person pronominal prefix is not gender-differentiated) got a bellyache; we the audience understand that this explains why she is lying down.

But we know by the fact that the person who answers is designated the "little sister" by the narrator that this person answering is in fact NOT a man; the narrator's lexical selection reveals that she is in fact a woman, and not the husband. So at this point we, the audience, know a few things: women, not men, used to hunt. This is scene-setting. Najik is not to be trusted: his voice quality signals this. The audience also knows from the beginning that Najik's always on the lookout for women. He suspects the two people he has encountered are women but tries to confirm this.

There is also some kind of collusion represented as going on between the two women about their identity. One has lain down (we begin to suppose, to hide that she is a woman), and the other, asked a question, answers AS IF they were a husband-and-wife pair to satisfy Najik's curiosity. But we know this isn't the case because the narrator tells us directly that the person who answers is a "little sister" of the other, NOT a man. Her saying that the other person is lying down because of a belly-ache begins to emerge as (possibly self-preserving) prevarication.

Yes, says Najik, she's got a bellyache MAYBE (*ngarra* revealing his doubt). *Ngarra* expresses doubt. More particularly, it is often used at the end of a rhetorical question, such as: *ngiyn-borr'mamang ngarra*? 'are you deaf?' where the thrust of the question is to create the effect of doubt, rather than actually ask a question expecting a substantive answer. So the first attempt to deceive is represented as on the part of the women: they are trying to make Najik think they are a husband and wife. But Najik is not easily taken in, and expresses his doubt.

He looks at her hard and says, "That's a woman" (not the "husband"). Immediately: how could she refuse me? This tells us more than we could have known, namely, that Najik had designs on the woman and is affronted by a seeming refusal. But she seems to have known that, and that is why (we later surmise) she tried to make Najik believe she was a man.

The focus returns to the women. They prepare kangaroo and put it in the ground oven; in lines 21–22 they give some of it to Najik, a choice piece of liver.

The narrator then tells us that Najik goes back to his humpy and articulates his plan to do them in: he's going to roast them. Slightly out of sequence, Najik then tells the women to cook, assuming that they will soon open the oven up. Then in lines 29–33 he really goes back to his humpy and gets a big piece of paperbark, enough to cover them up, the narrator says, with the kangaroo. He gratuitously calls the women loafers, bludgers; and he also expresses resentment that they lied to him: *ga-warrpmar*, he says, 'she is lying', "those two are women". Their lying is represented as fueling and justifying his resentment.

Lines 34–36: Najik goes back with the paperbark, slips into a hole (a tricksterish ability he has); they continue to prepare. Lines 42–51: He sneaks up on them, and sees them sharpening a blade, covering up the meat, putting stones on top to cook the meat. He runs over and covers them up with the paperbark, sweeping them into the pit. "Grandfather!", they cry out – but it's done. Najik proclaims, "That's what I do to you two sisters". He adds insult to the injury, calling them *na-bok-yurr'yurr-yark* 'two sluts', or 'sex-hungry'. Here the narrator makes an overtly evaluative remark: *na-baranggu ni nabay* 'he was a cheeky bugger'.

Lines 57–60: Najik waits while the two cook, and then in an often-repeated motif, he listens as their eyes burst, *dum-dowk*. (This motif occurs again in the next story).

Lines 63–64: Najik eats the contents of the pit, women and kangaroo and all, to repletion, and explicitly states the normative message: Those women shouldn't kill kangaroo.

The scene then changes. Lines 69–78: Najik sees a mob of kangaroos and turns his mind to confusing them – with the result that they become endowed with the capabilities they currently have, to smell people and other things. But he does this in a ridiculous way, by going upwind of them and farting. The narrator describes this metaphorically, as *gemo-barr'muwum* 'he broke open their nose'. In so doing he accustoms them to smelling people and everything else.

At the end Peter combines the two main themes: that women used to hunt (but the implication is they shouldn't) and a subsidiary theme, that they were sluts; and that kangaroos lacked some basic capacities, and Najik fixed that situation. There is only a loose connection between the first main set of events – doing away with the sisters – and the second, breaking open the kangaroo's nose.

The audience is left with these messages. Only men hunted after that, establishing things as they are today. Women were always up to no good anyhow – they should be compliant, and (we are given to understand) it was not right that they hunted, or at least that's not how things are. Never mind that the *trickster* is represented as sex-hungry – the characterization doesn't carry any negative moral weight (a gendered near-universal, perhaps).

Overall Najik is a caricature more than a rounded character. His main features are that he is peering, intrusive, scheming, lecherous. He does not talk much to the sisters nor does he reveal his intentions or thoughts to them. His talk is directed to himself, as he plans "I'll do those two in", and so forth. The sisters, though perhaps apprehensive and therefore cautious about presenting themselves as two women, also do not appear as full personalities. They are hospitable and give Najik meat; they call him "grandfather"; they are surprised and overwhelmed when he covers them up with paperbark and proceeds to cook them. Duplicity inheres in what Najik is said to do, planning to himself while enjoying the food the sisters give him.

The narrator's laughter is mainly at points where he characterizes the women as sluts. That is the point which is, all in all, most outrageous both in terms of defying any kind of propriety, and in focusing audience attention on Najik's insouciant malice in doing away with them after their benign treatment of him. Laughter is a significant aspect of conversation and narration, and it is worth considering what meanings it may have here (Grønnerød 2004; Blythe 2011). Laughter, I propose, here occurs in heightened interactive moments (this is almost a tautology). But what heightens those moments, and makes them funny? Peter's direct interaction in this telling was with me, and so one might suppose that Peter laughed out of a sense of the impropriety of what he was saying at those points. That may be part of the explanation, but probably not all of it. Peter was my Aboriginal father, we'd known each other a long time and we had discussed many improper topics. An additional reason for his laughter comes out of the narrative event more directly: maybe not only because of the impropriety of Najik's actions, but at the same time his own mischievous alignment with them – that is, his amusement at and sense of identification with the outrageousness of Najik's behaviour.

11.4.2 Story 2: Na-Balukgayin, the ritual guardian, content and expressive features

The second trickster story has a somewhat more involved and connected plot.

Old "Blind-Eye" (*dum-muya*) was to be ritual sponsor to two young boys, his grandsons, and take them to ceremony in the north. "They're going to make them young men, take them, Blind-Eye", people said to him.

Along the road, he told the boys to go into a cave to get a rock wallaby. They went inside and he kept urging them further and further. The young boys heard a whishing sound, *Widjidiwidjidi!* "What's that whistling, grandpa?" they asked. "It's the little wallaby", he said. But really, he was twirling a firedrill. "Grandpa might kill us, wrong ones!" the boys said (meaning, mistakenly, in the sense 'we do not deserve this'). But Blind-Eye made them go in, "You two are shit-scared", he said. He piled up some spinifex and lit a fire, Poof! in the cave. The eyes of the two young boys popped, Pow! Pow! in the heat. Old Blind-Eye collected their bones in a basket and kept going north.

As he got towards the ceremony ground he raised large whorls of dust. He let it be known that he was bringing lots of participants to the ceremony, people of all sorts of different languages (*ngani-barlarr* 'language-other'). He asked people at the ceremony for honey for all these participants. But really it was just himself who whooshed in and out and raised big whirlwinds of dust. They brought him honey and he ate it all himself.[6]

Lots of people were dancing on the ceremony ground. Blind-Eye looked for a little mouse-hole on the ceremony ground to go into. "Make the dance-ground really big", he said, as if he had lots of people with him. From there, the trickster whooshed and swirled and blew up clouds of dust. He jumped up from the mouse-hole and poked the dancers in the arse, even the women!

"That's it, they're going to kill me", he thought to himself. And yes, they did! The sun had gone down. He was making lots of dust whirlwinds. His forehead poked out through the dust. He whooshed up in front of the mothers and fathers of the boys, and the basket of bones spilled out. He whirled and jumped up and poked them in the arse. People tried to spear him but he kept on going, whooshing and poking.

Finally, a "clever" (a "doctor", or person with special powers) put a stone under him. He slid on it and they speared him. He ran and slipped, Woops! into a hole in an ironwood tree. He jumped out and went back and poked them some more and then slipped back into the tree. Then they lit the ironwood tree on fire, and they watched as his innards ran out as it burned.

Let us consider some of the tropes and features of the narration more closely.

Blind-Eye agrees to take the boys north. On the trip north they are obedient (13, 28) and continue to call the guardian "grandfather", even though he swears at them obscenely (16, 25) (similar to the way in which Najik called the women "sluts" but to himself only; here Blind-Eye swears directly at the boys, whom he is supposed to protect and bring safely to ceremony). Blind-Eye orders the boys around so that, in this story, unlike the women of the Najik story, they begin to suspect he might injure them (15) – but they say he might do so "mistakenly" ("hit

---

6 Honey figures prominently in many Aboriginal stories. In Haviland and Hart (1998: 19), for example, a key character positions himself over a hole and pours honey down his throat, so it courses through his body and out, a pure figure of wish-fulfilment. The figure in that story has some tricksterish characteristics according to the criteria of Hynes and Doty (1993).

us wrong ones"). He orders them into the cave, supposedly to get a small wallaby, but then lights them on fire, and waits to hear their eyes burst (34) (a common motif; this also occurs in the Najik story). He puts their bones in a large basket and carries it with him. He arrives at the ceremony place and is greeted with an approving shout by the waiting public (55), and the assembled people seem to be impressed and credulous for a time (63). The trickster orders them to bring large quantities of honey but he sucks all of them up himself (Peter laughs heartily at this greed, 78). The guardian acts as if he is bringing many people from many different groups to the ceremony (59), which would be highly praise-worthy; but in fact he is by himself. He creates whirlwinds of dust, sending them up into the air. This provides the camouflage for the most outrageous of the guardian's actions: he dashes about in the dust-clouds poking people in the ass. As he tells this, Peter laughs heartily after each utterance (100, 104, 106, especially 108 where he says the trickster did this to women, too; 109). The guardian, like Najik, expresses resentment that women "should've given me their vaginas" (45), the apparent reason for his vengeful treatment of the boys (and similar to the characterization of Najik). The guardian has scattered the boys' bones on the ceremony ground (43), truly a profanation of his supposed guardian's role in relation to initiands. But the guardian realizes that his time is almost up and that people will kill him. He runs about looking for a mousehole to slip into; eventually he slips in and out of an ironwood tree, returning to the ceremony ground to poke people and then slipping back into the tree. Eventually a "clever" (or doctor) manages to slide a stone surface beneath him, and he is speared. He slips back into the tree, and the people burn the tree down (121), as his innards ooze out and down the tree.

In several utterances Peter voices the guardian with a hint of the special nasal quality that he had used to represent Najik (3, 12). The narrative involves a number of reported speeches, the longer of them typically set off by a framing form of the verb 'to say' ("he said", "they said" etc.), usually delivered by Peter after a slight pause following the report, and typically with lesser intensity and volume (5, 6, 16, 98).

Peter repeats a particular loud shout (rendered *arrarr'*! 54, 98) by which the guardian is represented as marking his entry into the ceremony ground. There are other special sonic effects, such as the *diiit* (14) representing the guardians throwing and (nearly) hitting the boys (with an unnamed object, presumably a spear or piece of wood).

As Radhakrishnan (2016) pointed out in an earlier examination of expressive aspects of this story, there are other onomatopoeias and sonic effects, including a number of vowel lengthenings; *widjidiwidjidiwidjidi* the sound of the firedrill being twirled; *bul jurrurdu*, the whirling sound of the willywilly; and some conventional particle interjections, such as *wart* ('chuck! Throw!', 43), and numerous uses of *Yo* 'yes', to introduce a new development in the story, or as a brief pause, but which is also internal to the story as a representation of assent on the part of a character; also *Yowoyn* 'yes', representing the assent of characters (the assembled public) to what the guardian is doing.

Neither story is framed in a comprehensive way, either as Narrative or Narrated Event. Story-tellers like Peter are not, in my experience, given to announcing a narrative framework (who is present, who the storyteller is, etc., as is found in some narrative traditions). This is quite typical of Indigenous language story-telling as I have experienced it in northern Australia; and very different from, for example, the New Guinea Highlands where there is much attention to framing, setting the stage, announcing who is present, who the storyteller is, and so forth.

Each of the stories begins with an action (searching for; taking boys) and these introduce the main (trickster) character into the narrated event. The guardian's story begins with an exchange of a request to him to take the boys north; and his response that he will. As the narrator proceeds he asks himself questions which are suspended between the event of telling and the story itself: To where was he to take them? And so on, another indication, as Peter treats them jointly, of a relatively at-ease attitude about the relation between Narrative and Narrated Event.

The next section is a series of exchanges between guardian and boys, in which the former orders them to go into a cave and to make a wallaby go in further, intending to trap them in there. But the guardian says nothing of this. He works a firedrill, making noise which alarms the boys. The guardian puts them off by saying the noise is being made by a young wallaby – in short, he tricks them, lights them on fire, waits for their eyes to burst, and returns home, ending a first dramatic sequence.

In an interlude (36–49) the guardian goes back to camp, and gathers the boys' bones. He then enters the ceremony ground, puts the bones there; and in a newly dramatic moment (54) appears on the ceremony ground. Over a long portion of the story (50–79) the guardian commands people to prepare the ground, to bring honey; he deals with their questions about whether he is alone, somehow convincing them that he has brought many people (whose language the people say they cannot understand, somehow the unintelligibility coinciding with their invisibility).

From around 80 onwards, the guardian is represented as knowing he will be killed; and in a subsection of this part, 87–100, his dashing and appearance from the dust is conveyed by repetition of *merng yi'* 'forehead out'; he particularly appears provocatively to the mothers and fathers of the boys (101–102), and pokes people in the ass (104, 106, 108, 109, 117), scatters the bones (103), and slips in and out of the ground and the ironwood tree as he persists in his chaotic mischief.

At line 121, as I thought the story was coming to an end, I intruded to ask what kind of being the guardian was. (I had in mind the fact that Najik is understood to be Owlet Nightjar – I thought something similar might be true of the guardian). Peter says, however, that he was thought of as a man (122); and having said that, says that he doesn't know a name for him.

11.5 Concluding observations

This version of these stories was told while I was camping overnight at the storyteller's home. The minimal framing of Narrative Event is consistent with the way in which Peter, among the most talented storytellers, typically told stories he knew. Telling stories in language was becoming less common among his family group, as Jawoyn (and Mayali) language competence was increasingly restricted to people of his age group. Other family members were present (a daughter, and her son) but attending much less closely than I was. I asked him to tell these stories in order to tape them; I had heard him tell them on other occasions.

Peter begins stories with an action or event, and supplies relatively few contextualizing remarks. Some of the narrative is carried forward by conversational exchanges between the trickster figure and others. Sequences of reported speech are often framed with a 'say' verb, but occasionally they are not (especially when there is a key word such as *Yo* 'yes', which makes it clear that a particular turn is a response). There is no descriptive characterization; the character of the trickster emerges through description of his actions, and by conversational exchanges. Other characters remain fairly backgrounded, and mainly appear in response to what trickster says or does.

The additional characters thus appear mainly in their responses to actions and orders of the guardian. His depiction as a norm-breaker and -inverter seems to be a key element of the humour for the narrator. From his laughter one gathers that Peter was most highly amused by the transgressive moments in each story, most notably his characterization of women as sluts in the Najik story, and his amusement at the guardian's poking people, especially women, in the behind in the second story. There is no sense of moral weighting to these transgressions in the way Peter tells this story. Neither interiority nor reflexivity is developed in relation to the trickster characters. The trickster does not reflect on his own actions or the responses of others. The guardian is self-aware, and knows that his run of behavior will end. But there is absolutely no hint that the guardian, for example, thinks about his having killed the boys, or about his disgraceful treatment of their parents. The events are presented for the audience to grasp and enjoy their presentation.

With respect to Narrated Event (q.v. diagram above) the possibility of action is developed, and largely consists of acts of ostentation and aggression on the part of the trickster with respect to a relatively passive, and limited, set of other characters. Narrated speech events, a subclass of narrated events, are an important means of development of the narrated event as a whole, but again, largely consist in orders given by the trickster figure to others, and their relatively acquiescent responses. There is no internal reflection on the part of any character.

These trickster stories contrast with some others within the repertoire of this narrator (and some of his close associates) in not having a moral focus at any point. There are other stories (such as one of a greedy emu, and others of strange encounters in which there are unexpected exchanges of food and other items) that clearly do embody a moral lesson about sharing and not depriving others. Such stories exemplify the importance of norms of generosity. But these stories, again are largely without any explicit moral commentary or reflexivity on the part of the characters (Bohemia and McGregor 1995). They make their point by exemplifying what happens to those who do not share.

These trickster figures do conform to a wider pattern of making clear certain norms, by highlighting trickster's subversion of them rather than by verbal articulation of them. For example, Najik accepts food but returns only harm to the women, illustrating what an aberrant character he is. He swears rudely about the women and metes out violence to them. In the guardian story, trickster undertakes a morally important task – that of initiating the younger generation – but turns that into a festival of violence, gluttony and aggressive mischief. He comes to a violent end himself, but only after he has wrought havoc – and no doubt created a lot of fun for the audience.

Peter as narrator says relatively little outside the frame of the Narrated Event. Of Najik, he comments that he was "cheeky" (dangerous). Of the guardian, he answers my question about what kind of being he was by saying he was supposedly a man. As a narrator, in his vivid style and laughter, he appears to identify strongly with the trickster figures.

The Jawoyn speech community, when I first got to know it in the latter 1970s, included a range of older women. Although some were good narrators, none ever told me a story of this kind. For that reason, I have consistently treated the trickster figure as male. Telling of stories of this trickster genre was, in fact, limited to a particular, closely related group of older men. I tentatively conclude that these stories, though probably told to mixed audiences, were the province of male narrators of southern (and perhaps wider) Arnhem Land, at least over the latter part of the last century.

Abbreviation

NSg   nonsingular

Appendix: The stories, Najik and Balukgayin

These are the two stories referenced above, told by Peter Jatbula at Werrenbun near Katherine, Northern Territory on 13–8–1998. He told them to me on a number of occasions in slightly varying versions and arrangements. These are reproduced here in Jawoyn at the word level. For grammatical rendering of the stories, and audio, refer to the sound files and the Appendix in Merlan (2016).

Najik – How women used to hunt – Peter Jatbula

This is a story Peter used to tell of the trickster Najik, Owlet Nightjar – also known as Najik-were. He made hunting what it is today.

Women used to hunt, not men.

Najik was going along and saw the two of them, they were roasting in a pit. One was lying belly-down. He reached them and said, "You and your wife, you're by yourselves?"

"Yes", one said, "she's got a bellyache" (and that's why she's lying down).

Najik looked hard at her. "That's a woman", he thought.

He ate some of the innards from their kangaroo, and went back to his camp. "I'm going to roast them", he thought. He went back. "Maybe you're going to open the oven now?" he asked. "Yes."

He got a big sheet of stringybark to cover them up with, along with the kangaroo meat.

"These two are lying", he thought. "One says he's a man, but these are two women."

The two prepared the kangaroo, put cooking stones and laid out the kangaroo. He ran over and Wup! into the ground oven they went, and he covered them with paperbark. "That's what I do to you two sisters, you two sluts always looking for trouble."

He waited as they cooked, their eyes burst. He took them out and ate them with the kangaroo. "I should mess up (confuse) these kangaroo", he thought.

Kangaroos were gathering. He went upwind of them. He farted. "Maybe I've opened their noses", he said (meaning, now they'll know to smell people, and dogs, and whitefellas).

Now, only men hunt. Those women should have made their vaginas available. "That's what I do to them", said Owlet Nightjar.

1. *nabay ngalmukayek ley'leymay* — He just looked for women.
2. *bonyukley'leymay ngalmuka* — He just looked for women.
3. *lay bonnanay* — He saw kangaroos.
4. *lay* — Kangaroos.
5. *bumbunay ngalmuka bonyi anbay* — Women killed them, women at that time.
6. *mungguy gerrung walbunay wakay* — Men didn't, no.
7. *ngalmuka bumbunay* — Women killed (game).
8. *bonlakwolakwonay* — He caught up to them.
9. *bonwalakanay* — He peered at them.
10. *ngalwula gaderk gabololo niyarnbay buyuknanay* — This one's lying on her belly, they saw him there.
11. *gun* — There.
12. *yo* — Yes.
13. *ngalnongiyngu nurrangyiwa* — "You and your wife, you're by yourselves."
14. *yowoyn gajingbarang jungay . . . ngalarnbay ngal-wo- ngaljajangayu* — "Yes, she's got a belly ache", her little sister here.
15. *yo, gajingbarang ngarra jungay* — "Yes, maybe she's got a belly ache", he said.
16. *yukyongnanay properly* — He looked hard at (her).
17. *ngalmuka nabay jungay* — "That's a woman", he said.
18. *gurni wurra ngangeywunay jungay* — "How could she refuse me" he said.
19. *yowoyn* — Yes.
20. *wangarrewunay ngukmangay nganwotjalwotjal mangay buyalwunay buwonay bonyi* — She partly cooked it, gutted it, got out the lungs, they cooked it and they gave it.
21. *yowoyn nganmayang bonyi ngajarwu nen* — "Yes, maybe I'll eat the liver now."
22. *nganmayang jay uhuh* — He ate the liver.
23. *ja'ngajaaay ngagoyindin jungay* — He aaate it, "I'm going back", he said.
24. *gukal lakwolakwonay* — He reached his humpy.
25. *ngawonngolunggu ngawonderrpmar* — "I'm going cook 'em. I'll roast 'em.
26. *gen gurnjin ngagoyin* — "Ah, no, now I'll go back."
27. *gaynwurra nuwerr'mang nen bonyi bungolu* — "Maybe you're going to open it up soon, now cook it."
28. *yowoyn buynjungay* — "Yes, they said."

29. *goy'goyinay gukal gukmangay ngan-berndak ye* — So he went back, and he got a big sheet of stringybark.

30. *nuffor twofella na bla coverim up laymuyuk* — To cover the two of them up, along with the kangaroo.

31. *nawula nabay lubra loafer jungay I killim that twofella bonlakwolak-wonay* — "These useless women" he said, "I'm gonna kill these two", he caught up to them.

32. *nawula gawungeya gawuwarrpmar yemboyi mungguy ngeya ngalmukayarrk ngalbay jungay* — "This one, they're whatsit, lying, it's supposedly a man, but it's what's it, those two are two women", he said.

33. *more better ngawonderrpmanggu jungay* — "Better if I roast the two of them", he said.

34. *goy'goyinay gukmangay bonmorl-kyongnanay* — He went back and got the stringybark, and he watched the two of them secretly.

35. *gawuynjapma'japmar gawum-buylayang layluk* — They are poking them in, filling the kangaroo up with stones.

36. *bonmorlkyongnanay mot dunngap-ngapmay* — He watched those two secretly, lifted the paperbark, slipped quietly into a hole.

37. *Bepa* — Wait.

38. *gaya ganay* — He went close up.

39. *uynjutbererkoyinay gen darra* — They were sharpening (a blade) maybe.

40. *gukalmuyuk narnbay* — And with the stringybark.

41. *narngula najamorrwu ganamjiyi niyarngula* — He's standing here watching.

42. *buynjutbererekoyinay yo* — They were sharpening (the blade).

43. *bumarr'mangay* — They lifted it up.

44. *marr' bumangay got buynjungay wurrkluk* — They lifted it up, and put it on the hearth.

45. *gun'ba gun'ba* — From one side and the other.

46. *bumbuy weynja'weynjangay na* — They put it on top now.

47. *bumbuyweynjangay layluk niyarn-bay* — They put the stones on top of the meat.

48. *niyarnbay wurra warnlakminay wup* — He ran over there and wup!

49. *yakay yakay yakay jamuyn buyn-jungay finish* — "Ow! Ow! Ow! Grandfather", they said, finish.

50. *wanyuynjunggu nabay ngalgorrang* — "That's how I do to you sisters."
51. *nabokyurr'yurryarrk jungay* — "You two sluts", he said.
52. *nabay nabokyurr'yurryarrk nabay-yarrk jungay* — "Those two sluts those two", he said
53. *nabaranggu ni nabay* — He was a cheeky bugger.
54. *buynjungay warngarriyay bulerrlur-rplurrpmangay wakay boyn* — They did like that, he had them, they struggled, nothing, finished.
55. *bungeya bumorlpmay yowoyn ngawongaywum boyn* — They what's it, they went quiet, I took it from those two
56. *bonngolu'ngolungay darra* — And he cooked them.
57. *bongenduyay bonbengjiyay dumdowk*
    Buynjungay yo — He tended them, he heard them, their eyes burst.
58. *wiyn'gu wanyunjunggu nabay ngalgorrang* — "That's what I do to the two of you, sisters"
59. *ngalbokyurr'yurryarrk* — "Those two sluts."
60. *Najikwere* — The owlet nightjar.
61. *bongenduyay bonwerr'werrmay na* — He waited for the two of them, and he took them out now.
62. *narnbaymuyuk nen bonjay nen* — He ate them with that (kangaroo), maybe.
63. *warngapgapmay narnbay layluku jungay*
    bonwarnjay arayt — He kept on guzzling it with the kangaroo, he kept on eating them, all right.
64. *a! nabay ngalmuka warrulebunbun lay jungay* — "Aah, those women shouldn't kill kangaroo", he said.
65. *maku narnbay larruk jay* — It's good, he ate full up, it filled him up now.
66. *bidenbamborr'may na*
67. *ooo gurni nen ngajung* — "Ooh, what'll I do?"
68. *more better lay ngawirriwirriwon jungay* — "I should mess up the kangaroo."
69. *guppu nay gameren guppurlangbu* — He saw a big mob of kangaroos gathered.
70. *narnbay najik ga'ngangay lerrwot juy* — That Owlet Nightjar went and stationed himself.
71. *bulku* — In the middle.
72. *matjyongnanaaay gurni gila ngalak-min ngayewun* — He kept on watching the wind, "which way will I run? That way!"
73. *gun matjgom budiyangiyn* — There upwind he sat down.
74. *ngukdiiiiirrng juy* — He farted.

75. *bunguknomayn na* — They smelled him now.
76. *lay narnbaywu* — Those kangaroos.
77. *o! nganbunguknomayn nen leku* — "Ooh, they've smelt me, maybe that's good."
78. *buwarnwukayn wurra gawungen-nomar mungguy juy* — They took it. "Maybe they smell people", he said.
79. *gaynwurra ngalmuka gawungen-nomar* — "They smell women's sweat."
80. *ngukdirrng'may narnbay finish gem-obarr'muwum nabay lay* — He farted and that was it, he broke open the nose of the kangaroo.
81. *that's the way nyanngennomar na* — And they smell us now.
82. *waruk nen gangennomar mungguy gangennomar whitefella nen gan-gennomar moticarlukku nawarngu-lawu lay* — It smells maybe dogs, it smells people, maybe it smells whitefellas, and cars, these kangaroos.

83. *najik narnbay bonwirriwirriwoy* — Owlet Nightjar messed them up.
84. *mungguyyek buwelangyamay na* — Only men hunted after that.
85. *nabay bonyukwolipum ngalmuka nabay bumbunay* — He finished them off, women used to hunt.
86. *ngalmarri'marriyn too nabokyurr'yurr waywo yembo nabay* — Girls too, they say they were always after sex.
87. *lay narnbay nyanngennomar na* — Kangaroos smell us now.
88. *mungguyyek* — Only men.
89. *yanganbo ngalmukayek bumbunay* — Long ago only women hunted.
90. *ngalmuka wanganbuwonay ngan-gunyoyngu jungay* — "Those women should have given us their vaginas", he said.
91. *ngawonbungu nabay nabokyurr'yurr* — "That's how I knock them off, those sex-hungry buggers."

Na-Balukgayin The ritual sponsor

1. *Naway darra mululuk buyukwo* — "Another one, You lot give him young boys (to initiate)."
2. *Gurni wurra nabay ngeniyay* — "What was that one's name?"
3. *yowoyn* — "Yes."
4. *dummuya ngiynbonyukwukan merre nawula nagomdutjyarrk* — "Blind-Eye (old man), you take them north – these two young boys."
5. *Gawumbeyingu buynjuy* — "They are going to make them young men", they said.
6. *yo gandiynngerrwuy ngawonwu-kan juy* — "Yes, I'll take the two (I'll take my two grandsons)."[7]
7. *bonwukangay niwula wurra merre nen* — He took them, maybe it was here to the north.
8. *gurniwu nen* — To where was it?
9. *bonyukwukanay warnyukbeng-gowanay nibay dorriya* — He took them, he became aware of a rock wallaby there
10. *10. Dorriyawayn ngeme'ngemenay* — Where that rock wallaby had gone in
11. *bulakbulakbu nagorrang* — "You frighten it! you two brothers!"
12. *bulakbu dunluk nyambungu* — "You shoo it into the cave! We want to kill it!"
13. *yo gandiynngerrwuy bonjungay* — "Yes grandsons!" he told them
14. *yowoyn jamuyn* — "Yes, grandpa."
15. *Bonbulakbunay nabay najuway-woyarrk bonbunay diit* — He frightened them, those two kids, and he hit them.
16. *jamuyn wanyanbun wanyanway-irrbun* — Grandpa, you might hit us, you might hit us, the wrong ones (the boys think).
17. *numolyerrmar buyukjarr'ma nabay jungay* — "You shit run down! You poke it", he said.
18. *Yo bonngeya.. gilkanmarrk. nawula gabokjarrayi wurritjma* — He what's it to them, right inside, "Its rear end is sticking out here. You get its tail!" [the boys say to him]
19. *wakay nabay buyukjarr'ma gilkan-marrk gerru nyambun dunluk jungay* — "No, poke it right inside, then we'll kill it in the cave", he said.
20. *Yo gilkanmarrk bungemeng jungay* — "Go right inside", he said.

---

7 The old man calls the boy "grandsons".

21. *nawula gawitjwitjmar* — "What's that whistling?"
22. *lay nabay nawalkwalk* — "It's a little kangaroo (wallaby)."
23. *Narnbay garwarwungay* — But it was him (Blind-Eye) working a firestick.
24. *narnbay jalkwarak war'mi bur'mi aaaa jamuyn* — He'd gotten a lot of spinifex, he blew on it. "Grandpa!"
25. *too dark inside, gilkanmarrk darra bolkmorokjiyay* — Inside it was very dark.
26. *gilkanmarrk bungemeng numolyerrmar* — "You go right inside! You shit run down!"
27. *marrk jalkwarak warngotmay uhuh bambal'mayn* — Grass, spinifex, he kept on putting it, he filled it up (the cave).
28. *Witjitwitjitwitjit witjitwitjitwitjit* — *Witjitwitjitwitjit witjitwitjitwitjit* (sound of firestick being twirled).
29. *nabay yenang gawitjdimamang jamuyn* — "What's that going whish whish grandpa?"
30. *nabay ngeya nawula nawalkwalk* — "That's what's it, a little one (wallaby)."
31. *walkjilkmay* — "The little kangaroo (wallaby) has fallen over."
32. *yo* — "Yes."
33. *garwarwu jurdu ngum! dul' bonmuwum* — He twirled the firestick, it sparked and caught! He lit the two of them.
34. *jitjwarr oh goodness! bondul'muwukangay* — Poor things! Oh goodness! He lit them!
35. *bonyukgenduyaaay burndum-dowkdorowkmay* — He waited for them, and their eyes burst.
36. *goy'goyiyn lerrluk* — He went back to camp.
37. *goy'goyiyn niyarnbay burroywayn* — He went back there where he camped.
38. *bumburroy* — They were sleeping.
39. *borong mi na borong war'warmay ngeya waywo butbut waywo* — He got a rope now, he loaded up what's it, kurrajong rope and everything.
40. *boynja'boynjangay na* — He twisted it now.
41. *boynjangay darra ngeya basket lolbasket narnbay* — He wove it like a what's it, like a basket.
42. *murrka nganberndak gen nganmo lang jungay* — He loaded the bones, it was a big basket."
43. *burrongiyn burrongiyn burrongiyn burrongiyn garlayak malnguyn'mayn* — He camped, camped, camped, many nights.

44. *wart yembo layiyay narnbay murrka, yarlarr' juy*
Then supposedly, chuck! He threw the basket, and it spread out (the contents scattered).

45. *ngawonmolakwon nagorrang*
"I get the bones of those two, those brothers."

46. *Ngangunyoyngu ngalgarrangn-gayu nganwonaywa yembo jungay*
"Their mother should've given me her vagina!" he supposedly said.

47. *bonmowar'war bongotmaaay ngangarrawarra ngandakmorakmo bongotmay*
He loaded up, put their bones, he put in their leg bones and pelvis bones.

48. *gerrung walwarlarrkmay wukan-gay jalkmi murrkaluk*
He didn't wash them, he took it just like that in the basket.

49. *bonlerrkoyiyn*
He took them back.

50. *goy'goyinay na lerrluk*
He went back to camp.

51. *niyarngula jamba ring place galalniyay*
Like here, there was a ring place (ceremony ground).

52. *gilkan narnbay*
Inside that.

53. *niyarnbay bonmogotmayn*
There he put the bones.

54. *Ja bonyi jawurritjmayn ngayiwa*
And now he appeared himself!

55. *arrarr! juy dirn'mi*
Wow! Wow! he came out!

56. *nawula jawurritjmay nabaluk-gayin! buynjuy*
The sponsor has come out! They said

57. *warngangay lerrwot*
He went and sat down.

58. *gotim bim*
With white paint on,

59. *dil'miyinaywayn*
Where he'd painted himself up,

60. *yemboyi mungguymuyuk*
Supposedly accompanied by men.

61. *bonmangay*
He'd fetched them.

62. *yeko nginyiwa*
"Hey, are you alone?"

63. *yembo gerrung wanyanganingan bunganibarlarr nawula ngawonmangay*
"I guess we can't hear that language, they're a different language, the one's I've gotten."[8]

64. *yo*
"Yes."

65. *ngawonmangay namalnguyn*
"I've gotten lots (of people)."

66. *ja bumbolkbirr'ma*
"So clear the ground."

67. *bunggalalmakwo*
"Make a ring place (ceremony ground)."

68. *Bolknay o gajalngbam nabay*
He looked at the place and there was a log.

---

8 The sponsor lies to everyone, pretending to have collected people.

69. *bop too yukley'may*
He was looking for a mouse.

70. *dunley'may bop gayn ngangemen jungay*
He was looking for a mouse-hole, maybe I'll go in there, he said.

71. *yo nge'ngekuluk*
Yes, in the afternoon

72. *gaynwurra bulorlkanay wurrpu bulorlkang bumbolkbalpmiwo jungay*
Maybe they were dancing. "You dance! wurrpu! Make the place really big!" he said. [dance style]

73. *wam bonbubijarrkbu*
"You send them (the imaginary guests) honey!"

74. *mungguy nabulkan ngawon-wukanay nanganinganibarlarr*
"I've brought strangers, people of different languages."

75. *bonmogotmay niyarnbay nge'ngekuluk gula ngawonyukwukan gaynwurra wurrpu wow bumbolkbirr'ma nanumbuyn'gu*
He put the bones there. In the afternoon, "I'll take them this way." Maybe they were dancing. "Clear the place! Over yonder."

76. *bop darra yukley'ma gadunwayn niyarnbay ngawarnngemen jungay*
He was looking for a mouse, where its hole is. "I'll go in there", he said.

77. *yo ooo wam gomen*
"Yes, and what about honey?"

78. *wam niyarnbay gun'ba gun' ba buynjotjwo namalnguyn wurra bonjarrkbu nganberndak jungay*
"You give honey there from all sides, there are a lot of them, send them a large amount", he said.

79. *lerrkoyinay jowkmay ngayiwa jowkmay jowkmaywayn larruk burroy bonyi darra jowkmay oh Christ*
He took it back and sucked it by himself. He sucked and sucked it. He slept full up, and then he sucked some more.

80. *jowkmay darra boyn*
He sucked some more, that's all!

81. *laswan nganbubunwayn jungay*
"(This is) the last one, where they kill me", he said.

82. *true all right they been killim im*
True, they killed him.

83. *yowoyn*
Yes

84. *o ngoy'miyn geben*
The sun had gone down

85. *mowe nay*
He looked at the sun.

86. *aaaaa WAAAA juy ngayiwa*
"Aaaah! Waaah!" he said, just himself.

87. *gawunggangan bumbolkbirr'ma*
They are ready (= they go), "Clear the area!"

88. *bul jurrurdu julwu narnbay buyn-julwunay like a ngaljurlum*
Whirlwhirl, dust, they saw dust, like a willy-willy.

89. *ooo mungguy nawula merng yi'*   Oooh! A person's forehead emerged!
    merng yi' merng   And another and another, supposedly
    yi' yembo menay narnbay   from the dust.
    julwuwa

90. *bbbb julwu dowkmay ngayiwa*   He threw the dust around himself.

91. *nawunmalnguyn all right*   Over there, a big mob!

92. *dil'miyinay guwarrk merng*   He'd painted himself, so his forehead
    dirn'mangay   came out there from the dust.
    niyarnbay julwuwa

93. *merng dirn' gula darra merng*   His forehead appeared there, and
    dirn'mangay   appeared again.

94. *yo namalnguyn buynjuy*   "Yes, there are a lot of them!" they said.

95. *got jungay niyarnbay ngeya*   He put down that what's it, that bone
    nganmorlerreyn   package.

96. *bonbuwarnnay gayakaya o*   They saw them close up, o, this is a lot of
    nawula malnguyn mungguy   blackfellas.

97. *niwula gayarlok*   Here close up.

98. *ooo bbbbb merng dirn' yembo*   Oooo, bbbbb (sounds). "Forehead come
    mangay   out! Forehead out!" and he peered at
    merng dirn' bonyukwalakang   them, he looked at them.
    walakang bonjungay

99. *arrarr narnbay nayukjirriyn*   There that one person, supposedly came
    yembo bonyi lerryi'meyn niyarn-   out, the messenger.
    bay mirdiwakan

100. *julwu ngani'nganiwonay darra*   He was talking to the dust, and he came
    gun'ba ngayiwa jawurritjmay   from there by himself.

101. *ngurrebepmeng ngurrebepmeng*   "You come out! You come out!"[M], his
    wulp ngemeyn merngyi' merngyi'   forehead came out.

102. *warnjungay gayakaya niyarnbay*   He kept on doing it, close to where they
    buwarnbudiyaywayn   were sitting, the two mothers.
    ngalgarrangngayuyarrk

103. *najartngayu*   And fathers (of the boys).

104. *Gayakaya bbb merng yi' bon-*   Close up, his forehead came out and
    walakangay darra mongeyapu   he peered at them, and then spilled the
    bonyi   bones out.

105. *yeko dorlmurr dakjarr' bonjuy*   "Hey!" bash . . . and he poked them in
    yembo   the arse, hit them and poked them in the
    dorlmurr bonbum dakjarr'   arse.
    bonjuy

106. *gilkanba yoynba yoynngemeyn na* — From inside the ground. He went into the ground now.

107. *yembo bonbunay nawula dakjarr' bonjungaywayn* — He hit them as he poked their arses.

108. *gukway' bumeyn* — They jumped.

109. *Ngalmukaluku bonjarr'may* — And he poked the women too!

110. *dakjarr' dakjarr' bonbunay darra yoynyek buyoynbunay darra dakjarr' jungay* — Poked their arses! Poked their arses! They just hit the ground, and he poked their arses.

111. *ngalmuka darra bonbum.. lol! Buyoyngamjongay dakjarr' juy* — He hit the women too . . . they stabbed the ground and he poked arse.

112. *buwarnjuy yembo dirl bumbum* — They kept on, but at sunrise they killed him.

113. *bat nawungurang nawula bat bibatgotmay na underneath* — The "clever" put a stone underneath for him.

114. *jurlurlumiyn na lolgiyowk* — He slid like a fish.

115. *den.gop buyamayn* — They speared him properly.

116. *layn worrombokangay ngeya marukal* — He ran and hid in a what's it, tree, ironwood.

117. *dunwulpngemeyn* — He went into the hole, slip!

118. *bulukuyn buwarnbunay yembo darra lurra goyinay darra dakjarr' bonjungay* — They nearly- they kept on hitting him, and he went back and poked them in the arse again.

119. *bonjungaywayn laynngemeyn marukal* — As he did it to them, he went inside that ironwood tree.

120. *niyarnbay burndul'muwum* — They burned him there.

121. *dul' bumuwum* — They lit it on fire.

122. *buyongnanaaaay ngukjorr' borr-porr ngukjorr' gepya yembo juy bornayingwayn* — They watched, his innards ran down, and his innards spilled and spread as it burned.

123. *mungguy niyay yembo* — He was supposed to be a person/blackfella.

124. *narnbay nabalukgayin ngange-bengmupmayn* — I've forgotten the name of that sponsor.

References

Abrahams, Roger. 1968. Introductory remarks to a rhetorical theory of folklore. *Journal of American Folklore* 81(320). 143–158.

Beidelman, Thomas. 1980. The moral imagination of the Kaguru: Some thoughts on tricksters, translation and comparative analysis. *American Ethnologist* 7. 27–42.

Blythe, Joe. 2011. Laughter is the best medicine: Roles for prosody in a Murriny Patha conversational narrative. In Brett Baker, Ilana Mushin, Mark Harvey & Rod Gardner (eds.), *Indigenous language and social identity: Papers in honour of Michael Walsh*, 223–236. Canberra: Pacific Linguistics.

Boas, Franz. 1914. Mythology and folk-tales of the North American Indians. *The Journal of American Folklore* 27(106). 374–410.

Bohemia, Jack and W. B. Mc Gregor 1995. *Nyibayarri: Kimberley Tracker*. Australian Institute of Aboriginal and Torres Strait Islander Studies.

Carroll, Michael P. 1981. Lévi-Strauss, Freud, and the trickster: A new perspective upon an old problem. *American Ethnologist* 8(2). 301–313.

Carroll, Michael P. 1984. The trickster as selfish buffoon and culture hero. *Ethos* 12(2). 105–131.

Douglas, Mary. 1970. *Purity and danger: An analysis of concepts of pollution and taboo*. London: Pelican.

Evans, Nicholas. 2003. *Bininj Gun-Wok: A pandialectal grammar of Mayali, Kunwinjku and Kune*. Canberra: Pacific Linguistics.

Evans-Pritchard, E. E. 1967. *The Zande trickster*. Oxford: Clarendon.

Grønnerød, Jarna Sailevuo. 2004. On the meanings and use of laughter in research interviews. *Young: Nordic Journal of Youth Research* 12(2). 31–49.

Haviland, John B. with Roger Hart. 1998. *Old man Fog and the last Aborigines of Barrow Point*. Washington/London: Smithsonian Institution.

Hynes, William J. & William Doty (eds.). 1993. *Mythical trickster figures, contours, contexts and criticisms*. Tuscaloosa: University of Alabama Press.

Jakobson, Roman. 1984. Shifters, verbal categories and the Russian verb. In Roman Jakobson, *Russian and Slavic grammar: Studies 1931–1981*, 41–58. (Edited by Linda R. Waugh & Morris Malle). Berlin: Mouton de Gruyter.

Lame Deer, John (Fire) & Richard Erdoes. 1994. *Lame Deer, seeker of visions*. New York: Simon & Schuster.

Lévi-Strauss, Claude. 1963. *Structural anthropology*. (Translated by Claire Jacobson and Brooke Grundfest Schoepf). New York: Basic Books.

Lowie, Robert H. 1909. The hero-trickster discussion. *The Journal of American Folklore* 22(86). 431–433.

Lowie, Robert H. 1918. *Myths and traditions of the Crow Indians*. New York: American Museum of Natural History.

Merlan, Francesca. 2016. *Tricksters and traditions: Story-tellers of Southern Arnhem Land*. Canberra: Pacific Linguistics.

Radhakrishnan, Mahesh. 2016. The expressive voice in Jawoyn Story-Telling. Paper presented at Australian Linguistic Society meeting, ANU, Canberra.

Radin, Paul. 1956. *The trickster: A study in American Indian Mythology*. (With commentaries by Karl Kerényi and Carl Gustav Jung). London: Routledge/Kegan Paul.

Turner, Victor. 1986. *The anthropology of performance*. New York: PAJ Publications.

Rosita Henry

12 Narratives of self and other: Auto/biography in Papua New Guinea

It is currently a widely held view among scholars in the humanities and social sciences that one of the ways humans construct selfhood is through the stories that we tell about ourselves and about others. Yet, anthropological and linguistic studies on Papua New Guinea (PNG) reveal that, while humans may indeed construct selfhood through narratives, such narratives do not necessarily involve the teller as a character in the story. In other words, they are not autobiographical in the way this genre is typically defined in literature studies – that is, as a literary genre denoting the retrospective telling of one's own life – often synonymously termed "life writing". This paper discusses the idea of the narratively constructed self by drawing on ethnographic research the author conducted in the Western Highlands of PNG for the auto/biography of Maggie Wilson and on comparative anthropological literature examining various narrative genres found in PNG. It is argued that it is important to distinguish between the concepts of "self" and "person". If selfhood is constituted narratively, which is debatable, then it is important to consider in tandem with the cultural concept of person, what type of self is thus constructed.

12.1 Introduction

Narratives of various kinds are an important part of the way people communicate with both humans and non-humans in their worlds. Both the nature of the narra-

Acknowledgments: I am grateful to Alexandra Aikhenvald, Luca Ciucci, Rob Bradshaw, and Pema Wangdi, for inviting me to contribute a shorter version of this paper to the workshop they convened on "Celebrating Indigenous Voice: Legends and Narratives in Languages of the Tropics" (Cairns Institute, JCU, 25–27 November 2020) and for then persuading me to develop it for this publication. I am particularly grateful to Alexandra Aikhenvald for her encouragement and supportive editorial comments. Special thanks go to my late friend, Maggie Wilson, and her extended family, for sharing her remarkable life story with me and leading me to reflect upon the link between autobiographical narratives, self and personhood. These reflections are also based on research conducted for the Australian Research Council (ARC) funded project "Planning for Later Life among Papua New Guineans in North Queensland" (DP140100178).

Rosita Henry, James Cook University

https://doi.org/10.1515/9783110789836-012

tive form and the interpretation of the messages encoded in narratives that they record in the context of field research are of great interest to both linguists and anthropologists.

Among scholars in the humanities, arts and social sciences it is widely accepted that humans construct selfhood narratively, that is, through telling stories about ourselves and our relationships with others (Brockmeier and Carbaugh 2001; Nelson and Fivush 2020). "More precisely, we are characters – usually the protagonists – of the stories we tell or could tell about ourselves" (Vice 2003: 93). However, if the self is indeed created narratively, through discursive practice, a claim which is itself debatable (Zahavi 2007),[1] then we must consider not only if this is the case in all cultural contexts, but also what kind of self is thus constructed?

In this chapter, I consider the problem of the "narrating I" in relation to the concept of self and how personhood might be constructed, with reference to the auto/biography of Maggie Wilson (2019) and to anthropological scholarship on various traditional narrative genres in Papua New Guinea (PNG). Maggie Wilson's mother was from the Western Highlands of Papua New Guinea and her biological father was a brother of Michael and Daniel Leahy, who were among the first Australian explorers to venture into the Highlands. Maggie's life spanned the last twenty-five years of the Australian administration in PNG and the first three decades after Independence. Maggie's uncle, Daniel Leahy, sent her to a Catholic boarding school in the far north of Australia (Mt St Bernard College in Herberton, North Queensland) in 1970. There, we began the life-long friendship that drew me to complete the autobiography she began before her sudden death.

The book that resulted is part autobiography, part collective biography. Maggie's life story chronicles a complex entanglement of social worlds. The narrative involves an interplay of many life stories, not only Maggie's but also those of her family and friends, including mine. The stories about Maggie that her Penambi Wia kin of Kunguma Village in the Western Highlands told me provide a rich resource for reflecting on the problem at the heart of this chapter – the narrative construction of the self.

---

1 Zahavi (2007) challenges the claim that the self is a narratively constructed entity. He argues that while self-narratives can tell us something about who a person is, the self is not reducible to what can be said narratively.

12.2 Autobiographical consciousness in Papua New Guinea

Classically within literary studies, autobiography is "auto-diegetic",[2] that is, it is told in the first person[3] where the narrator is also the protagonist, based on memories of experiences the narrator had in the past, but told from the point of view of the present. In other words, the author occurs within the world of the narrative rather than external to that world. The 'autobiographical person' is the both the narrator and the person who has experienced or is continuing to experience the events, situations or feelings narrated. Thus, autobiographies are often critically analysed in terms of the peculiar temporal qualities that emerge:

> At the heart of its narrative logic lies the duality of the autobiographical person, divided into 'narrating I' and 'narrated I', marking the distance between the experiencing and the narrating subject. Whereas the 'narrated I' features as the protagonist, the 'narrating I', i.e., the 1st-person narrator, ultimately personifies the agent of focalization, the overall position from which the story is rendered, although the autobiographical narrator may temporarily step back to adopt an earlier perspective. (Schwalm 2014)

The concept of the self that is expressed in autobiography by this duality (the "narrating I" and the "narrated I"), and the associated spatial and temporal dimensions, are not just a construction of the narrative itself. While life narratives work to create and reproduce a concept of the self, culture has a dynamic impact on autobiographical remembering (Wang 2016) and narrators bring to their narrations already formed cultural ideas about what makes a self and what constitutes a person.

Much of the critical scholarship on PNG postcolonial literature today is framed in terms of a comparison between how narratives were once told traditionally and how they are told today by PNG writers. For example, in his book, *Imagining the Other: The Representation of the Papua New Guinean Subject*, PNG scholar and author Regis Stella (2007) compares "the precolonial oral representation of landscape and place as a focus of identity and sense of belonging" with "the postcolonial salvaging, reconstituting, and reinscribing of that oral representa-

---

2 Genette (1980) distinguishes between a narrator who is also a character in the story – a homodiegetic narrator, and a narrator who is not a character in the story but knows everything about it – a heterodiegetic narrator. If the homodiegetic narrator is also the protagonist of the narrative, it is an autodiegetic narrator.
3 However, there are examples of autobiographical writing told in the second and third person (Schwalm 2014).

tion, primarily through the medium of writing". Similarly, anthropologist Michael Goddard (2008: 35) compares "the mythopoeic, and therefore non-historical, worldview of the Motu-Koita", where he argues "an autobiographical individual could not exist", with the rise of the autobiographical genre written in English in the postcolonial era.

This distinction can be understood with reference to debates among anthropologists regarding concepts of the person in Melanesia. Based on her research among Melpa speaking people, Marilyn Strathern argued that in Melanesia persons are predominantly understood as 'dividuals' rather than individuals (Strathern, M. 1988: 131, 185). While this distinction has been challenged by some scholars (e.g., Josephides 1991; Macintyre 1995; LiPuma 1998; Englund and Leach 2000), it has now become commonplace among anthropologists to refer to dividuals and the 'relational self'[4] as being a feature of Melanesian society that is rapidly being replaced by an autonomous inward looking possessive individual (Martin 2007; Sykes 2007a, 2007b). Following this line of thinking, Goddard (2008: 40) argues that "traditional Motu-Koita did not acknowledge themselves as the autonomous, ego-oriented entities, imbued with temporal continuity, which we might call individuals. Consequently, they could not have an autobiographical consciousness". He argues that it was only in the postcolonial context that such consciousness started to appear. He provides examples of some very early transitional works to evidence his point – one being a story that a prominent Koita woman in Port Moresby, named Kori Taboro, dictated in the 1940s. Her narrative was published in both English and Motu. However, as Goddard notes, her account is not so much a life story as a story about "migrations, warfare, missionary and other colonially related activities".

The Motu title of Kori Taboro's story, *Kori Taboro Ena Sivarai*, specifically means 'the story told by Kori Taboro'. According to Goddard (2008: 41):

> To indicate a story *about* Kori Taboro, a different phrase, *Kori Taboro Sivaraina*, would be required, and the speaker would be someone other than Kori Taboro. *Sivaraina* (*sivarai* with a possessive suffix) is the inalienable case, the story and its subject are inseparable ... Such a construction cannot sensibly occur with the speaker as the object, such as *lau sivaraigu*, 'the story of me'. In order to use the inalienable construction in a reflexive manner, Kori Taboro would have to tell a story about her *participation in* an event (e.g., *lau Mosbi nala sivaraina*, 'story about my trip to Moresby'). In conformity with the mythopoeic conception of the persona, Kori Taboro cannot represent herself as an entity with its own life history.

---

4 This concept of the "relational self" can be, and has been, applied to humanity in general without cultural distinction (Gergen 2011).

"Autobiographical consciousness", following Nelson and Fivush's (2020: 73) definition of the concept, means the ability to integrate "an extended subjective perspective within an extended narrative framework", which they argue is universal. They argue that humans develop autobiographical consciousness through "language and linguistically mediated cultural narratives" but "the form of language and narrative structure may be culturally variable and thus the form of autobiographical consciousness may be variable as well" (Nelson and Fivush 2020: 74). This would include, for example, pronominal choice.

In English, it is usual when speaking and writing about oneself to use the first-person pronoun, although there are some exceptions within the autobiographical genre. However, there is, as Zahavi (2007) reminds us, a difference between having a first-person perspective and being able to articulate it linguistically: "Whereas the former is simply a question of enjoying first-personal access to one's own experiential life, the latter obviously presupposes mastery of the first-person pronoun". Thus, the fact that the first-person pronoun may not be used, or that it may not be possible in certain languages to *represent* oneself narratively in the first person does not mean that a first-person perspective, or a sense of a self, does not exist. According to Zahavi (2007), the "experiential core self is an integral part of the structure of phenomenal consciousness and must be regarded as a pre-linguistic presupposition for any narrative practices". Zahavi, thus, suggests using the terms "self" and "person" to distinguish between an "experiential self" and a "narrative self" (that is, the self as a "narrative construction") respectively.

12.3 Self and person in relationship with the other

The terms and 'self' and 'person' are quite often conflated or used interchangeably in the literature (Harris 1989) although many scholars have attempted to differentiate these concepts (Josephides 2010). While there is a close link between subjective experience, or 'self-consciousness' and the way that persons are imagined in any cultural context, it is important to distinguish these concepts. Josephides (2010) questions the assumption among some anthropologists and others that selfhood is a "culturally alien concept for many societies" (Josephides 2010: 23). She argues their narratives demonstrate that Kewa people derive great pride from their selfhood "which they burn to have recognised as something they have authored". Josephides uses both terms, self and person, but not contrastively. She uses the term 'person' when she is considering "how characteristics are ascribed and 'self' when discussing consciousness and the construction of the self and its relationship to the other" (Josephides 2010: 23–24). Self here is understood as always being constituted in relation to other. Consciousness of self involves a process of othering, as theorised by Hegel ([1807] 2019: 91):

> A self-conscious being exists in being present to a self-conscious being. Only thus does it in fact exist at all, since only thus does its oneness within itself in its otherness become evident to it.

Pippin (2010: 90), in interpreting Hegel's notion of self-consciousness, notes that it is about mutual recognition. The self-other relationship is a 'recognitive relation', in which "any putative pair of self-consciousnesses must be ascribed a practical teleology, the ultimate outcome of which is that 'They recognize themselves as mutually recognizing each other'".

A recognitive relation is required for auto biographical consciousness. As the foundation of any social relationship it also lies at the heart of the concept of the person. Harris (1989) helpfully differentiates the related concepts of 'self' and 'person' as follows. While self is a concept of the human being "as a locus of experience, including of that human's own someoneness" (Harris 1989: 601), person is "an agent, the author of action purposively directed toward a goal . . . an agent-in-society" (Harris 1989: 602). In some societies, according to Harris (1989) the self is subordinated to the person and in others the person is subordinated to the self, as, for example, in America where agency-in-society is subordinated to subjectivity and the concept of the person is "shaped by a psychologistic concern with the self" (Harris 1989: 607). The self is closely tied to the concept of the individual, defined by Harris (1989: 600) as "a single member of the human kind", not all of whom may be granted or achieve social recognition as agents-in-society.

Harris's is a useful distinction that may provide some resolution to the debates regarding dividual personhood in Melanesia and whether it is possible for such persons to linguistically represent themselves as self-conscious entities with their own life histories. In concert with Josephides, Strathern, and Stewart (2000: xix) write in their introduction to the new edition of the life story told by Ongka, a leader among the Kawelka people of Mount Hagen, which Andrew Strathern had recorded and transcribed in 1974, that:

> The view that societies such as the Hagen society in the past did not have a concept of the individual and that this emerged only with modernity is in our opinion untenable on the basis of Ongka's narrative as well as materials from the very earliest ethnographic writers on the region. . .

For Strathern and Stewart, Ongka's narrative exemplifies that, while he is a relational person (i.e., a person constituted by and embedded in relationships with others), he is also capable of representing himself as an individual self. The question remains, however, regarding which is dominant in Ongka's narrative. Is it the relational (or dividual) person as 'agent-in-society' or is it the self as introspective 'locus of experience'?

Sarvasy (2021) has recorded narratives in Nungon, a Papuan language[5] of the Morobe Province, where the tellers feature themselves as protagonists. One story, by a woman of about 40 years old, Roslyn Ögate, which concerns an exciting multi-day journey she made with her sister-in-law across perilous terrain, begins with the narrator using the first-person singular, and reiterating that it is she who will tell the story.

(1) Nok,   wo-rok, homu-na   Dono
    1SG.PRO   DIST-SEMBL fem.same.gen.in.law.of.fem-1SG.POSS   Dono
    oe-no=rot,
    woman-3SG.POSS=COMIT
    I, that is, with my sister-in-law, Dono's wife,
    Yupna ha-in   ongo-go-mok=ma=hon hat   yo-wang-ka-t.
    Yupna area-LOC   go-rp-1DU=SUB=GEN   story say-PROB.SG-NF-1SG
    went to the Yupna area's story, will I tell.

The story is autobiographical in that Roslyn is both the 'narrating I' and the 'narrated I', and she clearly has a first-person perspective. Similarly, another of Sarvasy's Nungon informants, a man by the name of Waasiong, narrated a story about an important event in his own life history, using the first-person singular and prefacing it with: 'Another story, that is, I will tell about myself' (see Sarvasy 2017: 601).

(2) Hat   au   Wo=ma-i
    Story   other   that
    Another story, that is
    Naga=ha   yo-wang-ka-t
    1SG.PRO.EMPH=BEN   Say-PRPB.SG-NF-1SG
    I will tell about myself

A close examination of these short stories, and Ongka's narrative reveals that they are typical of the kinds of stories Kulick (1992: 234) has defined as personal narrative accounts of places to which the narrators went and what they saw there.

---

5 Details on Nungon grammar can be found in Sarvasy (2017).

Such stories characteristically are told in terms of an action, an encounter, or a difficulty and a return to the point of departure (Kulick 1992: 238). They are "event-dominated narratives displaying strong temporal referencing and ordering of event lines, roles, and entities are the basis upon which experience and the self are represented as socially authentic and credible . . ." (Pickford 2014: 182). In other words, the narratives are sociocentric and concern the actions of relational persons. The use of the first-person singular does not necessarily equate to an 'I' that is an egocentric, self-reflective, introspective individual self. If, as Ricoeur (1992: 18) argues, "to say *self* is not to say 'I'", one could also argue that to say "I" is not to say *self*, at least not always and everywhere.

There are other genres that, I argue, make it is possible for people express themselves as autobiographical persons, or "autodiegetic narrators" (Genette 1980), even though they are not commonly understood as autobiography – myths, public speeches, confessions, and songs – where in some cases to say 'I' is not to say self and, in others, to say self is not to say 'I'.

There are clearly oral narrative genres in Papua New Guinea, such as ancestral myths, songs, sung tales, public speeches, migration histories and confessional speeches that, I argue, can be, or at least become, autobiographical, when employed in the service of self-representation. Such narrative genres are, and continue to be, a way for people to tell stories that feature themselves as protagonists and that enable them to express their own introspective desires, hopes and fears, joys and sorrows, shame and anger, while at the same time expressing and celebrating relational personhood.

12.4 Oral narrative genres and the self

12.4.1 Public speeches: The segmentary person

Oratorical uses of grammatical person categories from the Western Highlands have been extensively studied by Alan Rumsey and Francesca Merlan (Merlan and Rumsey 1991) specifically among Ku Waru speakers in the Nebilyer Valley. Ku Waru belongs to a linguistic continuum that includes Penambi Wia *tok ples* and also Melpa in the Hagen area. As Merlan and Rumsey (1991) have documented, and I have also observed while conducting research for Maggie Wilson's life story, it is common in public speeches given at intergroup events such as brideprices, *haus krai* and funerals and compensation payments for the orators to use the first-person singular when referring to their entire tribe, even if the orator himself had not personally participated in the historical events recalled, and may not yet have been born. In other words, an orator, through the use of the first-person singular, "presents the entire clan as a homogeneous collectivity" (Strathern 1991: 211). For example, a Mogei orator might say "I killed that old woman" (Maggie's grandmother, was killed in a tribal war back in the 1920s) meaning not him personally but his segmentary group and/or their allies in that war. Rumsey refers to this use of the first-person singular as the 'segmentary I' or the segmentary person. However, use of the segmentary person in such oratory does not preclude the orator also being a protagonist in his narrative. As Rumsey writes, "in personifying his clan, he amplifies himself by representing its unity as the outcome of *his* single will (*numan*)" (Rumsey 2000: 109). Additionally, it is often not clear when a speaker is referring to himself or to his whole segmentary unit. Rumsey (2000) notes the co-presence of two tendencies "the simultaneous amplification of the everyday self and partial eclipse of it" (2000: 109). He writes:

> The Ku Waru orator can, within the space of a single sentence, speak as one man, and then as a body of men, which would still have survived as the 'one man' whom he was instantiating even if some of its component 'men' had been killed. (Rumsey 2000: 111)

Thus, the use of the first person in public oration in the Highlands, I would argue, could be deemed to be autobiographical, whether the orator is speaking as one man or as a body of men, depending on how autobiographical selfhood or the autobiographical person is conceptualised. Whether a Highlands orator narrates his own personal lived experiences, or whether he narrates the experiences of the group that he instantiates, he orates as a 'world-immersed' self (Zahavi 2007: 6), as a relational person, or 'dividual', who at the same time seeks to enhance his own *noman*, "variously glossed as mind, consciousness, intention, will, social sentiment, and understanding" (Strathern and Stewart 1998a: 170).

12.4.2 Confession

Another oral genre in which autobiographical consciousness is expressed is confession. In my discussion here I draw on my own understandings of confessionals among Maggie Wilson's Penambi Wia family, but also rely heavily on papers on the topic by Rumsey (2008) and by Strathern and Stewart (1998b). After Maggie died, and the *haus krai* (funeral) was over, Maggie's lineage (the Penambi Wia Ulgamp Komp) held a special meeting to give members of her lineage an opportunity to confess (*outim sin*) any wrong they had done Maggie during her life so that, as Maggie's daughter Bernadine put it, "behain, behain we will be okay as a family" and no one will get sick or die as a result of harbouring their own wrong doing or their own resentments against others (see Wilson 2019: 193–194 for details). Such confessional practices, while merging today with Christian ideas, are traditional in the Western Highlands. Rumsey (2008: 457) discusses the various *tok ples* (vernacular) terms for confession. For example:

1. *ung kis pára si-*, where si- is a verb root that takes suffixes indicating grammatical person and number (*ung kis pára sid* 'I confessed'; *ung kis pára sing* 'They confessed').

    Para si- means neutralise or disarm so literally 'to confess' translates as 'talk-bad-neutralise-I/they'.
2. *ariribe mons- pára si-*
    anger (resentment)

Communal confessions bring the agency of the person into focus and, as such, are a mode of definition of personhood (Strathern and Stewart 1998b). However, Christianity has led to a shift in the traditional confessional mode from a communal inquiry to a private statement before God, which, according to Strathern and Stewart (1998b: 63), has led to a change the definition of personhood "toward a new kind of individuation".

I argue that the confessional narratives people tell of their relationships with others, and the wrongs they may have done towards those others, or the resentments that they harbour towards them for perceived wrongs perpetrated against them, can be treated as a form of autobiography, if not whole life stories, then at least auto-diegetic micro-narratives. In such confessions people will use the first-person pronoun and, although I have not done this myself, I think there is potential to study such confessional narratives in depth to explore the duality of the autobiographical person, where the confessor features herself as *both* the protagonist (the narrated I), *and* as the 1st-person narrator (narrating I). Such a study might also shed further light on changing concepts of personhood and how this might relate to the emergence of autobiographical literature in the postcolonial context.

12.4.3 Songs

A variety of genres of song in PNG also lend themselves to introspective self-expression. Maggie Wilson includes songs that her kin composed about her during her lifetime in her autobiography, and I followed suit in my biographical completion of her book. After Maggie died in 2009, several songs were composed about her by women in Kunguma Village. As the finale to her book, I included one of these songs, which the women danced during a sing sing they held for my benefit and that of a group of undergraduate students I took to her house in the village for an ethnographic field school.[6] The song was composed by a woman named Mawa Pil, an Ulga woman who had married into Maggie's sub-clan:

Weldo we, ya weldo we: Chorus
Knep ya morgup kantmegl: Looking from Knep I can see
Kunguma kapa lo penem: The Kunguma house with the tin roof all locked up
Ina werel tigi pont: I am so lost
Mogpe nenba ampbegl agimp: The only person I could talk to
Kuguma mey rawa ngump: Is buried at Kunguma
Klanda mana ora kilt penem: Tears run over my pillow
Pep ropeldop pelepent: I cannot sleep at night, thinking of you
Weldo we, ya weldo we Chorus

In reflecting upon the songs in Maggie's book and also the genre of sung tales (*tom yaya kange*) discussed by Alan Rumsey (2006, 2011) it seems to me that such songs (or at least some of them) could be analysed as micro-autobiographical narratives – stories in which the narrators feature themselves at a particular time of their lives and that enable them to express or reveal their own *noman* – their own inner desires, hopes and fears, joys and sorrows. As Rumsey (2011: 269) writes,

> *tom yaya* performers tend to present tales as if they themselves are stepping into the narrated world and taking the part of the protagonists or interacting with them. This is a two way process, in that by doing so performers also bring aspects of the narrated world into the here and now, identifying themselves with the protagonists, implicitly or even explicitly . . .

12.4.4 Myths

It is not only songs that can used as a vehicle for autobiography, but also myths. Young (1983) in his classic study of 'living myth' in Kalauna, Goodenough Island, argues that "it is invalid to contrast unique biography (lived experience) with impersonated myth (exemplary experience), for biography in Kalauna is shaped, even contaminated by myth in its very construction" (Young 1983: 19). Personhood in Kalauna, Young writes, is "underwritten by myth" (1983: 21). He presents the intertwined biographies of three male leaders – Didiala, Iyahalina, and Kimaola – each who presented their life histories to him in terms of how they converged with their myths, at the same time reciprocally creating the mythical

---

6 The field school was funded by the Australian Department of Foreign Affairs and Trade (DFAT) as part of its New Colombo Plan programme.

heroes in their own images. For example, when Young asked Iyahalina to tell him "the story" of his life, instead of autobiographical details about his childhood, his marriage and so on, that Young was expecting, Iyahalina recounted a myth about a culture hero named Kiwiwiole, with whom he closely identified. Through his rendition of the myth he constructed his own identity and represented himself as the embodiment of his clan, a clan that, through its ancestral hero Kiwiwiole, provided food to all the other Kalauna clans. Iyahalina claims respect from other lineages for himself and his Lulauvile lineage for this act of food-giving, insisting that if it were not for him "everyone would still be licking stones" (Young 1983: 188):

> Kiwiwiole went hither and thither . . . and fetched food. He brought together yams, taro, bananas, coconuts, pitpit, sugarcane, betel nut, and pigs. He put them down and he said: "This is our real food". Then he shared them out . . . So in this way each clan got its pig, its yam and its other food. We Lulauvile had many things and we distributed them thus . . . These were mine and I shared them out . . . You came from the ground with empty hands and carried nothing of value. But I came from inside the ground with my possessions and my wealth. I shared them out and now there is abundance for all. I am Lulauvile Man: I feed large pigs, I preserve yams in my house, I hoard coconuts and betel, I tie sugar cane. My customs adhere to me like the dirt of my ancestors. The body dirt of my ancestors sticks to my comb and my limepot. (Young 1983: 187)

Similar to the use by big men in the Western Highlands of the 'segmentary I' (Merlan and Rumsey 1991) and the way *tom yaya* performers present their sung tales "as if they themselves are stepping into the narrated world" (Rumsey 2011: 269), Kalauna leaders appropriate the myths of their lineages to tell of themselves and their own life projects, but also of themselves as relational persons instantiating their lineage identities.

The genres discussed above – public speeches, confessions, songs, and myths – are all oracular. What can be concluded about the written autobiographies that have emerged in the colonial and postcolonial context in PNG? To address this question, I return to Maggie's autobiography.

12.5 Maggie's memoir

The narrative that is considered to be the first true PNG autobiography, i.e., defined as one that is auto-diegetic (having both a "narrating I" and "narrated I") is Albert Maori Kiki's (1968) *Kiki: Ten thousand years in a lifetime*. Many similar autobiographies soon followed, usually structured first by a narration of early childhood experiences growing up in the village, then an account of first encounter with Europeans, followed by opportunities for gaining a Western education, and so on.

This chronological structure was also followed by Maggie in her memoir. She began with an account of her birth as follows:

> My grandmother said, "Kuan, indeed you have the spirits on your side; it is a strong healthy baby girl. Just wait until we settle her in the *bilum* and pass her out to you for a look. Grimel, put some more *pit pit* grass in the fire, so I can see what I am doing!"
> *I was there but I don't remember this.*

Here, Maggie identifies herself clearly as the 'narrating I' (I was there but I don't remember this), but she is also the narrated I (herself as a baby). Maggie continues her life story with an account of the history of her lineage (tribe, sub-tribe, clan) and their first contact with the Whiteman, beginning the chapter with identifying herself as a member at the highest segmentary group level of the paired tribe – the Elti Penambi.

> *Na eltika penamb ampael* 'I am an Elti Penambi woman'

Maggie then moves on to discuss the colonial relationship of the Australians with her people, especially the Leahy brothers at the goldmine near her birthplace; and her own encounters with these 'others'. She writes of her school life, including boarding school with me in Australia, her return to PNG, her working life and her political and business ventures.

Yet, while Maggie's narrative can be categorised as an autobiography in the classic definition of the genre – i.e., a retrospective telling of one's own life – she is spare in terms of self-reflection. She generally states what she did and what she saw in quite a straightforward matter of fact manner, rarely revealing an inner self, or directly disclosing what she might have felt or thought about something or someone. Her emotional states need to be gleaned by the reader mostly through what she does, the practical actions she takes, and the nature of the social relations in which she was engaged. In this sense, her narrative reflects vernacular oral genres. Her narrative is event-dominated rather than characterised by introspective self-reflection. It has the "go-come" structure that Kulick (1992) identified as characteristic of the *stori* genre – "strong temporal sequencing of material action; . . . references to local people, school, and community events as mutually informing contexts; and . . . restrained use of direct evaluation" (Pickford 2014: 188). Maggie presents a 'self' through her practical deeds, exchanges, temporally emplaced social actions and her relational engagement with others. She draws into her narrative, the stories that members of her family tell about her and the songs they sing about her. In this way, she is able to narratively construct herself sociocentrically through others, rather than just through her own self reflections.

In telling tales of Maggie, her kin and friends in turn are able to tell something of themselves. As a result, the book is effectively a relational auto/biography in which the distinction between both self and other, and self and person collapse.

References

Brockmeier, Jens & Donal Carbaugh (eds.). 2001. *Narrative and identity: Studies in autobiography, self and culture*. Amsterdam/Philadelphia: John Benjamins.

Englund, Harri & James Leach. 2000. Ethnography and the meta-narratives of modernity. *Current Anthropology* 41(2). 225–248.

Feld, Steven. 1996. Waterfalls of song. In Steven Feld & Keith Basso (eds.), *Senses of place*, 91–135. Santa Fe: School of American Research Press.

Genette, Gerard. 1980. *Narrative discourse: An essay in method*. Translated by Jane E. Lewin. Ithaca: Cornell University Press.

Gergen, Kenneth J. 2011. *Relational being: Beyond self and community*. New York: Oxford University Press.

Goddard, Michael. 2008. From 'my story' to 'the story of myself': Colonial transformations of personal narratives among the Motu-Koita of Papua New Guinea. In Brij V. Lal & Vicki Luker (eds.), *Telling Pacific lives: Prisms of process*, 33–50. Canberra: Australian National University Press.

Harris, Grace Gredys. 1989. Concepts of individual, self, and person in description and analysis. *American Anthropologist* 91(3). 599–612.

Hegel, Georg W. F. 2019 [1807]. *The phenomenology of spirit*. Notre Dame, IN: University of Notre Dame Press.

Josephides, Lisette. 1991. Metaphors, metathemes, and the construction of sociality: A critique of the new Melanesian ethnography. *Man* (N.S.) 26. 145–161.

Josephides, Lisette. 2010. *Melanesian odysseys: Negotiating the self, narrative and modernity*. Oxford/New York: Berghahn Books.

Kiki, Albert Maori. 1968. *Kiki: Ten thousand years in a lifetime: A New Guinea autobiography*. London: Pall Mall Press.

Kulick, Don. 1992. *Language shift and cultural reproduction: Socialization, self, and syncretism in a Papua New Guinean village*. Cambridge: Cambridge University Press.

LiPuma, Edward. 1998. Modernity and forms of personhood in Melanesia. In Michael Lambek & Andrew Strathern (eds.), *Bodies and persons: Comparative perspectives from Africa and Melanesia*, 53–79. Cambridge: Cambridge University Press.

Martin, Keir. 2007. Your own buai you must buy: The ideology of possessive individualism in Papua New Guinea. *Anthropological Forum* 17(3). 285–298.

Macintyre, Martha. 1995. Violent bodies and vicious exchanges: Personification and objectification in the Massim. *Social Analysis* 37. 29–43.

Merlan, Francesca and Alan Rumsey. 1991. *Ku Waru: Language and segmentary politics in the Western Nebilyer Valley, Papua New Guinea*. Cambridge: Cambridge University Press.

Nelson, Katherine & Robyn Fivush. 2020. The development of autobiographical memory, autobiographical narratives, and autobiographical consciousness. *Psychological Reports* 123(1). 71–96.

Pickford, Steve. 2014. Narrative modalities, identity and the (re)contextualisation of self in teacher education in Papua New Guinea. *Journal of Language, Identity & Education* 13(3). 171–194.

Pippin, Robert B. 2010. *Hegel on self-consciousness: Desire and death in the Phenomenology of Spirit*. Princeton: Princeton University Press.

Ricoeur, Paul. 1992. *Oneself as another*. Chicago: University of Chicago Press.

Rumsey, Alan. 2000. Agency, personhood and the 'I' of discourse in the pacific and beyond. *Journal of the Royal Anthropological Institute* 6. 101–115.

Rumsey, Alan. 2006. The articulation of indigenous and exogenous orders in Highland New Guinea and beyond. *The Australian Journal of Anthropology* 17(1). 47–69.

Rumsey, Alan. 2008. Confession, anger and cross-cultural articulation in Papua New Guinea. *Anthropological Quarterly* 81(2). 455–472.

Rumsey, Alan. 2011. Style, plot and character in Tom Yaya tales from Ku Waru. In Alan Rumsey & Don Niles (eds.), *Sung tales from the Papua New Guinea highlands: Studies in form, meaning and sociocultural context*, 247–273. Canberra: Australian National University Press.

Sarvasy, Hannah. 2017. *A grammar of Nungon: A Papuan language of Northeast New Guinea*. Leiden: Brill.

Sarvasy, Hannah. 2021. Nungon narratives by Roslyn Ögate and Fooyu (Finisterre-Huon, Morobe Province, Papua New Guinea). Recorded, transcribed, glossed, and annotated by Hannah S. Sarvasy. *Languages and Linguistics in Melanesia*, Texts in the Languages of the Pacific (TILP) series, vol. 3. https://www.langlxmelanesia.com/tilp

Schieffelin, Bambi. 2002. Marking time: The dichotomizing discourse of multiple temporalities. *Current Anthropology* 43(S4). S5–S17.

Schwalm, Helga. 2014. Autobiography. In Peter Hühn, John Pier, Wolf Schmid & Jörg Schönert (eds.), *The living handbook of narratology*. Hamburg: Hamburg University.

Stella, Regis Tove. 2007. *Imagining the other: The representation of the Papua New Guinean subject*. Honolulu: University of Hawaii Press.

Strathern Andrew and Pamela J. Stewart. 2000. Introduction. In Ongka, Andrew Strathern and Pamela J. Stewart. *Collaborations & conflicts: a leader through time*, xvii–xxx. Fort Worth, Tx., Harcourt College.

Strathern, Andrew & Pamela J. Stewart. 1998a. Seeking personhood: Anthropological accounts and local concepts in Mount Hagen, Papua New Guinea. *Oceania* 68(3). 170–188.

Strathern, Andrew & Pamela J. Stewart. 1998b. The embodiment of responsibility: "confession" and "compensation" in Mount Hagen, Papua New Guinea. *Pacific Studies* 21(1–2). 43–64.

Strathern, Marilyn. 1988. *The gender of the gift*. Berkeley: University of California Press.

Sykes, Karen. 2007a. The moral grounds of critique: Between possessive individuals, entrepreneurs and big men in New Ireland. *Anthropological Forum* 17(3). 255–268.

Sykes, Karen. 2007b. Interrogating individuals: The theory of possessive individualism in the Western Pacific. *Anthropological Forum* 17(3). 213–224.

Vice, Samantha. 2003. Literature and the narrative self. *Philosophy* 78(303). 93–108.

Wang, Qi. 2016. Remembering the self in cultural contexts: A cultural dynamic theory of autobiographical memory. *Memory Studies* 9(3). 295–304.

Wilson, Maggie. 2019. *A true child of Papua New Guinea: Memoir of a life in two worlds*. Edited and with additions by Rosita Henry. Jefferson: McFarland.

Young, Michael W. 1983. *Magicians of Manumanua: Living myth in Kalauna*. Berkeley: University of California Press.

Zahavi, Dan. 2007. Self and other: The limits of narrative understanding. In Daniel D. Hutto (ed.), *Narrative and understanding persons*, 179–202. (Royal Institute of Philosophy Supplement 60). Cambridge: Cambridge University Press.

Michael Wood
13 The origin of death in Kamula futures

In this chapter, I discuss how various expectations, questions, interactions and events were attached to a Kamula narrative about the origin of death as it was transcribed in late 2019 in the village of Kamiyame in the Western Province of Papua New Guinea (PNG). The transcription took place after the forestry industry had operated in the area for the last 20 years and, along with Christianity and White Australian colonialism, it had transformed people's sense of self, security and what they desired for their future. The paper outlines how this narrative entered into a series of interactions primarily between myself and Kamula and how many of these interactions were attempts to make me more responsible to the Kamula, their history and to the potential they and Europeans might contain to create a better future.

13.1 Introduction

In this chapter I want to explore how Kamula men I worked with understood certain ancestral beings who remain active in the present. Involved were a series of narratives concerning Kaiyalo and Yolisi that continue to have a creative role in the constitution of Kamula social life and its problems. Kaiyalo is the most important Kamula creative ancestor who provided the foundational structure of the world and Yolisi is an ancestor who disordered aspects of that world. In particular, I emphasize how, in 2019, these ancestral figures and their associated narratives positioned the dead as a salient political concern for a number of Kamula. In exploring these concerns, I take an interactive approach to outlining the power and effectiveness of the narratives among those Kamula interested in the topics. I want to describe how the Kamula made parts of the narrative relevant to their engagement with Europeans, understood as both different and similar to Kamula. The narratives I outline informed my and some Kamula's mutual interactions that explored each other's differences. At times we also explored our limited understandings of each other, including moments of radical incomprehension that destabilised coherent subject positions that might have been thought to obtain in such inter-cultural self-other relations (Merlan 2005). We were at times producing considerable social ambiguity, mystery and semi-recognition (Stasch 2006: 333) while also being able to assume we had known each other for many years.

Michael Wood, James Cook University

https://doi.org/10.1515/9783110789836-013

The chapter emphasizes how narratives can take on an interactive quality beyond their telling, transcription, and translation by being enmeshed in local issues. Narrative is not something that is freestanding or detachable from such events. Rather than treat any narrative as a somewhat isolated self-contained text whose interesting properties primarily involve plot structure and the poetics of analogy, obviation, metaphor and image, an emphasis on interaction provides a different entry point to contexts that could generate further, even if at times uncertain, meanings and interpretative possibilities. Rumsey clarifies this point by arguing "the appropriate unit of analysis is not the tale as repeatable text (as in Levi-Strauss 1969; Propp 1968; Wagner 1978), but particular performance events, with all their specificities of context in which the tales are performed . . ." (Rumsey 2001: 203). Such an approach, adopted in this chapter, entails a historical account of narrative in performance and in its circulation in space, time and different media.

Insofar as narrative performatively overflows into forms of interaction analysis of the event of narrating, and of the narrated events, needs to be supplemented by knowledge of other events that are not contiguous with the key sequences of narrated events (De Fina and Georgakopoulou 2008: 380). Many of the referential processes and other values of narrative depend on resources "beyond the event of narration" (Worthanm and Rhodes 2015: 162). Consequently, any narrative sequence can involve not just a teller and a passive listening audience, but a wide set of different types of story recipients who may reject, modify or undercut any narrative event (De Fina and Georgakopoulou 2008). This would undercut the old role of the ethnographer as a story recorder who would avoid interruptions or challenges in the course of recording a story's telling. These different understanding of narrative raise different types of tasks for different actors. In the example outlined below a number of narrative recipients actively reworked material from the narrative into their social and political interactions with me, such that I became a party to the narrative which was understood by the Kamula, and myself, as having effectively created a community of shared, and disputed, practice and understanding. In the process, the narrative emerged as open to renegotiation and interactional contingency where different actors took up different tasks in sequences of interaction, significantly defined by the narrative. These interactions were often defined in "otherness charged terms" (Stasch 2009: 47) and also at times involved a certain transformation of ancestral characters into real-time persons and their movement into narrative events (De Fina and Georgakopoulou 2008: 3008; Wortham and Rhodes 2015; Wood 1995). My own transposition into an ancestral participant was debated and emerged as a horizon of possibility rather than as something that was concretely materialised in the present. Despite such limits, this process of transposition was a part of a political project that sought to make me a more responsible actor to the Kamula.

In this way, the narrative helped generate new forms of social interaction and the possibility of more to come. In such contexts effective narrative emerges, not just as semiotic or grammatical achievement, but as a collective social and political achievement. As presented here, the narrative tensions involved in our interactions were partially resolved by my incorporation in different ways into the narrative. But while this sometimes took the form of a polite but excessive upward revaluation of who I might be, of more interest to me here is the way this process also succeeded in making me partly responsible for the distinctly Kamula project of seeking liberation from some of the persisting ordering or regulative values of the ancestral narrative. By taking some responsibility in such projects, I was indicating I had been persuaded by my Kamula interlocutors to act in terms of a normative framework defined largely by them and by Kaiyalo's story. As a result, for a time, I became a somewhat normative actor while also being a norm-exceeding other. I was partially synchronized into the narrative, its temporalities, politics and spatial transformations. But this "synchronisation" was only partial and sometimes involved relationships that were not clearly definable as between self and other but involved less distinguishable, fragmentary subject positions and even the absence of such a possibility.

Such expansion of the narrative into a variety of social relations and interactions can be understood as relying on a strong contrast with earlier foundational definitions of narrative as a "verbal technique for recapitulating past experience, in particular a technique of constructing narrative units which match the temporal sequence of that experience" (Labov and Waltetzky 1967: 13). In such an account, narrative is largely monological with the teller as the main producer of meaning. In approaches linked to such definitions, analysis of narrative primarily involves the linear temporal and causal ordering of event clauses linked to an unfolding plot with a beginning, middle and end (Ochs and Capps 2001: 20).

Problematizing such forms of "natural" chronological linear time as defining features of narrative has long been a key business of narrative studies. The counter-argument suggests that historical and narrative texts contain multiple, alternative and overlapping times that can be non-synchronic (Bakhtin 1981; Blommaert 2015; Wenzel Geissler and Lachenal 2016). Any narrative involves a multiplicity of socially conditioned temporalities that are layered, of different duration and origin and which are nonetheless present and effectual at the same time. Such ideas are evident in Bakhtin's account of a chronotope:

> Chronotopes are mutually inclusive, they co-exist, they may be interwoven with, replace or oppose one another, contradict one another or find themselves in ever more complex interrelationships . . . The general characteristic of these interactions is that they are dialogical (in the broadest sense of the word). (Bakhtin 1981: 252)

13.2 Arrival as rehearsing and recreating multiple pasts

Accounts of first contact and anthropological arrival stories often involve the kinds of multiple temporalities and dynamic fields of complex, dialogical interaction that Bakhtin (1981) evokes in the above quote. The fieldwork that elicited much of the data in this chapter relates to my long-term absence from the village of Kamiyame, and the possibilities contained in returning. I returned to Kamiyame in November 2019 after a twenty-year absence. This trip was an exploration of how someone who was a virtually permanent physical absence can actually return. Certainly, any such return demanded a series of highly self-conscious re-enactments and re-engagements with what had already happened on those long past earlier visits. This occurred in preparatory off-site rehearsals and as deliberate on-site re-enactments of the past.

Preparing for my return trip often involved me looking at photos of my earlier trips to Kamiyame and wondering if there would be people at Kamiyame who could help me re-enact myself in versions of my earlier relationships. and this moved me beyond nostalgia for times long past, and beyond my rather too comfortable mourning for those who had died, into concerns about my own life and legacy. I planned to actively re-enact the past by creating a public slide show of people who had lived at Kamiyame many of whom passed away. Using a small portable computer as a screen I held a week of scheduled evening slide shows in the church hall.

A second evocation of the Kamula's past was part of my attempt to train some male Kamula teachers and high school graduates in transcribing audio recordings of Kamula stories. I wanted to employ them to transcribe other prior recordings of Kamula talk and narrative and recordings made while I was at Kamiyame. I did not spend much time actively engaged in the transcription training process. During most of the time in which the text was being transcribed, I worked in another room recording men's and women's accounts of how they had cared for the elderly and sick.

The first narrative the new team transcribed involved a 2015 video recording of a man from Wawoi Falls telling a foundational story about Kaiyalo, a significant creative ancestor, and the origin of death. I thought working off a video would be more interesting for the transcribing team than just listening to an audio tape. It took my team of new transcribers five days of solid work to complete a transcript of this narrative and we did not really finish negotiating a more or less agreed-to translation into English while I was there.

13.3 Contextualising the return in the violence of industrial logging and the promise of a new concession

During the first week of my stay at Kamiyame, while the narrative about Kaiyalo was transcribed, we were also hearing stories about the murder of two Chinese at Sasalema, the base camp of the Makapa logging concession. The murders were part of a raid by criminals from Tari that took place two days before I arrived. We heard of Chinese threats to respond to the murders by attacking Tari. The day before I arrived people had seen planes flying north in layered formation, repeating memories from World War II of allied planes flying from Merauke. The councillor reassured me that the Americans had talked against the Chinese intervention in PNG and as a result war had been avoided. The police were said to be expelling, beating and possibly killing Highlanders living in and around the Makapa concession. From my perspective, these violent events, the stories and their multiple temporalities destroyed the idea that logging had the ability to provide the Kamula with progress understood as a linear, teleological unfolding of the development of infrastructure and wealth. These stories seem to provide critical insight into the failures of logging to provide anything like a good life; but at the time they were circulating, people were saturated by the fearful, apocalyptic, intensity of stories about what one man rather proudly noted were the first multiple killings in the concession.

And similar violence continued into the future. In June 2020, two Chinese staff were kidnapped at Sasalema by another gang, apparently from Tari. The logging company apparently paid the kidnappers around K300,000 to release the Chinese. In August there was a raid on Kamusie, the headquarters of the Wawoi-Guavi concession run by Rimbunan Hijau. In one story, resident land owners were kidnapped and taken to the Kamula village of Wawoi Falls; some residents there were also kidnapped and then released once several thousand kina was paid. The police were also said to be disabling suspects by cutting their arms, knees and tendons and another suspect was burnt to death by the police. The 2019 events foreshadowed a new kind of life under conditions of permanent warfare.[1]

But during my time at Kamiyame in 2019, people were also expecting something very different. They were expecting forestry officials to arrive, bringing a contract to allow a significant extension to the Makapa logging concession's oper-

---

[1] In 2021 there were further attacks by "sweet potato people" on Wawoi Falls and the surrounding region.

ations. This was to be achieved by adding part of what was formerly known as the Kamula Doso concession as an extension to the Makapa concession. The signing of the contract was an important attempt to realizing some Kamulas (and other land-owners') hopes of development through perpetuating logging. The appeal of more logging was in its promise of another successful transformation of the forest into an ecology of site-specific temporalities that could create and regulate potential flows of money without the need for much work. The logging landscapes the Kamula were yearning for involved a repetition of highly effective socio-cultural and phys-ical transformations found in the existing adjacent Makapa TRP forest concession that had regulated earlier flows of money and development into the region. If the murder of the two Chinese reflected certain aborted dreams associated with logging, the contracts to be signed were saturated with living potentialities and traces of a different far better future. This imagined future was palpably close. The tension between the imminent fulfillment of long-delayed expectations concerning further logging and the intensifying violence and precarity of the Kamula's past experiences of industrial logging continued up until the day further rights in timber were apparently signed away to the state, which was also the day I left Kamiyame.

13.4 South Papuan narratives and the origin of death

These two events – the long-awaited renewal of logging and the collapse of logging social order into violence – provided a dynamic intensity, oscillating somewhere between utopian hope and deep fear, to the transcription of the nar-rative concerning Kaiyalo and his son's death. The story of Kaiyalo's son and the origin of death is part of a series of narratives, songs and rituals and a specific language that relates to Kaiyalo as the key foundational creator of the world and its manifest forms. Certain initiation rituals, while not explicitly serving as an introduction to Kaiyalo, contained opaque symbolism that made links with Kaiyalo. Kamula ritual and narrative are part of a broader revelatory economy where any prior or restricted knowledge may have to be re-evaluated in the light of new revelations (Robbins 2001). Kaiyalo and his associated narratives provide a scaffolding around which such events can be ordered. As a result of this orienta-tion to knowledge production, the figure of Christ is understood by some Kamula as already prefigured in stories about Kaiyalo and his son.

External analysts such as myself have positioned Kamula ancestors as part of a South Papuan genre of narrative concerning travelling ancestral heroes (Wagner 1972, 1967; Busse 2005; Landtman 1917; Wood 2013) and heroines (Wood and Dundon 2014). However, in this chapter, the emphasis is on stories and allusions to the death of Kaiyalo's son that outline certain "laws" or "rules" about the dead that still persist in ways that highlight how the Kamula continue to be subject to these laws. Stories of recent Kamula encounters with the dead are also relevant but are only briefly considered here.

The story about the death of Kaiyalo's son is central to how post-colonial Kamula redefined themselves in the 1980s and early 1990s when I recorded some accounts of how the death of Kayla's son was linked to the origin of death and social relations between the Europeans and the Kamula (Wood 1995). Yolisi is a character who often lacks proper sense and cannot control his desires. He is someone who does not think or do things properly. The term 'Yolisi man' can be applied to someone who cannot do things well or carefully. A 'Yolisi bow' is a term that is used to describe a black palm bow in contrast to a gun (literally 'fire-bow') and Kamula sometimes talk of themselves as 'Yolisi people' in contrast to Europeans. In the foundational narrative of the origin death, Yolisi failed to show deference to Kaiyalo and consequently Kaiyalo did not allow Yolisi to marry any of his daughters. As a result of this, Yolisi, angry at this outcome, told Kaiyalo's son not to come back to live among the Kamula after he had died. If Yolisi had not created this prohibition, all the dead would be able to return to live among the Kamula. In other narratives, the son's response to his own death is to kill a Kamula couple – Kamki and Ikwapa – whose bodies contain some of the promises of European modernity and technologies which he takes to Australia where the whites get to use these technologies. The key point of such narratives is that Kamula ancestors' bodies contain these things and because of such transfers, Australia has always been part of a Kamula moral community. Australia is now the place where Kamula dead live, leaving the Kamula to deal with their sorrow for the dead.

13.5 The story of Kaiyalo's son's death transcribed at Kamiyame

The story that was transcribed at Kamiyame was perhaps not so grand in its ambition to explain the structure of the world. It was recorded in 2014 at Wawoi Falls, some 80 kilometres northeast of Kamiyame, on a lazy afternoon when I was experimenting with a new video camera. I asked Bakadiye, a very skilled and entertaining storyteller, to talk about Kaiyalo. No one else in the house was listening or paying much attention to Bakadiye's efforts and he was perhaps uncomfortable with having a large video camera aimed at him. It was possible that without an audience he got a bit bored. Due to problems with a shortage of power and time, I decided not to transcribe the story while staying at Wawoi Falls.

To oversimplify, the story is composed of two smaller stories.[2] One story concerns the transformation of the production of sago that is sometimes attributed to Yolisi. In the following account, the transformation in sago production is correlated with his arrival on the scene, angry at Kaiyalo's failure to provide him with a wife. Prior to Yolisi's arrival, sago that was ready to be cooked could be taken directly from the opened trunk of a sago tree and placed immediately on the fire. There was no need to rinse and pound sago prior to collecting it from a settling tray. Sago production was easier and more like effortless work before the events in this micro-narrative. The transformation of sago – the Kamula's staple food – into stone is also an ominously dramatic change and a somewhat analogous precursor to Kaiyalo son's illness and death that listeners know is coming next.

13.5.1 Transformations of sago into stone at Keketapa

This is a story of Kaiyalo going inside a mountain. He came to Keketapa – the stone's name. His daughters made sago with an axe splitting open the sago tree and then they just pulled the sago out. They got the [unprocessed][3] sago and sat down and while cooking it on the fire Yolisi was there. While they were sitting and eating the sago he came. They [the daughters] were sitting there with his [Kaiyalo's] only son Su. While they were sitting there they were startled by Yolisi. They left the cooked sago there. The sago changed to stone. Its name is Keketapa. The stone's name is Keketapa. The tongs [used for cooking the sago] were stuck. The sago had changed to stone. The cooking tongs stayed stuck [in the stone]. Its name is Keketapa. He [Kaiyalo] travelled to a place. While he was coming, in the middle, his son got sick. His son was sick so what to do? What did he do? There was some other sago there. He pushed the sago into the ground with his feet. He pushed all the sago in the ground by stepping on it.

Yolisi presence restricts Kaiyalo's family's access to food and induces sickness in Kaiyalo's son. Kaiyalo then attempts to move away from Yolisi and he moves to Kukolo where he creates some other mountains:

While he was staying there Yolisi followed his footsteps. "Hey Kaiyalo is there? Kaiyalo stay on that side and I will stay on the other side". He stayed on that side and Kaiyalo on

---

2 For details on Kamula as related to other languages in the region see Suter and Usher (2017) and for an account of Kamula bridging techniques often employed in their narrative see Routamaa (1997a, 1997b). I have divided the text into what might be called "scenes" following Dobrin (2012) but her quite precise definition is not followed here.

3 Square barackets are used to indicate my clarifying additions to the text.

the other. They stayed there without Kaiyalo saying anything. And then Yolisi cut chopped down tree and cut up the tree trunk to make a house. He went around cutting down trees. And then Kaiyalo's son sickness got worse. The pain got larger and he became thin. And he [Kaiyalo] watched him about to die. "Oh my only boy is about to die. Who will go and get stinging nettles?"

13.5.2 Talking to the birds

This section of the narrative is famous among Kamula and often a real delight to hear. The narrator moves between his narrator's voice, Kaiyalo's voice and the sound of the bird's movement in the air that in this version is given full acoustic expression. A narrator can extend the story and display verbal artistry by adding more birds and thereby multiplying dazzling often funny sonic effects that supplement the more constant sound of flapping wings "to to to!" These supplementary sounds form part of the sonics of wind flapping and are not marked by reported speech markers even though one of the birds is defined as a person and another briefly speaks Kamula and certainly the assumption underlying Kaiyalo's interaction is that the birds can understand his Kamula. There is not a simple contrast between birds who don't speak and humans who do but a range of possibilities that could be further explored.

It is also the case that at a couple of points in this particular transcription, it is not quite clear if the voice being articulated is that of the narrator, Kaiyalo or Yolisi. Another feature is the use of a switch reference mechanism, not just in this section, but throughout the text, which is instrumental in signalling subject shifts. And, as will become clear in the following, I also enter into the narrative briefly.

> While he [Kaiyalo] was there *yekati* [possibly quail thrush] came. Yekati man. Kaiyalo said "Hey *yeakati* you get my stinging nettle! My boy is very sick". "Taka'ummu to to to to". *Yekati* ran way.
> And then *kakolomi* [black backed or hooded butcherbird] came. "To to to to to". "Hey *kakolomi* you cut my boys stinging nettles and give them to my boy". "Ka ho ka ho ka ho" and ran away. That's not the way . . . [Then white cockatoo, hornbill and gouria pigeon came and refused to get the stinging nettles].
> Hey – the Red Bird of Paradise's tail feather – nothing else. He [Kaiyalo] was there and said "Red Bird of Paradise what is happening? Get my boy's things he might die. You go and get stinging nettles to wipe on my boy". He [Kaiyalo] stayed there . . . [The Red Bird of Paradise flew away] "To to to to". And then the *kolepi* tree [Anonnaceae Polyathia sp] – you have seen it.

The narrator, Bakadiye, is addressing me directly here. He is breaking out of the narrative frame as a self-enclosed event to bring in new knowledge concerning the tree and simultaneously seeks to bring me to the actual place where the narrative's events are taking place by reminding me that many years ago I had been to the site – Kukolo Mountain – where the *kolepi* tree was located. According to my notes, Kamula recognise *kolep*i has a number of varieties and is sometimes associated with evil spirits that can kill people. Some stories about the Yolisi's role in the production of death link it to his creation of these evil spirits.

The narrative continues:

> While [Kaiyalo] was waiting at Kukolo mountain near the *kolepi* tree Bosavi mountain became dark. Ke come quickly! come quickly! If only this had been done. His boy's heart stopped . . . he died. And then he said "Don't cry. Let it be". He just waited and then Red Bird of Paradise came. "To to to to". He saw red Bird of Paradise coming bringing a bundle of stinging nettles and he said "Red Bird of Paradise the boy is lying dead". And then the Red Bird of Paradise came and threw the stinging nettles there. Its name is Bukumi, Bukumi throwing place. At a big lake the nettles were thrown. "To to to". "This is Kaiyalo's stinging nettles". And then he [Kaiyalo] got the nettles and wiped his boy with them. [Kaiyalo's son] Cannot stand. There was no way [literally no path or road]. He was dead.

13.5.3 Yolisi makes death permanent

> And then Yolisi came. Kayailo's house was quiet. This is not the way to do it. Not like this. What are you doing? He (Yolisi) went to Kaiyalo's house and was surprised. There was no noise at all – it was all quiet. [The expectation is that the house would be full of the sounds, people crying and keening in mourning for the dead. This is not happening because Kaiyalo believes that his son will return to live with him and hence there is no need for grief.] While [Kaiyalo was] sitting quietly women came. The women were Anapa and Kowame and one man came. And then [the woman] Betowame and her kin and clan came and stayed there. And then Yolisi came and was surprised it was so quiet. He asked "Kaiyalo what happened to your boy?" "My boy is dead". "You should be crying for your boy. Kaiyalo you would cry beautifully ye -e-e-ee. Kaiyalo e – e – e, Kaiyalo e – e – e. You will cry". And then Yolisi left him.
>
> In the late afternoon when the cicadas were calling Yolisi heard someone coming saying "father". He [Kaiyalo's son] came close to the cleared are around Yolisi's place. "Father what happened? Father I am coming back". He [Kaiyalo] was just about to say yes. But Yolisi said "child the dead go away forever. Do not come back. Take your net-bag with your things and go away forever. You go and stay in your house forever". Yolisi replied "Father you turned me back". And Kaiyalo said "Children what has happened will continue into the future. You will not return at the end of life. Oh children". And then he dug the grave for his son and put him in the grave. And then his son's spirit started moving around.

Kamula continue to engage in sometimes productive, and sometimes futile searches for a sign or indication of the end of death. One of the stories I recorded in December 2019 was a women's experience in a Port Moresby hospital where she met two recently deceased Kamula who were travelling to Australia. They had dropped in to say goodbye before they caught the afternoon's plane. Another man explained to me that the hospital ship that comes into the region from Australia brings back some of the dead Kamula as staff. They can speak Kamula and by curing diseases help the living Kamula – they are Kamula Europeans who come back to look after their kin. What is clear is that these kinds of stories and the story of the origin of death functioned as a summons to me and made every visit of mine their further affirmation and a responsibility.

13.6 Stories with Tom, interactions and sites of excess almost beyond the self-other dialogue?

After all, in a somewhat similar fashion in 2019, I had returned from Australia and made the origin of death central to my own agenda and work. Perhaps not surprisingly some of my transcribers began to redefine me in terms of the Kaiyalo narrative they were transcribing. And a couple of my good friends recruited me into a project they hoped to implement in Australia that would allow the Kamula dead to return to the living. These moves involved my immersion into Kamula concerns about their own future with the dead. We did achieve occasional, momentary co-presence in temporalities but such a possibility was also enmeshed in an awareness of what could be called a "substrate of underlying radical polytemporality" (Geissler and Lachenal 2016: 26). Despite such awareness, we assumed our experiences of time were, at least in principle, more or less synchronisable and that through certain shared practices we might actually be able to cause something of significance to happen in some future shared time and place.

This was a temporary achievement and during my time we were not always easily sharing the same time or history (Fabian 1983). I found my partial shift into responsibilities as defined by Kamula to be destabilizing, at times intrusive and beyond my capacities to enact them. The conversations that caused such discomfort moved beyond the kind of conventional rapport that allows exploration of the different kinds of moral mutuality at the heart of an intersubjectivity of self and other. Instead of such moral mutuality, other temporalities and entangled positions emerged in ways that ruptured coevalness and co-presence (Geissler and Kelly 2016: 916). These were temporary sites of destabilizing excess often beyond more conventional forms of inter-dependency and relationality. They were attempts to create novel forms of interaction where claims to responsibility

might be recognized and enacted across and with recognition of radical difference. Such processes emerged as we began to explore the possibility that I was a
manifestation of what was originally contained in Kamula bodies prior to Yolisi's
curse on Kaiyalo's son. While never explicitly stated, I might have been a Kamula
who, though dead, had returned.

One example of our conversations around such themes involved Tom, an
enthusiastic lay preacher in a local church that had broken away from the Evangelical Church of Papua. He was staying in the same house I was in and worked
every day in this house transcribing text with the group of transcribers I was
employing. The house where this work was undertaken was owned by the Kamiyame pastor of the Evangelical Church of Papua.

Tom once told me:

> I want to talk to you on Sunday and listen to you. You are a white man. You are different to
> us. You are Malana we are Yolisi. We are nothing. Jesus came to your people first. He belongs
> to you. Kaiyalo is our God. Jesus is other people's God. He is not our God but your God. So
> people want to hold on to Kaiyalo and understand where his son is. The white man like you
> understands everything. We are Yolisi our understanding is lower . . . I am nothing. But you
> understand everything . . . we have been looking at your ways of doing things. [Tom at this
> point made a gesture with both hands to form a screen or camera which he held up to his
> eyes as if filming me]. You are Jesus and Malana and so we want to know you. Even if I was
> different to the Kamula, and very confusing, I was very welcome to be here again with my
> family and friends . . . Tom said he did not really understand God because it was not really
> clear where Jesus or Kaiyalo or his son were now living. Where were they now? (Fieldnotes
> 29 November 2019).

I think Tom was trying to define our proposed Sunday talk as a social space where
could we could explore Kaiyalo's story and ourselves via a radical openness to
otherness.[4] This was a space where Tom could articulate some of his own issues
with Christianity and equivalences between God and Jesus and Kaiyalo and his
son. Tom's aim was to emphatically reposition his Christianity in Kamula concepts linked to Kaiyalo. His Church was de-colonial in its repudiation of the European God. However, Tom was trying to establish more complex points for debate
in our proposed Sunday meeting – he indicates that all the gods and ancestral
characters were sources of confusion to him given their shared inability to be
manifestly co-present in the Kamula's world.

The second issue Tom wanted to discuss was my own status and who I was.
This emerges when he signals in the quote above that I am possibly like both Jesus
and Malana. Malana is a name commonly used by Kamula when they are seeking
to praise Europeans and when they want to highlight perceived differences and

---

4 The phrase is commonly used, but I owe this version to McDougall (cited in Schram 2018: 213).

inequalities between Europeans and themselves. There are many Kamula stories where Malana serves as the opposite of Yolisi. In these stories, Marana, who is something like a secular embodiment of Kaiyalo's attributes, is more likely to be effective, competent and powerful when compared to Yolisi who is involved in sorcery, jealousy and the production of suffering and disorder. In contrast, the self-controlled quick-thinking Malana is someone who often fully exhibits the character and moral virtues the Kamula most admire and who often overcomes the chaos unleashed by Yolisi. Yolisi and Malana are different aspects of the Kamula's reflexive self-understanding of their own character and its often extreme and absurd possibilities. The idea that Yolisi represents the Kamula, and Malana the Europeans, converts the Kamula's auto-critique of who they might be into a comparative critique of the Kamula's social and moral limits as Yolisi while Malana exemplifies the European's superior wealth, power and moral virtue. If Yolisi is a projection of Kamula inadequacies, Kaiyalo, Malana and the European – who is in some contexts really a Kamula – contain all that is good among the Kamula.

Over the first week I was at Kamiyame, Tom and I developed a mode of interaction that could be defined as an interrogative interview. Tom questioned me almost every evening. He explored some implications of Kaiyalo, my presence and his work in transcribing the Kaiyalo text through a series of question and answer sessions with me. One evening he rather enthusiastically pointed out that no one in the village knew who I was or why I was here. They could not understand why I had come back. It seemed to me I had no place in their history whereas the reason I had come was to resume my place in what I thought was an already existing history. Tom was forcing me into recognizing my own alienation[5] from people at Kamiyame where some of my fears about returning would be realised – that I had been forgotten and that I was responsible for the death and suffering of many Kamula at Kamiyame because I had not been there to help people.[6] I had in a sense betrayed them.

Nonetheless, when talking with Tom I declined to explicitly define our interaction as a space where we could together productively grapple with the problem of the dead. I did not want to own, or take responsibility for, the story in the way Tom was suggesting. I did not always fully articulate this – partly because at times I did not occupy a coherent speaking position and at other times I felt that explicitly repudiating my possible role would have been counter-productive.

5 Alienation can be a form of powerlessness where a person cannot determine the outcomes he or she wants (Seemen cited in Ladwig 2021:78)
6 Some of this sensibility was amplified by my own daily work at Kamiyame which involved recording and transcribing stories of care for the elders, the self and others. Many of these stories outlined forms of intense suffering that had occurred while I was away.

Sometimes I became angry at Tom's seemingly relentless interrogation. I became somewhat mute and passive and felt I was in an involuntary position.[7] Deferring any clear response rather than directly refusing to be substitutable for the dead or Jesus at times seemed a more polite way forward. What my conversations with Tom developed was not so much a set of agreed facts or coherent arguments, but what Geissler and Kelly (2016) have called an "awkward intimacy" where both Tom and I reflected on our own contradictory positions on the past, present and future as defined by Kaiyalo and by the Christian God. While attempting to define ourselves in terms of stories of Kaiyalo and the dead, we were also critically evaluating the possibilities of taking responsibility for something new and hopeful in our emerging relationship.

Toms's comparative analysis of our relationship and his own critiques of himself and myself often took the form of a parable or compressed narrative that was somewhat dazzling and a challenge to understand. Once, while asking me "who are you?" Tom, without waiting for an answer, went on to immediately explain to me that Jesus had asked his disciples the same question "who am I?" While it was not entirely clear who was Jesus in this interchange what was clear is that I was not really fully present. I did not give any direct answer to Tom's question nor articulate my sense of the impossibility of me being, like Jesus, fully responsible for the Kamula. In this discussion there was no easy "reciprocal recognition" between myself and Tom about what kinds of acts or relationships could exist between us – the issues seemed beyond language and beyond an easily definable moral standpoint.

On another evening Tom asked me if the Kaiyalo story was mine or the Kamula's. At one level this kind of question was yet another invitation for me to define myself. My initial response was to treat the question as one of possession, of intellectual property and argued it belonged to the Kamula. I also mentioned I had already published parts of Kaiyalo's stories (Wood 1995), that some Europeans were interested in them. This point was in a way redundant as I had already dramatically enacted such European interest by making the narrative and its transcription central to the first week of my return. Tom's question was also pointing to the way I might be implicated in and authorised by the story and its revelatory economy in ways that enabled me to appear as one of its outcomes. Such authorisation emerged more clearly in a later conversation with a long-term friend, John, who noted that Kaiyalo had given the Kamula the power to make Europeans visit the Kamula.

---

7 Points developed here loosely replicate accounts of responsibility developed by Levinas (1981, 1991) and Blanchot (1986) who were seeking to move beyond a harmonious model of inter-subjectivity as the foundational ground of sociality and responsibility.

13.7 Talking with Grant, John and John and my responsibilities in reforming existing Law

Conversations with long-term friends highlighted additional features of Kaiyalo's history in ways that I felt I could respond to, even if ambivalently. What John, a member of the Kuyala kin group, told me on the 26 November is paraphrased below:

> he was not happy with the video version of the Kaiyalo story that was being transcribed because it did not give sufficient emphasis to the fact that Kaiyalo and his son were Kuyala ancestors. He also argued it was not true that that the dead did not come back. Kayailo's son did come back, bringing lots of edible things such as pig meat at Kamki spring a few kilometres from where he had died at Kukolo mountain. He then took the bodies of the Kamula he had killed there to Australia without eating them even though he singed their body hair at Balimo, now a government station, a typical procedure to prepare a pig for cooking pig meat (Fieldnotes 26 November 2019).

John emphasised this link between consumption of valued food and Australia by noting the word in Kaiyalo's language *hastani* means 'eat' and is the real name of Australia.[8] Australia is here presented as an outcome of Kaiyalo's son's actions. Following Inoue (cited in Blommaert 2015: 112) we can understand this as a form of Kamula post-colonial nationalism that posits Kamula belonging as embedded in a deep history reaching back to Kaiyalo and his son. It involves the continuous time of Kaiyalo's language and the narrative's events that placed Australia within the realm of the Kamula and their dead. To further emphasize the link, with the Kamula dead with Australia, John immediately made the point that a pilot had told him that his mother was living in Australia. If John came to Australia he would see her there. As a result, John was planning to get a passport and come to Australia with me.

My notes of conversations with Grant outline further implications of Kaiyalo's story and the dead. Grant was my key organizer of events during my stay at Kamiyame and many years before had been one of my co-initiates.

> Grant asked me if it is true the dead come back. Is it true that Kaiyalo's son went to Australia and Moresby? Can we remove the law preventing the dead coming back? Is it possible for us to live like Europeans – sit in the house and the food comes. Or that our houses will be able to fly to the sago swamp and then come back. One problem is that we don't we don't

---

8 *Hastani* in ordinary Kamula is the imperative form of 'throw away'. In what may have been a hospitable further emphasis of this thinking John spent several days hunting for meat and delivered some of the outcomes for me to eat.

know the language of the law. Was it Kamula or was it Kaiyalo's language? (Fieldnotes 1 December 2019).

Grant here was making the point that the Europeans, who may be dead Kamula blocked from fully returning to the Kamula by Yolisi's curse, defy gravity. They travel by flying, moving without weight. As Bashkow (2006: 64–94) has argued, for the Oraikaiva, Grant is emphasizing that such attributes are manifested in the things of this European world and are not just properties of the Europeans' bodies (Bashkow 2006: 64–94). Their houses and planes as well as their bodies are mobile beyond anything manifest in the Kamula world and contain the promise of effortless food production and here the over-coming of space.

On another day Grant persisted in questioning me about whether I had seen dead people in Australia. Did I know if they were there? Would they come back here? He also explained to me that the Kamula had taken up the customs of Christianity and understood that the dead will come back. But the problem was how to get money in your pocket and food into your house – that was unclear. Grant made the point that money and food just turn up for the Europeans. Grant said he:

> wanted to come to Australia to understand the origin of money. Did it have another name (like Kaiyalo's secret names)? Kamula see the planes flying and know that the Europeans are travelling, but the Kamula just stay here (at Kamiyame) doing really hard work to make food. They are blocked from achieving this kind of state of development because Yolisi's law (*aiyalama*).

Later that evening at around 9 pm, Grant came to my house with John and Moses. Earlier in the day Moses had introduced himself and shown me his passport and outlined how he was hoping to come to Australia with John and Kame. At this meeting, we were discussing the making of a trip to Australia. But in our evening meeting, Kame started our discussion via questions – do the dead live in Australia? Is Kaiyalo or his son living there? Did I think they have the power to bring Europeans here (to Kamiyame)? I put up a very ambiguous response – I had not seen the dead in Australia but noted Australia is a big place and so rather unconvincingly suggested I could have missed something. John cut across such qualifications by arguing that Kaiyalo has the power to make Europeans come here (and in a sense indicating that my presence was a function of Kaiyalo's agency). He said while he was living at Wawoi Falls a few years ago, Sisiyo's son and another boy, both having recently died, came back to Wawoi Falls with a book that explained details of the timber company's plans. This was the dead helping their brothers, sisters, mothers and fathers. Moses then changed the topic to a discussion of how to get passports to come to Australia and how we might develop a guest house at Wawoi Falls and get a high school built there. I talked quite a bit about how Kame and John would have to spend some time in Port Moresby getting a passport and then a visa from the

Australian High Commission. We ended our discussion on this note of effectively planning future travel that would remove Yulisi's prohibition on the dead returning. We were narrating ourselves into future do-able plans. And a few days later as I travelled just before dawn in canoe to the airstrip to fly back to Port Moresby, Grant reminded me of what we had talked about and how I should help him and John get to Australia so they could overthrow Yolisi's law concerning the dead.

13.8 Conclusion

The conversations I had with Tom, John, Grant and others were essentially retellings derived from earlier stories of the death of Kaiyalo's son. Such stories manifested as narrated texts and conversations have provided a persisting template involving trajectories of causality and relatedness between otherwise different events, especially involving characters who might be both aliens and extensions of oneself – such as the dead, Yolisi, Malana, evil spirits and the Europeans. Our conversations over two weeks did not explicitly position specific events in the same way as the controlling script, but we did all assume the existence of roughly the same text. This allowed us to assume we shared elements of a common narrative tradition, involving certain events, plots and themes which we as actors could improvise on in the course of our linguistic interactions (Hanks, 1987: 668; De Fina 2021). Our various retellings of the narrative depended on, and were held together by, an emergent community of narrators and characters (Wortham and Rhodes 2015: 169) who all interacted in different ways to create various partial and contingent instantiations of the story. As a result of such processes, the story of Yolisi's invention of a non-returnable death has remained a crucial moral problem for many Kamula I have known ever since my first few days with Kamula in 1976 at Wasapeya, then the site of a longhouse not far from Kamiyame, when I first recorded an account of Kaiyalo son's death.

However, this is perhaps to overplay the kind of holism and continuity thinking that might be associated with the flow of this canonical narrative across speech events, time and space. While my Kamula interlocutors and I generated forms of unity and community through our interactive engagement with Kaiyalo's son's narrative, we also generated forms of disunity and difference. We created gaps, ambiguities and degrees of incomprehension in the sociality that emerged from our engagement with the narrative of Kaiyalo's son's death. We did not create a spatially and temporally unified community, but rather sets of interactive relationships that implicated different projects and responsibilities for different interacting actors. Nonetheless, these contextually specific interactions were extensions of the scaffolding of Kaiyalo's narrative – as Bauman argues narrated events and any acts of narration are indissolubly bound together (cited in Wortham and Rhodes 2015: 127).

What I recorded in 2019 at Kamiyame was Kaiyalo's narratives moving forward in new, often tense, contexts defined not just by my long absence and subsequent interactions of my return, but also by industrial logging and the failure of neo-colonial development. The narratives about Kaiyalo's son's death did not provide particularly effective mechanisms for Kamula resistance to processes of legal dispossession of timber or the violence linked to the history of existing local concessions. The hopes and longing for the return of something that cannot easily be returned, such as the dead, could in some arguments be understood to facilitate the development of capitalism, dependency on logging and related political and economic inequalities. In this argument, what is salient in the narratives is their ideological effect in mediating and disguising the real tensions and contradictions between Kamula hopes for exchanging their timber rights for money and the brutality of life in a logging concession evident in the murder of the two Chinese store men. Alternatively, the narratives linked to the origin of death and its consequences could also be read as a critique of the racial order of the world system and the Kamula's place in it (Wood 1995). Ultimately both arguments do not help us fully understand the long persisting faith people mobilize around a promising future with their recent dead.

The continuing relevance of Kayailo's story is also to do with Kamula patience, faith and stoicism. Kamula have also known for many years that over-turning Yolisi's curse, like the promise of Christ's final coming and the promise of development, is always deferred to the day when such promises might be fulfilled. They know their hopes for capitalism, Christianity, and those contained in the Europeans remain possibilities even if they are never realised. It is in this gap between hope and unrealised past futures that many Kamula interactions with others, such as myself, take place and it is in these social interactions that foundational narratives such as the Kaiyalo narrative are renewed and transformed to once again play a role in defining potential futures.

While a practice-oriented approach to narratives cannot in itself fully explain the persistence of Kamula speaker's specific faith in a particular set of foundational narratives, it does put the analytical emphasis on the activities of different narrators and on the way they communicate with others, rather than on the texts themselves. To fully understand the hold narrated events may have on people requires knowledge of how other events and actors are actually brought into relationships with each other as part of narrative-based conversations and interactions of the kind outlined above. As De Fina (2021: 49) has argued, this is to move beyond the artificial constraint of "speech events" as the central analytic category of narrative analysis to one based on an understanding of narrative as not detachable from conversational interaction with others. It is these interactions that help define the persisting relevance of such narratives to Kamula.

References

Bakhtin, M. M. 1981. *The dialogic imagination: Four essays* [translated by Caryl Emerson & Michael Holquist, edited by Michael Holquist]. Austin: University of Texas Press.

Bashkow, Ira. 2006. *The meaning of the whitemen: Race and modernity in the Orokaiva cultural world*. Chicago: University of Chicago Press.

Blanchot, Maurice. 1986. *The writing of the disaster* [translated by Ann Smock]. Lincoln: University of Nebraska Press.

Blommaert, Jan. 2015. Chronotopes, scales, and complexity in the study of language in society. *Annual Review of Anthropology* 44. 105–116.

Busse, Mark. 2005. Wandering hero stories in the Southern Lowlands of New Guinea: Culture areas, comparison, and history. *Cultural Anthropology* 20(4). 443–473.

De Fina, Anna. 2021. Doing narrative analysis from a narratives-as-practices perspective. *Narrative Inquiry* 31(1). 49–71.

De Fina, Anna & Alexandra Georgakopoulou. 2008. Analysing narratives as practices. *Qualitative Research* 8(3). 379–387.

Dobrin, Lise M. 2012. Ethnopoetic analysis as a resource for endangered-language linguistics: The social production of an Arapesh text. *Anthropological Linguistics* 54(1). 1–32.

Fabian, Johannes. 1983. *Time and the other: How anthropology makes its object*. New York: Columbia University Press.

Geissler, Paul & Ann H. Kelly. 2016. Field station as stage: Re-enacting scientific work and life in Amani, Tanzania. *Social Studies of Science* 46(6). 912–937.

Geissler, Paul & Guillaume Lachenal. 2016. Introduction: Brief instructions for archaeologists of African futures. In Paul Wenzel Geissler, Guillaume Lachenal, John Manton & Noemi Tousignant (eds.), *Traces of the future: An archaeology of medical science in twentieth-century Africa*, 14–30. Chicago: University of Chicago Press.

Hanks, William. 1987. Discourse genres in a theory of practice. *American Ethnologist* 14(4). 668–692.

Labov, William & Joshua Waletzky. 1967. Narrative analysis: Oral versions of personal experience. In June Helm (ed.), *Essays on the verbal and visual arts*, 12–44. Seattle: University of Washington Press.

Ladwig, Patrice. 2021. Non-correspondence in fieldwork death, dark ethnography, and the need for temporal alienation. In Irfan Ahmad (ed.), *Anthropology and ethnography are not equivalent: Reorienting anthropology for the future*, 71–92. New York: Berghahn Books.

Landtman, Gunnar. 1917. *The folk-tales of the Kiwai Papuans* (Acta Societatis Scientiarum Fennicae 47). Helsinki: Finnish Society of Literature.

Levi-Strauss, Claude. 1969. *The raw and the cooked: Introduction to a science of mythology*. New York: Harper and Row.

Levinas, Emmanuel. 1981. *Otherwise than being, or, beyond essence*. The Hague: Martinus Nijhof.

Levinas, Emmanuel. 1991. *Totality and infinity: An essay on exteriority*. Dordrecht: Springer Netherlands.

Merlan, Francesca. 2005. Explorations towards intercultural accounts of socio-cultural reproduction and change. *Oceania* 75(3). 167–182.

Ochs, Elinor & Lisa Capps. 2001. *Living narrative*. Cambridge: Harvard University Press.

Propp, Vladimir. 1968. *Morphology of the folk tale*. Austin: University of Texas Press.

Robbins, Joel. 2001. Secrecy and the sense of an ending: Narrative, time, and everyday millenarianism in Papua New Guinea and in Christian fundamentalism. *Comparative Studies in Society and History* 43(3). 525–551.

Routamaa, Judy. 1997a. *Events and participants in Kamula discourse*. Summer Institute of Linguistics. Unpublished manuscript.

Routamaa, Judy. 1997b. *Tail-head linkage in Kamula*. Summer Institute of Linguistics. Unpublished manuscript.

Rumsey, Alan. 2001. *Tom Yaya Kange*: A metrical narrative genre from the New Guinea Highlands. *Journal of Linguistic Anthropology* 11(2). 193–239.

Schram, Ryan. 2018. *Harvests, feasts, and graves: Postcultural consciousness in contemporary Papua New Guinea*. London: Cornell University Press.

Stasch, Rupert. 2006. A society through its other. *Anthropological Quarterly* 79(2). 325–334.

Stasch, Rupert. 2009. *Society of others: Kinship and mourning in a West Papuan place*. Berkeley: University of California Press.

Suter, Edgar & Timothy Usher. 2017. The Kamula-Elevala language family. *Language and Linguistics in Melanesia* 35. 105–131.

Wagner, Roy. 1967. *The curse of Souw: Principles of Daribi clan definition and alliance in New Guinea*. Chicago: University of Chicago Press.

Wagner, Roy. 1972. *Habu: The innovation of meaning in Daribi religion*. Chicago: University of Chicago Press.

Wood, Michael. 1995. "White skins", "real people" and "Chinese" in some spatial transformations of the Western Province, PNG. *Oceania* 66. 23–50.

Wood, Michael. 2013. Mesede and the limits of reciprocity in fieldwork at Kamusi, Western Province, Papua New Guinea. *Asia Pacific Journal of Anthropology* 14(2). 126–135.

Wood, Michael & Alison Dundon. 2014. Great ancestral women: Sexuality, gendered mobility, and HIV among the Bamu and Gogodala of Papua New Guinea. *Oceania* 84(2). 185–201.

Wortham, Stanton & Catherine Rhodes. 2015. Narratives across speech events. In Anna De Fina & Alexandra Georgakopoulou (eds.), *The handbook of narrative analysis*, 160–177. Malden: John Wiley & Sons.

About the contributors

Alexandra Y. Aikhenvald is Professor at the Jawun Research Centre of Central Queensland University (Cairns), and Australian Laureate Fellow. She is a major authority on languages of the Arawak family, from northern Amazonia, and has written grammars of *Bare* (1995) and *Warekena* (1998), plus *A Grammar of Tariana, from Northwest Amazonia* (CUP, 2003), and *The Manambu Language of East Sepik, Papua New Guinea* (OUP, 2008), all based on extensive immersion fieldwork, in addition to essays on various typological and areal topics. She edited numerous books, among them *The Oxford Handbook of Evidentiality* (OUP, 2018) and, jointly with R. M. W. Dixon, *The Cambridge handbook of linguistic typology* (CUP, 2017). Her other major publications include *Classifiers: A typology of noun categorization devices* (OUP, 2000), *Language contact in Amazonia* (OUP, 2002), *Evidentiality* (OUP, 2004), *Imperatives and commands* (OUP, 2010), *Languages of the Amazon* (OUP, 2012), *The art of grammar: a practical guide* (OUP, 2014), *How gender shapes the world* (OUP, 2016), *Serial verbs* (OUP, 2018), *The web of knowledge: evidentiality at the cross-roads* (Brill, 2021), and *A guide to gender and classifiers* (OUP, forthcoming), in addition to a general interest book *I saw the dog: how language works* (Profile books). Her current focus is on the integration of language and society and the ways of conceptualizing disease and well-being in minority languages and cultures, and a comprehensive grammar of Yalaku, from Papua New Guinea.

Robert L. Bradshaw is a linguistics consultant and translation advisor with SIL International. He recently completed a PhD thesis at the Language and Culture Research Centre (LCRC), James Cook University: *A grammar of the Doromu-Koki: A Papuan language of Papua New Guinea* (2022) and is an Adjunct Research Fellow at JCU. Robert has been a member of SIL-PNG in Papua New Guinea since 1987, where he has been involved in research of three Southeast Papuan languages of Central Province. He is author of 'Fuyug Grammar Sketch' in *Data Papers on PNG Languages Volume 53*, (SIL-PNG Academic Publications, 2007), 'Doromu-Koki Grammar Sketch' in *Data Papers on PNG Languages Volume 58* (SIL-PNG Academic Publications, 2012), and *Doromu-Koki – English Dictionary* (LINCOM Europa, 2021).

Luca Ciucci is Adjunct Research Fellow at James Cook University. In 2007, he began his research on the Zamucoan languages (Ayoreo, Chamacoco, and †Old Zamuco). During his PhD years, he discovered the earliest grammar of Ecuadorian Quechua, which was later published in 2011. In 2013, he completed his PhD at Scuola Normale Superiore in Pisa. His research activities include grammatical description of Ayoreo and Chamacoco, the reconstruction of Proto-Zamucoan, and the analysis of the historical data available for †Old Zamuco. In 2017, he began documenting Chiquitano (also known as Bésɨro), an isolate. He is particularly interested in language contact between Chiquitano and the surrounding languages (such as Zamucoan), and in the comparison between the different Chiquitano varieties spoken nowadays plus the historical documents available on this language.

R. M. W. Dixon is an Adjunct Professor at the Jawun Research Centre, Central Queensland University in Cairns. It could be said that Bob Dixon sports a linguistic cloak of many colours. For forty years he revelled in on-the-spot fieldwork – in Brazil (*The Jarawara Language of Southern Amazonia*, 2004), in the South Pacific (*A Grammar of Boumaa Fijian*, 1988) and especially in Australia (grammars of Dyirbal, 1972, and Yidiñ, 1977, amongst others). He

https://doi.org/10.1515/9783110789836-014

has also put out two general books on Australian languages (1980 and 2002). Being equally intrigued with his native language, he has published *A Semantic Approach to English Grammar* (1991, 2005), *Making New Words: Morphological Derivation in English* (2014) and *English Prepositions: their Meanings and Uses* (2021). Bob Dixon also enjoys looking for inductive generalisations which reveal the nature of human language, resulting in *Ergativity* (1979, 1994), and the three-volume *Basic Linguistic Theory* (2010, 2012), among other works. His enterprise extends outwards from these foci, to kinship systems, the poetry of songs, the nature of linguistic evolution (with The *Rise and Fall of Languages*, 1997) and *Are Some Languages Better than Others?* (2015). His newest book (2022) is *A New Grammar of Dyirbal*, featuring new insights gathered since the 1972 volume on that language.

Nicholas (Nick) Evans (CoEDL Director), focusses his research on linguistic diversity and what this tells us about the nature of language, culture, deep history, creativity, and the human mind. His 2022 book *Words of Wonder: Endangered Languages and What They Tell Us* sets out a broad program for the field's engagement with the planet's dwindling linguistic diversity. Nick has carried out fieldwork in Northern Australia and Papua New Guinea, with grammars of Kayardild (1995) and Bininj Gun-wok (2003), and dictionaries of Kayardild (1992), Dalabon (2004, with Francesca Merlan and Maggie Tukumba) and Nen (2019), as well as numerous edited books, most recently *Insubordination* (with Honoré Watanabe, 2016) and *The Oxford Handbook of Polysynthesis* (with Michael Fortescue and Marianne Mithun, 2017). His CoEDL projects include SCOPIC (with Danielle Barth), a cross-linguistic corpus study of how diverse grammars underpin social cognition, ongoing work on Nen and Dalabon, and Parabank (with Simon Greenhill and Kyla Quinn), a large cross-linguistic database of paradigm structures focussing on pronoun systems and kin terms.

Rosita Henry is Professor of Anthropology at James Cook University. Her research concerns relationships between people and places across Australia and the Pacific as expressed through cultural festivals, the politics of public performances, cultural heritage, material culture, land tenure conflict and the relationship between Indigenous peoples and the state. Professor Henry is author of the book *Performing Place, Practicing Memory: Indigenous Australians, Hippies and the State* (Oxford and New York: Berghahn Books, 2012). She is also co-editor of the book *The Challenge of Indigenous Peoples: Spectacle or Politics?* (Oxford: Bardwell Press 2011) and *Transactions and Transformations: Artefacts of the Wet Tropics, North Queensland* (Memoirs of the Queensland Museum (Culture) Volume 10, December 2016. Her most recent work is an 'ethnographic biography' of Maggie Wilson entitled *A True Child of Papua New Guinea: Memoir of a Life in Two Worlds* (McFarland 2019).

Christoph Holz is a PhD student at the Jawun Research Centre at Central Queensland University in Cairns. He is working on the documentation and description of Tiang, an undescribed Oceanic language of New Ireland Province in Papua New Guinea. He has a passion for the languages and cultures of the Pacific region and Asia. His current typological work is centred on topics related to the noun phrase, classifiers and registers. He has published a number of papers dealing with youth registers in the languages of Papua New Guinea and counting systems across Oceanic.

Gwendolyn Hyslop received her PhD in Linguistics from the University of Oregon in 2011. She is currently a Senior Lecturer in Linguistics at the University of Sydney. She has worked on several Tibeto-Burman languages and is a specialist of the East Bodish languages of Bhutan and Arunachal Pradesh. Publications include articles on tonogenesis, ergativity, and historical linguistics. She has published a grammar of Kurtöp (Brill, 2017) and has a forthcoming Kurtöp/English/Dzongkha dictionary. She was awarded a prestigious Humboldt Fellowship for Experienced Researchers in 2020–2022.

John Mansfield is a Senior Lecturer in Linguistics at the University of Melbourne. He has studied language with the Murrinhpatha, Marri Tjevin and Anindilyakwa people of northern Australia, and his research has drawn on a diverse range of languages including Chintang (Tibeto-Burman), Matukar Panau (Austronesian), Pitjantjatjara (Pama-Nyungan area) and German (Indo-European). He is particularly interested in processes of language change, and how cognitive, communicative and social pressures shape language structure.

Francesca Merlan was professor of anthropology in the School of Archaeology and Anthropology, Australian National University; she became Emerita in 2021. She has conducted field research since the latter 1970s in northern Australia, the 1980s in Papua New Guinea with Alan Rumsey, and the 1990s in Europe (Germany). She has long been interested in critical, empirically accountable theorization and description of social and cultural change. She has also done research over many years on languages of Northern Australia, having published several grammars (including Mangarayi, Wardaman, and Ngalakan). She continues her work on Jawoyn and Wardaman, with both on language maintenance and revital-ization, and with the latter, a dictionary project. Her books include *Ku Waru: Language and Segmentary Politics in the western Nebilyer Valley, Papua New Guinea*. Coauthored with Alan Rumsey. 1991, Cambridge University Press; *Caging the Rainbow: Places, Politics and Aborigines in a North Australian Town*.1998, University of Hawai'i Press; *Tricksters and Traditions: Story-Tellers of Southern Arnhem Land*. Canberra: Pacific Linguistics, 2016; and *Dynamics of Difference in Australia: Indigenous Past and Present in a Settler Country*. 2018, University of Pennsylvania Press.

Alan Rumsey is an Emeritus Professor in the in the College of Asia and the Pacific at The Australian National University, and Chief Investigator in the Australian Research Council Centre of Excellence for the Dynamics of Language. His research fields are highland Papua New Guinea and Aboriginal Australia, with a focus on linguistic anthropology, comparative poetics, and child language socialization. He is a Fellow of the Australian Academy of Humanities and past president of the Australian Anthropological Society. His recent publications include "The sociocultural dynamics of indigenous multilingualism in northwestern Australia" (in Language & Communication, volume 62, 2018), "Melanesia as a zone of linguistic diversity" (Hirsch, Eric and Will Rollason eds. 2019 The Melanesian World) and "Intersubjectivity and engagement in Ku Waru" (Open Linguistics volume 5, 2019).

Hannah Sarvasy (PhD James Cook, 2015) is an Australian Research Council DECRA Senior Research Fellow at the MARCS Institute for Brain, Behaviour and Development. She is a field linguist active at the intersection of language documentation, language acquisition studies, and psycholinguistic experimentation. Her publications include over 50 books, articles, and book chapters, including a reference grammar of the Papuan language Nungon, spoken by 1,000 people in the Saruwaged Mountains of Morobe Province, Papua New Guinea (Brill, 2017), a volume of fieldwork autobiographies (Benjamins, 2018), learning grammars for the endangered Sierra Leonean languages Kim and Bom (Linguistics Publishing, 2009), and studies of child language development, linguistic typology, Papuan and Bantu languages, field methods, ethnobiology, and language processing. She previously taught at the University of California, Los Angeles and served as a research fellow at the Australian Research Council Centre of Excellence for the Dynamics of Language.

Elena Skribnik is Emeritus Professor and former Director of the Institute of Finno-Ugric and Uralic studies at the Ludwig Maximilian University of Munich (2001–2019). Her main areas of research are syntax, especially clause combining, grammatical categories and grammaticalization processes, and language contact of the languages of Siberia. She has carried out fieldwork on a number of Altaic and Uralic languages of Siberia (1977–2008) and published studies on these languages as well as teaching materials for national schools and pedagogical institutions. She led the ESF EuroCORES/EuroBABEL project 'Ob-Ugric languages' (2009–2012), co-organized three Strategic partnerships (Erasmus+) between nine European universities focusing on Finno-Ugric studies (2015–2024), and co-edited together with Johanna Laakso and Marianne Bakró-Nagy "The Oxford Guide to the Uralic languages" (OUP 2022).

Pema Wangdi received his PhD degree in 2021, with his PhD thesis on a comprehensive grammar of Brokpa, an indigenous language of Bhutan. He received Graduate Diploma and MA in Linguistics from Australian National University in 2003 and 2005 respectively. He worked for Dzongkha Development Commission (National Language Commission of Bhutan), producing bilingual dictionaries in Dzongkha and English. He carried out parts-of-speech tagging and morphological segmentation in Dzongkha, used for writing dictionaries and developing Dzongkha Natural Language Processing systems. He has taught International Baccalaureate courses in language and literature at Institut Le Rosey, Switzerland, from 2009 to 2013. His research interests include studying indigenous languages and culture and their interconnection. he is currently a Research Fellow at Jawun Research Centre, Central Queensland University.

Michael Wood is an anthropologist working at the Cairns Campus of James Cook University. His research interests are primarily located in Papua New Guinea. He is currently exploring how proponents of industrial logging and carbon trading are competing to develop the rainforests of the Western Province. He has recently worked on describing some of the cultural components of the World Heritage values of the Nakanai Ranges in New Britain and is about to finalise co-editing a collection of articles on the Chinese in PNG. During the COVID lockdown Michael watched many episodes of the Sopranos, the Wire and VEEP and consequently sometimes claims to be an expert in American politics and cultural studies.

Index of authors

https://doi.org/10.1515/9783110789836-015

Index of languages and language families

https://doi.org/10.1515/9783110789836-016

Index of subjects

absolute 3, 23, 25, 145
agency 294, 298, 320
alienation 317
anaphora 7–8, 161–6, 181–2, 190–214
areal diffusion 6, 89, 98, 100, 105, 111, 114,
    158, 205–11, 221, 241
article 182, 239, 241
aspect 8–9, 34, 74–5, 99, 143–4, 157,
    165, 183–4, 224–5, 232, 270, see also
    imperfective aspect, perfective aspect
autobiography 3, 11–13, 37, 96, see also
    biography

backgrounding 5, 7, 10, 74–8, 84–8, 104–5,
    254, 274, see also foregrounding
biography 3, 11–12, 200–1, 289–304
borrowing, see areal diffusion, language
    contact, loan
bridging construction 74, 99–115, 126,
    133, 136, 312, see also recapitulative
    bridging, summary bridging

capitalism 322
case 7, 17, 23, 91–2, 143–7, 151–3, 157–9,
    164, 172, 175–6, 183, see also ergativity
cataphora 8, 181–2, 192, 196–7, 200–214
Christianity 12–13, 298, 305, 316, 318–20
clause chain 5–7, 73–79, 85, 88–9, 98–101,
    109, 113–14, 121–25, 129–39, 143–50,
    165, 174, 224, 229, see also medial clause
code-switching 6, 95, 111
cohesion 85, 95, 103
command 5, 39, 80, 84, 87–9, 125, 172, see
    also imperative
confession 12, 296, 298–301
conjunction 5–6, 95, 98–101, 104–16, 143,
    147, 157–8, 161, 169–71, 176, 182, 194,
    202, 213, 241, see also connective
connective 147, 164, 169–70, 182
constituent order 75, 77, 123, 144, 183
content question 82, 125, 131, see also
    question
conventionalization 88, see also
    grammaticalization

conversation 5–9, 33, 47, 67, 73, 76–7, 83,
    87, 100, 104, 121–5, 130, 144, 160, 232,
    270, 274, 316–21
coordinating conjunction, 105–109, see also
    conjunction
copula 9, 145, 156, 162, 167, 171, 176, 182,
    224–5, 228–32
co-verb 43

definiteness 55, 91, 143, 154–7, 200
demonstrative 7–8, 23, 42, 101, 157, 161–2,
    172–6, 181–218, see also anaphora,
    cataphora
desubordination 80–1, 245, 247
different subject 74, 77, 81–7, 99–101, 113,
    125, 129, 133, 146, see also switch
    reference
direct speech 38–9, 44, 196, 201–2, 250, see
    also indirect speech, quote, reported
    speech
discourse continuity 5, 11, 73–9,
    87–9, 103, 321, see also discourse
    discontinuity
discourse discontinuity 73, 105, 116, see also
    discourse continuity
disjunction 169–70
dual 183

egophoricity 9, 143–4, 171, 224–7
engagement (of addressee or audience)
    12–13, 49, 302, 305, 308, 321
ergative-absolutive, see ergativity
ergativity 3, 17, 23–6, 46, 145, 159, 224
evidentiality 2, 8–9, 74, 143–4, 157, 188,
    224–5, 228–30, 238–9, 242, 245–52,
    255
exclusive/inclusive distinctions in
    pronouns 35, 183

focal clause 5–7, 74, 77, 143–80
focus 75–6, 182, 198, 243
foregrounding 7,-8, 96, 261–2, see also
    backgrounding
framed quote, see quote framer

https://doi.org/10.1515/9783110789836-017

www.ingramcontent.com/pod-product-compliance
Lightning Source LLC
Jackson TN
JSHW050737261224
76011JS00006B/41